Into the Hands of the Soldiers

DAVID D. KIRKPATRICK

Into the Hands
of the Soldiers

FREEDOM AND CHAOS IN
EGYPT AND THE MIDDLE EAST

VIKING

VIKING

An imprint of Penguin Random House LLC

375 Hudson Street

New York, New York 10014

penguin.com

Map illustration by Jeffrey L. Ward

ISBN: 9780735220621 (hardcover)
ISBN: 9780735220645 (ebook)

Printed in the United States of America
1   3   5   7   9   10   8   6   4   2

Set in Times LT Pro
Designed by Amy Hill

For Laura Bradford, who never signed up for any of this.

Contents

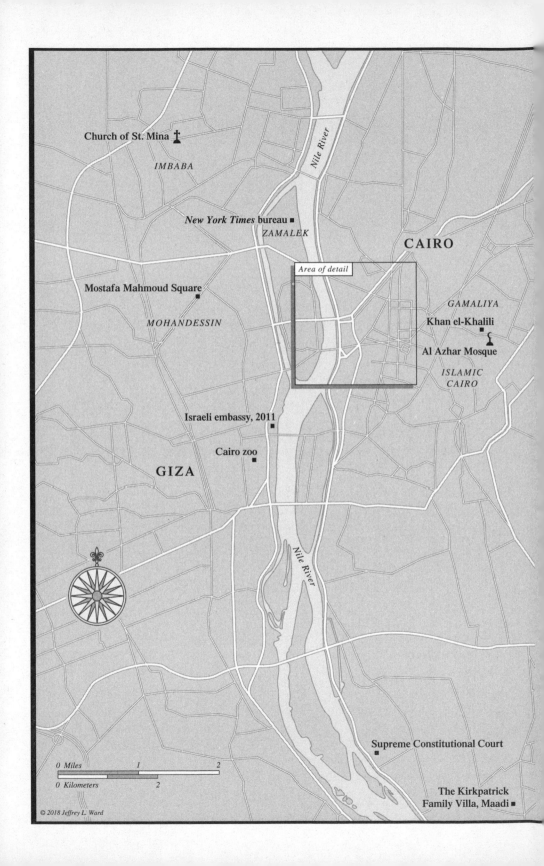

Church of St. Mina ✝

IMBABA

New York Times bureau ■

ZAMALEK

CAIRO

Mostafa Mahmoud Square ■

GAMALIYA

Khan el-Khalili ■

MOHANDESSIN

Al Azhar Mosque

Area of detail

ISLAMIC CAIRO

Nile River

Israeli embassy, 2011 ■

Cairo zoo ■

GIZA

Nile River

Supreme Constitutional Court ■

0 Miles   1   2

0 Kilometers   2

The Kirkpatrick
Family Villa, Maadi ■

© 2018 Jeffrey L. Ward

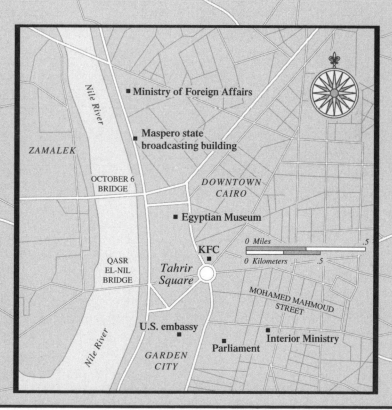

Presidential palace

Ministry of Defense and
Military Production

Republican Guard complex

Al-Nour Mosque

Cathedral of St. Marks

Rabaa al-Adawiya Mosque

Rabaa al-Adawiya Medical Center

NASR CITY

CAIRO

Cave Church

Muslim
Brotherhood
headquarters

Nile River

Ministry of Foreign Affairs

Maspero state
broadcasting building

ZAMALEK

OCTOBER 6
BRIDGE

DOWNTOWN
CAIRO

Egyptian Museum

KFC

0 Miles   .5

0 Kilometers   .5

QASR
EL-NIL
BRIDGE

Tahrir
Square

MOHAMED MAHMOUD
STREET

U.S. embassy

Parliament

Interior Ministry

Nile River

GARDEN
CITY

Into the Hands of the Soldiers

1

Whoever Drinks the Water

Driving east from Tunis may be the best way to take in the miracle of the Nile. The road follows the Mediterranean coast for about seventeen hundred miles. Almost every inch of it is brown twelve months a year—rock and sand baking in the sun. Then you cross an invisible line at the edge of the Nile Valley. Everywhere is an eruption of green. Not even the congestion of Cairo can contain the riot of vegetation.

For millennia, no other territory in the Middle East produced such a bounty. Where the yearly flooding of the Euphrates was violent and destructive, the cycles of the Nile were gentle and predictable. A truism holds that the histories of Egypt and Iraq follow their rivers. Medieval sultans dug a well, known today as the Nile-o-meter, on Rawda Island in Cairo, to measure the water level. The annual rise determined how generous the crops would be that year, and the sultans taxed the peasants accordingly. Farming was that easy. The Nile Valley became the breadbasket of the Arab world. Egyptians swelled with pride in their river. Whoever drinks the water of the Nile will return again to Egypt, the old saying goes.

Egyptians also like to say that they have been rallying around grand national projects since the Pharaohs built the temples of Thebes. After taking power in 1952, President Gamal Abdel Nasser decided to build a great dam at Aswan, near the Sudanese border, to harness the Nile for hydroelectric power. Abdel Nasser promised a dam "more magnificent and seventeen times greater than the Pyramids."

Secretary of State John Foster Dulles announced in 1955 that the United States and the United Kingdom would provide $70 million in assistance for construction of the dam. But he did not like Abdel Nasser's denunciations of colonialism, or his refusal to ally exclusively with Washington. After seven months, Dulles withdrew the offer. Abdel Nasser turned to Moscow.

The dam became a monument to Stalinist engineering. Its construction displaced one hundred twenty thousand Nubians, the dark-skinned Egyptians indigenous to the area. The lake formed by the dam nearly demolished the breathtaking Pharaonic temples at Abu Simbel; UNESCO saved them by paying Western European contractors to relocate the complex, stone by stone, on drier ground. The finished dam stopped the flow of silt and nutrients that had kept much of the Nile Valley so fertile for centuries. The depletion of the water devastated the farmlands downstream and the fishing around the mouth of the Nile. The slowing of the current led to an explosion in waterborne diseases like schistosomiasis.

To fight the disease, Abdel Nasser's successors launched a massive campaign of inoculations. But government health workers reused unsterilized needles. That set off a hepatitis C epidemic that raged on for decades. About one in five Egyptians was infected with "virus C," as Egyptians called it, in imported English. Barbers spread the disease by reusing blades, so sensible Egyptian men carried their own personal shears to haircuts, and I did as well.

The adage about drinking the Nile water lives on today as black humor. The river is so filthy that your first stop would be a hospital. Yet Egyptian schoolchildren are still taught to celebrate Abdel Nasser's High Dam as an unalloyed triumph. I think of the dam whenever I get a haircut: a parable of centralized planning and unaccountable power.

I had the luck to be an American journalist living in Cairo during the thirty months when Egyptians broke free of the autocracy that ruled them. Their escape set off revolts from Benghazi to Baghdad. But the old authoritarian order had only hidden underground, not shattered. It returned to take revenge. A reinvigorated autocracy did its best to blot out the memory of those thirty months of freedom. Let me tell you the story.

2

City of Contradictions

August 14, 2010–January 23, 2011

My introduction to Egypt was an *iftar*—the ritual meal at dusk to break the Ramadan fast—on a gritty day in August 2010.

My family and I had moved that week into a one-story villa in Maadi, a leafy district about six miles up the Nile from the *New York Times* bureau on the island of Zamalek. Both neighborhoods—Maadi and Zamalek—are full of Western expats and Egyptian old money. I had a twenty-minute drive to work if the streets were empty. Usually the lawless traffic made the trip more than an hour. Mercedes sedans and Land Rovers veered around donkey carts stacked with carrots or garlic. Families of four or five crammed onto the backs of Korean motorcycles, and mothers rode sidesaddle with infants in their arms. My wife, Laura, and I had hauled our one-year-old's car seat all the way from Washington. We felt so fussy.

I was drawn to Egypt in part by the terrorist attacks of September 11, 2001. I knew the roots of Al Qaeda and its ideology ran back to Egypt. Also, I had turned forty in 2010. I wanted a change from Washington, where I had reported for the previous six years. That was about the extent of my preparation for my posting in Cairo.

I was thrilled with the job. Egypt, home to a quarter of all Arabs, had set every major trend in religion, culture, and politics across the Arab world for more than half a century. Egypt commanded the largest Arab army and held together the region. It kept the peace with Israel. After Israel, Cairo had received more United States aid over the decades than any other country—over $70 billion, at a rate of $1.5 billion a year at the time I arrived. Whatever happened in Egypt was in a way an American story.

The skinny apparatchik in charge of the international news media had welcomed me to Egypt just a few days earlier. He told me that the Foreign Ministry had recalled him from the San Francisco consulate to apply his public relations expertise to the upcoming reelection of President Hosni Mubarak, who was then eighty-two and seeking his seventh five-year term in office. But the genial bureaucrat, Attiya Shakran, talked mostly about how sorry he was to leave San Francisco. Expect laziness and dysfunction from Egyptians, he told me. IBM in Egypt stood for *Inshallah, Bokra, Malesh*—God willing, tomorrow, sorry!

About three dozen people had gathered for the *iftar* in a private dining room high in the Sofitel hotel on the tip of Zamalek, with a sweeping view of the river. U.S. ambassador Margaret Scobey opened the event by recalling the *iftar* President Thomas Jefferson had hosted at the White House. She reprised the main themes that President Barack Obama had laid out in a speech in Cairo the previous year, about "a new beginning" for American relations with the Muslim world. But she left out the indelicate parts, like Obama's Quranic admonition to "speak always the truth," or his nod to the universal right "to speak your mind and have a say in how you are governed."

My table felt like a scene in a World War I movie where warring generals meet for tea during a break in the battle. The embassy had invited some of Egypt's most notable dissidents and they were seated with me. One was a shaggy-haired, foul-mouthed blogger known for publicizing videos of police abuse and sexual harassment; the security services had recently shut down his website. Another was an Egyptian political scientist at the American University in Cairo who specialized in the defects of Arab authoritarianism. And a third was a researcher for Human Rights Watch. Mubarak kept the organization in a legal limbo, refusing to either fulfill or reject its license application, which meant that at any moment his police could jail its researcher, Heba Morayef.

On the other side of the table were American diplomats and Mubarak officials, all chatting amiably with the dissenters and me. Was I familiar with the figs and soup traditionally served first after a day of fasting, to reawaken digestion? Had I tried *kushari,* the beloved staple of Egyptian cuisine? (Rice and pasta mixed with lentils and garbanzo beans, flavored by three different sauces at once—vinegar and garlic, tomato, and hot pepper.) Or how about roasted pigeon? It was a delicacy here. We made small talk about politics in Washington and Cairo.

So many contradictions hung out in the open in the late summer of 2010. Facebook pages borrowed Silicon Valley marketing techniques to agitate against Mubarak and attracted an audience running into tens of thousands. A left-leaning activist group calling themselves the April 6 Youth Movement, after the date of a wildcat strike at a textile plant, claimed more than seventy thousand online members. But a newspaper columnist who questioned the president's health was sentenced to jail for destabilizing the country. Membership in the Muslim Brotherhood was illegal, but eighty-eight of its members served openly in Parliament. They made up 20 percent of the otherwise docile chamber and constituted Mubarak's only real opposition. Egyptian papers covered the sayings and doings of the Brotherhood's "general guide," a sixty-eight-year-old veterinarian, in the same way the New York tabloids might cover the city's Catholic archbishop (or, for that matter, the way the Egyptian papers covered the pope of Egypt's Coptic Orthodox Church, whose members made up about 10 or 15 percent of the population).

Conservatives in the Brotherhood's leadership—including an obscure engineering professor from the Nile Delta named Mohamed Morsi—had recently forced off its governing board their movement's most charismatic moderate, a physician named Abdel Moneim Aboul Fotouh. But in the summer of 2010 the Brotherhood was collecting signatures for the presidential candidacy of Mohamed ElBaradei, the Noble Prize–winning diplomat who had become the Arab world's best-known liberal. Strange bedfellows. Of course, Mubarak would never allow ElBaradei to run. The state newspapers were busily besmirching him with bogus reports that he had abetted the American invasion of Iraq. One paper published pictures of ElBaradei's daughter in a bikini—a shocking indecency to most Egyptians. ElBaradei's aides found audio surveillance bugs in his office that summer, and the government made almost no attempt to deny or censor reports that intelligence agencies—the *mukhabarat*—were behind it. I was the only one surprised.

No one saw any chance that the character of the regime might change any time soon. That is why government officials and prominent dissidents could dine together so comfortably. Yet the daily dysfunction of the state boggled my mind. Fiefdoms within the government bureaucracy sparred publicly with one another. Judges protested that the police threatened their independence. Diplomats rolled their eyes at their geriatric president. And the military and interior ministries more or less openly competed with one another for influence and power. In 1986, several thousand police conscripts had staged an armed insurrection. Army troops fought them with gunfire in city streets and hotel lobbies. Now the gossip buzzing around the embassy *iftar* was about how much animosity the military commanders felt toward the president's son and heir apparent, forty-six-year-old Gamal Mubarak. He stood to become the first Egyptian head of state from outside the military in fifty-eight years, since Abdel Nasser's Free Officers overthrew the British-backed monarchy.

Gamal—or Jimmy, as hip Egyptians called him—had gotten rich as an investment banker in London and Cairo. Then his father installed him atop the ruling party and began grooming him for high office. Everybody was doing it. Hafez al-Assad had bequeathed power over Syria to his son. His fellow dictators in Tunisia and Libya were in the process of passing on their jobs to members of their families. Plenty of Arab states were straight-up hereditary monarchies (Jordan, Morocco, Saudi Arabia, and four of its Persian Gulf neighbors). So why not Gamal? He was pitching himself as the leader for a new generation: the three out of four Egyptians under forty, and the two out of three under thirty-five.

I was seated next to a close friend of Gamal's, Tamim Khallaf. He was a diplomat who had gone to college with the researcher for Human Rights Watch. Now he had been seconded by his ministry to help tutor Gamal. Khallaf told me that he had watched the 2008 American presidential election from a fellowship at Harvard, and when he learned I had covered the race he was full of questions. What had happened to Hillary Clinton? Had Sarah Palin hurt John McCain?

I had a question for him, too. Would his friend Gamal really run for president to succeed his father in 2011? Khallaf practically winked at me. The Mubaraks were treating the presidential palace as a personal plantation.

I would later learn that the chief of military intelligence, General Abdel Fattah el-Sisi, was in the midst of tackling the same question. Intelligence in the Arab world sometimes includes spying on a head of state himself, and Sisi had reported to the top generals that summer that the president might hand his office to his son as soon as the elder Mubarak's eighty-third birthday, in May 2011. Sisi predicted to the generals that Egyptians would rise up in revolt. Mubarak would respond by ordering the army to quell the unrest. Then the generals would face some decisions.

The army had crushed bread riots under President Anwar Sadat in 1977 and the police mutiny under Mubarak in 1986. But the military was a barony of its own. It held the heavy weapons, and its obedience to any civilian was still a matter of choice. Would the generals answer the president's call?

As recently as January 2010, at a ceremony for his promotion to chief of military intelligence, Sisi had publicly praised Mubarak as a father to his country. "Egypt's flag will always continue to fly high under his leadership," Sisi had said.

He recommended to the generals just a few months later that they reject Mubarak. Sisi told the generals to declare loyalty to the people, not the president. They should shape their own transition. A modern state might call that treason. But the time was still ripening as we gathered that summer at the *iftar.*

I had skipped lunch. As soon as the sun went down I dived into the hummus, grape leaves, lamb, couscous, and anything else I could reach. The Muslims around me only picked at the food. They were pacing themselves, they told me, for a long night of festive eating. They had just woken up, and they would nap the next day. Night is day and day is night during Ramadan in Cairo.

In the middle of the twentieth century, Egypt had led the Arab world to independence from the former colonial powers. It became the wellspring of Arab nationalism, political Islam, and global jihad. Everything in the Arab world had seemed to start in Cairo. Anyone in the region who cared about local politics also followed politics in Cairo. The vibrancy, nightlife, and climate lured the princes of the oil-rich Gulf to holiday at the beaches of Sharm el-Sheikh or the Marriott in Zamalek. The people of neighboring basket cases like Yemen, Jordan, Libya, or the Palestinian territories looked to Egypt as a big brother. Cairo was the place for education and culture, the big time.

But the experts in Washington had all assured me that nothing else interesting would happen in Egypt. It had now set the template for the stagnation of the region. Its docile citizenry would never challenge their corrupt rulers. Its corrupt rulers could never meet the needs of their exponentially expanding population. In economics, politics, and culture, the ancient Arab heartland was in irreversible decline.

Most Egyptians lived a world apart from Zamalek or Maadi. There were 78 million of them in 2010, up from 66 million a decade before. Nearly a quarter lived in Cairo, and 95 percent in the valley of the Nile. More than 40 percent of Egyptians—and the vast majority in many rural areas—lived on less than $2.00 a day. A fifth survived on less than $1.25. At about $5.00 a pound, beef was an extravagance. Nearly one in four Egyptian adults could not read. Forty percent of households lacked access to sewage systems, and 10 percent lacked running water (including many in the urban slums of Cairo and Alexandria). Only 8 percent of the population owned a car, and that was still more than enough to clog the streets of the capital.

I brought with me the standard Western assumptions. Islam fused religion and politics, mosque and state could never be separated, and so Arabs were all but doomed to choose between secular strongmen and religious extremists. Arab and Islamic culture, I was told, was uniquely resistant to the spread of democracy. Over the last two decades, democracy had taken root in Eastern Europe, Latin America, East Asia, and sub-Saharan Africa, but not yet in the Middle East—except for Israel. Arab exceptionalism, political scientists called it.

I pictured Egypt and Israel as enemies held in a fragile peace only by American payments to both sides. But the $70 billion in American military aid over decades had made Egypt's generals into Washington's best Arab allies. Arab families were tribal, Arab culture antimodern, Arab women treated almost as chattel. And so on. Almost all of it was wrong.

I was surprised at what I can only call the colonial feel of our lives. We drank gin and tonics at picnic tables among palm trees on the lawn of the

Maadi British Club, a vestige of the occupation. We swam at an even more exclusive club, run by the American embassy for its staff and contractors (and for the non-Egyptian faculty of the American University in Cairo, where Laura taught law and advised the administration). The embassy commissary provided the club with imported wine, beer, pork, and other products that were almost impossible to find anywhere else in Egypt. Our friends in Zamalek spent weekends at a former British Officers' Club with multiple swimming pools and a stable for horses. Abdel Nasser had nationalized it decades ago, but having a low membership number was still a status symbol. It meant your family had belonged longer.

The police invariably sided with foreigners—*khawagah* is the derogatory term—in any dispute with Egyptians. The Arab wife of a Western journalist I knew showed her husband's business card to any traffic policeman who stopped her, and the policeman always sped her on her way. In the Egyptian film *Hassan and Marcus* (2008), a general in the Interior Ministry announced that seventy-five people had died "pushing" to escape from a terrorist bomb blast. "And thankfully they are all Egyptians! No foreigners!" Big laughs from Egyptian moviegoers.

Working-class Egyptians tumbled over themselves to help foreigners like us, only sometimes fishing for *baksheesh.* ("The taxi drivers see you as a bag of money," an Arabic tutor told me.) But members of the Anglophone elite invariably tried to bond with us over the failings of their poorer countrymen, like the bureaucrat who had told me about "Egyptian IBM" and missing San Francisco.

The Egyptian novelist Naguib Mahfouz wrote in the 1950s of an autobiographical character, Kamal, whose rich Egyptian friend pined for Paris or London. "How it hurt Kamal whenever his friend let slip some hint of his sense of superiority over the Egyptian people [as if] he was talking about a people to which neither of them belonged." Many in the elite talked that way sixty years later. The minister of culture used to pontificate on state television about the tragic "backwardness" of his fellow Egyptians. Affluent Egyptians were often zealously chauvinistic about their homeland—"the Mother of the World," as Egyptians called it. How could the same people identify so snobbishly with the West and condescend so deeply to their own countrymen? I was still new to the postcolonial world.

Exclusive clubs, hotels, and restaurants had almost entirely blocked off the breezy banks along the Nile in Cairo by the time I arrived. Desperate for air, poorer Cairenes gathered at night in rows of plastic chairs on the narrow sidewalks of bridges, sipping juice or tea from vendors who paraded back and forth with tanks on their backs. On the edge of Maadi, families picnicked on a tiny patch of grass between the Total gas station and the busy road along the river.

Only over the last decade had the rich begun fleeing to gated communities in newly built suburbs. Many were designed to look like Palm Springs, with pools, golf courses, and ceaseless irrigation. Mubarak's ministers had sold off publicly owned desert land around the city at bargain prices to well-connected cronies. After the land grab, the race to build the suburbs had sucked so much capital away from other investments that it helped trigger a nationwide recession. An upscale project across the Nile in Giza was sold as "European CountrySide"—transliterated into Arabic letters that would spell "Eurobean" if pronounced correctly. A rich developer (and ruling-party lawmaker) marketed one of his projects as "Mayfair," after the neighborhood of London. Another, on the Mediterranean, he called "Virginia Beach Village."

Khedive Ismail Pasha, the hereditary ruler who led Egypt into vassalage to Britain in the late nineteenth century, once proclaimed, "My country is no longer in Africa; we are now part of Europe." He might have felt right at home in the early-twenty-first-century suburbs. Their development meant that for the first time in centuries Cairo no longer forced the rich and poor to mingle in the streets.

One night in the summer of 2010, Laura and I dined at the suburban home of the Pakistani-born executive who ran Citigroup in Egypt. As we looked out over his pool and a golf course, he was explaining to an assortment of Western guests and Anglophone Egyptians that no population as poor and uneducated as Egypt's could ever govern itself through democratic elections. He had learned that in Pakistan, he said. All nodded in agreement.

Then an American executive of an international tobacco company, enjoying the wine, posed a question to the table. Was it true, he asked, that the Arabic language contained no word for "compromise?"

For even the snobbiest Egyptian, this was too much. The Arabic language had developed over centuries across a vast swath of countries on three continents. It had accumulated a daunting multitude of synonyms for everything, including compromise. This supposed deficit was an urban myth in the West. The Arabic speakers politely corrected him. The wine flowed on. But I knew then that whenever I heard someone say, "Arabic has no word for . . . ," I was in the presence of a racist.

The most visible champion of the privatizations that created the new suburbs was a steel mogul and ruling party power broker named Ahmed Ezz. His face appeared almost daily on the front pages of Egypt's privately owned newspapers. In his college days he had played the drums in a Fleetwood Mac–style rock-and-roll band. Then he took advantage of the opening up of the Egyptian economy under Sadat by expanding his father's business selling building materials. By the 1990s, Ezz was rich and connected enough that Mubarak appointed him to a joint U.S.–Egyptian trade council. There he befriended another council member, Gamal Mubarak.

That was also the time when, in 1996, Ezz managed to buy control of the massive state-owned steelmaker. He said that he had been the only one willing to inject needed capital; his critics said he got a sweet deal through his Mubarak connections. Either way, he now controlled at least two thirds of the booming steel market. He amassed a personal net worth of more than $2 billion. He became chairman of the Parliament's most important finance committee, and he joined his friend Gamal atop the ruling party.

Every Arab despot had an Ezz in those days. Egypt, Syria, Tunisia, Libya, and other Arab states all followed Western advice and opened their state-dominated economies to competition and markets. But their authoritarian rulers made no effort to open their political systems, or to make the government officials who were selling off the assets accountable to the public. Privatization ended up giving enormous windfalls to a handful of cronies. And in each country, a single well-connected businessman emerged as the grinning face of economic reform—Ezz in Egypt, Sakher el-Materi in Tunisia, Hassan Tatanaki in Libya, Rami Makhlouf in Syria, and so on. I pictured them all around a table at the Four Seasons in Dubai, raising their glasses to toast the Washington consensus.

Ezz looked like a capitalist elf. He was about five and a half feet tall,

with wavy dark hair parted to the side and sideburns down to the bottom
of his ears. He favored platform shoes, Italian suits, spread collars, silver
cuff links, and Cohiba cigarillos. He kept three wives—a practice allowed
by Egyptian law and Muslim tradition but practical only for the rich and
the bold. He was forty-nine years old in 2007 when he married his third
wife, Shahinaz el-Naggar—an heiress, businesswoman, and fellow member of the ruling party's parliamentary block (he insisted she resign after
their marriage). Cairo gossip columnists reported that he had paid her a
dowry of $5 million and bought a $175,000 ring. They flew to Switzerland
for the wedding, and she moved into an apartment in the Four Seasons.
(His second wife lived in another apartment in the hotel, and his first lived
in a suburban compound.)

By 2010, Ezz could boast that privatization had worked wonders. The
economy had grown by about 50 percent over the decade, the highest rate
in forty years. More Egyptians were buying cars and air conditioners.
Home building was booming. So was the steel business. But to the majority
of the population, Ezz embodied the widening gulf that divided them from
the lucky few inside the new gated suburbs.

O strich! Ostrich! Over here, ostrich!" "Psst! Zebra, want to see zebra?"
We took our sons to the Cairo zoo, and the animal keepers reminded
Laura and me of the pot dealers who used to call out to passersby in Washington Square Park in New York City. Instead of caring for the animals,
the keepers were there to pimp them out. For a dollar tip you could touch,
feed, or ride whatever animal you fancied. We snapped pictures of our four-
year-old riding a zebra, feeding an elephant, mingling with kangaroos, and
petting lion cubs. One keeper convinced us to let our son pose with a
mother tiger, as the attendant himself looked on with a menacing stick in
his hand. He suggested we put a hand in the mouth of the lion. That we
declined.

Empty cigarette packs floated beside the crocodiles. We saw a keeper
beat a tiger with a rod. Animals stared dazedly. I later learned that the
World Association of Zoos and Aquariums had expelled the Cairo zoo for

violating international standards for the treatment of animals. When we thought of the cruelty, it ruined the fun.

Khedive Ismail, who once proclaimed Egypt part of Europe, founded the zoo in 1881. He commissioned no less than Gustave Eiffel to design a bridge for its garden. But the most glorious part of the original zoo lay along the Nile, and that had been sold off long before our visit. A Four Seasons Hotel now blocked the view of the river. Egyptian families looking for a few yards of grass to picnic on or play in swarmed over the remaining eighty acres. And the animals, for practical purposes, belonged to the zookeepers. Each saw his charge as a chance to profit off what was left of the zoo.

In 2010 the Egyptian government spent more than a quarter of its budget on the salaries of more than six million civilian employees like the zookeepers, and that number excluded millions more in the army and police. Those six million were about 20 percent of Egypt's civilian workforce—more than twice as many as the number of government employees that the United States and the United Kingdom employ together, or three times the size of the public sector workforce in Turkey, where the population was slightly smaller but the gross domestic product was three times as large. Turkey, infamous for its bloated bureaucracy, was a model of efficiency compared with Egypt.

Most Egyptian public employees saw their positions as assets to rent out or withhold, a source of *baksheesh*. Traffic policemen took small bribes to forget moving violations (so, of course, the traffic was lawless). Or a policeman might stop you from parking in a perfectly legal space, but then require only a few pounds to let you park in any space you wanted—no matter what that did to the flow of cars and pedestrians. Civil servants brought vegetables to work, peeled them at their desks, and went home to cook lunch.

It was the Nasserite social contract, and versions of it prevailed across most of the region. A paternalistic state had once furnished an abundance of jobs along with generous food and fuel subsidies. Abdel Nasser had guaranteed a job to everyone with a university degree, no matter how overcrowded the classes or poorly trained the graduates, and until 1990 Mubarak had kept up the pretense. Egyptians, in turn, put up with a government over which they had no say at all. But by 2010, the bargain was breaking. Anyone could see it. Just take a walk from the Four Seasons through the squalor of the zoo.

For a police state, though, I found Egypt in 2010 remarkably open. Mubarak had first allowed the private ownership of news organizations about a half dozen years before I arrived. They were not fully independent: All the newspapers and television networks belonged to a small handful of businessmen close to Mubarak, and the owners were usually dependent on the state for other business interests. Their journalists worked within clear boundaries. Criticizing the military, Mubarak, or Islam would land you in jail. But within those lines, newspapers like *El-Masry El-Youm—Today's Egyptian*—or talk show hosts like Mona Shazli managed to call attention to many of the state's deficiencies, including the terrible economy, the soaring price of vegetables, or even the epidemic abuses of the Egyptian police.

I heard a great deal that summer about a minibus driver named Emad el-Kabeer. A couple of years earlier, the police had accosted his cousin in a parking lot, and Kabeer made the mistake of attempting to intercede. The police arrested him, stripped him half naked, hung his feet from a ceiling, beat him senseless, and shoved a black pole into his anus. Using a mobile phone, an officer recorded a video of Kabeer's humiliation.

"Oh, pasha, forgive me, I beg your mercy, forgive me," Kabeer pleaded.

"Everyone in the parking lot will see this tomorrow," the officer replied.

The video reached the internet, and it was still circulating a few years later when I arrived in Cairo. The blogger at my table at the embassy *iftar,* Wael Abbas, had brought the Kabeer video to widespread attention. Talk shows took it from there. Emad el-Kabeer became one of the most recognized names in Egypt.

Questioned about the video, the Interior Ministry responded by arresting Kabeer a second time. This time he was sentenced to three months in prison for assaulting an officer. Only after an overwhelming outcry did the police detain two of the officers involved. Or was that just a pretense? The torturers were soon released and reinstated.

Emad el-Kabeer was back in the news in the summer of 2010 because of an echo. In June, policemen in Alexandria had dragged a clean-shaven young man out of a café for an uncertain reason. The ministry later said the policemen had suspected him of smoking or dealing pot, but their motives were hazy. They pulled him into a nearby apartment building, beat him, and slammed his head against a marble staircase. In front of witnesses, the police watched him die of his wounds.

One onlooker took a picture of the bloody remains with a mobile phone, and remembering Kabeer, Egyptians knew what to do. Within weeks two competing Facebook pages dedicated to the name of the latest police victim—"We are all Khaled Said"—had accumulated tens of thousands of followers. Interior Ministry officials said Khaled Said had choked to death on a clump of marijuana, trying to swallow the evidence. They barely tried to sell the lie. They seemed not to care if anyone believed it, and the new openness of the media made the ministry's cynicism especially stark.

A hit film, *This Is Chaos,* had reached satellite television that summer. Released to theaters in 2007 by the Egyptian directors Youssef Chahine and Khaled Youssef, the film began with a disclaimer to placate the censors: "We appreciate the patriotic role played by the police establishment to maintain stability and security. These are just isolated acts." But that only added a laugh line. As the disclaimer faded, the film showed hundreds of riot police carelessly destroying a neighborhood vegetable market to chase down a handful of nonviolent demonstrators. The police beat them with batons, locked them in a dungeon, and tortured them on and off for the duration of the film.

The main character, a policeman named Hatem, became an icon. "If you are not good to Hatem, you are not good to Egypt!" he forced local shopkeepers to repeat as he shook them down for bribes. "Law? Here, there is only one law. Hatem's law," he told a prisoner, administering electric shocks to his chest while the captive hung suspended from the ceiling. "Now let the law help you!"

In one scene, Hatem attempted to steal a valuable oil painting from the office of a police commissioner by substituting a fake. It was common knowledge in the ministries of culture and antiquities that officials had been pilfering Egyptian treasures for years using similar methods. Western and Egyptian archaeologists groused to me that so many cheap knockoffs had been left in the storerooms of the Egyptian Museum that it was becoming hard to know what was real anymore. Those sticky fingers, too, became a public scandal in the summer of 2010. *Poppy Flowers,* painted by Vincent van Gogh and worth more than $50 million, was stolen from the walls of an Egyptian government museum. It was obviously an inside job. The same painting had been stolen from the same museum before, in 1977, although later recovered in Kuwait. No one was held accountable, and this time the painting has never resurfaced. In *This Is Chaos,* the policeman Hatem was such a philistine he ripped the canvas, tearing it from its frame, cheerfully unaware that he had destroyed its value.

The climax, though, was what made *This Is Chaos* memorable. Fed-up residents of the neighborhood stormed the police station—scaling fences, throwing rocks, and sending the policemen fleeing in terror. Anxious senior police officials facing the crowds even put Hatem under arrest. Or was that just a pretense, like the brief detention of Kabeer's torturers? "Hatem, don't you know that we love you? We are trying to protect you!" the police commissioner stage-whispered as he led Hatem away.

Years after the film, a newspaper columnist called Egypt "A Nation of Hatems." Every reader understood.

Washington was a mainstay of Mubarak's nation of moguls, zookeepers, and Hatems. The American embassy in Cairo was one of the largest in the world. It occupied a city block, looked like a fortress, and oversaw an enormous aid budget. The United States sent $1.3 billion a year in hardware and services to the Egyptian military and another $250 million to the civilian government. *New York Times* boilerplate called Egypt "the cornerstone of the American-backed regional order." "Mama Amreeka," Egyptians called their government's Western patron.

I had assumed the United States adopted Egypt after Camp David, in 1979, but the story went back to the early 1950s. In those early days of the contest with the Soviets, American cold warriors had worried about the popular appeal of communism across the region and especially in Egypt. Kermit Roosevelt Jr., the grandson of Theodore Roosevelt and a senior American spy, wrote an internal government report imagining an ideal Arab ally, one "who would have more power in his hands than any other Arab leader ever had before, 'power to make an unpopular decision.'" Roosevelt knew Egypt well. He had established the first American intelligence operation in Cairo during the Second World War and then set up a CIA-run military training program. Back in Cairo in February 1952, he met with a small group of officers who included thirty-four-year-old Colonel Gamal Abdel Nasser. (The next year, in 1953, Roosevelt orchestrated a coup to remove the prime minister of Iran.)

A few months after Roosevelt's visit to Cairo, in July 1952, Abdel Nasser and his Free Officers wanted to get back in touch with the American government. Some later said they had contacted the United States Air Force attaché in Cairo, David Evans, as early as July 19. And at 3:00 A.M. on the morning of July 23, Abdel Nasser sent an emissary to knock on the door of the Maadi home of the American ambassador, Jefferson Caffery, with an advance warning: the Free Officers planned to remove King Farouk that day in a military coup. They wanted Washington with them.

"The image of the United States was closely associated in our minds with championing the cause of freedom and supporting liberation movements," one of the plotting Free Officers, Anwar Sadat, wrote in his memoir, only partly seeking to flatter. "Besides, by establishing such a link we sought to neutralize the British."

Three days later—on July 26—Ambassador Caffery escorted Farouk to his yacht for a voyage into exile. In the years that followed, the ambassador reputedly referred to the Free Officers almost like protégés: "My boys."

Abdel Nasser's men later said that after the takeover Kermit Roosevelt passed the new strongman at least a million dollars under the table in a bid for his loyalty. Legend holds that Abdel Nasser used the money to build the Cairo Tower, a 614-foot-high pillar in Zamalek. Nasserites call it Roosevelt's erection.

But America stood by Caffery's "boys" at a critical moment. Four years after the coup, Abdel Nasser nationalized the Suez Canal. In retaliation, Israel, Britain, and France conspired to invade Egypt, seize the channel, and oust him. Westerners know the episode as the Suez Crisis. Egyptians call it the Tripartite Aggression.

President Dwight D. Eisenhower was furious. Although the United States and the United Kingdom had withdrawn aid for the Aswan Dam just a few months earlier, Eisenhower now threatened to cut off vital American financial support and petroleum imports to all three allies if they persisted in their operation. He deployed the Sixth Fleet to face down British and French ships on the way to Egypt, and he hinted that the fleet might block-ade Israel.

He was exerting America's postwar preeminence, but in rhetoric, at least, he sounded like the friend of the revolution that the Free Officers had hoped for. "As there can be no second-class citizens before the law in America . . . there can be no second-class nations before the law of the world community," Eisenhower proclaimed, invoking the struggle of the American founders. "There can be only one law—or there will be no peace." Abdel Nasser survived, and he owed his thanks to Eisenhower.

The escalation of the Cold War, though, tempered the American pro-nouncements about "no second-class nations" and "only one law." Abdel Nasser tried to cultivate the support of the Soviet Union as well as Wash-ington, and in 1965, President Lyndon Johnson punished Egypt by cutting off crucial imports of subsidized wheat. Johnson backed Saudi Arabia in a crushing proxy war against Egypt in Yemen; Egypt had backed Nasserite rebels there in an ugly war that became its Vietnam. And two years after the wheat cutoff, Johnson joined with Israel decisively in its devastating Six-Day War against Egypt and the Arabs.

"There was one power that ruled Egypt and the world, and that is: America," Anwar Sadat concluded after he succeeded Abdel Nasser at his death in 1971. In the Middle East, "the U.S. holds 99 percent of the cards."

Acting on this assessment, Sadat secretly courted Henry Kissinger, who had become national security adviser to President Richard Nixon in 1969 and secretary of state in September 1973. Kissinger worked avidly to thwart Egypt in the opening days of its next war with Israel, in October 1973. But at the same time, Sadat was privately reassuring Kissinger in a secret cable that Egypt had no intention of "intensifying the engagements or wid-ening the confrontation."

Mohamed Hassanein Heikal had been Abdel Nasser's adviser, confi-dant, and ghostwriter from the earliest stages of the Free Officers' coup, and he continued to play a central, behind-the-scenes role in Egyptian af-fairs until his death in 2016. (I knew him in Cairo.) Heikal called Sadat's gambit with Kissinger "the first time in history that a country at war disclosed its intentions to its enemies, and gave them a free hand on the political and military fronts."

But Sadat won his game. Five years after the war, he stood at Camp David with President Jimmy Carter and Israeli prime minister Menachem Begin. "I shall sign anything proposed by President Carter without reading it," Sadat told his aides, to their shock and dismay.

The resulting Camp David Accords did little about the underlying Arab-Israeli conflict and nothing at all about the plight of the Palestinians. But Washington committed for the first time to backing just the kind of Arab autocracy Kermit Roosevelt had proposed in 1951—a leader "with 'power to make an unpopular decision,'" a leader, as Roosevelt also wrote, who wanted power "primarily for the mere sake of power."

I met Carter in Cairo, and he said he understood Egyptian complaints about that arrangement: Washington was supporting a dictatorship in Cairo for the well-being of Israel. "I think that is true, we were," he told me. "And I can't say I wasn't doing that as well."

President George W. Bush tried, for a time, to nudge Egypt toward democracy. That was part of what he called the "Freedom Agenda," and his prodding may have spurred Mubarak's decision in 2005 to hold Egypt's first presidential vote with more than one candidate. (His sole opponent, Ayman Nour, was allowed to win only 7 percent of the vote and then was jailed promptly after losing.) Mubarak had also allowed the spread of a grassroots opposition movement under the banner Kifaya!—Enough!—as in three decades of Mubarak had been more than enough. Almost everyone I met in Cairo who played any role in politics or activism cut their teeth in Kifaya! Its emergence in 2005 was more political freedom than Egyptians had ever known.

But by then the American military saw Egypt as uniquely vital: the guarantor of the peace with Israel, the gatekeeper of the Suez Canal and strategic flight routes, the crossroads of three continents, and the regional bellwether. I heard the same litany many times from American officials.

Washington now had more urgent concerns than democracy, and even small doses of it could be unnerving. The Muslim Brotherhood had railed against Western dominance of Egypt for nearly eight decades, and it won big in the first round of the 2005 parliamentary elections. The next year,

Hamas, the Brotherhood's militant Palestinian offshoot, won the first legis-lative elections in the Palestinian territories.

Alarmed, the Bush White House stayed silent as Mubarak cracked down on the Brotherhood to limit its gains in the runoff round of parlia-mentary voting (the Brothers still took an unprecedented one fifth of the seats). In the Palestinian terroritories, the United States actively backed Israeli intervention to overturn the election and keep Hamas from power.

Ten years later, Obama authorized a secret study questioning the viabil-ity of the authoritarian order in Egypt and a few other countries in the re-gion. His National Security Council recognized, in an abstract way, that the autocratic regimes of the previous six decades could not stand much longer. "The region's foundations are sinking into the sand," Secretary of State Hillary Clinton warned the leaders of the Arab world in a speech in Doha, Qatar, on January 13, 2011. But she urged only vague reforms. The study about regime viability was not yet complete. Aside from Obama's speech in Cairo, American policy had not changed much. The "Freedom Agenda" was dead.

"God help us if something ever happened to Mubarak," a senior State Department official told a group of diplomats heading to the region in 2010, summing up the American view. I did not understand until years later the role that Washington continued to play in the struggle of Egyptians to real-ize their freedoms.

I was studying Arabic full time in the fall of 2010, learning how to order Turkish coffee with the "just right" (*mazbut*) amount of sugar, or to ask for a bathroom (*hammam*) instead of a pigeon (*hamam*). I worked with two tutors, both Cairenes, but from two different worlds.

Jehan was the wife of a rich businessman who lived in a large villa in our neighborhood, Maadi. She had earned a doctorate at the American Uni-versity in Cairo and become a professional translator of books, working in Arabic, English, and French. She wore a headband, slacks, and pastel-colored blouses, and her housekeeper served us Turkish coffee *mazbut* as we reviewed lessons at a polished wood table overlooking a well-tended garden.

"Do you know why everyone is always catching a cold in Cairo?" she asked me one day with disgust. "Because Egyptians never wash their hands!" I had not noticed the colds. But I was getting accustomed to the elite repudiations of ordinary Egyptians.

My other tutor, Hatem, was the son of a stable hand at the elite Gezira Sporting Club in Zamalek—the former British Officers' Club. His father had been an extra in *The Ten Commandments,* he told me with pride. Hatem came to my villa in a rusty, red Fiat, and he often interrupted teaching me Arabic to vent about his life. He suffered from high blood pressure and diabetes. He shared a two-room, un-air-conditioned apartment with his wife and infant son, and he often lost his temper with them for keeping him awake at night. I suspected he dragged out our lessons to enjoy the cool of my villa. But he was uncomfortable in Western-run houses and always lowered his eyes to avoid looking at Laura. He told me that if I ever used the bathroom in an Arab household, I should keep my eyes on the floor at all times, lest I accidentally glimpse a wife or a daughter.

Where Jihan shook her head over the backwardness of Egyptians, Hatem fumed at the venality of their rulers. One of the first words Hatem taught me was *fesad*—corruption. He always referred to Mubarak's circle as "that gang of thieves," the way observant Muslims repeat the words "peace be upon him" whenever they name the Prophet Mohamed.

I read the daily paper aloud to him in Arabic for practice, and we followed the case of Hisham Talaat Moustapha, a ruling party parliamentarian and the millionaire developer behind "Mayfair" and "Virginia Beach Village." Moustapha, who was fifty-one, had paid a retired Egyptian police officer $2 million to kill his mistress, the thirty-year-old Lebanese pop star Suzanne Tamim. A trial court had sentenced Moustapha to death, an appeals court had invalidated the ruling on a technicality, and now a new judge had sentenced him to fifteen years in prison. Wasn't Hatem pleased that justice was served?

No. Moustapha must have run afoul of Mubarak, Hatem reasoned. Surely that was the only reason he had been convicted.

Who knew? Moustapha was transferred out of prison for health reasons three years later. His sister took over his parliamentary seat.

I could scarcely imagine a meeting between my two Arabic tutors. Hatem would look at his feet; Jehan would look for dirt on his hands. They both agreed on one thing, though. Something had to give.

Although I was not yet on duty, I volunteered to help the *Times* cover the parliamentary elections that fall, and I learned two new words: *fowda*, for chaos, and *baltagiya*, for thugs.

Progress on all fronts had seemed to skid to a halt. The global recession of 2008 had interrupted the rise of Egyptian living standards. And Mubarak, no longer under American pressure, was closing down the newly opened political space. He had added new amendments to the constitution that had eviscerated any hope of a fair vote and any right to a fair trial. Cynics guessed that he was laying the groundwork for a succession to Gamal.

I watched the vote on November 28, 2010, from Alexandria, a city I associated with Lawrence Durrell, C. P. Cavafy, and trans-Mediterranean cosmopolitanism. I was curious about the place because I knew that since Abdel Nasser's coup the city had become an Islamist stronghold. At a polling place in an elementary school, waiters rushed in and out with free pastries for the voters, in boxes labeled with the ruling party logo. But the registered election observer for the Muslim Brotherhood—a balding, portly man in an ill-fitting suit, with a clipboard—was stuck outside. The police guards refused to honor his credentials. As I stood with him, three police trucks rolled by with Islamist anthems booming through tiny, barred windows. Inside were Muslim Brothers the police had rounded up all over Alexandria, to prevent them from getting out the vote.

The local Brotherhood headquarters was squalid and dull. A couple of bearded men were working the phones under fluorescent lights. When I turned on the bathroom faucet, water ran through a drain without a pipe and splashed on my shoes. On a television, a Brotherhood lawmaker from Alexandria was holding up a handful of bullet shells. A minibus of *baltagiya* had chased his supporters with knives, and a policeman had fired his gun.

"You're trying to kill us, you tyrants!" he was shouting. "You're killing us on the streets for not electing you!"

I raced to find the man on TV, Sobhi Saleh, and caught up with him as he was leaving a hospital. He was a clean-shaven lawyer, and he showed me his torn necktie and the streaks of blood on his neck and collar. The *baltagiya* had beaten him, he said. Then Saleh turned away and began walking down the center of an empty street of tenements, shouting the Brother-hood's perennial slogan at the top of his lungs: *Islam hua el hal*—Islam is the solution.

Hundreds of voices echoed back from the windows. Scores of young men poured from the doors and fell into step chanting behind him. I shiv-ered, wondering, what "solution" did these men have in mind?

Nine people were killed that day in clashes around the polls, according to human rights groups. Saleh lost his seat. So did every Islamist. For the first time since 1984, the Brotherhood was shut out completely. Their 20 percent of the Parliament was reduced to no seats at all.

Ahmed Ezz, the steel baron, published an op-ed column in a state newspaper declaring 2010 to be the cleanest election in Egyptian history. The paper identified him as "the man behind the sweeping win by the rul-ing party."

Mohamed ElBaradei—the sixty-eight-year-old liberal, former diplomat, and presidential hopeful—was no Muslim Brother. With his horn-rimmed glasses, balding head, and wispy mustache, he was nobody's idea of a rev-olutionary either. But he sputtered with rage at the fraud. "Keep a record of every case of torture and oppression and the violation of personal liberty, because there will be a reckoning," he urged Egyptians in a videotaped message from his den that circulated over social media. "There will be violence."

3

Police Day

January 24, 2011–February 11, 2011

A dozen men and women had gathered over sugary tea and Nescafé in a Cairo law office. They were all in their late twenties or early thirties, which made them older than most Egyptians. Some were leftists, others liberals, and others Muslim Brothers. Several had been friends since they were students at Cairo University. They had been organizing together for years—against the Israeli occupation, against the American invasion of Iraq, and always against the Egyptian police. Now they were doctors, lawyers, and engineers. Some had young children. Yuppies, we might call them. None of them had known any other president besides Hosni Mubarak.

It was a Monday night, January 24, and the next day was Police Day, the annual holiday that commemorated the massacre of fifty policemen who had resisted the British army in 1952. The same clique of yuppies had used the same day every year to demonstrate against police abuse, always in Tahrir Square—Liberation Square, in English. Almost no one else showed up. The police chased them away in about fifteen minutes. But there seemed a small chance that this year might be different.

My first official day on the job as an international correspondent was January 9, and I had flown that day to Tunis. A young street peddler had burned himself to death about three weeks earlier after an encounter with a bullying police officer in an interior town. His self-immolation had inspired a rash of imitators, including a few in Egypt. I imagined an article about the psychology of suicide.

Tunisia, a former French colony, was once the most benign example of Arab autocracy. Unlike Abdel Nasser, the father of Tunisia's independence had been a lawyer, Habib Bourguiba. Even while he plotted to overthrow colonial rule, he was also scheming to expand commercial ties with France and Europe. Tunisia broke away in 1965, and he invested in education and literacy. He championed women's rights, encouraged birth control, and ended polygamy, successfully lowering birth rates and expanding the middle class. (Tunisia was the only Arab state to outlaw polygamy.)

But even the best autocracy had limits. Bourguiba jailed his opponents, bowed to no court, and never contemplated any possible successor. In 1987, his security chief, Zine al Abidine Ben Ali, seized power through a medical coup, enlisting doctors to declare the president no longer fit for office.

In contrast to his predecessor, Ben Ali had no education except military training in France and the United States. Five years after he took power at the age of fifty-three, he left his first wife for a woman two decades younger—Leila Trabelsi, a hairdresser. By 2010, a sprawling clan of Ben Alis and Trabelsis was sucking up so much of the economy that Tunisians described them as a ruling mafia: the Family. The Family had muscled its way into control of banks, telecommunication companies, an airline, hotels, car distributorships, radio stations, a newspaper, prime real estate, a property developer, and much more. The first license to provide internet service had gone to Ben Ali's daughter. The *Assabah* newspaper belonged to his son-in-law, Sakher el-Materi, who was considered a potential successor. Two younger Trabelsis, on a lark, had once stolen a yacht from Bruno Rogers, the chairman of Lazard Frères, and the Ben Ali side of the Family included a noted drug dealer.

"Seemingly half of the Tunisian business community can claim a Ben Ali connection through marriage, and many of these relations are reported to have made the most of their lineage," reported a cable from the U.S. embassy that was disclosed by WikiLeaks. "Contacts tell us they are afraid to invest for fear that the family will suddenly want a cut." The diplomats summarized: "There are no checks in the system."

Other journalists told me not to bother visiting. The Tunisian police state put Egypt's to shame. *Mukhabarat* would follow me from the airport, bug my hotel room, and scare everyone away from me. Tunisians had even less experience than Egyptians with civic debate or competitive politics.

But the chain of events set off by the fruit peddler's suicide on December 17 had led in unexpected directions. The funeral erupted in chants against Ben Ali. Police fired into the crowd. Grainy mobile phone footage spread over Facebook and Al Jazeera. Within days a widening spiral of martyrs, funerals, protests, and more martyrs was spreading from town to town, toward the capital. Police gunfire had killed more than thirty civilians by the time I landed in Tunis. Ben Ali had denounced the demonstrators as foreign spies and Islamist terrorists—the perennial bogeymen—and he vowed to crush them.

Using Skype to avoid telephone surveillance, an activist I knew in Cairo sent me the contact information of a Tunisian human rights lawyer, Radhia Nasraoui. When I reached her apartment that Wednesday, I saw that its front door had been torn off its hinges. A child's toys were strewn around the floor. Nasraoui, with a deeply creased face and short curly hair, was sitting in a housedress weeping on the couch.

A group of armed men in plain clothes had broken in and dragged off her husband, Hamma Hammami, who led Tunisia's outlawed Communist Party. (Arab politics had been in such a deep freeze that there were still Communist parties.) He had given interviews on French television commending the rural protests. "So we were waiting for his arrest," Nasraoui told me. Her ten-year-old daughter had shrieked in terror when the police broke down the door, and Nasraoui had sent all three of her daughters away for fear the assailants might come back for their mother.

Nasraoui ran a Tunisian rights group that opposed the use of torture, and the police had jailed and beaten both her and her husband many times before. But this time the security forces were jittery and unpredictable. Would I please write about her husband's disappearance? she asked. The abduction of another Tunisian dissident was hardly newsworthy, but I said I would try.

As I left her, a taxi driver checking Facebook on his mobile device had tipped me off about an upcoming protest. It materialized an hour later outside the French embassy, and I was introduced to tear gas. So the next day I checked Facebook first thing in the morning. I saw calls for a protest in

Hammamet, the East Hampton of Tunis, where Ben Ali's family kept their summer homes, and I made it there by the early afternoon.

A police car and garbage piles were burning in the streets. Rioters had already set fire to every bank in town, including one next to the police station. Most police had fled. The handful remaining—all from local families—stood in front of the station asking the mob for mercy. Leave us alone and go sack the mansions of the Ben Ali family. The police pointed the way.

At the beachfront mansion of Sofiane Ben Ali, the president's uncle, looters were carrying coffee tables and color televisions out through a broken picture window. Others set fire to a pair of all-terrain buggies on the lawn. Motorcyclists did wheelies around them. Someone "liberated" a sailboat. A chestnut-colored horse ran loose on the beach while a Tunisian coast guard boat observed from the water.

"Look, the people of Tunisia, the people of Tunisia," rioters told me, showing me mobile phone videos of themselves in action. They were giving me their names, without fear of reprisal. "Now, we can say what we want," said Cheadi Mohamed, a thirty-two-year-old airport worker. "It has started to change."

On the road back into Tunis, I saw tanks and armored personnel carriers (APCs) heading the other way. I wondered what other protest they intended to crush.

Ben Ali declared a curfew and delivered a third speech. But this time he no longer called the demonstrators terrorists or vowed to restore order. His hands shook at his podium. He jostled the microphone. He had dyed his hair black but he was seventy-four years old and it showed in his eyes. "I am telling you I understand you, yes, I understand you," he tried to assure Tunisians. Even with my amateur Arabic, I could hear the fear in his voice.

He pledged not to run for reelection. He promised to open up the media. Blocked websites were back online by the end of his speech. From now on, he said, the police would no longer shoot demonstrators.

Outside my hotel, drivers were ignoring the curfew, honking horns and waving placards in celebration. But all the cars were the same, and so were the placards. They were government cars, in a staged demonstration. Tunisians were not fooled.

But they had heard Ben Ali's promises. Early the next morning, on Friday, Radhia Nasraoui made for the headquarters of the Interior Ministry, on Avenue Habib Bourguiba. She had learned that her husband had been held there since Wednesday, and she wanted to bring him a change of clothes.

She arrived with a handful of Tunisian journalists, and the police guards seemed more anxious than ever. At around 9:00 A.M., about two hours after she arrived, they invited her inside to meet the ministry's political director, and he offered to let her see her husband—if only she would send away the journalists.

She refused and kept waiting. The journalists were joined by a growing crowd outside, and the numbers swelled further when midday prayers ended. "See what you have done with these demonstrations?" a plainclothes policeman told her accusingly, as though she and her husband were responsible. "Now are you happy?"

As the throng grew, a lawyer called her with a message from the interior minister. Then a Ben Ali crony called with a message from the president. She could take her husband home, they both said, if she sent away the crowds.

"I am not the leader of ten thousand people," she told them angrily, "and I can do nothing for Ben Ali!"

Hamma Hammami could hear the chants from his cell. This was his third day spent in solitary confinement, much of the time with his arms bound behind him. Around noon, a senior ministry official walked in and told him, "I am bringing you good news. You will leave, you will leave! If you say a word to the people, things may calm down, and we will let you leave."

The noise outside rose suddenly, and police started running in the halls. The ministry is under attack, they shouted.

I was outside, and by early afternoon a crowd in the tens of thousands stretched for several blocks of the broad boulevard, as far as the old French cathedral. A sign in English read YES WE CAN, mimicking Obama's campaign slogan. "What happened here is going to affect the whole Arab world," Zied Mhirsi, the thirty-three-year-old doctor who held the sign told me. Maybe someday, I thought.

By then the protest felt more like a celebration. Ben Ali was still in his palace but his authority had already fled. Political power is like fairy-tale magic: it works only if you believe in it.

Some time after 3:00 P.M., a group of men made their way in front of the Interior Ministry with a coffin on their shoulders. A rumor spread that they carried the body of another victim killed by the police, and the ministry lost patience. Hundreds, maybe thousands of police in riot gear stormed into the throngs.

Almost blinded by their tear gas and doubled over from coughing, I stumbled around a corner. A middle-aged man in an overcoat and with a small mustache grabbed me by the shoulder. I panicked, taking him for a policeman, but he pulled me into the bottom of a stairwell with a half dozen others. There he handed me half of a lemon. Rub it on your face, he told me. A home remedy for the tear gas.

My editors were in a fright, too, I later learned. I had never covered anything grittier than Congress, books, or business—not even a house fire. It was too late to fly in a more experienced hand. Tunisia had closed its airports.

By the time the gas cleared and I'd hiked to my hotel, Ben Ali had fled to Saudi Arabia. The police gave Hammami a ride home to his wife. On January 14, 2011, a popular uprising had removed an Arab ruler.

Experienced Egyptian activists used to send encouragement in online messages to the novices in Tunis. Now Tunisians were writing back with "advice to the youth of Egypt": "Put vinegar or onion under your scarf for tear gas." Apolitical Egyptians were trading jokes online: "Mubarak, your plane is waiting!"

I wanted to head back to Cairo for Police Day, eleven days later, but my editors told me to stay in Tunis. The transition there was the big story. "Nothing is going to happen in Egypt."

Ninety thousand Egyptians had clicked a link on the six-month-old "We are all Khaled Said" Facebook page to say that they would join this year's Police Day demonstration—a number that would exceed any organized rally in the four decades since Abdel Nasser died. The friends in the law office planning for Police Day hoped that if the crowds were large enough, they might demand the resignation of the interior minister.

With Tunisia in the news, though, someone suggested that this year they try a new twist. They had always reached out to their friends in Cairo's small middle class. This year, they thought, why not the poor? "We always start from the elite, with the same faces," one later recalled. "So this time we thought, let's try."

Many Westerners would come to see these worldly, middle-class yuppies as more like us than they were like other Egyptians. They were harnessing the technologies of Silicon Valley to the nonviolent tactics of Martin Luther King Jr. And we Western journalists in Egypt naturally accentuated the details that resonated with Westerners. I am sure I had a hand in fostering the feeling that these charming organizers had more in common with readers of the *New York Times* than they did with their compatriots. But that Police Day their clique galvanized something much broader. The shakedowns and self-dealing, the broken bargains of the Nasserite social contract, the shamelessness of the police, the rollback of rights, the rigging of the vote—the Tunisian revolt had brought it all into focus in a moment of common cause among Egyptians of all ages, classes, and creeds.

The organizers fanned out across poor and working-class neighborhoods on the morning of Police Day, January 25, 2011. They chanted old standbys, like the one mocking the paramilitary state security police, *"Amn el-Dawla—Amn fein? Dawla fein?"* "Where is security? Where is the state?" The Mubarak government had failed to provide any of the public services or accountability that citizens expect of a modern state, least of all security. Egyptian police were a menace. But this Police Day the organizers also hit bread-and-butter issues, like grocery prices and the minimum wage.

"They are eating pigeon and chicken, and we are eating beans all the time."

"Oh my, ten pounds can only buy us cucumbers now, what a shame, what a shame."

"Come down, Egyptians! Come down," marchers called to the balconies. And down they came. Contingents of a few dozen in each neighborhood swelled into thousands. The tributaries merged into rivers, and all converged toward the central traffic circle at Tahrir Square. "We entered Nahyan street with two hundred and we came out with ten thousand," one of the organizers told me later. Rich and poor, young and old: this was no yuppie revolt.

The leaders of the Muslim Brotherhood kept their distance, mainly to protect themselves. They knew that they made a big, easy target. Because of their numbers, their members would overwhelm any march that the organization joined. Mubarak's propagandists would easily dismiss all the marchers as Islamist extremists, and Mubarak's police would hit the Brotherhood. Besides, compared with Abdel Nasser or Sadat, Mubarak was gentle toward the Brothers. There was no need to risk what they had won.

But some younger Muslim Brothers in their twenties and thirties were among the core organizers who met in the law office and planned Police Day. Thousands of other members joined the marches as individuals, without waiting for a go-ahead from their leaders. And hundreds more gathered at a parallel Police Day demonstration led by former Brotherhood lawmakers at a Cairo courthouse. One of them, Mohamed Beltagy, brought the police a bouquet of flowers, to say thank you for all the abuse and incarceration. A female Brotherhood lawmaker led a contingent of Islamist women who pushed through police lines all the way to Tahrir Square. Islamist women may have been the first to make it.

My friend and *Times* colleague Kareem Fahim was in Cairo to cover the marches. "Bedlam," he emailed at midday. But that was just the beginning. "This shit is nuts," he wrote back that night. "The battle is spreading."

Amn el-Dawla met the marchers with tear gas, clubs, rubber bullets, and eventually live ammunition; a handful or more were killed by police gunshots. It took the security forces until late at night to expel the demonstrators from the square. Some turned then to Zyad el-Elaimy, who had convened the planning meeting in his law office. What happens now? they asked.

"We are going to jail," he told them assuredly.

The White House seemed to concur. "Our assessment is that the Egyptian government is stable," Secretary of State Clinton told journalists in Washington. Vice President Joe Biden, who said he knew Mubarak "fairly well," told a television interviewer not to call him "a dictator."

What did Washington know? The American intelligence agencies, I later learned, knew the top generals well and eavesdropped on them, too. But the U.S. government knew very little about what was going on inside the police force, among left-leaning activists, or within the Muslim Brotherhood. Washington more or less depended on Egypt's own intelligence services. "The leadership we were relying on was isolated and unaware of the tidal wave that was about to hit them," Michael Morrell, the deputy director of the Central Intelligence Agency, later acknowledged.

The embassy had ordered its personnel off the streets that day, and the intelligence agencies were thin on the ground. Steven A. Cook, an American political scientist who happened to be in Cairo, posted an observation on Twitter and a few moments later he got a call from the White House.

"You are my eyes and ears," Daniel Shapiro, senior director for the Middle East and North Africa on the National Security Council, told Cook. "Can you tell me what is happening?"

I called Mohamed ElBaradei, Egypt's great liberal hope. He had been working on his memoirs in his office in Vienna. "Frankly, I did not think the people were ready," he told me. Now we were both racing back to Cairo.

We awoke on Friday, January 28, to discover that the government had shut down all internet and mobile phone service. The Police Day organizers had told me to attend noon prayers at a mosque near Giza, and as a few thousand of us were leaving the prayer hall, some started chanting for bread and freedom. The police hit us all with tear gas and water cannons. Our driver had parked our Mitsubishi SUV nearby. A tear gas canister broke through the rear window, destroying the toddler car seat Laura and I had hauled all the way from Washington.

I had been directed to that mosque because Mohamed ElBaradei had also prayed there. He was wearing a suede jacket and clip-on sunglasses, and younger men held him by each arm to steady him against the force of the fire hoses. With their help, he stood his ground for a time, drenched and sputtering, even in the fumes. It may have been his finest hour.

When we both retreated back inside the mosque, he wanted to remind the *New York Times* that the police had soaked and gassed a Nobel Peace

Prize laureate. "This is the work of a barbaric regime," he told me, still dripping wet and panting. "They have told the Egyptian people that they have to revolt." Then he retired to his grand villa in a gated community in Giza.

A pudgy twenty-seven-year-old with floppy hair and a baggy sports coat pulled me to a corner of the prayer room. He said he was Waleed Rashed from the April 6 Youth Movement, best known for using the internet to rally opposition to Mubarak or to support striking workers. "Do not worry about ElBaradei," he told me. "We are making a revolution—not a protest, a revolution."

On his advice, I made my way back across the river to the downtown side of the Qasr el-Nil Bridge, a flat span with colonial-era stone lions at each entrance. It was midafternoon by the time I made it, and in front of me was a phalanx of more than a thousand policemen in black riot gear, armed with clubs and rifles. Five armored personnel carriers were moving with them and blasting tear gas. Two fire trucks were using their hoses as cannons. But all together they were somehow unable to repel the mass of demonstrators trying to push across the bridge from Giza.

I stood transfixed. The black mass of police surged forward, shooting and smashing, protected by helmets and flak jackets. I braced myself for a massacre. I was sure the police would break through, but they never did. The demonstrators wore motorcycle helmets and scraps of plastic under their shirts. They wrapped onions or lemons under scarves around their nose and mouth (as the Tunisians had suggested), or sprayed their faces with vinegar or cola—more home remedies for tear gas. They picked up hot, smoking canisters of tear gas and hurled them into the river; long trails of gray fumes arced majestically behind them.

As one wave faded back in exhaustion, a fresh one rotated to the front lines. The bridge was thick with marchers; they outnumbered the police. On the sidewalk around me, scrawny police conscripts fresh from the battle sat with their helmets off, panting, soaking with sweat, and shaking their heads in disbelief.

The shadows lengthened, and the battle continued. Phones were dead. The streets were in chaos. The taxis had fled. The three bridges from downtown Cairo back to Zamalek were all closed or obstructed. Worried about getting back across the Nile to my office on the island, I walked by the river to look for a passage by foot across one of the bridges.

Two policemen caught me under the overpass of the May 15 Bridge. *Sahafi*—journalist—I repeated. But they tore up my full notebooks and then shooed me off. Forget about getting back to Zamalek, they told me.

I set off half running into downtown, turning corners with no idea where I was going. Mubarak had decreed a 6:00 P.M. curfew and my newspaper deadline was approaching. I raised a thumb to hitchhike.

A tall, bearded man let me in his beat-up blue Fiat and introduced himself as Mohamed el-Masry—Mohamed the Egyptian, surely not his real name. I said I was a journalist for the *New York Times*, and without further explanation he spun his car around. He drove south until, after several tries, he found a passable bridge to Giza, on the far side of the Nile, so he could loop back to Zamalek. It was an hour-long detour on a dangerous night. Mohamed el-Masry asked only one thing: Would I take a message for Obama?

"I call on President Obama, at least in his statements, to be in solidarity with the Egyptian people and with freedom, truly, as he says," he dictated into my audio recorder. I managed to squeeze his quote into the newspaper, which I hoped might reach the president's desk.

Late that night the demonstrators on Qasr el-Nil Bridge finally broke through. Looters torched the ruling party headquarters and hauled out computers, televisions, briefcases, file cabinets, and assorted souvenirs with the ruling party logo. Then the crowd proceeded directly to the business headquarters of Ahmed Ezz, steel tycoon and friend of Gamal.

By midnight mobs had set fire to nearly a hundred police stations. As many as two thousand burning police cars littered the streets. I could hardly blame the rioters, but I winced each time I heard Westerners call the demonstrations "peaceful" or "nonviolent." (I qualified my own coverage, calling the protests "largely" nonviolent.) We were projecting our own ideals onto these "Facebook youth."

An Egyptian government inquiry later concluded that 849 civilians were killed during the uprising, almost all by police bullets and almost all on that night. (The tally from independent rights groups is roughly the same.) By midnight, though, the defeated police had vanished from the city.

Mubarak stuck to the script. The protests were "part of a bigger plot," he said in a televised address around midnight. "A very thin line separates freedom from chaos."

Obama, perhaps remembering the tumult he lived through as a child in Indonesia, told his advisers that day that Mubarak was doomed. "He took one look at what was happening in the streets and he thought, 'We ought to get on the right side of this,'" Ben Rhodes, the deputy national security adviser and a longtime aide to Obama, later told me.

"He knew that the old order was rotten and the status quo was unsustainable," Rhodes said. "Obama thought this was an opportunity that had to be tested. He wanted the future of Egypt to be the people in the square—not Mubarak."

Virtually every senior figure on Obama's National Security Council wanted to stand by Mubarak: Secretary of State Clinton, Vice President Biden, Secretary of Defense Robert Gates, National Security Adviser Tom Donilon, and others. They invoked the Iranian Revolution of 1979. They worried about other autocratic Arab allies across the region, like the hereditary monarchs of Jordan, Morocco, and the Persian Gulf. What if citizens marched on those royal palaces, too? The United States should not "throw them to the wolves," as Gates later put it.

"The dynamic was established that day that the president wanted to get rid of Mubarak," Rhodes told me, "and most of his government didn't."

After placing a phone call to Mubarak, Obama delivered a statement from the White House. Mubarak "pledged a better democracy," Obama said. "I told him he has a responsibility to give meaning to those words." Despite what he had said inside the White House, Obama talked like Mubarak had years in office still ahead of him.

Tahrir Square was unlike a city square that you might find in New York or London. It was an unplanned urban void of dirt and pavement sprawling over several city blocks, in the shape of an elongated triangle rounded off at its two bottom corners, like a tear. A mosque and government administration building occupied one side of the lower circle, with a KFC opposite. At the northern point the Egyptian Museum stood beside a wide corridor under the overpass to the October 6 Bridge.

That Friday—remembered as the Day of Rage—demonstrators had converged on the square from all over the city. By night they had taken it over. After that the numbers never fell below a few thousand and sometimes swelled to ten times as many—or even to hundreds of thousands. After the success of Police Day, the leaders of the Muslim Brotherhood had come off the sidelines and told every able member to march on Tahrir Square and stay there.

With the police gone, the army had stationed hundreds of soldiers inside the iron fence of the Egyptian Museum, presumably to protect the mummies. A few tanks and personnel carriers were parked around the periphery of the square, but the soldiers did nothing. They looked down from their tank turrets with rifles across their laps, or sipped juice through straws from little plastic bags (cheaper than cups) sold by roving street vendors. Protesters—usually young Muslim Brothers—slept at night under the tank treads, to prevent surprise movements.

Military helicopters and jets buzzed low over downtown, and the crowds cheered as though the pilots had turned against Mubarak. I never understood what all those soldiers were waiting for behind the fence of the museum. Was the army replacing the police, turning against them, or waiting to roll out and crush the demonstration? Compared with modern states—where both the army and police answer to the same civilian authority—the Arab world was confounding.

Between the tanks and soldiers a booming tent city quickly sprang up. Smiling volunteers patted me down at the entrance to the square with exaggerated apologies, advertising the contrast with the haughty and brutal Egyptian police. More tents, blankets, chairs, and loudspeakers were arriving each day (from rich donors somewhere). Street vendors hawked drinks, tea, roasted sweet potatoes, and corn on the cob. Tens of thousands surged in again on Tuesday, beginning a biweekly rhythm of larger and larger rallies each Tuesday and Friday. Even in the middle of the night the population of Tahrir Square was still at least a few thousand. The internet returned on February 3, but organizers no longer needed it to spread their messages; satellite networks carried them now.

Politicians, preachers, and pop singers took turns at the soundstage. The Muslim Brothers centered in one spot in the square, the leftist activists in another, and the rich kids from the American University in their own "Gucci corner," near Qasr el-Nil Bridge to Zamalek. Each constituency had its place. It was a pluralistic little republic, through the looking glass from Mubarak's Egypt.

Western journalists, myself included, struggled not to sound starry-eyed. The reality of Tahrir Square was hard to fathom even as you witnessed it. Men and women mingled freely, and safely, by day and by night, in galabiyas and suits, niqabs and V-necks. Most were under forty. But there were plenty of older people, too, both rich and poor. Coptic Christians stood guard around Muslims at prayer; Muslim Brothers guarded a Coptic Mass. Patriotic anthems sung by midcentury crooners played from giant speakers. Handsome young troubadours led sing-alongs urging Mubarak to get out already. Couples held weddings there. In the small hours, poets—some well known—held readings.

Doctors established field clinics, with central "hospitals" in the mosque and behind the KFC. Volunteers used Twitter to coordinate donations to a Tahrir "pharmacy" stocked with everything from bandages to insulin and asthma inhalers. Makeshift kitchens doled out cheese sandwiches and flat *baladi* bread—"country" bread. Social services were efficient and honest. The square felt more like a functioning state than the Egyptian government did.

Incandescent graffiti spread over the walls: Islamic crescents with Christian crosses, mummies screaming in rage, a black king toppled over on a red-and-white chessboard, the Statue of Liberty in an Islamic niqab, dark angels with luminous wings holding Molotov cocktails. My favorite was a sad, pudgy panda staring down a tank. One Western journalist took pictures with her iPhone and covered the walls of her Zamalek loft with 8½ x 11 prints of revolutionary graffiti. We all loved it.

I heard rumors of "revolutionary" counterpolice, vigilantes who would catch and beat suspected government infiltrators, then lock them in the closed subway station below the square. "The people's jail," they called it.

"We did not like to report it, but of course it happened," my friend Ahmad Abdallah, a young engineering professor active with the April 6 Youth Movement, later told me. I tried without success to confirm those rumors at the time. Maybe if I had been less dazzled by the graffiti and poetry readings I would have tried harder.

One day a stranger with a tripod shared a taxi with me from Tahrir Square to Zamalek. He was an Egyptian about my age, and he turned out to speak not only the native dialect and formal Arabic but also fluent French and English. Before the uprising he had produced satiric online videos about police abuse, under the pseudonym Ahmed Sherif. After the police denounced the video of Emad el-Kabeer's torture as fake, Ahmed Sherif had released an online video in which Jerry Seinfeld appeared to present a best director Oscar to the policeman who sodomized the bus driver. Kabeer took best actor. The Oscar video was a big hit on Facebook.

Now my fellow passenger was filming videos in the open—hence the tripod—under his real name, Aalam Wassef. At forty, he had already made his mark in Paris and New York as a successful publisher, software designer, photographer, and artist. He contributed a regular column about Egypt to the website of *Le Monde*.

Extraordinary people like Wassef seemed to pop up all the time around Tahrir Square in those days. Educated young Egyptians were as fluent in my culture as they were in their own, and more sophisticated about both than I was about either. They were easy to like, easy to root for, easy to render appealingly for remote Western readers.

Take the clique behind Police Day. One day I was helping Zyad el-Elaimy, who had hosted the planning meeting in his office, to put some folding chairs in the square. How did you end up here? I asked. Without looking at me, he told me that the Egyptian police had detained him for his socialist activism for the first time when he was sixteen. He had been imprisoned three other times after that. When he was twenty-three, the police had tortured and beaten him, broken his leg, and lacerated his back. "Amnesty International did a report—you can look it up," he told me flatly, unfolding a chair.

Zyad was now thirty and he was running ElBaradei's presidential campaign effort when the uprising broke out. He and the same circle of organizers who had met in his office before Police Day convened every day in his mother's apartment downtown to orchestrate the daily demonstrations.

Zyad's partner, thirty-two-year-old Islam Lotfy, was a rising star in the Muslim Brotherhood. But he worked by day as a lawyer for USAID (a fact he asked me not to print in the newspaper then). He was a liberal when it came to women's equality, cultural pluralism, and freedom of expression, and he scorned the Brotherhood's leaders for distancing themselves from the Police Day protest. "On Tuesday, they said, 'You are making a mistake.' On Wednesday, it was 'We are not sure.' And on Friday, 'You have done a great thing and we are right behind you.'"

Lotfy and Elaimy took a businesslike approach to their organizing. After the surprise success of Police Day, they ran "field tests" the next night. At 6:00 that evening, each set out for a different neighborhood and chanted for bread and freedom, to find out what kind of crowd he could raise. "And the funny thing is, when we finished up the people refused to leave," Lotfy told me. "They were seven thousand and they burned two police cars." They knew Cairo was ready.

Lotfy said the organizers had imagined Mubarak meeting his predecessors, Abdel Nasser and Sadat, in the afterlife. When the dead presidents asked, "What got you? A gunshot? Or poison?" Mubarak would answer, "Facebook."

Lotfy and Elaimy were close to Sally Toma, a thirty-two-year-old Coptic Christian psychiatrist of Irish and Egyptian parentage. (She used her Irish father's last name, Moore, when she talked to Western journalists.) She was an outspoken leftist and feminist, and she had helped plan the Police Day demonstrations. She also set up the first Day of Rage field clinic. One day in the square I watched several young Muslim Brothers commend her for an interview she had given to the BBC.

"I like the Brotherhood, and they like me," she told me. "They always have a hidden agenda, we know, and you never know when power comes how they will behave. But they are very good with organizing. They are calling for a civil state just like everyone else, so let them have a political party just like everyone else. They will not win more than ten percent, I think."

I had known that trio's mutual friend Shady el-Ghazaly Harb, also thirty-two, for about two weeks before he let slip that he was a practicing surgeon trained in London. He had been arrested at the Cairo airport for his activism in 2010, trying to fly back to take the exam for the Royal College of Physicians.

Another day I spotted Ahmed Maher, a thirty-year-old left-leaning civil engineer who led the April 6 Youth Movement, at the edge of a crowd in the lobby of an Egyptian newspaper building. How did you do it? I asked him. How did you break through the Qasr el-Nil Bridge? How did you overcome and shatter the Egyptian police?

"Gene Sharp," he said immediately.

I had to look him up: Sharp was a political scientist at Harvard who studied the use of nonviolent tactics against authoritarians (overt violence plays into their me-or-chaos self-justification). Maher and his April 6 friends had traveled to Serbia to meet with a group called Otpor!—Resistance!—who had relied on the Sharp playbook to oust their own auto-crat, Slobodan Milošević. April 6 had borrowed its clenched fist logo from Otpor! They learned tricks like putting scraps of plastic under your clothes to protect against rubber bullets, or jamming up the wheels and exhaust pipes of armored police vehicles. All from a Harvard professor! Of course, I put that in the *New York Times* as fast as I could.

Wael Ghonim, then thirty-one, became famous in the West. He was "the Google guy": a Google executive based in Cairo with an American wife and a degree from the American University. "I worked in marketing," he told me, "and I knew that if you build a brand you can get people to trust the brand." He was the anonymous creator of the most popular "We are all Khaled Said" Facebook page. Ghonim had used Silicon Valley salesman-ship to rally opposition to Mubarak. He held online polls, solicited user content, and turned his own anonymity into a marketing gimmick: "My name is that of every Egyptian who has been tortured or humiliated in Egypt." The Police Day organizers all corresponded online with the page's anonymous administrator and they had no idea that they were writing to a friend they already knew, like unwitting friends of Bruce Wayne emailing Batman.

The police arrested Ghonim at the start of the uprising and held him for twelve days, often blindfolded, in solitary confinement. Why had he trav-eled to the United States? his interrogators demanded. Despite their own close partnership with the American intelligence agencies, Ghonim's inter-rogators were sure he was an American spy. "Do you think we are idiots? You are an undercover agent to the CIA," they told him as they beat him.

After his release, a television interviewer showed him photographs of young demonstrators killed in the streets. "To the mothers and fathers, it's not our fault," Ghonim sobbed. "It's the fault of the people in positions of authority who don't want to leave power."

They were all so heroic, so ingenious, but also so familiar. Of course I fell for them. We all did, even Obama.

"What I want is for the kids on the street to win and for the Google guy to become president," Obama told an aide, who promptly relayed the comment to my colleagues in the Washington bureau so they could put it in the paper.

We set ourselves up for disappointment. Where did it go? I was often asked later, in New York or London. What happened to the nonviolent, secular-minded, Western-friendly, Silicon Valley uprising that we cheered in Tahrir Square? Who stole that revolution? That image of the revolution was as much about Western narcissism as it was about Egypt.

Laura spent the Day of Rage with our sons at the home of a neighbor. Mubarak had declared a curfew, and she set out to walk home before dusk. One-year-old Emmett was in his Bugaboo stroller and five-year-old Thomas was standing in back. But as she pushed them out of the neighbor's gates, she saw clusters of men in the streets. They were armed with baseball bats, crowbars, tree branches, and anything else they could find, and they had hauled rebar, sand, and garbage to build roadblocks on each corner. Was this an ambush? How would she get home?

In retrospect, I think she was safer that night than on any other night we spent in Cairo. After the police had fled, the authorities filled the airwaves with warnings of impending chaos and looting; the military sent text messages to every mobile phone. So the men in every city neighborhood had organized themselves into squads for community protection. And when the men of Maadi saw Laura with the boys, they sprang into action. At each roadblock strangers lifted up the Bugaboo and handed it over. Emmett rode inside like a Pharaoh on a litter. Laura reached our door beaming with gratitude. I shuddered to think what would have happened if the police had vanished from New York or Washington, D.C. Cairo held it together.

Still, neighborhood justice goes only so far. One morning on the way to the square I stopped at our usual supermarket, part of the French chain Carrefour. We needed breakfast cereal, and I wanted to check on rumors of a break-in. It turned out to be much worse than that: the mall around the store had been ransacked. Mannequins in dark abayas and bright head-scarves lay dismembered in puddles of water from the overhead sprinklers. Shattered glass cracked under my boots. Two men working on the cleanup told me that the police who normally stood guard had invited in a gang of Bedouins in a pickup truck. Then the police abandoned their stations to let the Bedouins smash the place and take what they pleased.

I called Laura from the wreckage. How would you and the boys like to take a vacation? All the commercial flights and embassy charters were full, so a friend who worked for an oil company stowed her and the boys on the plane his employer had hired to get its staff to Dubai: her first evacuation.

Cairo felt like it was splitting into two cities. One was the sunny city of Tahrir Square and the neighborhood watches. The other was the shadowy city still shaped by the security agencies, businessmen, and news media of the Mubarak regime. The latter was the city where unidentified looters ran wild in the spaces between residential neighborhoods, such as the Carre-four strip mall, and where the state media's warnings of chaos became self-fulfilling. Both the police and civilians who dwelled in that city were turning increasingly hostile to Westerners like me.

Every voice on the state-run television and radio stations insisted that the protests were all the handiwork of foreign spies. Call-in shows buzzed with theatrical rage at the "hidden hands" and "foreign fingers," and in the Egyptian imagination the perfect cover for a spy was as a journalist with a notebook. State television reported that foreigners were handing out free dinners of fried chicken to bribe the indigent to demonstrate in the square. Someone called in to report that he had seen two "foreigners" order eight hundred sandwiches at an Egyptian fast-food restaurant, implying conspir-atorially that the order was for distribution in the square. Police raided rights groups, arrested liberal activists, and rounded up Muslim Brothers (including a former parliamentarian by the name of Mohamed Morsi). They even detained a few Western journalists, briefly including two work-ing for the *New York Times*. We all felt the xenophobia.

A distorted narrative of those days would later become a touchstone in future debates about American policy around the region. So it is worth remembering the interplay of events between Washington and Cairo.

The drama in Washington began when Obama convened an emergency meeting of his National Security Council on the morning after the protesters had broken the police and taken the square. After a heated debate, he had agreed with his advisers on a State Department plan to encourage Mubarak to hand power to his seventy-four-year-old spy chief and alter ego, Omar Suleiman.

Suleiman had been Egypt's main liaison to both Washington and Israel. American lawmakers, diplomats, generals, and spies all knew him well. "He was very wise," Mike Morrell of the CIA later wrote. "You could ask Suleiman a single question about any regional issue and then sit back for what might turn out to be a half-hour lecture packed with insights."

But Suleiman was known inside Egypt primarily for his brutality and torture. State Department cables released by WikiLeaks had identified him as an avid player in the American rendition program after the invasion of Afghanistan. "He was not squeamish," as Edward Walker, a former American ambassador to Egypt, later put it.

Obama was skeptical about the Suleiman idea. To Obama, "you were not going to be able to put the genie back in the bottle," Ben Rhodes later told me. "But he was not going to tell people, 'Don't try that.' His view was, 'Let's try to see what we can do.'" Obama went along with the plan.

Frank G. Wisner, a seventy-two-year-old former ambassador to Egypt, had developed an unusually strong bond with Mubarak, so senior State Department staff picked Wisner as a special envoy to the Egyptian president. The White House sent him talking points on Saturday, January 29. Obama spoke for ten minutes over the phone with Wisner on Sunday morning, and he set off the next day in a military jet for the ten-hour flight to Cairo. He had been instructed to make only a few specific short-term requests of the aging autocrat: Do not use force to crush the demonstrations, and let a successor outside the Mubarak family take over the presidency after the elections in September. The White House demanded neither an immediate exit by Mubarak nor fundamental immediate change to the Egyptian regime. Its goal was to let Suleiman manage a succession, possibly to himself.

Wisner met Mubarak at his palace in Cairo on Monday, January 31, the third day that the protesters had held the square, and events in Cairo were accelerating. At 9:00 P.M. an anonymous general with a gravelly voice and hard-brimmed cap appeared on state television with an unexpected announcement from the Supreme Council of the Armed Forces (SCAF). "Your Armed Forces have not and will not resort to the use of force against this great people," he said, and he praised "the legitimate demands of the honorable citizens." As far as I could tell, that could only mean Mubarak's immediate departure.

The generals—taking the advice General Sisi had given them in 2010— had given Mubarak no warning. His irate staff called the chief of the state media's news division demanding to know how the military's statement reached the airwaves. Suleiman rushed to a television studio an hour later to respond with a two-minute statement. Mubarak, Suleiman announced, had named him vice president. He was deputized "to contact all the political forces" about constitutional reforms.

Mubarak spoke the next night and in effect complied with Wisner's requests. By naming Suleiman vice president, Mubarak had taken Gamal out of the succession. And the security forces had stopped shooting. Now Mubarak declared that he would leave office at the end of his term, after elections in September. The White House—despite Obama's instincts— had not abandoned Mubarak, and Mubarak was doing as the White House requested.

Mubarak's tone, though, was so defiant that he sounded as if he had conceded nothing at all. "This is my country," he said. "I will die on its soil." Protesters in Tahrir Square threw shoes at a television broadcasting the speech.

Obama again called Cairo. "I know you care about Egypt, I know you have given your life," Obama told Mubarak, according to Dennis Ross, a veteran Middle East diplomat who listened to the call.

"You don't know Egypt. I know my people. This will be over in a few days," Mubarak insisted.

Thirty minutes in, Obama was losing patience: "Why don't we talk again tomorrow?"

"No, we don't need to," Mubarak replied.

Obama hung up. "There is no hope for this guy," he told Ross and others.

"What I indicated tonight to President Mubarak," Obama said in another televised statement on Egypt, "is my belief that an orderly transition must be meaningful, it must be peaceful, and it must begin now."

But a White House spokesman struggled the next morning to explain what Obama meant. Was the emphasis on "now" or "orderly"? The spokesman finally clarified that Obama was not seeking Mubarak's immediate exit. The administration's vision of "an orderly transition" was still under Suleiman.

The division between the president and his Cabinet over Egypt, though, was no secret in the region. Crown Prince Mohammed bin Zayed of Abu Dhabi, the de facto ruler of the United Arab Emirates—known as MBZ—complained to U.S. officials that Obama advisers like Ben Rhodes were describing one Egypt policy while Robert Gates and Joe Biden were describing another. And Gates sympathized with the complaints. He had always had a high regard for MBZ's "insights and judgments," Gates later wrote, and the prince "gave me an earful."

The crown prince and the Emiratis had deep ties to Egypt and its military. MBZ surely shared his view of the discord behind Obama's speech with Egypt's top generals. If the Emiratis knew, then the Egyptian military knew that most of the officials around Obama hoped to preserve a version of the Mubarak regime. The White House's messages were mixed from the outset, and players in the region could see that Obama sat at a distance from the cabinet around him.

It was late at night in Cairo when Obama finished speaking, and I had a telephone conversation with a former Egyptian diplomat, Mohamed Shokry. I knew he was close to Suleiman.

"What will happen if there is a flare-up, a few bullets shot into the young men, a Molotov cocktail?" Shokry mused aloud. "A million people in the streets. How will we keep the peace?"

Egyptian state radio and television networks reported the next morning, Wednesday, February 2, that a counterdemonstration was forming in the Giza neighborhood of Mohandiseen—a rally to thank Mubarak for his service and say "Enough!" to the Cairo of Tahrir Square. My *Times* colleague Liam Stack headed over.

A handful of Mubarak supporters spotted him as a Western journalist and started beating him. So Liam snuck back around from another direction.

Organizers were passing out signs that said WE ARE SORRY MR. PRESIDENT, or depicted the face of Mohamed ElBaradei under a Star of David. This crew did not let the first name "Mohamed" get in the way of its anti-Semitism. Hundreds had gathered, and a fair number seemed to Liam to be plainclothes security agents. When he picked up one of the provocative signs, a security agent snatched it away.

The pro-Mubarak crowd began moving, mostly by foot, across a bridge over the Nile to another square on the far side of the Egyptian Museum from the entrance to Tahrir Square. Liam and a photographer, Scott Nelson, took a car to catch up. Rough-looking men armed with clubs, bats, and machetes were disembarking from microbuses. Others brought jerry cans of fuel and crates of empty bottles, for gas bombs. *Baltagiya*. Liam compared it with *The Lord of the Rings*. "Like the Orcs pouring out of Mordor."

I was strolling Tahrir Square with Mona el-Naggar, an Egyptian journalist working for the *Times*, and men kept stopping us, one after the other. Each one wanted to tell us the same thing: Mubarak's speech had changed his mind. The president had conceded enough. This chaos in the square was too much. It was time to go home. We could hear the same arguments in the murmurs all around us. Time to go home, time to go home!

Suddenly the tone heated up, and we heard shouting. The clock on my phone read 2:15 P.M.

A middle-aged man with a furrowed brow grabbed my arm. "We don't know who is with us and who is against us now—we are lost," the man, Abdel Raouf Mohamed, said.

"I love Mubarak! I need Mubarak!" a burly stranger screamed over his shoulder, cutting him off.

A third, older man—one of the protesters against Mubarak—pulled me away. "In ten minutes, there will be a big fight here," this man, Reda Sadak, told us. "It is an old game, the oldest game in the regime."

He was wrong: it took less than eight minutes. He spoke at 2:22, and by 2:30, shoving and punching had broken out all over the square. The Mubarak men had evidently set their schedule in advance. Rocks and sticks

rained down on the pavement near the Egyptian Museum, hurled by a phalanx of "thank you Mubarak" demonstrators. Anti-Mubarak demonstrators
all over the square banged bricks against metal lampposts—a noisy alarm
system improvised to warn of intrusion.

Some of the anti-Mubarak crowd tried to preserve their celebrated ethic
of nonviolence, the hallmark of the sit-in. A half dozen bearded men in a
tight row held up their hands and presented their chests in a display of pas-
sivity, as though ready for martyrdom. Rocks crashed around them. Mona
and I saw a clean-cut young man clutching a tree branch as a weapon and
rushing to fight the oncoming Mubarakites.

"Put it down," an older man implored.

"Three of my friends are bleeding inside, and my friend lost an eye,"
the young man yelled back, pointing to an apartment building. But he put
down the branch, sitting down and sobbing. His name was Sameh Saber,
he told Mona.

By 3:15, the last pretense of nonviolence was gone. A battle line between the opposing forces had formed perpendicular to the pink granite
hulk of the Egyptian Museum, below the October 6 Bridge overpass. Anti-
Mubarak demonstrators were dragging sheets of corrugated steel from a
construction site on the edge of the square to build barricades against the
attackers. Men and women used scraps of steel to break the pavement into
rocks. Others ferried this fresh ammunition to the front line in milk crates
or scarves used as slings. Hundreds of young men were crowding to the
front to hurl the missiles.

The Muslim Brotherhood, with its disciplined cell structure, provided
organizational backbone for the defense of Tahrir Square by the anti-
Mubarak demonstrators. But the front ranks belonged to "ultras"—trash-
talking soccer fans. They had made sport of clashing with the police for
years before the uprising; they had sprayed walls all over Cairo with the
English graffiti motto A.C.A.B., for All Cops Are Bastards. Other demonstrators volunteered as medics, carrying away the injured on cardboard
stretchers. Motorcycles—"the ambulances of the people"—ferried the
wounded to field clinics.

I climbed an abandoned backhoe (left near the construction site, a future Ritz-Carlton hotel) to get a better view of the action. Hundreds of

soldiers were still standing inside the iron fence of the museum, but they were just watching, too. They came alive only when firebombs landed inside the fence, and only to put out the flames with fire extinguishers.

When I looked behind me, the scene was surreal. Camels! At least a pair of Mubarak men on camels and eighteen others on horseback were attacking the square. The riders had usually used their animals to sell rides around the Pyramids, and now they were quickly beaten back. But their ludicrous charge gave the day its name: the Battle of the Camel, after a battle between Sunni and Shia in the early history of Islam. (No self-respecting Western journalist ever missed a chance to mention a camel in writing about the region.)

Surely the soldiers would intervene, I thought. Surely the army would crush the protests, which were now clearly violent. But the bloodshed went on—hundreds were hit by rocks, wounded or stabbed in close combat, or burned by the fire of the gas bombs. The soldiers did nothing. Darkness fell and I had to write for the next day's newspaper before knowing who won.

I finished the edits for the last edition shortly before dawn in Cairo. I was leaving the bureau to hunt for a cheap hotel—there were no taxis home that long after curfew—when an editor called from New York. Al Jazeera was reporting gunfire in the square.

I hitched a ride from a stranger to the base of the October 6 Bridge and set out on foot over the Nile. But on the way across I realized that I had picked the wrong span: the overpass looking down on the square was controlled by the pro-Mubarak thugs. I could see dark figures with clubs milling around the bridge or looking over the railings. I was sure they would pummel me if they guessed who I was. As far as they were concerned, an American walking alone here at this hour and armed with a notebook could only be a spy. I looked at my feet and kept walking.

A stairway! I ducked off the bridge before I was noticed, and at the bottom another group of men was hauling a burned-out car frame into place to reinforce a barrier. I tapped the shoulder of a middle-aged man in a gray hooded sweatshirt. Excuse me, I asked gingerly, in my rudimentary Arabic. Are you with the president, or are you with the square?

Are you kidding? he asked in perfect English, with a yellowing smile. He was a Muslim Brother, he said, and he handed me a business card that identified him as an engineering professor at Cairo University. He led me to a field hospital run by Muslim Brothers in the alley behind the KFC. A short doctor in a white lab coat was standing on an upside-down crate, barking orders. He stepped down to meet me. Volunteers pulled back sheets to show me the bodies of two dead demonstrators, killed by gunshot wounds just before dawn. More than twelve hundred Egyptians had been seriously wounded in the battle that day and at least thirteen had died, though only a few were killed or injured by gunshots. I had never been so close to a corpse, or seen one outside a funeral coffin, but no one else was flinching. I playacted foreign correspondent and pretended that I had seen it all before.

The witnesses all told the same story: At least one of the plainclothes thugs on the Mubarak side had started shooting shortly before dawn. Instead of rolling out onto the tent city, the uniformed soldiers had fired their own weapons into the air in the direction of pro-Mubarak attackers. At that, the thugs scattered, thanks to the intervention of the soldiers.

Several people in the Obama administration later told me that the Pentagon and the State Department had organized systematic call lists to press their contacts at every level of the Egyptian armed forces. Hold back from attacking the demonstrators, the Americans urged. Remember your bond with your people. Do not turn on your own civilians.

But the thugs had attacked the demonstrators at 2:30 P.M. The army had waited until nearly dawn the next morning to stop it, after more than a dozen deaths and hundreds of hospitalizations. Why did the army wait fourteen hours? The Supreme Council of the Armed Forces had pledged four days earlier, in the televised message from the anonymous soldier, that it would not act against civilians.

When the eagerness for credit had cooled, several senior American officials—including Leon Panetta, then head of the CIA—later told me that they believed the generals had made up their own minds, for their own reasons, about how to play it. The Egyptian army relies on mandatory conscription. Turning against the body of Egyptians gathered in the square—Egyptians of every stripe—was unthinkable. It might have been different if the crowd was only Islamists. But I learned that only later.

"We are reeling a bit," Jon Finer, a senior State Department official wrote later that day to my colleague Anthony Shadid, an old friend of Finer's, who forwarded me the email. "I've heard from a bunch of people who got the shit kicked out of them," Finer wrote. He said the *Times* report was one of the few that "explicitly called it what it was—a government crackdown, not 'clashes' between rival groups."

"Shocking how much pushback there was to that notion here," Finer added. Even after the Battle of the Camel, many in the United States government sympathized with Mubarak and distrusted the revolt. The White House did not realize that the square—that pluralistic little republic—had already won.

Two days later, Wisner, Obama's envoy, publicly backed Mubarak. "President Mubarak's continued leadership is critical," Wisner told a security conference in Munich. Mubarak should "write his own legacy" and "show the way forward."

Clinton, at the same conference, backed Suleiman. "It's important to follow the transition process announced by the Egyptian government, actually headed by Vice President Omar Suleiman," she told journalists, as though the old spy were perfectly well suited to lead a transition to democracy. "That is what we are supporting."

Clinton worried privately that she came *too* close to pressuring Mubarak toward the door. "I am afraid that what I said yesterday is being used to support the idea that we are pushing his leaving," she wrote in an email to her closest adviser, Jake Sullivan.

But Obama, who had written off Mubarak on that first Day of Rage, wished she had come closer to doing just that. He "took me to the woodshed," Clinton later wrote.

"There was substantive discord," Rhodes later told me.

Nine days after the Battle of the Camel, shortly before the end of Friday prayers on February 11, I received an email from the White House telling me to call as soon as I could. The sender was someone I had known in Obama's Senate office. When I reached him, around 7:00 A.M. in Washington, he sounded like he had not gotten much sleep.

"Mubarak has left the capital," he said, slowly. "He is no longer in the presidential palace."

He would not tell me how he knew; officials invariably declined to answer that question in roughly the same way when the information came from classified intelligence or electronic surveillance. What did it mean for Egypt? "I leave that up to you," he told me.

Why he was telling me was becoming clear enough. The previous day, Thursday, the Supreme Council of the Armed Forces had released "Communiqué #1" to announce that the generals had begun meeting "in continuous session." Photographs showed the council without Mubarak. His associates hinted publicly that he would soon step aside. Panetta suggested the same thing, in open testimony to Congress.

Instead, Mubarak on Thursday night had delivered a harangue full of righteous self-justification, fatherly condescension, and vows to soldier on. "The worst speech he had made in his life," Abdel Latif el-Menawy, the chief of the state news service, later recalled. "It was arrogant. It was senseless. It was a disaster."

Some in Tahrir Square called for a march on the heavily guarded presidential palace—a walk into a firing squad. The Police Day organizers worried to me that they were losing control.

Now, on the morning of February 11, aides close to Obama had concluded that Mubarak's ouster was indeed the winning bet. "We were sensitive to the idea that Obama was late to that," Rhodes later told me, "because we knew that he was there early." Obama had been right all along, and if Mubarak was going, they wanted him to own it.

I hung up with the White House, posted a tentative article on the *Times* website about the reports of Mubarak's movements, and hurried to the square. I was unsure whether to expect violence or exultation. But the tent city was as cheerful as ever. I found Anthony Shadid and told him what I had heard. We called our colleague Kareem Fahim, and he turned back from a trip to Suez. Then we waited, and kept waiting.

At the beginning of late afternoon prayers, I turned to go. Thousands of men were prostrating themselves in neat rows across the asphalt, and I stepped between them as politely as I could, my mind on the placement of my hiking boots.

I heard a shout and looked up. A skinny adolescent sprang from a tent clutching a transistor radio. What was he saying? Soon everyone knew. Thousands rose from their knees as one—a tidal wave across the square.

Omar Suleiman had read a terse statement broadcast over the Egyptian state news media. Mubarak had handed power to the generals. The Supreme Council of the Armed Forces announced that it had now taken control. And the anonymous officer with the gravelly voice lifted a hand to his hard-brimmed hat in a salute to those he now called the martyrs of the revolution.

I braced for rioting, maybe looting beyond the square. I expected to hear the signature chants of the sit-in, about bread, freedom, and social justice. But the moment was much deeper and more primal. I had often heard Egyptians laugh off their country's corruption, incompetence, and complacency, or joke that history had left them behind. Now Egypt lurched forward so fast that I felt my gut sinking. The humiliation had been lifted. The square was filled with a sense of relief. I heard a new chant arise from all corners. "Hold your head high, you are Egyptian."

4

"We Don't Do That Anymore"

February 12, 2011–September 11, 2011

A council of generals had taken power from a president. One might call that a coup. But Arabs everywhere saw a revolution in Egypt. Protests erupted in Libya, Yemen, Bahrain, Syria, Baghdad, Jordan, Sudan, Morocco, the Palestinian territories, and beyond. The *New York Times* did not have enough reporters or column inches to cover it all. Even the Persian Gulf monarchs handed out pay raises to their subjects as inoculation against the contagion. Everything was up for renegotiation.

I landed in Libya on February 25, 2011, about two weeks after Mubarak's exit. Security officers were using whips and clubs to beat back thousands of dark-skinned African migrant laborers trying to push their way into the Tripoli airport, desperate to get out of the country before it imploded. The rule of Colonel Muammar el-Qaddafi was in a way the most honest of the Middle East autocracies. He made barely a pretense of the rule of law, a written constitution, or even a rubber-stamp Parliament. He kept the rank of colonel in homage to his idol, Gamal Abdel Nasser. But Qaddafi never even bothered to give himself a formal title like president or prime minister. He was simply "the leader." He ruled through undisguised coercion.

Cynicism defined the regime. Even Qaddafi's most vocal supporters did not seem to believe in what they were selling. Covering it felt like watching bad theater. Qaddafi's henchmen invited me and scores of other Western journalists to Tripoli but then tried to keep us locked in the five-star Rixos hotel. When the United Nations authorized a NATO bombing campaign to restrain Qaddafi's military, his right-hand man, Musa Kusa, delivered a prepared address to us that was supposed to convey only defiance. But his hands, like Ben Ali's, were visibly shaking, and within days he had defected to Europe.

Everyone seemed to be playacting. Ideology or loyalty was hard to pin down. Qaddafi militiamen cruised the streets of the capital with the barrels of the Kalashnikovs protruding from the windows of their white Toyota Hilux Double Cab pickups, and it was prudent to display a green Qaddafi flag in your car window to keep yourself safe. But when I escaped the hotel, I noticed that the same faces turned up at demonstrations for Qaddafi on one day and against him the next. "When NATO bombs at night, I hear my neighbors clap and cheer 'bravo,' and in the morning they are with the leader," the Egyptian who led the only Protestant church in Tripoli, Rev. Hamdy Daoud, told me when I managed to sneak out unnoticed for a Friday morning service. (Christians in the Muslim-majority world often worship together on Fridays.)

One night civilian homes were destroyed in a NATO air strike. A Qaddafi spokesman awoke everyone over the hotel loudspeaker with undisguised glee, eager to bus us all there to see for ourselves. "Attention all journalists, come immediately to the hotel lobby," he intoned slowly into every hotel room. "There are bodies in the rubble. I repeat, there are bodies in the rubble."

"Okay," the same spokesman, Musa Ibrahim, confided to me one night over espresso in the hotel café. "This is not the most *legitimate* regime."

One morning in late March, a Libyan woman with a badly bruised face burst into the lobby of the Rixos asking for journalists from Reuters and the *New York Times*—presumably the only two international news organizations she could think of. She gave her name as Eman al-Obeidi and started telling her story over breakfast in the main dining room. Qaddafi soldiers had stopped her at a checkpoint, detained her because she belonged to a tribe (Obeidi) based in a rebel region, and repeatedly raped and beat her until she escaped, she said. There was a large scar on her upper thigh, narrow and deep scratch marks on her lower leg, and binding marks around her hands and feet. "They violated my honor," she said.

Before she could finish, our official escorts, translators, hotel waiters, and even the shy hijabi barista from the hotel café were crashing into the room, trying to apprehend her. It turned out that even the uniformed hotel staff serving lattes and clearing plates were all Qaddafi agents. Scuffles broke out as journalists tried to protect her. At least two of the hotel staff threatened her and us with kitchen knives. One of our "escorts" pulled out a handgun. Others snatched and destroyed a CNN camera.

"Turn them around! Turn them around!" a waiter shouted to the other employees, imploring them to keep us away from her.

"Why are you doing this? You are a traitor!" the barista screamed at Obeidi, trying to force a heavy, dark coat over her head to cover her face.

Some journalists wrestled with her pursuers. But she was hauled away, imprisoned again, and eventually deported. I was vigilant after that about what I said in earshot of the hotel staff, certain that the receptionists, barmaids, and bellboys were spies playacting.

In the middle of a night at the beginning of August, one of those escorts drove me to a shuttered and darkened Radisson Blu Hotel where Qaddafi's son Seif al-Islam was waiting inside on a love seat in a borrowed sitting room. After styling himself for years as an Anglophone liberal reformer, he had grown a beard and he was fingering prayer beads. He told me that he and his father were forming a partnership with Islamist militants to fight off the liberal rebels and rule as a team. "The liberals will escape or be killed," he told me. "Libya will look like Saudi Arabia, like Iran. So what?" He enjoyed his own irony: "It is a funny story," he said. He was making it all up, presumably to scare the West, but he insisted he spoke in earnest.

It was his last scene in the play. Tripoli fell to the rebels just two weeks later. On a visit to the headquarters of the rebels' transitional government I ran into the same Qaddafi functionary who had corralled us into buses for propaganda trips and tracked us down when we escaped the Rixos (I was always caught eventually, including after my visit to the church). The day after the rebel takeover he had found a job organizing transportation for the new government's leaders.

"My uncle and my son were soldiers for the revolution," the man, Khalid Saad, told me when I bumped into him. "Everyone will be happy now. Everything is changed now. Everyone is free."

Many of Qaddafi's former henchmen switched sides that way. "It is legitimate, all these things they are doing—freedom of the press, the rule of law," the former chief of Qaddafi's foreign media operation, Abdulmajeed el-Dursi, told me, sipping coffee at a Tripoli café full of rebels. "We always thought it was the right thing to do." I came to love Libya, and its bad theater was part of the reason. Everyone seemed to know that everyone else was just pretending.

I felt silly saying the word "revolutionary" aloud, as though I had never read George Orwell. But there was no other word to describe the mood in Cairo. The day after Mubarak's exit, the organizers of the sit-in had called for another day in the square to clean the mess, and thousands of volunteers had worked late into the night. Our sons' nursery school was caught in the spirit and the kids had picked up litter in Maadi. New restaurants served high-end versions of Egyptian peasant food, like *kushari* with brown rice and organic lentils, or fancy *fuul*—slow-cooked beans, the classic breakfast—in bright pastel *beladi* flatbreads made with spinach or beets. Egyptian friends told me that for the first time they sought out Egyptian-made products in stores instead of avoiding them. Workers all over the country were holding wildcat strikes demanding better wages, continuing a wave that started during the uprising.

The generals in Cairo insisted that Egypt's era of coercion had ended with Mubarak's ouster. The top brass rushed to get pictures taken with the revolt's best-known leaders, and General Abdel Fattah el-Sisi was as eager as any of them. "They were very cute," Ahmed Maher of the April 6 group later told me. "They smiled and promised us many things and said, 'You are our children; you did what we wanted to do for many years!'"

Field Marshal Mohamed Hussein Tantawi, the seventy-five-year-old defense minister and highest-ranking military officer, declared himself interim head of state, ruling on behalf of the roughly two dozen generals of the Supreme Council of the Armed Forces. The council postured as the guardian of the revolution and promised to move quickly toward elections that would replace Tantawi with a civilian government. They put Mubarak under house arrest in his Red Sea vacation home.

The generals invited small groups of opinion shapers—intellectuals, professors, columnists, and newspaper editors—to a series of dinners at the gilded Al Masah Hotel and Spa in Heliopolis (owned by the military), where they drove home the message that they were proud that they had removed Mubarak and set Egypt on a path to democracy. Sometimes, a senior officer pointed to Sisi and recalled his prediction in 2010 of a popular uprising and his recommendation to break with Mubarak. "They had a plan to go to the streets and they simply moved it forward, to take advantage of the revolution," Hassan Nafaa, a liberal political scientist at Cairo University who attended one of the dinners, later told me. At the dinners, he said, "We did not recognize Sisi at all."

That spring, a state television camera followed Tantawi on a stroll through the streets in a business suit. Was he auditioning for the role of civilian president? Egyptians thought it was hilarious.

"Toys 'R' Us at Christmas: We have Tantawi in shorts, Tantawi in a tuxedo, Tantawi the sailor, Tantawi the doctor," ran one joke making the rounds on the internet. Mubarak, like every competent Arab autocrat, had long understood that the most immediate threat to his power was a coup by his defense minister. Tantawi stood out for his meekness. The other military officers derided him as "Mubarak's Poodle."

Some countries in transition invite international experts to share the lessons of South Africa, Latin America, Eastern Europe, South Korea, Spain, the Philippines, and so on. Egypt sought no such assistance. A senior general had a son who happened to work as a legal consultant to the Supreme Constitutional Court, and the military council tapped that son as the first of eight jurists on a panel to produce an interim charter. The panel then turned to Google, and it relied mainly on a website set up by Princeton University, "Constitution Writing and Conflict Resolution." It was all improvisation.

The goal of the legal experts was to transfer power to civilians as soon as possible. That way the generals would not have a chance to put their stamp on the drafting of a permanent constitution. But when the draft of an interim charter was put to a referendum on March 19, 2011, the Supreme Council of the Armed Forces surprised Egypt on the eve of the vote by revising the writ of its panel. A general in charge of legal affairs announced that the military council would still issue its own modifications to the transitional charter after the vote. And the military's tweaks allowed the generals to stay in control long past parliamentary elections and through the writing of a permanent constitution—undoing what had been the main objective of the panel.

Still, every weekend brought a new reminder of the generals' need to placate the public. Whenever the transition faltered, the organizers behind Police Day called for another Friday afternoon *millioneya*—a million-man march. And each Thursday night the generals caved in, just in time to appease the protesters.

The generals removed prime ministers, shook up cabinets, jailed Mubarak, put him and his interior minister on trial for murder, scheduled elections, repealed the so-called emergency law suspending due process rights, and more—all to defuse impending *millioneyas.* "The only thing that works is going back to Tahrir, but then they back down," one of the organizers, Shady el-Ghazaly Harb, told me. The "Thursdays of concessions," some Egyptians called them.

The anonymous officer who had announced the military's takeover in the name of the revolution now reappeared on television, shaking his forefinger at the camera and demanding an end to the protests. His name turned out to be General Mohsen al-Fanagry, and Egyptians compared him to a flip-flop sandal—*shib-shib,* in Egyptian Arabic—held on by a finger of plastic between the toes. "A *shib-shib* has a finger and Fanagry has a finger." No one was afraid of him.

You could scarcely walk a few blocks without noticing a difference in the status of the police. "We don't do that anymore, there's been a revolution," a young Egyptian woman I knew told a police officer, pushing him aside when he tried to shake her down for *baksheesh* to let her park her car. It was the police who were cowed.

"They treated people like pests, so imagine when these pests now rise up, challenge them, and humiliate them," said Mahmoud Qutri, a former police officer. "They feel broken."

Mohamed Ismail, a thirty-year-old who ran a mobile phone shop near a police station, said the officers had always demanded a 50 percent discount. Now they murmured "please" and paid the full price. "The tables have turned," he said.

Hisham A. Fahmy ran a trade association for multinationals operating in Egypt, and he, too, was amazed by the way he heard ordinary Egyptians talking to the police. "It's: 'Talk to me properly! I am a citizen!'" he told me, dumbfounded.

A small group of demonstrators started a sit-in outside the U.S. embassy to call for the humanitarian release from jail of Omar Abdel Rahman, the blind Egyptian sheikh imprisoned in the United States for plotting related to the bombing in 1993 of the World Trade Center. "If Mubarak were still around, those guys would be thrown in jail and sodomized with pipes," an American who worked in intelligence told a diplomat in the embassy.

Retreat was not defeat, of course, and the institutions of the old regime had hardly disappeared. Three days after the referendum, in late March, the generals sent every Egyptian news organization a letter reminding them of "the necessity of refraining from publishing any items—stories, news, announcements, complaints, advertisements, pictures—pertaining to the armed forces or to commanders of the armed forces" without prior approval. The satellite networks were still owned by the same small clique of Mubarak-friendly moguls, and they took it seriously.

One night the left-leaning blogger Hossam el-Hamalawy suggested modestly to a call-in show that "any institution of the country that takes taxes from us should be open to question."

"No, no, no," the host, Mahmoud Saad, interrupted. He hung up on Hamalawy. "I will not allow you to say those things on this network."

A military officer called in Hamalawy for questioning the next day. "When the military says 'please show up,' it is kind of like an order, especially when they are ruling the country," Hamalawy told me.

Curious about the shifting ground rules, I persuaded an officer in the military's propaganda arm, the Department of Moral Affairs, to invite me to its headquarters, in the neighborhood of Heliopolis.

His office was like a college radio station. The stuffing was coming out of a cushion in the couch. Audio headsets and coaxial cables were lying all over. Like every Egyptian military officer I ever met, my host wanted to tell me how much he enjoyed his American training—in his case in Maryland. But he insisted that insulting the army was still a crime in Egypt.

"If someone presents proof that any officer is corrupt, then the officer would be subject to the law," he said. "If the journalist doesn't present any evidence, then the journalist would be subject to the law."

A blogger had equated the Supreme Council of the Armed Forces— SCAF—with former president Mubarak. "That is why he is in jail," this officer told me. "If I call you a dictator, you can take that as an insult."

High stakes, if you took it seriously. But Hamalawy ignored the intimidation. He told his story to me, on his blog, and to anyone who would listen. Bottling up all the dissent coursing through Cairo seemed impossible then. Even atheists—previously afraid of arrest or ostracism, for the crime of insulting religion—were convening public meetings.

The White House and State Department now gushed with enthusiasm for the Egyptian revolution. The United States announced that it was shifting $65 million in economic aid into direct grants to promote democracy. The State Department bought advertisements in Egyptian newspapers to solicit grant proposals—after three decades in which the Mubarak government controlled every penny in American aid. To Mubarakite nationalists, Obama might as well have confessed to funding the protests in the first place.

But at the same time, the administration was more quietly embracing the Supreme Council of the Armed Forces as the best guarantee that the "revolution" would not go against American interests. "First you lean into the idea of Mubarak leading a transition," one senior State Department official later told me. "When that doesn't work, you lean into Omar Suleiman, and when that idea goes down, too, you think, 'Okay, let's work with the SCAF.'"

The Pentagon and National Security Council brought top Egyptian generals and intelligence chiefs to Washington, or sent senior officials to meet with them in Cairo. And the Pentagon made no secret of its backing for the military chief of staff, General Sami Anan, as Egypt's next ruler. Anan was "the Pentagon's man in Egypt," my *Times* colleague Elisabeth Bumiller reported from Washington.

The de facto American policy, Ben Rhodes later told me, was "to hug SCAF as closely as possible."

The security of Israel, an ever-present concern for American policy in Egypt, took on new urgency that August. An Israeli warplane chasing Palestinian militants inadvertently killed at least three Egyptian security officers inside their own border. Mubarak had smoothed over such incidents before, but now Egyptians demanded retribution.

Bowing again to street pressure, the generals recalled Egypt's ambassador to Israel. When protesters began gathering outside the Israeli embassy, several stories up in an office building near the Cairo zoo, in Giza, the military government erected a thin metal barricade along the sidewalk to protect the building.

A few weeks later, at an unrelated rally in Tahrir Square on Friday, September 10, I saw a group of demonstrators headed for the Israeli embassy armed with hammers and ropes. I tagged along behind them and found a mob of young men spearheaded by a core group of ultras, the soccer hooligans—conspicuous because they brought their trademark chants, drums, horns, and fireworks. (The Muslim Brothers were notably absent, perhaps conscious of the international attention now on their movement.)

The ultras climbed the barricade, secured rope to it, and used cars to pull it down in chunks. By nightfall it was flattened. The handful of Egyptian soldiers and police stationed outside the embassy did nothing to stop the marauders, who easily climbed a locked gate. Hooligans hauled down the Israeli flag and set it on fire.

The situation looked explosive, and I did not know the half of it. I later learned that a half dozen embassy employees were trapped inside, hiding in a secure room. And they had firearms for protection.

If the attackers had gotten any closer, the night would have ended in "a massacre," Steven Simon, then director for the Middle East and North Africa at the National Security Council, later told me. He was on an open phone line to his Israeli counterparts, who had the terrified embassy employees on speakerphone. Over the phone, Simon could hear the ultras banging on the door of the embassy's secure room.

Mustafa el-Sayed, a twenty-eight-year-old ultra who was milling around in the street outside, showed me mobile phone video of himself with about twenty friends inside the embassy. They had filmed themselves destroying furniture, rummaging through papers, and throwing binders out the window. He boasted that they had roughed up an embassy employee they found inside, too. Egyptian soldiers had eventually removed them without arresting them. They just regrouped in the street.

It was about 11:30 P.M. when riot-police trucks finally showed up. I counted as many as fifty. By then the rioters had set fire to a police kiosk in the street, and they began hurling rocks at the police in a game of cat and mouse through clouds of tear gas all around the neighborhood. I thought the hooligans might destroy the embassy while the police were preoccupied, and the generals were staying out of it.

Obama spoke with Benjamin Netanyahu. Marine Corps General James Mattis, chief of Central Command, talked to General Sisi, head of Egyptian military intelligence. Ehud Barak, the Israeli defense minister, placed a panicked call to Leon Panetta, who was now defense secretary. Would Panetta please get the Egyptian army to stop this?

But by 7:30 P.M. in Washington—2:30 A.M. the next morning in Cairo— Field Marshal Tantawi still had not yet picked up the phone to respond to Panetta.

"I am sure he was trying to figure out what was going on," Panetta later told me, charitably.

Panetta left the Pentagon to introduce a performance of Brahms's German Requiem at the Kennedy Center to commemorate the September 11 terrorist attacks. Aides pulled him from the audience to an adjoining room set up for a secure phone call when Tantawi finally called back. Tantawi made the usual courtly small talk, "so I tried to cut through that shit," Panetta told me.

"You have a serious situation there with the Israeli embassy," Panetta told Tantawi. "If this is allowed to happen, not only could it jeopardize lives, but it is going to make Egypt look totally incompetent at providing security."

Tantawi promised to do "whatever is necessary," and shortly before 5:00 A.M. in Cairo, Egyptian commandos finally rescued the six employees trapped in the embassy. Two Egyptians died fighting with the police, one of a bullet wound; twelve hundred were seriously injured, and nineteen were arrested.

Israeli officials blamed the "Islamization" of Egypt, but in this case the attackers were irreligious soccer fans and the negligent government was under military control. The Muslim Brotherhood had played no role in the attack. The next day, the Brotherhood condemned it.

I began that night to understand some of the many layers of Egyptian-Israeli relations. The two states were no longer hostile. Their generals got along fine, American military officers and diplomats in Cairo often told me. But Egypt's state and private news media fanned the flames of anti-Zionism and anti-Semitism with undiminished zeal. And state censorship had silenced any debate about the peace or its paradoxes. As a result, Egyptian public opinion had been frozen in place since the eve of Camp David. Egyptian leaders put on a performance of hostility for their citizens at home, and, intentionally or not, that stage show helped convince American policy makers that the peace was so fragile that it demanded constant attention and payoffs—the $1.3 billion a year in aid. In truth, the Egyptian military had no hostile neighbors or, for that matter, known enemies.

Now the supposed guardians of the peace, the generals, were in direct control of the government, and they were doing a lousy job protecting the security of Israel. Without any prompting, they had released from jail more than eight hundred convicted Islamist militants. Some had been imprisoned for assassinating President Anwar Sadat in 1981 because he had made peace. On five separate occasions in the six months since Mubarak's ouster, unidentified attackers had bombed pipelines carrying Egyptian natural gas to Israel without arrests or reprisals. Islamist militants based in the North Sinai had carried out a series of brazen cross-border attacks, including one that killed eight Israelis. (That set off the chase that ended in the accidental killing of the Egyptian security officers.) Direct military rule in Cairo was a disaster for Israel.

But Jerusalem saw only danger if the generals yielded more power, convinced that the alternative to military rule in Cairo would be far worse. Many in Washington seemed to agree. Even after Tantawi's dilatory response to the sacking of the Israeli embassy, Panetta had only kind things to say about the Egyptian defense minister. "That is what I liked about the guy," Panetta told me later. "Usually, if he gave his word about something, he did it." The generals could still count on Washington.

5

The First Lady and the Blue Bra

March 8, 2011–December 20, 2011

Three weeks after Mubarak's exit, on March 8, 2011, Laura brought our five-year-old son, Thomas, to Tahrir Square for a demonstration to mark International Women's Day. Laura's friend Joanna brought her six-year-old daughter. They all rode the women-only train car on the Cairo subway, a regular provision to protect against groping or harassment. When they got out, the two mothers carried the children on their shoulders. Thomas and his friend held hands in the air.

The crowd was smaller than Laura expected—a few dozen, mostly Western women. German and Egyptian teachers from our sons' preschool had come with flyers to hand out. A handful of other demonstrators were holding a separate sit-in across the square, to demand an end to martial law. It all seemed happy enough. Perched on the shoulders of their mothers, the two children passed out the flyers.

"Where are you from?" an angry man challenged Laura. She heard a child crying. A second man had torn the flyers out of the hands of Joanna's daughter and he was ripping them up in her face.

A gang of shouting men gathered around; they looked like neighborhood guys, not goons or Islamists. "The people want to bring down the women!" men chanted in Arabic. "Go back to the kitchen!"

Laura and Joanna fled with the children. Women who stuck around longer were groped and assaulted. Neither the police nor the "revolutionaries" protesting martial law did anything to stop it.

The question of what Mubarak's ouster meant for the rights and freedoms of Egyptian women became central to debates about the uprising, especially in the West. The safety of Tahrir Square for women was shattered the moment he resigned. An ecstatic throng had celebrated that night by mauling Lara Logan, the CBS television correspondent. Now the attack on the International Women's Day demonstration had happened in broad daylight, in a sparse crowd and in public view. Laura had always told me that pushing a stroller insulated her from street harassment. But these men had come after even mothers with children.

The question took on an uglier dimension the next night, March 9. Soldiers in riot gear moved in to clear out the last, lingering demonstrators against martial law, who had begun a small sit-in. The soldiers tore down tents, hammered demonstrators with batons, and detained nearly two hundred, including a small group of women. The army held its captives in the Egyptian Museum, where soldiers shocked them with electrical prods. Then a truck carried the women to a military base. Are you a virgin? the soldiers asked each of the women.

The question was worse than humiliating. Sexual experience can mean social stigma, isolation from family and peers, or disqualification for marriage in Egypt's patriarchal culture. And the interrogation was just the beginning. Each of the seven women who answered yes to virginity was forced to submit to the examination of her hymen by a male army physician. Soldiers stood guard and, according to the women, snapped pictures. The women were released a few days later, but none dared speak about their ordeal. The shame of their exposure could make them pariahs.

Those two days in March framed years of debates. Supporters of the military or Mubarak talked only about the International Women's Day attacks by civilians. The Islamists and self-described revolutionaries talked only about the virginity tests by the soldiers the next night.

Both sides "are just seeing women as prostitutes," Mozn Hassan, founding director of Nazra for Feminist Studies, later told me, looking back on the time.

Fears about the fate of Arab women always figured prominently in Western worries about the Arab revolts, including at the highest levels of the American government. "STOP LOSS OF FORWARD MOVEMENT FOR WOMEN in Egypt," Melanne Verveer, the United States ambassador-at-large for women's issues, implored that April in an email to her old friend Hillary Clinton.

Verveer worried about the removal of First Lady Suzanne Mubarak, who had been president of her husband's National Council of Women and was a friend of Clinton since her own years as first lady. Verveer felt that Suzanne Mubarak had been the exclusive source of improvements in Egyptian women's rights for decades. She had handed down laws making it easier for Muslim women to divorce their husbands (although the laws did not help Christians); setting the minimum age for marriage at eighteen (although child "engagement" or marriage remained commonplace in the countryside); and criminalizing the performance of so-called female circumcision (although no one was ever convicted). She had also persuaded her husband to decree a minimum number of seats for women in Parliament (which he filled with loyalists).

Egyptian rights advocates maintained that they deserved the credit. Their agitation had called the attention of the West to women's issues, they said, and that pressured Suzanne. But with scarcely any visible feminist movement in Egypt, the measures became known there as Suzanne's Laws, and Verveer argued to Clinton that some "youth leaders" now saw the laws as "illegitimate." The young women activists Verveer met on a trip to Cairo seemed naïve, she later told me.

Mrs. Mubarak's National Council of Women, though, had survived under the leadership of her close friend Ambassador Mervat Tallawy, previously its general secretary. Tallawy, then seventy-four years old, had been one of the first women to enter the Foreign Ministry, and it assigned her the job of accompanying the First Lady to events and conferences.

"In developing countries—Arab countries—things do not come from the grass roots," Tallawy explained when I visited her office, as though this were just a cultural quirk like the Egyptian preference for cats over dogs. She wore an enormous gold-encrusted brooch. The ring of her iPhone was a diva singing an aria.

"On the contrary, it is a top-down approach. Either it is a monarchy or a military authority that rules the country," she continued. So in Arab countries, "a president's wife handles issues affecting women and children."

Then Tallawy launched into the legacy of Huda Shaarawi, the

godmother of Arab feminism and a household name in Egypt whom I knew about already.

Shaarawi was born in 1879 in the province of Minya to a family so powerful that her father was known as "king of Upper Egypt," and she was married at the age of thirteen to a cousin three times her age. He helped carry her into the circle of the Egyptian political elite who were challenging British colonial rule. After World War I, Shaarawi organized women to demonstrate for independence. She traveled to Europe. She met with Western feminists. And in 1923, after returning from a conference in Rome and obtaining the approval of her son-in-law, she stunned the Arab world by disembarking from a train in Cairo without her face veil.

She founded an organization of wealthy and politically connected women who called themselves the Egyptian Feminist Union. She persuaded philanthropists and the khedive to expand education for women and girls, and she argued, without success, against the laws that allowed polygamy and restricted divorce. But she never sought women's voting rights, political power, or participation in Parliament. She was an elitist, pro-Western, progovernment nationalist through and through. She was celebrated for decades on street signs and in schoolbooks all over Egypt.

Neither Tallawy nor the schoolbooks mentioned the alternative icon of Arab feminism, Doria Shafik. Born in 1908 to a middle-class family in the Nile Delta, Shafik broke all kinds of rules. In 1935, she became the first Egyptian Muslim to participate in a beauty pagent, "risking my reputation," as she later wrote, and placing second in the contest to represent Egypt. She won a scholarship to study philosophy at the Sorbonne. For a time she became a protégé of the veil-bearing Shaarawi—until Shaarawi and her aristocratic circle blocked Shafik from joining their elite Feminist Union, evidently because of her middle-class background.

Shut out, Shafik started her own grassroots organization, the Daughter of the Nile Union, which focused on education and outreach for poor women who worked as housekeepers, nurses, or manual laborers. She published a magazine. She set up mutual-benefit schemes like a women-run employment agency for other women. And most of all she used collective action to demand a greater role for women in public life.

"No one will deliver freedom to the woman except the woman herself,"

Shafik wrote. "I decided to fight until the last drop of blood to break the chains shackling the women of my country."

On February 19, 1951, on the eve of Nasser's coup, Shafik stormed into a closed session of the all-male Parliament at the head of an army of fifteen hundred women. They seized control for four hours to demand changes to the laws on polygamy and divorce, women's political participation, and equal pay for equal work. During a 1952 uprising against the British, she led a uniformed female militia to shut down a Barclays Bank in Cairo. Two years later, Shafik conducted a ten-day hunger strike that commanded international attention and helped win Egyptian women the right to vote (albeit, under Abdel Nasser, in meaningless plebiscites).

If Shaarawi delivered charity from above, Shafik made demands from below, and Abdel Nasser, like any strongman, did not approve. When she denounced his "dictatorship" in 1957, Abdel Nasser put Shafik under house arrest, shut down her magazine and union, and banned her name from the news media and history textbooks. In 1975, Shafik threw herself off a balcony to her death. Outside Egyptian feminist circles, she was all but forgotten.

After that, virtually the only women's movement in Egypt was First Lady feminism—the feminism of Jehan Sadat, Suzanne Mubarak, and the National Council of Women. The Egyptian government effectively banned even United Nations agencies from working in Egypt if they did not work through the First Lady's council. Now the ouster of Mubarak seemed to threaten all that.

Economic changes had long ago upended many gender norms by the time I arrived in 2010. Seventy-five percent of women worked outside the home. Women in the tiny elite could be doctors, lawyers, economists, entrepreneurs, or almost anything; working-class women usually worked off the books in housekeeping, farming, retailing, or menial labor. Women were the primary breadwinners in 30 percent of Egyptian households. They were divorced, or their husbands were working abroad or underemployed. (Some supposed that the male anxiety about women's advancement contributed to harassment—blaming women for getting ahead.)

Suzanne's Laws had done little to alter the patriarchal culture. In 2011, women were more than twice as likely as men to be illiterate (a total of one in four Egyptians could not read or write). Also that year, under military rule, the chief judge of Egypt's family court publicly criticized Suzanne's Laws: the leading state newspaper reported that the judge had complained that the laws conflicted with the Quran and Sharia. This was the judge, Mohamed Ezzat el-Shazly, whom Mubarak had appointed in 2004 specifically to uphold those laws. While divorce was an absolute right for men, the judge argued, it should be granted to a woman only with the agreement of her husband.

Suzanne's Laws governed only Muslims, doing nothing for the Christian wives of abusive husbands. "It is very delicate," Tallawy said with a sigh. "The pope has to agree, otherwise the government would put itself against the church and this is not advisable."

The Suzanne's Law against female "circumcision" had accomplished almost nothing. Nine out of ten Egyptian women between the ages of fifteen and forty-nine had suffered genital mutilation, according to a United Nations survey. That included eight out of ten from twenty to twenty-four years old, and seven out of ten girls from fifteen to nineteen years old. It was almost as common among Christian women in Egypt—affecting three out of four—as it was among Muslims. (It is more common among Christians than Muslims in parts of Africa, but absent in some Muslim-majority countries.) Surveys backed by the U.S. government showed that 59 percent of men and 54 percent of women favored the practice.

Many seemed to describe it, perversely, as a matter of health and hygiene. That is why our driver circumcised his daughters, he told me. A female Egyptian journalist working with me at the *Times,* Mayy el-Sheikh, covered a seminar on marriage counseling sponsored by a nonprofit affiliated with the Muslim Brotherhood. The Brotherhood's leadership officially opposed the practice, but the male "expert" in charge of the seminar told the class to consult a doctor about the possible need. Sometimes the clitoris was simply too large, he said, like an inflamed appendix.

What solution did Tallawy, of the National Council, propose? Harsher punishments. "A firm attitude," she said. "They should do that about everything else—the attitudes, the behavior, the wrongdoing, in driving, in using words, and in all the social issues."

What did she think of the virginity tests? Tallawy made excuses for the soldiers. "We discovered that this test was an old thing. It had been a settled rule for ages, since King Farouk. And why? Because they think that this is a protection against any woman who might say that she was raped by X or Y in the military."

Couldn't a woman who was no longer a virgin claim to have been raped? I asked, incredulous. Of course, Tallawy said quickly, but Egypt was different than the United States. In Egypt, "if your ID card says you are a mademoiselle, or *anissa,* that automatically means you are a virgin. . . ." I was too embarrassed to press the question.

Not long before I had arrived in Egypt, a Dutch radio journalist had broadcast a translation of an Arabic advertisement for "fake hymens," aimed at brides who sought to feign virginity on their wedding nights. The Egyptian news media reeled in shock. Mubarak's rubber-stamp Parliament debated a ban, and the religious scholars at the state-sponsored Al Azhar Institute concluded that the devices were criminally deceitful. Commercial fraud statutes already prohibited fake hymens, they said. The ruse duped grooms.

I wondered if fake hymens were still around after the scandal, so a female Egyptian friend and I went on a hunt. She told me that the devices arrived from China and pharmacists procured them from the medical supply district, a crosshatch of narrow, filthy alleys off Qasr el-Aini Street near the Cairo University medical school. Rows of wheelchairs, stretchers, and treadmills gathered dust outside storefronts jammed with blood-sugar monitors, stethoscopes, and surgical clamps. Tucked into the corners of some windows, though, were handheld electrical "back massagers"—often long, narrow, and pink (but never labeled vibrators).

Everyone was as blasé as if we were asking about dentures. "Go ask Mena. He can help you!" a middle-aged customer in a head scarf told us when she overheard our question at RFA Medica. But if I—a male foreigner—was doing the asking, the shopkeepers were all sold out just at the moment. Each suggested another store up the street. So at a medical supply shop called el-Nour—"the Light"—my friend left me outside. A recording of a Quran recitation was playing in the background, and the female store clerk giggled slightly. But she happily called the male shopkeeper.

"Are you a patient or a doctor?" the shopkeeper asked. Did she need advice on the use of her new hymen? He offered a referral to a doctor who could help. Or perhaps my friend would like a large box of several hymens, for resale to friends, like Tupperware?

We paid the equivalent of fifty dollars for one; I later learned that the going rate was about ten dollars. It came in a reflective foil packet about the size of a playing card. Inside was a tiny, clear-plastic rectangle full of red dye, for insertion into the vagina before intercourse. Ideally, it would burst after penetration to simulate bleeding. The bride should avoid other strenuous activities—like running or dancing—to avoid a premature rupture.

Some brides went further. "Hymen restorations," performed by gynecologists, could entail suturing together fragments of the hymen, or lacerating the inside of the vaginal opening to induce bleeding. "Laceration is painful and could lead to infection," one gynecologist explained. "It takes up to a week to recover from it and it is usually done a day before the wedding. We would only do it to women who have been—I don't know how to say this— at it for a long time. . . ." The price varied from about two hundred dollars to about eight hundred dollars, depending on how affluent the neighborhood is or how wealthy the patient, the gynecologist said.

The mystery of virginity: are so many Egyptians unaware that not all virgins bleed, or that hymens break without sex? I heard agonizing stories of wedding-night ignorance (among Muslims and Christians alike). Yet the steady demand for virginity fabrications testified to a level of activity that defied the public prudishness.

"Sex in the Arab world is the opposite of sports," Shereen El Feki, a British Egyptian who wrote a book on the subject, once told me. "Everyone talks about sports but nobody plays. Sex is the inverse."

Feki perused the many, many lingerie shops of downtown Cairo that I never dared enter. "While the shopwindows are provocative, the sheer luridness of the stock inside is breathtaking. Mere words cannot do justice to the fevered imaginations that would create thongs adorned with plastic scorpions or a bra whose daisy-decorated cups play a tinny version of 'Old MacDonald Had a Farm' on contact," she wrote in her book *Sex and the Citadel*.

The Mubarak government controlled all public opinion polling and censored sex questions. But in surveys of Arab-speaking countries outside the Persian Gulf, more than a third of young men—sometimes much more— reported that they were sexually active before marriage, often with more than one partner. But less than a fifth of young women said that they were active at all. Either a few women were very busy, or some respondents were lying.

Arab sexual mores, of course, always fascinated Westerners, including me. Women in tentlike black abayas and niqabs glided down the streets in little cloisters of privacy like turtles in their shells. But young women hanging out along the Nile managed to follow an Islamic code of modesty to the letter but without the spirit. They covered their hair and arms. But they wore hijabs in eye-catching fuchsia or Hermès prints, and long-sleeve T-shirts stretched tight across their chests. They tottered in skinny jeans and high heels. One might throw back her head in laughter in a circle of young men, or stroll away along the sidewalk as half of a couple.

Seedy belly-dancing nightclubs near the Great Pyramids catered exclusively to men, but a performance by a belly dancer was also de rigueur at upscale weddings, even weddings where all the female guests covered their hair. Street prostitution in Cairo was illegal but common, and there were also "summer marriages." Those were temporary couplings of poor Egyptian women and Persian Gulf sugar daddies. The "groom" paid a dowry to the "bride," with the understanding that he would divorce her at the end of his vacation. At one point while I lived in Egypt, the justice minister of a secular government all but codified the practice. He required any non-Egyptian man who married an Egyptian woman twenty-five years his junior to pay a seven-thousand-dollar deposit into an account for the bride, explicitly to provide for "summer brides" left behind.

A decade before I arrived, an Egyptian-made movie called *Cultural Film* followed the quest of three medical students searching for a VCR and some privacy to watch a pornographic videocassette featuring Salma Hayek. They finally attempted to screen it in a mosque, and it was, predictably, a disappointment. But *Cultural Film* was a blockbuster: Even prudish Egyptians chuckled at their culture's cheerful hypocrisy.

I sometimes heard Westerners ascribe jihadist militancy to sexual frustration. The desire for martyrdom was said to derive from a Quranic verse that promised virgins in the afterlife. This notion had resurfaced so often in the West since the 2001 terrorist attacks that one dubious scholar had even named it: the "blue balls theory of terrorism."

It "reduces the political behavior of non-Western peoples to an elaborate mating ritual," the scholar, Gilbert Caluya of the University of Melbourne, concluded.

The "theory," of course, is absurd. Egyptian friends rolled their eyes and reminded me of mythic Western stereotypes as old as colonialism: the oversexed and animalistic Arab male was the corollary to the helpless Arab female in need of Western rescue.

After some effort I tracked down a self-described former jihadi who had immigrated to the United States and now insisted that in his youth in Cairo he had been drawn to violence by sexual frustration. "Sex-deprivation syndrome," this onetime sufferer, Tawfik Hamid, called it.

"You read that very sensual description of paradise, and you are willing to die for Allah just to have sex in paradise," he told me, sitting in his apartment in Manassas, Virginia.

In truth, he never got close to dying for anything. He had belonged only briefly to a nonviolent Islamist student movement in Cairo. Now he earned his keep telling conservative think tanks, conferences, and donors about his titillating theory of Islamic jihad. An invitation to Washington after September 11, 2001, from a conservative Senate staffer had led Hamid to publishing op-eds in the *Wall Street Journal* ("The Trouble with Islam" was one title) and to meeting with John Negroponte, the director of National Intelligence under George W. Bush. Hamid showed me an email from Antony Blinken, a senior official in the Obama administration, thanking him for a meeting and introducing him to a senior State Department official. Hamid had gone far playing into Western stereotypes about Muslims, sex, and gender. Most feminists I met in Egypt thought those stereotypes infused Western worries about the loss of Suzanne Mubarak, too.

First Lady" feminists never criticized the army, the police, the intelligence agencies, the generals, or the president. But these authorities all took advantage of the cultural stigmas around women's sexuality. The police tormented Islamists by intruding on their wives and daughters in raids on their homes. Domestic intelligence agencies spied on female politicians or rights advocates, then used information about their personal lives for blackmail. Or they snooped on the female relatives of their targets: the photographs of ElBaradei's daughter in a bathing suit were a mild example.

At street demonstrations, the soldiers, police, and *baltagiya* could assault female activists with extra impunity. Any woman who complained would end up taking the blame. Why did she expose herself like that? Where was her father, her husband, or her brother? Who, now, would marry her?

Female activists told me many times about the case of Nawal Ali, a journalist in her forties who happened to walk past a street protest in downtown Cairo in 2005. Dozens of police in riot gear watched in silence as thugs in civilian clothes attacked, groped, stripped, and abused the women in the crowd, including Ali. Unlike others though, Ali pressed charges.

The state closed ranks. The prosecutor could find no witnesses or evidence. The state newspapers and their private-media allies slandered her as a loose woman. She had ripped her own clothes off, some claimed, in a scheme to smear the police. Her husband divorced her. The National Council of Women never mentioned her. Four years after the attack—two years before the uprising—she died in shame and anonymity.

"Tell Her Father" was an old Egyptian folk song that reflected that patriarchal culture. It told the story of a wedding. "Tell her father to rest if he is worried. She is a tightly closed door lock and the key has come to it," the lyrics run. "Tell her father to have dinner if he was hungry. Go home, father, the blood has wetted the sheets."

Mozn Hassan never liked the song. After Mubarak's ouster, Hassan and Nazra for Feminist Studies saw an opening for a different kind of bottom-up, grassroots feminism, unfettered by the Mubarak government's restrictions on fund-raising or assembly, or by the need to coordinate women's projects through the National Council. She started organizing new cultural events, including improvisational music performances that made new songs out of the stories of women in the audience.

One of the songs that emerged was also called "Tell Her Father":

> *Tell her father: Cry for the calamity*
> *She was broken by your own hands and her tears spilled*
>   *on the sheets*
> *Tell her father they deceived you*

Her honor is not between her legs but they do not say
  that
Tell her father: she's not a commodity to be sold
They slaughtered and the wailing was public
Tell her father to rest if he was worried
She is not a door lock waiting for the key
Tell her father girls are in pain
They shoulder their pain, and they raise their heads high.

It was eventually recorded by a four-woman rock band, Bent al-Masarwa—Egyptian Girl—that also grew out of the Nazra performances. Soon the band was selling out shows at a Cairo art gallery. Egyptian Girl eventually released a commercial album of songs about virginity, harassment, head covering, and other gender-related subjects. "They are so cute," Hassan later told me.

Hassan turned thirty-two in 2011. She had grown up in Saudi Arabia while her father worked as a university administrator there. But she insisted that her childhood in the kingdom had less to do with her feminism than had watching the discrimination her mother faced as a professor of archaeology at the University of Alexandria. Hassan kept a biography, in English, of Doria Shafik in a prominent place in her Zamalek apartment. And after the eighteen days of protests drove out Mubarak, Mozn and the women at Nazra saw their chance to revitalize Shafik's legacy.

"We were so obsessed by the idea of a movement," Hassan told me.

Hassan and Nazra were the opposite of First Lady feminism. They focused most of all on expanding the public space for grassroots organizing. They started by holding training for scores of "women's human rights defenders," to provide legal services for female activists as well as to record their ordeals and triumphs. They advertised a national telephone hotline for women in need to reach them.

"Some were laughing at us," she said. "They were joking that we are searching for every stray cat in the street to call her a human rights defender. Others said 'they are just crazy feminists' and we should all have the same cause."

They collected the stories of women who suffered abuse at the hands of the police, or were abused by their families after their release. They helped foster grassroots groups like Operation Anti-Sexual Harassment, which trained men and women to police Tahrir Square and other public places, to combat sexual intimidation even among self-described "revolutionaries."

When a twenty-three-year-old woman named Merna Thomas complained that men dominated the graffiti scene, Nazra helped her set up seminars and design stencils to get female artists into the game. They sprayed slogans like WOMEN ARE EQUAL TO MEN around Cairo and other cities, along with graffiti portraits of notable women from Egyptian history—feminists, labor organizers, artists, writers, and so on.

Nazra staged women's theater productions on subjects like masculinity or sexual violence. Its "Young Feminist School" brought forty-five women and fifteen men under thirty from the provinces to Cairo for fifteen days of training in topics like women in politics, women in labor organizing, women in the arts, and violence against women. Only a few men were expelled for hitting on women.

A "cadres" program trained women to build parties. A "political representation academy" provided sixteen female candidates of any (non-Islamist) faction with training and tactical help on steps like collecting signatures, formulating a platform, and giving public speeches. Their programs were unlike the iniatives to foster democracy that the American government sponsored. Those counted how many hundreds or thousands of candidates they moved through two-day training conferences. Nazra stuck with its sixteen women candidates from registration through voting. When the promise of parliamentary elections was finally fulfilled—later, in 2012—one of the Nazra alumnae, Sanaa el-Saeed of Assiut, became the only woman to win a seat who did not come from either the Islamist parties or the former Mubarak legislature. (Of the 23 million women who were eligible to vote, about five hundred thousand cast ballots, and of the nearly one thousand female candidates, only nine won seats in the chamber. Five of the nine were Islamist women. But that was still to come.)

Hassan and Nazra were hardly well known in Egypt. But they represented a sea change: the rebirth of an independent women's movement, the first since Abdel Nasser shut down Doria Shafik's Daughter of the Nile Union. Nazra spawned independent, self-sustaining satellite groups in fifteen towns outside Cairo. Made up mostly of women who had never attended college, the Nazra satellites both reported local abuses and planned women's events. Some, like the group in Aswan, had as many as fifty members.

Trade unionists, free-speech advocates, and many other groups were taking advantage of the new opportunities to organize. But Americans and Europeans were always amazed by the women, Hassan told me. "The Western reaction was, 'Wow, women are in the streets!'" She widened her eyes in mock wonder. "Duh!"

Nazra and its women human rights defenders were also among the first to report the virginity tests, and they helped persuade three of the women to speak out by name. One, Samira Ibrahim, took the generals to court.

I met Ibrahim at a gathering of rights advocates taking up her cause. She was twenty-five years old, and she wore a purple hijab printed with flowers. She neither looked me in the eye nor shook my hand. I touched the left side of my chest instead, as I had learned to do when greeting conservative women. My colleague Mayy el-Sheikh asked the questions.

"I kept telling myself, 'People get heart attacks, why don't I get a heart attack and just die like them?'" Ibrahim told us. She was from a poor village near Sohag, in rural southern Egypt, where she worked at an office job for a marketing company. She and some friends had ridden a train for nine hours to join the protests in Cairo that March. They were spending the nights at an inexpensive hotel, she said, until the soldiers clearing Tahrir Square had hauled her into the Egyptian Museum.

When she returned to Sohag after her release from military custody, her mother told her to stay silent about her ordeal if she ever hoped to marry. Ibrahim was afraid even to tell her father, an Islamist who worked as a building contractor.

But as a young man he had been detained and beaten by the police himself, for belonging to a militant group. He recognized the electric-shock marks he saw on the skin of his daughter.

"History is repeating itself," he said. She told him of her ordeal, and to her surprise he said that now was the chance to take the army to court, to hold the generals accountable. "To get my rights," Ibrahim told us.

Cairo human rights lawyers filed multiple lawsuits against the soldiers on her behalf. But Egyptian news outlets reported that unnamed military sources had insisted Ibrahim fabricated the whole episode. She received anonymous phone calls at night threatening rape or murder. Critics in the news media demanded: How could she accuse patriotic soldiers of sexual abuse?

Then General Sisi publicly defended the virginity tests. "The procedure was done to protect the girls from rape, as well as to protect the soldiers and officers from rape accusations," he told Amnesty International. Sisi evidently expected the world to agree that, of course, only virgins could be the victims of sexual assault.

In the first verdict on her claims, a military court exonerated the army doctor who she said had carried out the examinations. It was her word against the army's. And her story might have disappeared there if not for another woman's more public encounter with Egyptian soldiers that December.

During another round of protests and clashes with the security forces around Tahrir Square, something—perhaps a Molotov cocktail or a canister of tear gas—set on fire a neoclassical library of rare books and manuscripts established by Napoleon in 1798 during the French occupation. Thousands of demonstrators fled as hundreds of soldiers swarmed forward around the burning building. A woman in a traditional dark abaya stumbled and fell, and a friend, Hassan Shahin, tried to carry her to safety.

Before he could, a group of four soldiers in helmets and visors caught up with them and seized her. They dragged her along the pavement, ripped her gown, and pushed it over her face, exposing her jeans, torso, and bright blue bra. The soldiers kicked her and stomped her and hit her with a club for several minutes while she writhed half naked on the ground. Then they hauled away her inert body.

It was hardly the first such attack. But this time an activist had caught it on film. Within hours the footage was everywhere. The next day, a freeze-frame photograph of a soldier's foot coming down over the blue bra covered the full front page of a new independent newspaper named for the square, *Tahrir*.

At a televised news conference, General Adel Emara of the military council insisted that the images had been taken out of context. "The Supreme Council of the Armed Forces has always warned against the abuse of freedom that leads to chaos and the fall of the state instead of the fall of the regime," he said, perhaps unwittingly echoing Mubarak's line about the "very thin line" that "separates freedom from chaos."

"There is a systematic plan to demolish the state," the general said, "to clash with the armed forces and show it in a bad and inappropriate light, using violence against protesters."

A female journalist tried to hold up the newspaper with the image of the beating. The general shouted her down. "Fold the paper, I know what I am talking about!" Then all the journalists started pressing. "No, I didn't open the door for questions," the general sputtered. "I didn't allow for talking! If you talk again I will kick you out! . . . We are securing the state."

Finally an older female journalist with the state media politely raised her hand. She identified herself as "an Egyptian woman first and the senior military editor second." Apologize and listen, she said calmly, "or the next revolution will be a women's revolution for real!"

Wait! the general told her, unfolding a note. The army had just learned of a new plan to attack government buildings, he said, and he steamrolled right past her.

The attack, of course, never materialized.

Many on television or in the papers again blamed the woman. Why didn't she wear an undershirt? Was that a blue bra or a bikini? Why so colorful? Did her abaya have snaps instead of buttons, and did that mean she *wanted* to disrobe? Why was a soldier in the picture wearing a tennis shoe instead of a boot? The photo's "genuineness is questionable," an announcer on state television averred.

Islamists called the photo a plot to distract from elections. "Regardless of what was written about her on the internet—about how she wasn't wearing anything under her abaya, about who she is and what she did, or that person who said she provoked the soldiers and was lying down for them for an hour—all this doesn't matter to me," summed up Khaled Abdullah, an ultraconservative Islamist host.

"The girl in the open abaya (the one with the snaps) performed a striptease show so that the cameras gush over her underwear and the poor military soldiers look like assassins who violate honor," wrote Lamees Gaber, a female screenwriter and columnist.

I thought she would end up like Nawal Ali, the journalist assaulted and disgraced under Mubarak. Thank God the soldiers covered her face.

Calls circulated on social media for yet another march—#bluebra. I foresaw a fiasco. No women's demonstration had attracted more than a few dozen people since before Abdel Nasser. The only news I expected to report from the event was more violence against the women.

But when I got out of a car downtown, I heard a roar blocks away. The crowd was not just dozens or hundreds. It was thousands, even tens of thousands. Women of all ages, from infants to grandmothers. And they were as diverse as the city—unveiled hair, head scarves that covered only the hair, longer veils that covered the torso, niqabs that covered all but the eyes. Many held blown-up photographs of the woman in the blue bra under the boots of the soldiers. Others had made their own signs:

IF YOU DON'T LEAVE YOUR HOUSE TODAY TO CONFRONT THE MILITIAS OF TANTAWI, YOU WILL LEAVE YOUR HOUSE TOMORROW SO THEY CAN RAPE YOUR DAUGHTER.

IS IT A REVOLUTION OR A COUP?

SHAME IS ASHAMED OF YOU, COWARDS.

"Drag me, strip me, my brothers' blood will cover me!" the women chanted. Or, "Yes, she was wearing an abaya with snaps. How could she have known that you were depraved?"

Men were there, too. Some walked in front of the march, even waving their hands like conductors for the women to chant louder. Others walked alongside like shepherds, protecting the marchers from potential assault. Some of the signs and chants, too, were in their own way conservative, like the demands for gallantry from the men of Egypt. But the sheer number of women was overwhelming. No one had ever seen anything like it in Egypt.

"Come down," they cried to the balconies and upper-story windows, and at each block more and more women joined in. Male storekeepers stood in doorways, watching slack jawed as the river of women flooded past them. Public and private had been turned inside out.

"Where is the field marshal? The girls of Egypt are here," they chanted.

"Down with military rule!" *"Hureya, hureya"*—"Freedom, freedom." "Every bullet strengthens us."

Older activists marveled. Ghada Shahbander had demonstrated with Nawal Ali in 2005. "The wall of fear is gone," Shahbander told me. "That is the difference the Egyptian revolution has made. And now when we march for the Blue Bra Girl, we march for Nawal Ali."

The woman never revealed her name. Mayy el-Sheikh chided me for calling her the Blue Bra Girl. Egyptian women, Mayy said, called her the Lady of All Girls.

She had stirred the largest demonstration by women in modern Arab history. By the time I got back to my office that afternoon, while the march was still swelling, the generals had reversed themselves, accepted the blame, and apologized for unspecified "violations."

"The Supreme Council of the Armed Forces expresses its utmost sorrow for the great women of Egypt, for the violations that took place during the recent events."

I had never heard anything like it: the generals almost never apologized.

The next week, Samira Ibrahim won her vindication, too. Egypt's administrative court unexpectedly ruled in her favor and banned virginity tests. "These acts involve deliberate humiliation and intentional insult to women participating in protests" and "a violation of human rights and freedoms," the court ruled. Never before had a civilian court ruled against the generals.

Graffiti stencils of a floating blue bra and the face of Samira Ibrahim started appearing on the walls of downtown Cairo. FEAR ME, GOVERNMENT, read the sign below a blue bra hovering near the raised fist of a woman in a hijab.

Plucky Ibrahim was an instant hero in Washington. She was precisely the sort of activist Americans had pictured leading the revolution. Perhaps the fall of Suzanne Mubarak was an opportunity for Egyptian women after all.

The State Department invited Ibrahim to Washington to receive its International Women of Courage Award, to be presented by Michelle Obama. But Ibrahim, like Egypt, was complicated. In the summer of 2012, she wrote a Twitter post lauding a suicide bombing that killed five Israeli tourists in Bulgaria. "A lot of very sweet news."

A few weeks later, she commended the September 11 terrorist attack. "May America burn again every year." She quoted Adolf Hitler. "No act contrary to morality, no crime against society, takes place except with the Jews having a hand in it."

The State Department rescinded the invitation.

6

The Theban Legion

May 7, 2011–October 9, 2011

Why did churches look like fortresses? Why the walls of stone, the slits for windows, the guard tower? Our driver Mohamed was full of questions about Christianity. By guard tower, I learned, he meant church steeple.

I was on my way to the Cairo slum of Imbaba, where a mob had torched two churches the previous night. Along with the risks to Israel and women's rights, the threat to the Christian minority was a recurring fear in Western debates about the Egyptian uprising. I imagined that the former police state had kept a lid on these dark, sectarian passions for decades, and now they were boiling over. It was the kind of easy metaphor we journalists cherish.

The Mubarak government prohibited surveys about the number or demographics of the Christians in Egypt. They were often said to make up roughly 10 to 15 percent of the population. Some followed various small Orthodox, Protestant, or Catholic denominations. The vast majority—more than 90 percent—belonged to the main Coptic Orthodox Church, headed by the pope of Alexandria. It traced its roots to St. Mark the Evangelist, said to be the author of the Gospel of Mark. (The English words "Copt" and "Egypt" come from the same Greek root, *Aegyptos*.) Some Copts were poor, like the *zabaleen*—the garbage people—who survive off the refuse of Cairo. Others were among the richest in Egypt, like the brothers Naguib and Nassef Sawiris.

But Mubarak prevented anyone from learning how many, how rich, or how poor Egypt's Christians were. He took the position that asking questions about differences between the Christian and Muslim populations would create sectarian rivalries or resentments where none had previously existed. Such feelings, he often insisted, were alien to Egypt. If trouble broke out between Muslims and Christians, it could be only the mischief of foreign instigators or the manifestation of some private vendetta.

This was as willfully naïve as maintaining that racism was alien to the former Confederate states, and Mubarak's denial of the problem had perverse effects. A few months before I arrived in Egypt in 2010, three Muslims had gunned down six churchgoers and a Muslim bystander outside a cathedral after an evening Mass in Nag Hammadi, Qena, in Upper Egypt; prosecutors wrote it off as an isolated act of revenge for the rape of a local Muslim woman by a Coptic assailant. The local bishop complained that police had ignored his pleas for added security, and twenty-nine liberal politicians and activists traveled from Cairo to show solidarity with the local Christian community. But instead of being welcomed, the delegation was arrested. Police accused the visitors from Cairo of turning the killing into a sectarian issue.

On New Year's Day 2011, a church bombing in Alexandria had killed twenty-three Christians and injured nearly a hundred. The Interior Ministry blamed Palestinian terrorists from Gaza and insisted those killings had nothing to do with Egyptian sectarianism either. No one was ever charged with the crime.

In practice, though, discrimination was an open secret. Every Egyptian's government-issued identity card bore one of three labels: Muslim, Christian, or Jew. (There were no options for atheists or others.)

Differing family and estate laws had governed Muslims and Christians since the colonial era, in part because Westerners cared to codify only commercial and criminal rules. They left social issues to local religious leaders. Medical schools steered Christians out of certain specialties, like obstetrics, keeping them exclusively Muslim. The highest ranks of the military and intelligence services were closed to Christians, who could work only as lower-ranking civil servants. Most business owners favored their own sect. Christian writers or bloggers were sometimes arrested on charges of insulting Islam. And onerous permitting laws restricted the construction of churches. In November 2010, police said that Christians in a Giza neighborhood had built an unauthorized church disguised as a community center, and when the Christians protested—some allegedly throwing Molotov cocktails—the police killed one and injured several others. I was stunned, because I was still new to Egypt, but no one else was.

Pope Shenouda III, head of the Coptic Church, had once confronted President Sadat, who punished the pontiff for his audacity with house arrest in a monastery. But Shenouda and Mubarak got along fine. The church endorsed Mubarak whenever required, and Mubarak let the pope dictate Christian family law and provided other favors. Soon after I arrived, the pope had briefly withdrawn into seclusion to protest some grievance; Mubarak coaxed him back out by pardoning some jailed Christians. It was their periodic ritual.

Christian minorities in Lebanon, Syria, Iraq, and the rest of the region followed the same logic: better to trust a ruling strongman than the Muslims around them—even if the strongman failed to guarantee equal treatment or, like Mubarak, willfully ignored discrimination.

After the collapse of the police during Mubarak's last days in power, violence against Christians spiked visibly under the generals. Among other episodes, a feud over an alleged interfaith romance had culminated in a church burning in March in a village in Helwan, just south of Cairo. Christians in Giza had demonstrated against the negligence that allowed the arson, and thirteen people were killed in clashes—eight Christians and five Muslims, according to news reports.

Now, in May, I was on the way to the neighborhood of Imbaba, where a night of street fighting had led to two church burnings. A dozen were killed—six Muslims, six Christians. More than 230 were wounded. Sixty-five were either injured or killed by gunshots. I had no idea why.

My *Times* colleague Mona el-Naggar and I got out of our Mitsubishi in an Imbaba traffic circle that smelled like cheap plastic and rotting vegetables. The alleys of the neighborhood were too narrow for even a small car, so we hired a three-wheeled tuk-tuk to get us farther into the maze of overcrowded tenements. Imbaba was said to be more than four times as crowded as Manhattan, and here the tallest buildings rose only a few stories. I could scarcely stretch my arms between the walls of the alleys. Men, women, and children leaned out of most windows, which were usually covered by only a scrap of fabric instead of glass. Children in flip-flops bounced through garbage spilling out of overflowing bins. Around a corner, a flock of sheep strolled through the street.

Hard-line Islamist militants had taken over the neighborhood for a period in the early 1990s and forced Christians to pay a religious tax (*jizya*, as the practice was known in the Middle Ages). Journalists dubbed the district the "Islamic Emirate of Imbaba." It took twelve thousand riot police with bulldozers to retake control.

Now soldiers were again peering from the turrets of armored personnel carriers stationed every few blocks along the main thoroughfares. No one would talk to us within earshot of anyone else, and taking out a notebook risked attracting a crowd or tangling with a soldier. But one young man, twenty-five-year-old Alaa Ayad, hailed us into a doorway and up several flights to his family's apartment. We passed a rooster on the stairs. Inside, images of Coptic saints and Pope Shenouda hung on the wall. A television showed a man with a long beard on a Coptic satellite network railing against Islamist extremists. Two of Alaa Ayad's brothers pulled stools toward the couch to join us, and I could see crosses tattooed on their wrists. Many Copts wore the tattoos: thirteen hundred years of Muslim rule could not erase the faith.

The feud at the center of the violence, like so many others, had started with a woman. Abeer Talaat, also twenty-five, had grown up in a Christian family in Imbaba. She married a Christian in Assiut, a provincial capital two hundred miles south along the Nile, but it did not work out. And the only path out of a bad marriage led through a mosque.

Christian family law effectively prohibited divorce, but a Christian woman could convert to get one. That frequently led to allegations of forced conversion or kidnapping by one sect or another, and then often to violence. The police never seemed to resolve the facts about the episodes, and rumors or fantasies about the cases spread across Egypt and beyond. Islamist militants as far away as Baghdad and Libya had bombed churches or killed Christians in the name of Kamilia Shehata, a Coptic priest's wife allegedly kidnapped by Christians to prevent her conversion to Islam.

So, for faith or freedom, Abeer Talaat had converted to Islam, filed for divorce, and headed home from Assiut to Imbaba. A Muslim man she met along the way, Yassin Thabet Anwar, somehow got the idea that Abeer would marry him instead of her Christian husband. But she had continued home alone. Then, on Saturday night, May 7, the would-be Muslim groom arrived in Cairo looking for the recently converted woman he hoped would be his bride.

That is when it reached the attention of Hussein Qheder, a hard-line Islamist who had recently returned to Imbaba after fourteen years in prison. "I would be considered an extremist," he explained when we caught up with him later and he told us his story of that night.

"You get a phone call that says, 'Come quick. A big sheikh's wife has been taken into the church, and he is calling on people to help get his wife out.'"

But who was this supposed sheikh? Why was his wife in a church? The caller could not say, Qheder said, so he stayed out of it. "We cannot bear this kind of talk. This could kill the revolution."

Alaa Ayad, the Christian sitting with us in his home, had received calls at the same time as the Islamist extremist. Ayad's callers told him that a mob of hard-line Islamists was heading for the Church of St. Mina, off an unpaved road called Luxor Street. So Ayad rushed to defend the church.

About twenty Muslims showed up at around 6:00 P.M. on May 7. Seeing themselves outnumbered, they called for reinforcements, and by 7:00 P.M., there were about five hundred on each side. The numbers grew into the thousands before the night was over.

A Christian coffee shop owner, Adel Labib, took a gun to the roof of his building, and at about 8:00 he fired the first shot. Did he hit anyone or fire into the air? I could never settle those questions. But Alaa Ayad was sure a Christian was the first to use a gun.

"How can they say we started it when we are defending our church?" Ayad asked. "I am going to defend my church and my house, and if that injures someone, I can't help it."

Both sides fought with bricks, clubs, knives, and more gunshots from the rooftops or windows. A Molotov cocktail set fire to St. Mina Church. Part of the mob broke off to burn down the nearby Church of the Virgin Mary. The policemen stationed outside had fled, and the battle continued until nearly dawn. The priest of the Church of the Virgin Mary said that a thirty-eight-year-old guard, Salah Aziz, had burned to death by the altar.

Abeer Talaat, the bride, had gone to the police for protection during the violence. They arrested her on suspicion of bigamy and detained her for three months.

The next day, the Supreme Council of the Armed Forces followed the usual playbook and blamed a third party for stirring up trouble. This time it was unnamed Mubarak loyalists—the *felool*, or remnants. Everyone pointed fingers. Bishops blamed hard-line Islamists. Lay Copts blamed the army and the police, who seldom seemed to arrest anyone for attacking Christians. The metaphor of the boiling-over pot had been wrong from the start, I realized. The police state had not kept a lid on innate sectarian tension. Its discrimination and denials inflamed the hostility.

F ather Matthias and Father Filopateer were troublemakers. In the decade before the uprisings, Coptic Christians in Egypt had often lamented to one another that columnists in the state-run *Al Ahram* openly insulted the Bible, or that church burnings and crimes against Copts were going unreported. Even the quasi-official church newspaper had "red lines" precluding criticism of Mubarak, the army, or the police. So in 2004, Matthias, who was forty-five, and Filopateer, thirty-seven, started a newspaper for distribution in churches, to agitate for equal protection.

They named it the *Theban Legion,* after a legendary battalion of 6,666 Roman soldiers garrisoned at the ancient city of Thebes in the third century. The legend was that all 6,666 had converted to Christianity. When the emperor ordered pagan sacrifices, they refused. They chose mass execution.

The *Theban Legion* was fearless, even incendiary. One cover depicted Mubarak as a bearded Islamist. After a few months, police started confiscating issues. Some bishops and churches refused to distribute it for fear of retaliation. Pope Shenouda summoned the two priests to a monastery in the desert west of Cairo and told them to stop causing problems. He twice suspended Father Filopateer from the priesthood for his criticism of Mubarak—the first time for a month, and the second for two years—and by 2006, the *Theban Legion* had folded.

After Mubarak, though, the two priests saw a new chance. In March, some younger Christians had protested the church burnings by demonstrating in the plaza outside the Maspero state broadcasting building, a massive cake of concrete by the Nile near a street named for a French archaeologist, Gaston Maspero. (The Christians picked a smaller space than Tahrir Square so that their numbers would look bigger.) More than three hundred soldiers and a dozen armored personnel carriers were stationed around Maspero, and they started to push the Christians away. So Father Matthias told them to stay and camp out. "I ordered the youth to bring tents and blankets and we slept in the street for nine days," he later told me.

It was the genesis of the Maspero Youth Union—the first political movement by Coptic laity since before Abdel Nasser, as far as anyone could remember. "It was a shock to Egypt," Father Matthias said.

To appease the Christians, the generals agreed to rebuild the burned churches and release a jailed priest—a victory. So after the Imbaba riots, Father Matthias, Father Filopateer, and the young Christian organizers camped out again outside Maspero. The church hierarchy equivocated. No other clergy joined in the protests. A brawl outside Maspero injured thirty-three Muslims and twenty-two Christians, according to the Health Ministry, and in the aftermath the police arrested nineteen Christians (and no Muslims). Pope Shenouda won their release the usual way, as a personal favor from the generals. In an apparent exchange, he delivered an admonition carried on the front page of the state newspaper the next day telling the Copts to abandon the sit-in.

The sit-in "negatively affects Egypt's reputation as well as your own," the pope said. "The patience of the rulers is starting to end, and you will be the losers if you continue in the protest." But thousands of Christians defied their pope and rallied again to Maspero. "With our blood, with our souls, we sacrifice for the cross," they chanted.

Smaller iterations of the Coptic demonstrations came and went from Maspero that summer and fall. After more scuffles with the soldiers or Muslim civilians, some of the lay organizers in the Maspero Youth Union wanted to shift to less easily targeted protests, like marches. But then, in October, a mob attacked a church in Aswan, about six hundred miles south of Cairo. The army general serving as governor of the province took the side of the mob and questioned the permit for the church. So on October 5, Father Matthias and Father Filopateer led a march of hundreds of Copts from the heavily Christian neighborhood of Shobra back to Maspero, about an hour's walk north.

The military police dispersed it with force. An officer beat and kicked Father Matthias. His eyeglasses fell off and shattered. Others were filmed stomping and hammering a prone Christian, then dragging his limp body across the asphalt.

So the two priests called for another march from Shobra that Sunday, October 9. I was coaxing my sons into bed that night when Ben Solomon, a videographer for the *Times,* sent me an email.

"Are you seeing this news? In front of Maspero?" he wrote. "I think I might go over to shoot some of it."

"Check that," Solomon wrote a few moments later. "Twitter says cameramen being beaten. Holding off for now."

I put down the picture book and hailed a taxi, then made my way by foot for the final stretch across Tahrir Square. The scent of tear gas was everywhere; the security forces seemed to be shooting canisters at random. People were moving around me in herds, some carrying clubs, machetes, or rocks. Flames leaped from burning cars. Sirens and screams filled the air. But the battle lines confused me. Some people were chanting against military rule or for the unity of Muslims and Christians. Others were turning Tahrir Square favorites into sectarian threats: "The people want to bring down the Christians."

Military police in riot gear marched back and forth along the edge of the square. But a swarm of civilians was marching with them, and they were all chanting together, soldiers and civilians: "Islamic! Islamic!" or at other moments, "Egypt is Islamic."

Closer to Maspero, officers in riot gear were beating a group of protesters who kept shouting "Allahu akbar"—God is Great—the Muslim credo. I was not sure whether men in uniform were beating Muslims, too, or whether Christians were pretending to be Muslims.

A broken cross lay on the ground next to a pool of blood in front of the Maspero building. Ambulances were hauling away bodies on stretchers. A priest in a long beard and clerical robe showed me two bullet casings in the palm of his hand. He was Father Ephraim Magdy, of a church in Shobra, and he said that the soldiers had fired live ammunition.

"They were monsters," he said. "It's impossible for them to be Egyptians, let alone members of the army that protected the revolution."

The march had begun in Shobra at 4:30 P.M., with a larger crowd than expected—thousands, including whole families, led by Father Matthias and Father Filopateer. Young men in plain clothes had tried to throw rocks and bottle bombs at the Christians at two different points along the route, but the march was too large to stop or steer. "We lost control after the first few blocks," Mina Thabet, one of the organizers from the Maspero Youth Union, recalled.

"The blood of Christians is not cheap," "Raise your head, you are Christians," the marchers chanted. They demanded an end to military rule. But they were provocative in other ways, too. Some chants reminded listeners that Egyptians were Christian before the Muslim conquest.

"Egypt is ours," the marchers repeated.

At about 6:30, the crowd passed under the ramp to the October 6 Bridge and in front of the Ramses Hilton. Soldiers perched on armored personnel carriers fired Kalashnikovs into the air, then into the crowd. The APCs jerked into motion. One crashed into a nearby jeep and crushed it, then hurtled into reverse. Others plowed into the throng.

Thabet gasped as an APC passed within a meter of his leg. Bloody bodies lay under the wheels. Women screamed and cried. Demonstrators fled in every direction.

Within thirty minutes, twenty-three Christian demonstrators were dying or dead. A third of them died of bullet wounds; the rest were crushed to death. More than two hundred were injured. "At Maspero we saw clearly who did the crime, and it was military one hundred percent," Father Filopateer later told me.

But Egyptian state television inverted the news. "Breaking: Coptic protesters throw stones and Molotovs at soldiers from above the October 6 Bridge and burn cars" ran a news crawl along the bottom of the screen.

A newscaster, Rasha Magdy, accused Egyptians of abandoning their army under a Christian attack. "Eyewitnesses confirm that hundreds of Coptic demonstrators who blocked the road threw stones and Molotovs at the army and police assigned to guard the Maspero building," she said, citing false reports of dead and injured soldiers. Egypt's "honorable citizens," she urged, must defend their armed forces. Newscasters interviewed soldiers who complained of a Christian ambush.

Some Muslim viewers knew better than to believe the newscasts, and they rushed to stand with the Christians. "Muslims get what is happening," twenty-seven-year-old Nada el-Shazly told me, pulling down a surgical mask she had worn to protect against tear gas. The military "is trying to start a civil war," she said.

But "honorable citizens" had set up vigilante checkpoints all around downtown. They demanded that passersby hold out their wrists, to be checked for tattooed crosses, or they forced them to recite the Muslim profession of faith. A Christian friend of mine escaped by holding the arm of a woman in a hijab; she said he was her brother.

Father Matthias fled into a building full of private television studios, and one let him hide inside as soldiers searched door-to-door. "I could see out the window the thugs coming and chanting, 'Islamic! Islamic!'" he told me, "and then when they met the officers they stopped chanting and they were all smoking together by the side of the street."

Father Filopateer hid for three hours inside a parked car in the garage of the Ramses Hilton. Someone eventually found a Christian policeman who escorted him to safety.

The next morning, at the main Coptic Christian hospital, the doctors showed me seventeen corpses. Most had died of bullet wounds, about a half dozen had been run over by APCs. One skull had been crushed under a wheel.

The Maspero massacre was the deadliest episode of sectarian violence in the modern history of Egypt. The church blamed the priests. The Coptic synod met in the cathedral the next day to debate putting the two priests to a church trial, "for seducing the Coptic youth to their death," Father Matthias told me.

Pope Shenouda told the bishops to forgive the priests, but he also avoided confronting the generals. A church statement blamed the violence only on "infiltrators" who "got in the middle of our sons and committed mistakes to be blamed on our sons." The statement made no reference to the military or police.

Thousands of Christians gathered for the funeral two days later in the Cathedral of St. Mark, the preeminent Coptic sanctuary. Pope Shenouda's enormous jet-black miter weighed down his frail head, and his beard brushed his lectern. He praised the dead as martyrs and "unarmed children who never carried a gun." But he still said nothing about who might have killed them. Having lived in Egypt only fourteen months at the time, I was shocked at his reticence.

The military council summoned foreign correspondents to the headquarters of the state information service later that week. The council was at pains to please both the West and the street in those days, and two generals pleaded for our sympathy. They showed us photographs and videos of Coptic demonstrators chanting for the execution of the defense minister. Civilians carried sticks, rocks, and bottle bombs. One hit an APC with a large wooden cross. Soldiers carried an injured colleague on a stretcher.

"The armed forces would never fire arms on the people," General Adel Emara insisted.

The Christians, he said, had terrified the soldiers. "Imagine, as parents would, the soldier in his vehicle now who sees the scene and wants to run for his life. . . . He sees a car burning, and if someone jumps out, the crowd beats him up severely. So this is not safe either. What can he do, other than try to drive his car out of this hell to safety?" The poor soldiers were "traumatized."

While the generals talked, the military police were arresting more than a dozen Christian demonstrators on charges such as attacking soldiers, burning cars, and storming the state broadcasting building. The two priests were taken in, too, but released later that day.

Afterward, Ben Rhodes told me that the Obama administration found it hard to blame the military when the Coptic Church itself had not. Others on the National Security Council did not want to alienate the generals, counting on them to manage a transition.

Secretary of State Clinton played Pollyanna. "The army doesn't want to be a police force," she told Reuters. "They just have to figure out how to create a police force again that will restore law and order while protecting people's rights." She saw the generals as a source of stability.

I tracked down the two priests years later. Father Filopateer had fled to North America. His outspoken criticism of the Egyptian government made him controversial in the Coptic diaspora, and he had bounced from church to church.

"If you dig into it more and you inflame things, it will only get worse and more people may die. That has always been the attitude of the Coptic Church, wisely," one parishioner, Malak Isaac, in Richmond, Virginia, told me, urging me not to listen to Father Filopateer.

I caught up with him at a picnic table outside a strip mall in the Virginia suburbs of Washington. Activists against military rule had complained to me for years about Father Filopateer for a different reason. They said that at the Coptic hospital on the morning after the massacre he had told the families of those killed at Maspero not to seek autopsies, even though an examination of the bodies might have helped prove the soldiers were responsible. After leading the march, they said, he had covered up the killing. Father Filopateer denied it. He said that he had only yielded to the wishes of the families.

But Father Matthias, secluded in a medieval monastery in the mountains near the Red Sea, told me his friend was right not to push for autopsies. "He knew it would not make any difference and they would not get their rights. When we started the *Theban Legion,* we wanted to change the overall situation in society. But after what happened at Maspero, we knew we could not get our rights from the army. There was no way for the Christians to get their rights from the army, and they were against the army now. Nothing had changed in our country."

He understood the silence of the pope, too. "Politics in Egypt are very complicated," he said. "We have to lie all the time in order to live in peace."

7

"How the Downfall of a State Can Happen"

July 23, 2011–November 25, 2011

F or sure! Everyone believes in democracy," Omar Suleiman, the old spy chief, had told Christiane Amanpour of CNN in an interview during Mubarak's last days in power. "But when? Only when the people have a culture of democracy."

That was always the catch: how to get there? Everyone insisted that they wanted an open, accountable democracy, but they always feared that some rival clique or faction was conspiring to hog all the power. Christians feared Muslims. Cosmopolitans feared Islamists. Islamists feared the military. The generals feared the mob—at least, at the beginning.

By midsummer, the near weekly rallies and marches seemed never ending. The generals were still in direct control of the government, with the defense minister acting as head of state, and they appeared emboldened by the divisions in the streets. Their promised parliamentary and presidential elections were slipping further into the future.

General Hassan el-Roweini had once visited Tahrir Square during the eighteen-day sit-in against Mubarak. A crowd gathered around him, and he tried unsuccessfully to convince the protesters that the gunmen shooting at them had been Muslim Brothers, not police. Now, on July 23, Roweini brazenly boasted in an interview on state television that he had lied to manipulate the Tahrir Square demonstrations.

Take the case of Ahmed Ezz, the loathed steel mogul and power broker. "When I wanted to calm the square down, I would spread a rumor that Ahmed Ezz was arrested, and things would grow calm," the general said.

"You were the source of these rumors, sir?" a female interviewer asked.

"Yes, of course," Roweini answered. "I know the effects of rumors on revolutionary groups. I know how to calm things down in a square and how to make things rowdy."

He had new rumors to share. Six months earlier the generals had promised to be out of power in six months, so the April 6 Youth Movement, which had spearheaded the use of nonviolent tactics against Mubarak, was calling for a march that evening to the Defense Ministry to demand an end to military rule. A small test march had taken place the previous night, but this time, Roweini said, the April 6 marchers would be armed with bottle bombs.

"You have information that they will move with Molotov cocktails?" the interviewer asked breathlessly.

"Yes, I have this information," the general insisted.

No longer eager to get pictures taken with the leaders of the April 6 Youth Movement or other young activists, the military council issued a new communiqué—#69—accusing the group of committing treason. April 6 had accepted money from a foreign power in a plot to turn Egyptians against their army, the generals now warned. Everyone knew they meant money from Washington.

The new American ambassador, Anne W. Patterson, had talked approvingly in her confirmation hearings about millions of dollars in aid for nonprofit groups in Egypt to foster democracy. A state-run magazine had welcomed her with a cover illustration depicting her holding wads of burning greenbacks and a bomb wrapped in the American flag. THE AMBASSADOR FROM HELL WHO LIT A FIRE IN TAHRIR ran the headline. Alarms were ringing all over the nationalist Egyptian news media. An Egyptian general had lectured a Washington think tank in July about how unfettered American aid to nonprofits undermined his country's sovereignty and stability. It was some "thank you" for $1.3 billion a year in American aid. But the generals' patrons in Washington did not seem bothered.

Were the April 6 activists really foreign-funded and -trained traitors? "Some strategic experts have said they know this for a fact," the interviewer prompted Roweini.

"I will tell you some incomplete information," General Roweini replied, as though culling tidbits from a trove of spy secrets.

It was well known, as the *Times* and others had reported, that members of April 6 had traveled to Serbia in the late Mubarak years to learn from the opposition group Otpor! Now Roweini claimed that the April 6 movement was executing a Serbian scheme to wreck the pillars of stability in Egypt: the police, the judiciary, the media, the educational system, and, finally, the armed forces. "I am explaining to you how the downfall of a state can happen," Roweini told her.

Fortunately, Roweini continued, the patriotic residents of the neighborhood around the Defense Ministry were safeguarding the soldiers, by "dispersing people and making them go away."

I had no idea why Roweini was spinning like that. Previous calls for marches on the Defense Ministry had never amounted to much. Still, I took a taxi to catch up with the April 6 protesters at around 7:00 P.M., and this time I found perhaps two thousand demonstrators—mostly young, middle-class men, along with a decent minority of women. I knew a few faces, and I saw no one with a weapon. They had walked about an hour and a half to the northeast. But at Abbasiya Square, shadowed by the minarets of the giant Nour Mosque, a half dozen tanks and hundreds of soldiers blocked the way.

Soldiers started firing into the air almost as soon as I arrived. The voice of an imam crackled from the loudspeaker at the top of the mosque's minaret. "Peacefully, peacefully!" But when I turned to retreat, men from the neighborhood threw down rocks and bottles from the buildings. Soon others came out to square off against the march. Some of them brandished machetes and kitchen knives—"white weapons," as Egyptians call them. They closed off the road in the other direction, back to Tahrir. Many of the neighbors earned their livings directly or indirectly off the nearby Defense Ministry headquarters, and they had heeded Roweini's warning to arm and protect themselves. (I heard secondhand reports that soldiers had gone door-to-door to help spread the message.)

I was trapped with the demonstrators. Soon civilians on both sides were tearing up the pavement for missiles to hurl back at one another. I found a corner, pressed my back against the iron fence around the mosque, and took out a notebook.

Demonstrators pleaded with a man inside the mosque to open the gate so they could escape. *Baltagiya*—thugs—the marchers said. But as I was taking it all down a hand grabbed my right arm. A scrawny kid—he looked like a teenager—held on to me and shouted, *"Agnabi, agnabi"*—foreigner, foreigner—to call for reinforcements.

I am a little over six feet tall and a hundred sixty pounds. The kid was a foot shorter and no thicker than me. These were not *baltagiya*. Nobody would hire this kid as a thug. He had heard about the "hidden hands" and "foreign fingers" that the government kept blaming, and now he had caught one red-handed.

Some of his beefier friends were coming our way. I jerked my arm free, and the kid ripped off half my red Brooks Brothers button-down. I was standing in rags.

Thank God his friends were more civil. I was their guest in Egypt, they told the kid, touching their chests in apology to me.

The fight in the square went on for two hours, and the watching soldiers did nothing. Then police arrived and doused us all with tear gas. The gates of the Nour Mosque at last opened to take in the wounded. (Nearly three hundred were eventually treated for injuries.) I followed a few others around the back to escape, and I learned the next day that after a few more hours the soldiers had escorted the remaining demonstrators back to Tahrir Square and safety.

No one had died. The *New York Times* barely covered the skirmish. But the generals now had civilians fighting for them.

The events of July, I think, marked the turning of a corner. The generals' transition plan, spelled out after the referendum in March, called for them to hold still-unscheduled parliamentary elections, and the Parliament would somehow oversee the drafting of a new constitution. Around the same time as the aborted march, Field Marshal Tantawi and the military council enlisted a new panel of jurists and law professors to propose a set of "principles" that the generals would impose on the writing of a constitution. The idea of these binding principles appealed to some liberals, who feared that an Islamist Parliament might limit personal freedoms. The liberals imagined something like the Bill of Rights in the American Constitution.

But some jurists on the new panel had argued for months that the generals should never fully relinquish political power at all, for fear that elections might yield an Islamist government. Judge Tahani el-Gebali of the Supreme Constitutional Court was especially outspoken about that. And when the so-called principles were unveiled in November, they indeed gave the generals permanent power over any elected civilians. The rules insulated the military council from any oversight and authorized it to intervene at will in the civilian institutions. A plan for quiet coup d'état, some called it.

On November 18, tens of thousands of Muslim Brothers and other Islamists jammed Tahrir Square to protest the power grab. The next day, a police sweep of the square ignited a riot. A handful of families (who were not Islamists) had camped out overnight demanding compensation for the deaths of relatives killed at the start of the uprising. When the police pulled up their tents, someone commandeered a police truck. Protesters climbed all over it. Twitter hummed with pictures. And as more riot police stormed in, the crowd of protesters swelled faster and faster. Hundreds of young men and women rushed into the square, despite the tear gas.

"The people want to bring down the field marshal," they were chanting when I got there. "Down with military rule!"

"We saw that people were being attacked and we came down to help," said Huda Ouda, a thirty-year-old secretary in a dark red hijab, pulling her scarf over her face against the gas. "We are completely against the military ruling this country."

A young activist named Ahmed Harara had lost an eye to birdshot during the uprising against Mubarak; he lost his other eye that day battling the police.

The fighting went on for a week. It was confined, bizarrely, to a single block of Mohamed Mahmoud Street, leading from Tahrir Square in the direction of the Interior Ministry. But the supporting crowds in the square sometimes swelled to more than ten thousand.

One day, protesters paraded through the square with the dead body of a demonstrator killed by another police blitz. The Health Ministry had confirmed civilian deaths from live ammunition. But the next morning an army general stood on the steps of the Interior Ministry and insisted to the state media that neither the army nor the police had ever entered the space or used bullets. "An invisible hand in the square is causing a rift between the army and the people," he said.

It was a golden era for talk shows. Generals, sheikhs, politicians, activists, and intellectuals—everyone went to the airwaves each night to make their case about the future of Egypt. Every night was like Sunday morning in Washington, and everyone was watching.

But that fall the talk show hosts were turning on the generals. One program broadcast footage of a soldier shooting a man in the back. As the man's bloody body fell to the ground, the voice-over was the interior minister vowing that his forces had never once used a weapon.

"Do they want us to believe that our eyes do not see what they see?" the talk show's host, Yosri Fouda, asked his audience, "that even when they see they do not see, and that if they indeed see, it means nothing?"

The Muslim Brotherhood stayed out of it. The leaders saw a trap. The presence of Muslim Brothers could provide a pretext for a crackdown or a cancellation of parliamentary elections, now scheduled to begin on November 28. Other protesters said that the Brothers had sold out for a chance to win power. When a dissenting Brotherhood leader showed up to apologize, a mob hounded him out. Convinced that the Brothers' accommodation amounted to collusion, the liberals and leftists never forgave the Islamists.

The military council had begun backing down almost as soon as the fighting began, the day after the all-Islamist protest. First the generals downgraded their binding principles to mere suggestions. Then they dropped the suggestion that they hold on to their power. They replaced their prime minister. They set a date for presidential elections, to begin in May 2012. They pledged that they would exit civilian government fully when the new president took office.

Finally, on the night of Thursday, November 24—Thanksgiving in America—the generals called a halt. An army crane stacked cubes of concrete to form a ten-foot wall across Mohamed Mahmoud Street. A row of soldiers stood impassively on top of it. The generals had turned off the violence, as if they could have done so any time they had chosen. "Our hearts bled for what happened," they wrote on the Facebook page of the military council.

National Security Adviser Tom Donilon and other stability-minded senior staff had gone home for Thanksgiving dinner. The younger cohort left in charge, including Rhodes and Denis McDonough, a deputy national security adviser, were more eager for change in Egypt. At 3:03 A.M. Friday morning in Washington—10:03 A.M. in Cairo—the White House issued its first statement explicitly urging the generals to let go of power: "The new Egyptian government must be empowered with real authority immediately" for "the full transfer of power to a civilian government" to take place "as soon as possible."

The generals' inability to manage the transition "was becoming an embarrassment," one senior diplomat later told me.

When he woke up to the statement, Donilon was furious. "How could you let this happen?" he complained to Steven Simon, who oversaw Egypt on the staff of the National Security Council.

But Simon, too, had taken a rare night off for Thanksgiving. Talk to McDonough and Rhodes, Simon snapped back. He was fed up with the White House's tugs-of-war over Egypt.

8
Forefathers

November 26, 2011–January 22, 2012

Could a Muslim man marry a Jew or a Christian?

A tall and heavy-set sheikh was fielding questions from admirers in an Alexandria mosque. His name was Yasser el-Borhami. He wore wire-rimmed glasses and a beard so long and unruly that it seemed to form a tripod. One tuft grew from his chin and two more from each of his cheeks. The prayer bruise on his forehead was as big as a doughnut.

Yes, Borhami answered, but the Muslim husband must show his wife only "contempt" until she converted.

Contempt in marriage?

"Must every man love the woman he rapes?" Borhami replied.

Borhami's advice, recorded in an online video posted in the years before the uprising, took on new salience during the election that fall of a post-Mubarak Parliament. The voting began on November 28, just days after the wall across Mohamed Mahmoud Street went up that Thanksgiving night, and continued in stages through January 11, 2012. By early December, it was already clear that Sheikh Borhami and the movement he founded, the Salafi Call, were among the big winners. Virtually everyone expected that the Muslim Brothers would take the most votes. The surprise was the Salafis like Borhami, whose conservative, literal-minded, and chauvinistic understanding of Islam made the Brothers look like milquetoasts.

Al Qaeda, the Taliban, the clerics of Saudi Arabia—they were all strains of the same Salafi movement. All, like the Egyptian Salafis, shunned electoral politics. It was a source of strife among the faithful, and a foolish attempt to put man-made law above divine revelation. But now the Egyptian Salafis had somehow sprinted ahead of leftists, liberals, and nationalists who had been at politics for decades. Salafi parties had won a quarter of the vote. They were second only to the Muslim Brothers in political clout. No one—not the Brothers, not the American embassy, and certainly not me—had seen it coming. Had we all so badly misunderstood where "the revolution" was headed?

Although less influential than the Muslim Brothers in the events that followed, the Salafis turned out to be a good place to begin an education in political Islam. They were what most Westerners I knew pictured when they imagined an Islamist: bearded, puritanical, antimodern. Before I moved to Egypt, I had supposed that differences among Islamists were a matter of degree, from moderate to extreme. Liberal or secular-minded Egyptians in Cairo often insisted that the difference was only in degree of candor: Salafis were simply honest about what all Islamists secretly wanted. But more than anything, the Salafis demonstrated that the term "Islamist" can have many contradictory meanings. People who say they seek Islamic governance disagree profoundly, even bitterly, about what that should look like—the way that Protestants and Catholics split over theology, or socialists and communists clash about politics. Compared with the Muslim Brothers, Salafis were in many ways more rigid and doctrainaire (like communists), but at the same time less uniform in their teachings (like Protestants). Let me explain.

Salafiyya refers to the pious forefathers, the original Muslims who were companions of the Prophet Mohamed. But there is some irony in the use of the term. It was first popularized in the late nineteenth century by Sheikh Muhammad Abduh, who was arguably the progenitor of all modern Islamist movements, including the Brotherhood. Abduh used *Salafiyya* to mean almost exactly the opposite of what it means today.

Born around 1850 to a prosperous family in the Nile Delta, Abduh studied at Al Azhar—the centuries-old Cairo mosque and institute that remained the premier center for the study of Sunni Islam when I lived in Egypt. But after Al Azhar, Abduh also visited the great universities of Europe, including Oxford and Cambridge. He drank in the Enlightenment rationalism that he found there, and returned to Egypt convinced that Islam had once embodied all the same virtues—before Europe did, while Christendom was still in its Dark Ages. Europe leaped ahead in science and philosophy because centuries of despotism across the Muslim world had buried Islam's original rationalism under rigid intolerance and rote learning.

Abduh self-consciously modeled himself on the Protestant reformers of Europe. He taught that a return to the ways of the *Salafiyya* meant restoring the rationalism and openness of the early Muslims. Only by reviving that spirit, he argued, could the Muslim world shake off colonialism and catch up to the West.

Visiting Europe, he wrote near the end of the nineteenth century, always renewed his hope "of changing the conditions of the Muslims for the better by reforming the religion that they have corrupted." Or, more aphoristically: "I went to the West and saw Islam but no Muslims; I returned to the East and saw Muslims but no Islam."

Abduh became an influential enough agitator for Egyptian independence that in 1882 the khedive (the hereditary ruler of Egypt who was by then a British puppet) forced him into exile, in Damascus, Beirut, and Paris. But Egypt's British overseers appreciated Abduh's admiration for their culture. They especially valued his emphasis, as he mellowed, on putting pedagogical reform ahead of political change. (In 1884, sympathetic Brits outfitted Abduh in a bright blue gown and white turban for a visit to Parliament, to make him look more satisfyingly exotic.) With the blessing of the British consul general, Abduh ascended to become the grand mufti of Egypt—its highest Islamic authority—and he spread interpretations of Islam that still sounded liberal in 2011. He taught that Islam required limited and representative governments, that citizens should determine their own laws, that polygamy was neither required nor tenable under Islam, and that only God could know which sects were closer to His vision (so Sunni and Shia should stop fighting about it). Abduh defended Charles Darwin decades before the Scopes trial of 1925.

I have often heard Westerners talk about the need for a Muslim Martin Luther. I realized in Egypt that it is far too late for that: Abduh came and went a century ago. But Abduh's ideas never went far. Abdel Nasser nationalized Al Azhar in the middle of the last century, and the institution became more hidebound and authoritarian than ever. Without freedom of speech and assembly, there was little hope for religious freedom either.

Contemporary Salafis say that they, too, emulate the early Muslim companions of the Prophet Mohamed. Like Abduh, they are willing to set aside centuries of intervening tradition to get back to those roots. But instead of returning to a golden era of reason and debate as Abduh proposed, these Salafis seek the most literal possible meaning of the text of the Quran or the sayings of the Prophet. Salafis like Borhami say they want the seventh-century applications of the original texts. Abduh was a modernizer; these Salafis reject modernity. They despise Abduh as a Westernized stooge.

Salafis I knew in Egypt praised the Prophet's medieval penal code. They condemned the salutation "Merry Christmas" as sinful heresy. They taught that women were designed to stay in the home, not a workplace, and they forbade any mixing of the sexes outside an immediate family. If forced to talk to an unveiled woman, Salafi men stared at the ground and refused to shake hands. Salafi women did the same if they had to meet me. Some sheikhs urged women to shun Facebook: a male face on a screen was too intimate. In a gesture toward the inclusion of women in the new Parliament, the military council had required political parties to include at least one woman in each candidate list. The Salafis put up billboards blocking out the veiled faces of their token females: two rows of beards, with a flower in the corner.

I heard music everywhere in the cities of Egypt. Om Kalthoum, a mid-twentieth-century Egyptian diva who is the Edith Piaf of the Arab world, crooned from the stereo of every taxi. Profane homemade rap music stored on USB drives thumped from the tuk-tuk taxis. Outdoor wedding parties took over whole blocks and rocked until dawn. But many Salafis forbade all music, even at weddings. Salafis allowed only the singsong a cappella recitation of Islamic poems or Quranic verses. On the eve of the November parliamentary vote, a Salafi sheikh named Hazem Shoman crashed the stage of a rock concert in the city of Mansoura. He grabbed the microphone and implored the audience to repent, until he himself was yanked from the stage. How could a quarter of Egyptian voters cast ballots for such austerity?

I went to meet Sheikh Borhami, at home in Alexandria, in a building with a small sign reading BORHAMI MEDICAL CLINICS. A vegetable peddler outside called up, and Borhami leaned out his window to throw down a key.

He made his living as a pediatrician, practicing in the same building where his father once had, and also in a government health clinic around the corner. His sister was also a doctor and she practiced in the same building, he told me proudly—Salafi ideas about gender notwithstanding.

His father and an uncle had both been imprisoned for their Islamist politics, which were the kind that had threatened Nasser and Sadat. Borhami found their imprisonment "terrifying," he told me. He discovered a safer form of political Islam on a visit in 1979 to Saudi Arabia, in its austere, authoritarian formulation of Salafism. Saudi sheikhs taught that strict obedience to an earthly ruler (even Sadat or Mubarak) was a religious duty. Any dissent meant *fitna*—strife or unrest among believers.

Borhami volunteered to me that his greatest influence was Sheikh Abdel Aziz Ibn Baz, a blind scholar who had been Saudi Salafism's leading evangelist. He may be best remembered for insisting into the final decades of the twentieth century that the sun circled the Earth, a position he recanted only in 1985 after Saudi prince Sultan bin Salman returned from a week aboard the space shuttle *Discovery*. The word of a royal was enough for the sheikh.

Petrodollar Islam, some scholars called the Salafism of Saudi Arabia. Arabs from Egypt and other poor countries traveled to Saudi Arabia to work in the oil boom and brought back Salafi ideas. And the newly rich Saudi donors used their bank accounts to finance Salafi missions and mosques around the region. Borhami was an apostle of Saudi-style Salafism, and he acknowledged to me the helpfulness of Saudi Arabian money.

"Of course people in Saudi Arabia like to build mosques here in Egypt. It is much cheaper!" he said, grinning.

Borhami and other Salafi leaders would somehow always end up on the Saudi side of politics in post-Mubarak Egypt, with fateful consequences. But that would come later.

While Borhami was spreading Salafism in Alexandria, other Egyptians—especially in the rural south—were following a similar literalist Salafi methodology to an opposite conclusion. These Salafis seized on the Prophet Mohamed's exhortations to battle against the rivals of the early

Muslims. They deemed the Mubarak government apostate and fought a bloody insurgency against it. One of these Salafi jihadis, Ayman al-Zawahiri, a physician who grew up in my neighborhood of Cairo, went on to shape and lead Al Qaeda.

Borhami and the Alexandria-based Salafis wanted no part in any of that, and their deference to authority naturally met only encouragement from Mubarak's *mukhabarat*. The police occasionally detained Alexandria Salafis briefly in Islamist roundups but not as often or for as long as they arrested Muslim Brothers, and the *mukhabarat* developed a working relationship with the Salafi sheikhs. "The intelligence service is everything you need in Egypt," Bassem el-Zarqa, a Salafi leader who lives a few blocks from Borhami, told me defensively. "Do you mean that we are active agents of the intelligence, or just under surveillance like everyone else? If you really live in Egypt, then you don't have to ask this question."

Other Egyptian Islamists believed the answer was easy: the Alexandria-based Salafis were so accommodating to the authorities that they had effectively turned into active agents. As time went on, I understood their reputation.

The Salafis had always opposed protesting Mubarak. Borhami urged all Muslims to stay home on Police Day, to avoid *fitna* and bloodshed. But after Mubarak's ouster, Borhami pushed his fellow Salafis to start their own political party, arguing that otherwise the Muslim Brotherhood might dominate elections and push them aside.

Who was buying what these guys were selling? After the Salafis' surprise success in the first stage of the parliamentary voting, my colleague Mayy el-Sheikh and I set out in early December 2011 to see them on the stump, in the village of Shabramant, Giza.

We drove about an hour southwest through a patchwork of urban sprawl and sugar beet fields. Trash floated in irrigation ditches. Corroded diesel water pumps roared like eighteen-wheelers.

The dirt road narrowed. Cinder-block walls rose on either side of us, and when the space became too tight for our SUV, we knew we had arrived. The road smelled of fresh manure, and we continued on foot to an open plot in the center of the village. Donkeys harnessed to carts were grazing on straw in a makeshift parking lot. Beyond them were hundreds of folding chairs. Loudspeakers stood in the dirt at either side of an elevated platform, and floodlights had been rigged on the low building behind us. A gaggle of sheikhs was mounting the rostrum, and I noticed that Mayy was the only woman in the square. (She and I were also the only ones in pants; the men all wore galabiyas.) I glimpsed a niqab peeking out from a window in the brick walls around the square. Salafi views on gender, alcohol, and female modesty were only common sense in towns like Shabramant (and in much of rural Egypt).

The organizers unfolded two seats for us in the front row and pressed into our hands two cans of sugary Miranda orange soda. Sheikh Shaaban Darwish, with a fluffy white beard and a sizable paunch below his galabiya, was seated at the center of the platform, and he spoke into a microphone on the table before him.

Constitutions, elections, freedom of conscience, and the rights of religious minorities—Sheikh Darwish claimed that all these ideas had originated with the Prophet Mohamed.

"The Prophet, may peace be upon him, said, 'elect twelve deputies from among you,'" he said. "'Elect!' See the word, 'election,' it is ours! 'Elect twelve deputies from among you,' meaning representatives. So the idea of representation is ours. It is not from Western culture, as they claim. The West took it from us. It is ours and now it has returned to us."

The Prophet Mohamed "established the first written constitution in history," Sheikh Darwish continued, alluding to a charter Mohamed had promulgated in the multifaith city of Medina. The people of Shabramant nodded. "Anyone who said that citizenship is an invention of the modern culture of liberalism lied. Citizenship is from Islam. The West took it from us! They wrapped it and canned it and reexported it to us!"

As literalists go, the Egyptian Salafis could be remarkably squishy. Did they earnestly envision an Egyptian government stoning adulterers and cutting off hands? Or would those medieval punishments apply only in some hazy end-times utopia, when poverty and ignorance had vanished from earth? Should the state require women to veil their hair and cover their bodies, or was that just a nice idea for sheikhs to encourage? And what did the sheikhs really think about Christians like me? Salafi sheikhs and candidates gave more liberal answers in more liberal precincts like Port Said but conservative answers in places like Shabramant.

There was no pope or general guide to set Salafist policy, which varied among allied movements in different Arab countries. Like Protestant fundamentalists, the Salafis cared about the individual reading the text for himself (or for herself, but mostly for himself).

But the Salafi roots ran thirty years deep. They had never been chased from mosques by the security services, smeared by regime propagandists, or sullied by electoral mudslinging. They were running charities, clinics, and schools. They had village street cred. The Muslim Brothers were doctors, lawyers, and engineers. They were professionals who preached and ministered to peasants. The Salafis *were* the peasants. They stood shoulder to shoulder, looking up resentfully at the Cairo elites—including, implicitly, the Brothers.

"Where were you before the revolution?" This, Sheikh Darwish said, was the question the other parties now asked of the Salafis.

"Unfortunately, this question comes to mind through the media, the media that hears with only one ear and sees with only one eye, only the eye and ear of the liberal secular current. . . . The elite find it unbelievable and impossible for us to represent our children, our brothers, and our neighbors. These politicians think that it is them, and only them, who represent and speak for us. But, brothers, they did not come to our streets. They did not live in our villages. They did not walk in our hamlets. They did not wear our clothes. They did not eat our bread. They did not drink our polluted water. They did not live in the sewage we live in, and they did not experience the life of misery and the hardship of the people. They never experienced a gas crisis or a bread crisis and they never stood in a line to buy subsidized goods. It is enough for them to look fresh in the media. . . .

"Aren't people equal like the teeth of a comb?" he asked. "Is the vote of a person with a PhD greater than the vote of a high school diploma? . . . You, Egyptian people, do you accept that? Do any of you accept this insult?"

I felt for a moment that I was listening to a sermon in a megachurch in suburban San Diego. If the West had stolen constitutionalism from Islam, then the Egyptian Salafis had borrowed back the religious populism of Jerry Falwell and William Jennings Bryan.

"Brothers, we, the Salafis, the founders of Al Nour Party, were part of the silent majority," he said. "Those people do not live with us, they do not feel our pain or our hopes." These elites will try to "clone" the Mubarak regime, he warned, and re-create "the same 'democracy' with its errors, the same capitalism with its errors, the same liberalism with its errors, but after the revolution, we accept nothing but real change."

It was hard to quantify the popular support for the Salafi views on social issues, or to isolate that support from more general populist resentment. But taking a quarter of the votes in Egypt's first free national election gave them a mandate. Salafi leaders used it to vex everything they touched in post-Mubarak politics. Borhami, the sheikh with the giant prayer bruise, made the most trouble of all.

9

Parliament Grows a Beard

January 23, 2012–May 23, 2012

The People's Assembly sits behind tall iron gates a short and shady walk south of Tahrir Square, east of the British and American embassies and near the fortified headquarters of the Interior Ministry, which is as imposing as the Parliament. The white-domed assembly building, with neoclassical columns and papyrus-flower capitals, was built in 1923 by King Fuad as a monument to Egypt's nominal independence. But he remained a British puppet. The Parliament never held real power. And the pell-mell urbanization during the Abdel Nasser era all but buried the edifice in tenements, storefronts, gas stations, and carts of *fuul* (the slow-cooked beans beloved by Egyptians). In my first year of running around Cairo, I had never noticed the building.

The newly elected lawmakers convened nearly a year after the uprising, on January 23, 2012. If the Salafis' claim to a quarter of the seats in Parliament was the surprise of the election, the Brotherhood was the undisputed winner. Its candidates captured nearly half the chamber. Between the Salafis and Brothers, Islamists of one stripe or another accounted for three quarters of the votes. The liberals, leftists, social democrats, the Tahrir Square activists, and ruling-party incumbents each took a small share of the remaining quarter; they had all washed out at the polls.

The founder of the Brotherhood, Hassan el-Banna, had set his sights on a seat in the Parliament within a decade of starting his movement, in 1928. Now, after eighty years of struggle in the shadows, his heirs were poised at last to lead the assembly. I arrived by 8:00 A.M., and hundreds of Muslim Brothers were already there.

For a supposedly secret society, they were easy to spot. Where Salafis favored the unruly beards of storybook wizards, the Muslim Brothers kept their whiskers fastidiously trim. The archetypical Muslim Brother was middle-aged and middle class, perhaps with the slight potbelly that comes with age and *kushari*—but never with the kind of protruding abdomen that might suggest gluttony or indolence. He wore chinos and a button-down shirt with a button-down collar, never the traditional galabiya of a sheikh or a peasant. A pen or a mechanical pencil might protrude from a pocket. The Brothers—the *Ikhwan*—were upright, confident, sometimes arrogant, perhaps patronizing. They were professionals, small-business owners, or senior vice presidents of sprawling multinationals. Physicians and engineers filled the leadership; medical school and the hard sciences offered the surest paths to prestige for the strivers of the Egyptian middle class. Mohamed Badie, the general guide, was a veterinarian.

The image varied somewhat in rural villages, of course, and there were also university students and recent graduates—drawn by faith, fellowship, or the vision of a better, alternative Egypt. But even among younger Brothers, the outline of the older archetype was discernible: pleated pants, wire-rimmed glasses, argyle sweaters, and thinner, collegiate beards. *Ikhwany,* Egyptians sometimes called the look—Brotherhoodish.

Outside the assembly, Muslim Brothers and Sisters held hands and danced in the street. They sang religious and patriotic songs from the forties and fifties. I watched middle-aged men lift onto their shoulders portly lawmakers in suits and neckties, like a high school football squad hoisting a winning quarterback. Grown men cried tears of joy. "This is the most important day in our lives," said Abdel Moneim el-Tantawy, a sixty-seven-year-old mechanical engineer.

The celebrations followed weeks of deadly, on-again, off-again clashes in the streets abutting the People's Assembly. But as in most such protests over the previous year, the Islamists had stayed out of them. The battles had pitted riot police against liberal or left-leaning protesters demanding civilian rule. (There were three camps now: the security forces, the Islamists, and those self-described "revolutionary" activists.) The street cops were still missing in action. And the riot police did more to provoke than to disperse. Their signature tactic was picking up rocks and throwing them back at the civilian protesters. Just a month before, a makeshift missile a policeman had thrown from the top of the cabinet building had hit my left boot, sending me limping off to look for a helmet. Having successfully ended the weeklong melee before Thanksgiving by building a wall across Mohamed Mahmoud Street, the army had erected no fewer than five more cement barricades across streets around the neighborhood to stop other brawls between the riot police and protesters. Three more went up in February. The stately neighborhood of Garden City was becoming a labyrinth of walls. On one, graffiti artists had painted a trompe l'oeil image of the streetscape behind it.

It seemed clear enough to me that the generals were loath to cede power to an Islamist-led Parliament. To address that question, a barrel-chested general with a white crew cut had summoned me and eight other journalists from Western news organizations for a special briefing before the swearing in, on December 7, 2011. Egyptian news outlets were excluded.

Do not worry about the Islamist electoral victories, the general, Assistant Minister of Defense Mokhtar el-Mulla, told us. The Supreme Council of the Armed Forces would still name the prime minister. The army would still control the government. In fact, the generals had decided to oversee the writing of a new constitution—a job that all the candidates for Parliament had campaigned on as the chamber's main responsibility.

"In such unstable conditions, the Parliament is not representing all the Egyptians," Mulla explained. "So whatever the majority in the People's Assembly, they are very welcome, because they will not have the ability to impose anything."

Islamists, he insisted, could never represent the true Egypt. "Do you think that the Egyptians elected someone to threaten their interest and economy and security and relations with the international community? Of course not!"

Besides, he said, the Mubarak constitution was mostly just fine. "A lot of legislators are saying that we have a very good constitution, and a very unique one, except for only Chapter Five, about the presidential elections, so we will only amend this chapter." He promised that under the military's supervision, a committee of jurists could do the job in less than a month.

Just three weeks had passed since the generals had dropped their overt plan to preserve their power by dictating constitutional principles; now they were trying a more subtle approach.

I was incensed that Egyptian journalists had been left out of the briefing. So I arranged for the *New York Times* website to post my audio recording. The reaction to Mulla's comments was swift. Liberals and Islamists again accused the generals of attempting a coup. The Brotherhood pulled out of a civilian "advisory council" the generals had set up. Within days, the military had retreated back to letting the Parliament oversee the writing of the charter.

But as obvious as the mutual suspicions between the soldiers and the Islamists seemed to me, many non-Islamist politicians and activists saw a conspiracy. They were convinced that the Muslim Brothers were secretly cutting a deal with the generals. The Brothers had accepted the military's continued control of the government, the theory went. In exchange, the generals had scheduled elections on a quick timetable that enabled the Brothers' well-prepared organization to lock up a plurality of the Parliament.

Now, in the midst of the Brothers' celebrations outside the assembly, protesters arrived denouncing the supposed Islamist sellout and demanding that the Brothers in Parliament push harder to take power from the generals. "No to the military, no to the Brothers, the revolution is still in the square!" hundreds of demonstrators chanted. Some seized on a phonetic similarity between the Arabic word for "sell" and the family name of the Brotherhood's general guide, Badie. "Sell, sell, sell the revolution, oh, Badie." It was funny in Arabic.

The Brothers, though, were well coached that morning. Scores linked arms. A long chain held back the protesters. A few threw empty plastic water bottles at the Islamists, but the Brothers more or less held their ground, and, for the day, kept the peace. How long would that restraint last?

Every conversation about the Arab revolts eventually became a debate about the Muslim Brotherhood. Islamists inspired by Egypt's Muslim Brothers constituted the main opposition to every Arab autocracy. The

Cairo headquarters had no control over the many loosely aligned affiliates around the world, but every Arab autocrat sold himself to the West as a bulwark against the dangers of the Muslim Brotherhood and political Islam. Would participation in pluralistic politics now domesticate the Brotherhood? Or was the Brotherhood's promise of an "Islamic democracy" a Trojan horse packed with jihadis? Were we watching a triumph of liberal democracy, or a clash of civilizations?

The U.S. government had been trying to understand the group for nearly six decades. Eisenhower had invited a senior Brotherhood leader into the Oval Office: Said Ramadan, the son-in-law of the Brotherhood's founder. He had come to the United States in 1953 to attend a conference at Princeton, and a cable from the U.S. embassy in Cairo had warned against "offending this important body." Eisenhower hoped to court the Brotherhood as an ally against communism. But when the Cold War ended, there was less to discuss. Mubarak learned in the early 1990s that American diplomats in Cairo had talked with the Muslim Brothers, and he exploded in rage.

"Your government is in contact with these *terrorists* from the Muslim Brotherhood," he fumed to the journalist Mary Anne Weaver—tarring the Brothers with an accusation that had dogged them for decades without substantiation.

George W. Bush raised a fuss when Egypt jailed non-Islamists, but he did as Mubarak asked when it came to the Muslim Brothers. "We have not engaged with the Muslim Brotherhood. And we won't," Secretary of State Condoleezza Rice said during a visit to the American University in Cairo in 2005, after Mubarak had moved to thwart the early Islamist victories in the parliamentary voting. Egypt "has its rule of law, and I'll respect that."

The philosopher Tariq Ramadan—son of the Muslim Brother who met Eisenhower and a grandson of the movement's founder—was hired as a professor at Notre Dame in 2004. The Bush administration denied him a visa. Ramadan was forced to teach at Oxford.

Seven years later, in 2011, some in the Pentagon and the Obama White House still viewed the Muslim Brotherhood as a close cousin to Al Qaeda.

"They are all swimming in the same sea," General James Mattis of

Central Command later said in a speech looking back on the period. He meant not only the Muslim Brotherhood and Al Qaeda but also the Shiite theocracy in Iran. National Security Council staff presented Mattis with intelligence reports delineating the deep differences and even animosities among those three rival strains of political Islam. But Mattis stubbornly persisted in lumping them together.

"Is political Islam in the best interest of the United States?" Mattis asked in the same speech, at the Heritage Foundation. That was the "fundamental question," he said. "If we won't even ask the question, how do we get to the point of recognizing which is our side in the fight?"

He saw the fight against political Islam—in all its forms—as the central dynamic of the Middle East, and plenty of others agreed with him in Washington, including at the Pentagon, in the White House, and in Congress. "Islamists are not our friends," Dennis Ross, the president's adviser, later wrote in an op-ed in the *New York Times*, making the same case. "Their creed is not compatible with pluralism or democracy."

John Kerry, then chairman of the Senate Foreign Relations Committee and future secretary of state, was an inveterate foe of the Brotherhood. In a 2008 confirmation hearing to send an ambassador, Margaret Scobey, to Egypt, Kerry asked only about "the current state of threat" posed by the Brothers.

"I've heard this from President Mubarak," Kerry said, describing the theory that democratic elections in Egypt would precipitate a Brotherhood takeover on the hard-line model of Hamas in Gaza. "If you sort of open it up and the Muslim Brotherhood were legitimate, that you would in fact have a more radical outcome and greater instability in Egypt."

Then there was the question of public opinion. Even those in the administration who understood the difference between the Brotherhood and Al Qaeda knew that distinction eluded most lawmakers and voters. No American politician wanted to publicly support the Brotherhood. An Egyptian lawmaker from the Muslim Brotherhood had turned up at a reception at the Cairo home of the American ambassador in 2007, and it became a Washington scandal. During the eighteen-day uprising against Mubarak, Hillary Clinton and White House officials avoided any mention of either "Islamist" or "Muslim Brotherhood" when they met with think-tank experts. The White House stuck to the euphemism "nonsecular actors." Later that spring, Obama personally struck the words "Muslim Brotherhood" from a draft of a speech about the uprising.

When European diplomats invited their American counterparts to meet with Arab Islamists, Steven Simon of the National Security Council staff imagined the headline: UNITED STATES JOINS EUROFAGS TO MEET WITH TERRORISTS. The Americans skipped it.

Now Egypt (and Tunisia) could provide the real-world answers to decades of hypotheticals about what might happen if Brotherhood-style Islamists won free elections. They were poised to wield power, and some in the administration realized that apprehension had kept Washington from acquiring firsthand information about the Muslim Brothers or their internal dynamics.

The American embassy in Cairo, heeding the six-year-old promise from Rice, had eschewed all contact except rare meetings with lawmakers who happened to be Muslim Brothers. In the spring of 2011, the State Department knew no one in what was about to become Egypt's most influential political bloc. "Why were we not talking to these people?" one member of the White House national security staff later told me, recalling the exasperation. "We didn't know anything!"

Advisers to Clinton at the State Department and staff on the Egypt desk at the National Security Council drafted a cable formally instructing the embassy in Cairo to reach out to the Muslim Brothers. But Donilon was still nervous. He sat on it for more than a month.

Finally a Clinton adviser got his hands on a faxed copy of a cable with the same instructions from Prime Minister David Cameron to the British embassy in Cairo. Now Washington was falling behind London. Donilon immediately approved the American cable.

Then the embassy resisted. Its diplomats were too anxious about being seen with the Brothers, and too unsure of which ones to call. By the summer, Clinton's chief policy adviser, Jake Sullivan, decided to send the State Department's expert on political Islam, Peter Mandaville, to make contact. But the outgoing American ambassador, Margaret Scobey, exercised a seldom-used prerogative to block the visit. She acceded only after top State Department officials assured her that Mandaville would bring along an embassy diplomat to the meeting.

Finally, in July 2011, Mandaville and the embassy diplomat met for coffee at the InterContinental Semiramis hotel in Cairo with Mohamed el-Shahawy, a forty-year-old Muslim Brother who worked as a regional executive for 3M, the American multinational. Western diplomats, journalists, and academics were swarming over Cairo asking about the Muslim Brothers by then. That coffee was just another meeting for Shahawy, As it happened he was on his way out of the movement. He resigned soon after as part of a mass defection of moderates.

But for the Americans, a dam had burst. Diplomats and politicians began beating a path to the Brotherhood's newly opened Freedom and Justice Party. John Kerry never abandoned his suspicions of the Muslim Brothers, which became more consequential when he was secretary of state. But in December 2011, he became the first member of Congress to visit their new Cairo office. (The Brothers told me that they liked him already, because he had also been the first lawmaker to visit Gaza under Hamas.) "The United States needs to deal with the new reality," Kerry told my colleague Steven Lee Myers in Washington after the trip.

The Islamist Parliament was riddled with conflict from the start, on January 23, 2012, the day I watched the Brothers outside celebrating their victory and defending the chamber. Zyad el-Elaimy, the lawyer who hosted the Police Day planning meeting, was the only Tahrir Square organizer to win a seat in the Parliament. On the opening day he tried to squeeze "revolution" into his oath of office. So Salafi lawmakers tried to ad lib oaths to Sharia. Then a Brotherhood defector staged an insurrection.

The defector, Essam Sultan, had left the Brotherhood fifteen years earlier to start a moderate splinter party, the Center Party. In retaliation, the Brotherhood's leaders had gone to court alongside Mubarak's lawyers to try to crush the breakaway party. But now Sultan, with a grin, announced his revenge. He had formed a strange-bedfellows coalition of Salafis, moderates, and non-Islamists to try to deprive the Brothers of a chance to choose the Parliament's speaker. Islamists shouted down Islamists, and it took until nightfall for the Brotherhood to muster enough votes to beat back Sultan.

"This is democracy," the newly elected speaker, Saad el-Katatni of the Muslim Brotherhood, intoned wearily. "The people have grasped it."

Even after all the shouting, though, the Brotherhood-led Parliament never pried much power from the generals. Some complained that the Brothers did not try hard enough, afraid of confronting the military council. Others argued that any confrontation then could end only in allowing the military to tighten its grip. But in any case, without a new constitution or a new president, the generals made the rules. Defense Minister Tantawi still acted as head of state. His council still appointed the prime minister and Cabinet and issued the laws. The parliament of beards was noisy but impotent. A transition would wait until the election of a new president. In some ways, though, the Islamist-against-Islamist fracas on opening day was a fitting beginning to the presidential race, and, for that matter, a fair sample of the Brotherhood's history.

O ne evening in 1974, a tall, slender medical student slipped into a busy shoe store on Qasr el-Aini Street, not far from the hospital where he worked as a resident. He did not need shoes; he was asked there to meet a Muslim Brother who had been released that year after twenty years in prison in Qena, a six-hour drive south of Cairo. The storekeeper was another Muslim Brother. Shoe shopping was a pretense to allow them to speak outside the earshot of the secret police.

The medical student, Abdel Moneim Aboul Fotouh, was then the leader of a new and independent Islamist student movement that was sweeping campuses. He was a born politician, handsome and articulate, with a round face and a ready smile. He had grown up in an apolitical middle-class family in Cairo, and as a teenager he had been as enthralled as the rest of his generation by Abdel Nasser.

Then Abdel Nasser's promises of national greatness were shattered by his humiliation in the Six-Day War with Israel in 1967. As the depth of his defeat became clear, he called his ally, King Hussein of Jordan, to strategize about making excuses. "Shall we say the United States is fighting on Israel's side?" Abdel Nasser asked over an unsecured phone line. "Shall we say the United States and England, or only the United States?"

Both, the king agreed, as the world soon learned. Israel had recorded the two leaders scheming to lie, and played the tape over the radio in Egypt.

Tapping into the disillusionment with Abdel Nasser in the years after 1967, Aboul Fotouh and his young Islamists had swept the Nasserites (and communists) out of student government for the first time since 1952. He became president of the student union at his university and built a national organization of student Islamists on campuses across Egypt. By then, successive crackdowns had all but eliminated the Muslim Brotherhood; it had almost ceased to exist outside the prisons. At the moment of the meeting in the shoe store, Aboul Fotouh might have been the most influential Islamist in Egypt, or possibly in the region.

Sadat, who took power at Abdel Nasser's death in the fall of 1970, had recently begun letting Islamists out of prison as a counterbalance to the left. The aging Muslim Brothers emerging from the jails looked enviously at the youth, energy, and numbers in Aboul Fotouh's student movement, and they were eager to meet him.

Moved by the determination of the newly released Muslim Brothers to resume his dangerous vocation, Aboul Fotouh eventually led the student leaders around him into the moribund Brotherhood. They revitalized it, just as the elders had hoped, and the shoe store meeting began its rebirth. Many Muslim Brothers of his generation referred to Aboul Fotouh as their movement's "second founder," and his life was transformed as well. He wrote decades later, "When I remember that meeting, I cannot stop crying."

Three years after the meeting, in 1977, Aboul Fotouh attended a televised forum at Cairo University with President Anwar Sadat, who was still riding high after Egypt's "victory" over Israel in the Yom Kippur War in 1973. The audience dutifully applauded, until Aboul Fotouh raised his hand.

He wanted to know why Sadat's security agents had barred a popular sheikh from speaking in public. Was it because he criticized the government? Mr. President, Aboul Fotouh told Sadat, you are surrounded by "sycophants" and "hypocrites."

"Stand right there, stop!" Sadat shouted. "I am the president of the family, the president of the country!"

"I am standing, sir," Aboul Fotouh replied evenly.

Many had gone to prison for less. Aboul Fotouh became an Islamist icon. Video footage of the encounter was still circulating when I arrived in Egypt.

When I met him in March 2012, Aboul Fotouh was fifty-nine years old. He had spent seven years in prison for organizing against Mubarak. He was sitting behind a schoolteacher's desk in the small office he used as president of an umbrella group for doctors' syndicates in the Arab region, and he had just filed papers to run for president of Egypt, in what promised to be the first free and fair presidential election in any Arab state. But he was not running as a representative of the Muslim Brotherhood. Aboul Fotouh was running against it.

"You can say I am a liberal Islamist," he said. "Compared to the Muslim Brotherhood, I am more liberal."

He had the classic look of a Muslim Brother, including a white beard trimmed to within a half inch of his skin. But his demeanor was surprisingly informal for a Brotherhood leader or any Egyptian politician. His suit jacket hung over the back of his chair, and he leaned forward on his elbows to gesture with his hands. I had the feeling several times that he was laughing at my questions.

The Muslim Brotherhood had said during the uprising that it would not seek more than a third of the Parliament; then it had contested almost all the seats and won nearly half. Now the group had pledged not to field a presidential candidate. My Anglophone Egyptian friends were certain Aboul Fotouh was a stalking horse for the Brothers, feigning a break with them to run as their stealth candidate despite their pledge. I tried again and again to catch him out. But everything he said was not only left of Brothers. It was left of the Egyptian mainstream.

He wanted a strict separation of religion and government. "When we mix religion and politics, they both get ruined," he said. He would protect free expression and even blasphemy; he had once visited the Nobel laureate Naguib Mahfouz in the hospital to show solidarity after he was stabbed in the neck by a hard-line Islamist for writing a sacrilegious novel (Aboul Fotouh still had the pen the author gave him). Aboul Fotouh wanted full equality for women and non-Muslims. He looked forward to voting for a woman or a Christian as president of Egypt. He criticized the Brotherhood for its all-male governing board, known as the guidance council. His wife worked as an obstetrician and supported their family. Their daughter practiced medicine in California. "I am very close to Western values."

But Aboul Fotouh was not *only* a liberal. He backed his positions with verses from the Quran or Hadith. "God told our Prophet, 'You cannot control people, you can only advise them,'" Aboul Fotouh said. "'If I obligate you to adopt some religion—to adopt some behavior—I shall charge you as a hypocrite.' People must have free will."

Okay, then, how about gay marriage?

Now I had him. "I am running for the president of Egypt!" he said, exasperated at last. "This is a question for the United States—it is just out of the question in Egypt!"

Aboul Fotouh was forcing debate on the issues that had puzzled me since I first heard Muslim Brothers chanting their decades-old slogan, "Islam is the solution." The solution to what? And what would that look like? No Arab government had ever allowed an open argument over how to apply the teachings of Islam in public and political life. No free election had ever tested the case.

I would spend seven years studying debates about the true nature of the Brotherhood. What real agenda was it hiding behind its slogans? I learned that that question was all wrong. There never was a single, essential character of the Muslim Brotherhood, because the Brothers themselves never fully agreed with one another about any of these issues. Their ideology was not just ambiguous to the public; it was ambiguous even to them. Vagueness and flux, in fact, were the keys to the endurance of their movement.

Hassan el-Banna, who was born in 1906 and founded the Brotherhood at the age of twenty-two, had a knack for paradox. He was the son of a rural imam who owned one of Egypt's first phonograph shops, and both father and son had a keen interest in Sufi mysticism—even though both Sufism and music were deemed heretical by the most orthodox Sunni Muslims. The son trained as an Arabic teacher and worked in state schools. But he also briefly took over publication of the flagship of Abduh's Islamic modernist movement—*Al Manar,* or the Lighthouse. More than anything else, he dedicated the Brotherhood to Abduh's idea that returning to the roots of Islam was the only way to catch up with the West in rationalism and progress.

Into that core concept Banna mixed themes of Islamic traditionalism and anti-Western nationalism borrowed from some of Abduh's intellectual successors. Then Banna harnessed their abstract ideas to his own zeal for organizing.

"If the French Revolution decreed the rights of man and declared for freedom, equality and brotherhood, and if the Russian Revolution brought closer the classes and social justice for the people," Banna once wrote, "the great Islamic revolution decreed all that thirteen hundred years before."

Would it be a movement for spiritual renewal or political power? Militant or peaceful? Egyptian nationalist or pan-Islamic? Democratic or authoritarian? Banna took both sides of every argument, and he bequeathed to his acolytes decades of internal debate over their goals.

He was drawn to politics but insisted that the Brotherhood was much more than a party—"an athletic group, a cultural-education union, an economic company, and a social idea," among other things. He made deals with the British-backed king to restrict prostitution and alcohol sales. But Banna maintained that real change could come only from below, one believer at a time. "Eject imperialism from your souls," Banna often promised, "and it will leave your land."

He pledged to work for a new caliphate and declared that the "Quran is our constitution." But he made clear that he regarded the caliphate as only a gauzy, end-of-history paradise. He denounced theocratic rule and "ecclesiastical tyranny." At times he said the best model for Islamic government was a democracy with the sort of written constitution found in the West.

What might an Islamic state or society look like in practice? Banna mostly avoided the question, or insisted that the answer would vary with time, place, and public consensus. (That is part of the reason Brotherhood-inspired groups differ from one country to the next.) His bylaws demanded absolute obedience, but the first internal rebellions, splits, and defections broke out within four years of the founding. They were still roiling when I lived in Cairo. The Muslim Brotherhood was tethered to a core vision and history, to be sure. But it was always changing and never monolithic.

Should I fear the Muslim Brothers? Their reputation for violence was so pervasive in the West that I took special care to understand that legacy. Banna had talked avidly of jihad, martyrdom, and "the art of death" in defense of Islam. For a few years in the 1940s he went so far as to create a secret paramilitary wing—the so-called "special apparatus." But Cairo in the '40s was lousy with paramilitary outfits. Every faction had one—the nationalists, monarchists, and so on. Banna, in that sense, was keeping up with his times. The Brotherhood's special apparatus cooperated with Abdel Nasser's Free Officers to fight against the fledgling state of Israel and to plot against the British occupation. Anwar Sadat was the Free Officers' liaison to train and equip the Brothers.

Then the special apparatus appeared to go rogue. On November 15, 1948, King Farouk's government arrested all the Brotherhood's leaders, severing its chain of command. But the foot soldiers of the secret apparatus remained at large. On December 28, a twenty-three-year-old student veterinarian who belonged to the Brotherhood's paramilitary dressed up as a policeman and snuck inside the Interior Ministry when the prime minister, Mahmoud el-Nuqrashi, was visiting. The impostor saluted, shot the premier in the back, and then finished him off with a bullet to the chest when Nuqrashi turned to see what hit him. An older veteran of the secret apparatus was arrested two weeks later for attempting to bomb a courthouse holding the records of a case against the Brothers.

Banna denounced the perpetrators and their actions. "They are neither Brothers, nor are they Muslims," he declared in an open letter. In a second letter he pleaded with other wayward "young ones" to shun threats or weapons. Nonetheless, successive Egyptian rulers for decades seized on Nuqrashi's assassination as evidence of the Brothers' true character. After the uprising of 2011, Egyptian journalists and intellectuals opposed to the Brotherhood still cited the 1948 killing of the prime minister to explain their fear of the movement.

Banna himself was assassinated by an agent of the king barely eight weeks later, on February 12, 1949, as he got into a taxi off Ramses Square in downtown Cairo. His successor as the Brotherhood's general guide was a former judge, Hassan el-Hudaiby. He made it his top priority to purge violence from the organization and eradicate its secret apparatus. But a decade later, in the early 1960s, a small circle of Muslim Brothers tried again to reestablish another secret paramilitary unit, in defiance of Hudaiby.

Inspired and led by the Islamist thinker Sayyid Qutb, this new circle conspired to smuggle weapons from Sudan and talked of using them for retaliatory assassinations (justified as self-defense) if Abdel Nasser moved against them again. But they were too slow. Abdel Nasser learned of the scheme, broke up the plot, and, in 1966, executed Qutb.

Supporters of the regimes that ruled the Arab world over the next half century remembered Banna and Qutb as terrorists who were killed for their treason. To Islamists, they were martyrs. Banna had always warned that they would face persecution.

Some of Qutb's ideas—specifically about the apostasy of dictatorships like Mubarak's—became a starting point for the thinking of Salafi jihadists like Ayman al-Zawahiri of Al Qaeda. (Jailed for a time with al-Zawahiri, Aboul Fotouh once watched him pick a pointless fight with a guard just for the sake of the conflict and bloodshed.) But the Brotherhood leadership redoubled its commitment to nonviolence, codifying its position in a tract by their imprisoned general guide, Hudaiby. The tract, "Preachers, Not Judges," became a pillar of the Brotherhood canon.

The main Brotherhood-inspired organization of Palestinians, Hamas, has carried out violence against Israel, including attacks that have killed Israeli civilians. The United States has designated Hamas a terrorist organization. And the leaders of the Egyptian Muslim Brotherhood applauded Hamas. But they regard it as a special case. They consider Hamas resistance to an illegal occupation, and thus justified under international law in the use of violence to defend Palestinian independence.

But from Qutb to 2011, historians have found no evidence that the leadership of the Muslim Brothers ever again plotted violence in Egypt. Instead, those inclined toward militant jihad, like Ayman al-Zawahiri, left the Brothers in frustration. *The Bitter Harvest* was the title of his book-length jeremiad against the nonviolence of the movement.

Aboul Fotouh had started out in the 1970s as censorious as a Salafi. One of his proudest achievements as an Islamist student leader was segregating men and women in lecture halls. His Islamist students sold inexpensive head scarves to encourage women to cover up. They frowned on music, drama, movies, and almost any other entertainment. "We did not have any view of art except that it was forbidden," he later wrote.

But the Muslim Brotherhood loosened him up. The third general guide of the Muslim Brotherhood, Omar al-Tilmisani, also released from prison in the early 1970s, shocked Aboul Fotouh by announcing that he listened to Om Kalthoum and even performed music. Tilmisani said the founding generation of Muslim Brothers had organized art, film, and theater teams to elevate the culture. His wife wore her hair without a veil. Most important, Tilmisani convinced Aboul Fotouh and other students to shun violence at a time when others in their generation were joining the Salafi jihadi insurgency centered in southern Egypt.

"Some people said to me, 'You made a fatal mistake, Aboul Fotouh, because you made those Muslim Brothers our leaders,' and they still say it," Aboul Fotouh told me. "But I said to them, if we separated from the Brotherhood, you may have taken the option of violence."

Aboul Fotouh and the Islamist students he brought with him began pushing the Brotherhood to compete in elections in the state-sponsored professional associations, like the doctors' syndicate. Although Mubarak still outlawed the Brotherhood, its members eventually began running for Parliament, too, initially under the banners of existing parties and then as independents. By 1987, the Brotherhood's candidates were distributing booklets that forswore any imposition of Islamic law and affirmed the equal citizenship of Coptic Christians. In 2000, the Brothers fielded female parliamentary candidates, reinterpreting Quranic verses about male guardianship to refer only to the family. Some leaders even said the head scarf was not a religious obligation, but "merely a question of identity and belonging, just as saris are for Indians."

Aboul Fotouh was the Brotherhood's most prominent advocate of moderation and an increasingly visible spokesman. He belonged to a broader movement of like-minded Islamists around the region who advocated for religious values but secular governments—most notably including Aboul Fotouh's close friend Rachid Ghannouchi of Tunisia. Essam Sultan, who upended the opening day of Parliament, was part of the same trend. By around 2005, they were conspicuous enough that journalists and scholars needed a term for them: "post-Islamist."

Then to the shock of most rank-and-file Muslim Brothers, their governing board voted in 2009 to expel Aboul Fotouh from his seat. He had dissented from a prototype party platform that rolled back much of what he stood for. It declared that only a male Muslim could serve as president of Egypt, and that the Parliament should be required to take the advice of a council of Muslim scholars. Despite the outward transformation of the Brotherhood, a conservative faction had the upper hand after all. "They controlled the Brotherhood completely," Aboul Fotouh later told me. "There was no hope for me."

In June 2011, he was sitting in an airplane taxiing at the Cairo International Airport, having just returned from a visit to London, when his presidential campaign media adviser called with news from the Brotherhood. The same leaders who had removed Aboul Fotouh from its governing board had voted to expel him from membership in the Brotherhood. The board said he had defied its orders by running for president after the Brotherhood had pledged not to field a candidate. He wept in his seat.

The revolts of the Arab Spring had pulled once-hushed debates about the goals of political Islam into the open. We heard versions of it playing out everywhere—from the street cafés of folding chairs selling Turkish coffees downtown to the cacophony of nightly talk shows.

Aboul Fotouh, undaunted by the Brotherhood's opposition, built a presidential campaign aimed at the center of the question. Dozens or hundreds of young Muslim Brothers were defecting to join him (including Shahawy, the 3M executive who had met with the Americans). His campaign media adviser was a young liberal whose primary qualification was experience on Michael Bloomberg's mayoral campaign in New York. The campaign's political adviser was an outspoken feminist and socialist, Rabab el-Mahdi, who had taught political science at Yale before coming home to join the American University in Cairo.

I tracked her down at the end of yet another Tahrir Square rally against military rule, and she let me follow her to her car if I could keep up. She had wavy shoulder-length hair and colorful glasses, and she threw around words like "discourse" and "hegemony."

"Egypt needs to hear the core ideas of the left, but through an Islamist voice so it does not sound so alien," she said. The Aboul Fotouh campaign set out "to create a left that included Islamists and non-Islamists, so we could talk about politics and stop talking about religion."

She made no secret of her delight at inflicting pain on the Brothers. "Aboul Fotouh is very dangerous for them—a matter of life and death. If he succeeds, it means the Brotherhood loses its monopoly on moderate Islam."

Aboul Fotouh's views evolved, she told me years later. "At first he would say, 'Why do I need a special policy for Copts? Why are Copts different than the Muslim Brotherhood? Aren't the Muslim Brothers discriminated against, too?'" The day after the massacre of the Christians outside the Maspero building in October 2011, some of the ex-Islamists on Aboul Fotouh's campaign team sympathized with the soldiers, suggesting they were obliged to defend against a Christian attack. Mahdi was outraged and stormed out of the campaign office.

But after she left, Aboul Fotouh issued a stronger condemnation than almost any other party, stronger even than the Coptic Church itself. "Those who have fallen, the dead and the injured, are Egyptians, and we Egyptians have to unite to stop this threat to our national security," he said.

I came to consider Mahdi a friend, and she was merciless about any hint of sexism. But she was also critical of her fellow feminists who acted like political Islam was the only threat to the rights of Arab women. She knew from experience that Egyptian nationalists, liberals, and leftists were all sexist, too.

"When I hear Egyptian women say, 'The Muslim Brotherhood are going to put us down,' I tell them, 'Guys, we are already put down!'" she said. "In terms of sexism and patriarchy, the Muslim Brothers are very much in the Egyptian mainstream."

Like most Egyptian politicians, Aboul Fotouh started out referring to women as "girls," talking about "wives and mothers and sisters," or extolling the importance of women "to cultivate children and homes."

"I said, 'dump that shit,'" Mahdi told me. Soon Aboul Fotouh was talking about "minimum income" instead of minimum wage, stressing the value of work inside homes, and correcting interviewers who asked him about "poverty." Call it "impoverishment," he would tell them, because it was a product of an economic system and not an immutable condition.

"We sold him on everything," Mahdi said.

I followed Aboul Fotouh to rallies in Cairo and the Nile Delta. Whenever he was asked about religious issues, he replied that Egyptians were already religious enough. "Egypt has been proud of its Islamic and Arabic identity for fifteen centuries. Are we waiting for the Parliament to convert us?" he would say, or, "Egypt has enough mosques. What Egypt needs are factories."

Some of his younger supporters had recorded a song in the hip-hop-style computer-generated street music that blared from the speakers of tuk-tuks. "He is not American, not British, not Iranian. . . . He did not steal land. . . . He is a clean man. . . . Aboul Fotouh! Aboul Fotouh!" I was told that he hated it. I could not get it out of my head.

Khairat el-Shater was a business tycoon and the deputy general guide of the Muslim Brotherhood. He was its chief strategist, its top financier, and an old friend of Aboul Fotouh. That is, until 2009, when Shater emerged as the driving force behind Aboul Fotouh's expulsion from the governing board and then the movement.

Shater was sixty-two years old in 2012, and the tallest Egyptian I ever met. He stood well over six feet, and he was thick in the middle. Streaks of gray ran through his full beard, and his eyes were set deep below a high forehead. He had amassed a personal fortune investing in furniture, bus manufacturing, textiles, software, and other industries. We met in the headquarters of his holding company, in a high-rise in the neighborhood of Nasr City. Waiters served us cold glasses of freshly squeezed mango juice.

Shater had spent a dozen years behind bars on various politicized charges under Mubarak, longer than any other Brotherhood leader. He had run his business empire, the Brotherhood, and a family of ten children from inside a jail cell. He had married off all eight of his daughters to young Muslim Brothers—some of whom were his fellow inmates. The eight grooms visited him in prison to ask his consent. Five said their vows behind bars. The Brotherhood was an insular world.

If Aboul Fotouh had revitalized the Brotherhood, Shater had reorganized it. He had plotted and financed its political strategy, its expansion onto the internet, and its outreach to the West. He spoke with a time-is-money efficiency. Each utterance seemed to come out of his mouth already organized into roman numerals and capital letters. I am not sure he ever laughed.

He told me that he had been drawn to the Brotherhood because it answered every question. "It talks about building the individual, building the family, building the society, building the state," he said. "It talks about the economy. It talks about sociology. It talks about culture."

Shater had been as outspoken as anyone about the Brotherhood's embrace of democracy and respect for the West. NO NEED TO BE AFRAID OF US was the headline of an opinion column he had contributed to the *Guardian* in 2005. Now Shater had led the Brotherhood to abandon the positions in the old prototype platform—the same one over which the group had pushed Aboul Fotouh off the governing board just three years earlier. The board no longer taught that only a male Muslim could be president and that Muslim scholars should guide the Parliament.

But now that Mubarak was out, many younger Muslim Brothers complained that, in contrast to his calls for a democratic government, Shater was suppressing internal debate and dissent within the Brotherhood, running the group as a strongman. "We were deceived," twenty-seven-year-old Mohamed el-Gibba told me as he was leaving the group.

I was running into defecting Muslim Brothers right and left. Numbers were impossible to quantify, but there was clearly an exodus of Muslim Brothers leaving to express their own views. (Islam Lotfy, who helped organize the Police Day protests, was expelled, too, for starting a new post-Islamist party.)

"They tightened the screws on anyone who had different ideas," a former deputy general guide, Mohamed Habib, complained to me. "It should be a group for Muslims, not 'the' group for Muslims."

Why expel people from a religious movement over political disagreements? I asked Shater. Was that democratic?

Shater, for the first time in our conversation, sounded heated. "The Muslim Brotherhood is a value-based organization that expresses itself using different means—political, economic, athletic, health related, and social," he said. "You cannot take one part from one place and another part from another—this isn't how it's done." Islam "regulates life in its entirety—politically, economically and socially; we don't have this separa-tion," he said, referring to the line between religion and government.

"You can't adopt a different vision from the party that represents us, the party that represents the vision of the group," he continued. So he had told dissenters, "Either you stay in the Muslim Brotherhood and the Muslim Brotherhood's party, or if you insist on another party, then you'll be the ones leaving us!"

I was beginning to wonder about his avowed commitment to democ-racy, which clearly did not extend to allowing real debate within the Brotherhood. Where was the Islam in the Brotherhood's vision, then, if all faiths were equal under the law and if Muslim scholars played no role at all?

Islam should shape everything, Shater insisted. In an ideal world, the minister of finance would know economics and also Islam. The health minister should master medicine and Islam. The minister of transportation should understand traffic and Islam. And so on. "It is better, with time, to have someone who knows both subjects," he said. For Shater, I realized, Muslims were more equal. He supported elections. But he thought Muslims should win. No Christian could ever be so qualified.

Aboul Fotouh, the liberal Islamist, had gone to war against that all-or-nothing vision of the Brotherhood. On the campaign trail, he now vowed to force the Brotherhood to follow the same laws as any nonprofit, including disclosing its finances and severing its political arm. He would end the Brotherhood as Egypt had known it, and Shater's power with it.

The presidential race turned into an Islamist free-for-all. A moderate Islamist lawyer had jumped in on one side, a charismatic Salafi television preacher was sprinting ahead on the other. The Salafi, Hazem Salah Abu Ismail, promised all kinds of trouble: he vowed to cut back international trade, arrest women for wearing bikinis, and annul the peace with Israel. The Brotherhood risked losing its status as the standard of political Islam.

What's more, the military's repeated deferral of the handover of power meant that whoever won the presidency could have the decisive voice in shaping (or rolling back) the political transition. The Parliament would re-main impotent until a constitution was drafted, and the president could put his stamp on it.

Having expelled Aboul Fotouh for violating the Brotherhood's pledge not to run a presidential candidate, Shater broke the same pledge himself. In a close vote of its internal assembly, in March 2012, the Brotherhood voted to run a candidate after all. It nominated Shater to run against Aboul Fotouh. The fight over the future of the Muslim Brotherhood was out in the open now. Exposure to the sunlight promised to change political Islam, if that open debate was allowed to continue. Surely that was a development that liberals would cheer, or so I assumed.

10

Thug Versus Thug

May 23, 2012–June 17, 2012

The presidential election promised a decisive break with the Mubarak era. But daily life in the spring of 2012 reminded me of Mubarak's penultimate speech, in which he warned of the fine line separating freedom and chaos.

One spring day Laura took our sons and another family on a visit to the Cairo neighborhood known as Garbage City, high in the cliffs overlooking Cairo. The refuse of Cairo was removed by trash collectors—*zabaleen*—who hauled it in bicycle and donkey carts back to Garbage City. There, whole families, including children, sifted it into towering piles of glass, paper, cardboard, varieties of metals, types of plastic, and so on, for resale and recycling. The *zabaleen* were Coptic Christians who had lived there for decades, and in 1976, they had blasted and carved out an immense, majestic cave cathedral in the cliffs. Known as the Monastery of St. Simon, it could accommodate twenty thousand worshippers. The Garbage City cave church was one of the largest houses of Christian worship in the Middle East.

Laura and our friends had agreed in advance with two taxi drivers on a fixed price, about eighteen dollars, for the trips there and back. But upon their return, the two drivers demanded double. Laura had no more cash, and the two drivers refused to leave. They began banging on our metal gates and scaring the children. When Laura threatened to call the police, the drivers laughed in her face. What police? The police had been AWOL for more than a year, since the Day of Rage.

A cheerful walrus of a police guard was always stationed on our corner, outside the nearby South Korean embassy, and he sauntered over to the taxi drivers with his hand on his sidearm.

Pay up, he told Laura.

She called me in a panic. I was more than an hour away, so a neighborhood friend eventually coughed up enough to get the drivers to leave (we paid him back). We had been warned.

Under Mubarak, most Egyptians thought of the police as abusive, corrupt, and frightening. But they were ubiquitous. Even if arbitrary, their punishments had deterred blatant criminality. Of course, for rich people or Westerners, it had always been a different story. The police had taken much better care of us than they did of ordinary Egyptians. Maadi under Mubarak felt as safe as Bethesda.

Having lunch at an Italian restaurant in our neighborhood not long after the taxi incident, Laura watched a half dozen men run out of a jewelry store carrying long guns and bags of loot. We heard that thieves on motorcycles were snatching purses outside local international schools, and then one of them tried to grab Laura's. A private security team for an American oil company, Apache, caught one of the culprits. But the police did nothing.

Rena Effendi, a thirty-five-year-old photojournalist from Azerbaijan, was riding home to Maadi in a licensed taxi one night when the driver stopped the car, locked the doors, and pulled out a knife. He tried to rape her, but she fought back. He drove away with her handbag and left her in the dark by the side of the road.

Some days later, the police showed her a mug shot of a man they had caught using her stolen cell phone. But they made no effort to trace the chain of custody back to her assailant. "If they want to find him, they could," she told me. "I don't know if they are looking very hard."

Other taxi drivers were victims. Thirty-two-year-old Sayid Fathy Mohamed said two passengers had pulled knives on him in broad daylight while two other accomplices on a motorcycle—one with a shotgun—had pulled up next to his taxi. The four bloodied his face, left him in a field, and made off with his car, cell phone, and wallet.

The police seemed afraid and refused to visit the scene of the crime. So he called his cell phone and reached his attackers. He borrowed money from neighbors to pay the thieves a ransom equivalent to two thousand dollars for the return of his taxi. "I paid the money and took the car on the spot," he said.

Carjacking had become routine enough that thieves explicitly instructed victims to call their own phones to buy back their vehicles. Portions of the highway circling Cairo were so lawless that our driver refused to visit them even by day. Amani el-Sharkawi, a twenty-five-year-old English teacher, was riding in the back of a taxi when she saw men with chains and weapons stopping cars on a deserted patch of road just ahead. Her driver threw the car into reverse and backed down the highway. "Can you imagine that?" she marveled.

The poor inevitably bore the brunt of the crime, and in hard-pressed neighborhoods and towns some took matters into their own hands. In a small village in the Nile Delta province of Sharqiya, residents posted an internet video of two naked bodies hanging from a street lamp. Mayy el-Sheikh and I drove out to investigate.

A twenty-eight-year-old named Hazem Farrag had stepped from his family's auto supply store to defend the driver of a tuk-tuk against a threatening passenger, and his intercession triggered a cascade of killings. The passenger shot and killed Farrag. Farrag's friends strung up the killer. When one of the killer's relatives turned up during the hanging, Farrag's friends put a noose on him, too. No one in town could tell us their names.

"Disgraceful," said Mahmoud al-Herawy, a fifty-one-year-old Arabic teacher who found the bodies the next morning. "That is not the way to enforce the law."

In the nearby village of Ezbet el Tamanin we met a sixty-three-year-old farmer who invited us to sit with him on the carpeted floor of a shed his extended family used as a shared living room (none of the families had a private sitting space). The farmer, Mohamed Ibrahim Yousseff, said his cousin had been killed during a carjacking in February. At the funeral armed carjackers had attacked the vehicle of another cousin. When our host's two sons had tried to intervene, the thieves killed one, Mahmoud, twenty-nine, and crippled the other, Abdullah, twenty-four. Then a mob of villagers killed and incinerated one of the carjackers.

"It is becoming the culture of the Egyptian countryside to confront thuggery with thuggery, to take matters into our own hands," Yousseff told us mournfully. But what were the alternatives? "Should we surrender them to the police so they can release them in two hours?" (None of the vigilantes ever faced charges.)

Another farmer living near there told us that two of his sons, ages seven and ten, had recently been kidnapped. So the farmer, Hussein Abu Khisha, enlisted his neighbors to close down a highway, a pressure tactic to get the army and police to retrieve his boys. It worked: the army rescued his sons and the neighbors reopened the road. Such blockades had become a common sight, and now I understood why.

I later got to know a retired brigadier general in the Interior Ministry, Khaled Amin, who thought I should sympathize with the police. They felt "oppressed," he said one night over tea at a water-pipe café in the affluent neighborhood of Heliopolis, near the presidential palace.

"We were blamed for the revolution and we were blamed for the corruption of the last eighty years," he said. "The police felt abandoned and the regular officers were not listening to their leaders. So we spent more than a year after the revolution where we did nothing. We just did not deal with the people. The police essentially went home and even the ones who did show up did nothing. The traffic officers did not even look at the cars." Supervising officers like him were ordered to tolerate the negligence. "So we put up with it," he said, "for the sake of the unity of the ministry." See how you miss us! the police seemed to say.

Laura and I got in the habit of locking our car doors from the inside so that thieves could not climb in at an intersection. Laura stopped taking taxis. Then she stopped driving alone at all, except near our house. We raised our fence and fortified our gate. I began paying protection money every month to the police guards outside the South Korean embassy. Egyptian friends had exulted that the era of bribery had ended. I was just starting.

Three former Mubarak lieutenants were running for president, and the farmer who had barricaded the road told me that he would vote for one of them over any of the Islamists. "When you are sick like this, you go to a specialized doctor, you don't go to a beginner," Hussein Abu Khisha said. The Islamists "insult the police."

Voting in the presidential election began on May 23, 2012. More than a dozen candidates had qualified for a place on the ballot, and the top two vote getters were expected to face each other in a runoff in June. The first day of voting was scorching hot, but Egyptians seemed delighted to stand in line, often for several hours. Some held up scraps of cardboard to try to block out the sun. Anyone over eighteen was eligible to vote, more than fifty million Egyptians, and there had been a lot of voting since Mubarak: in a referendum, in two rounds for the main house of Parliament, and in two rounds for the almost powerless upper chamber. When I made the rounds of polling places for the first votes, many had said they doubted the process would be any fairer than it was under Mubarak. But after so many ballots with suspenseful results, Egyptians were confident of their power. One of Parliament's few accomplishments was modernizing the voting procedures. Ballots were dropped into transparent, sealed plastic boxes. The contents were counted in public view, in the same room, as soon as the polls closed. There was no way to stuff ballots.

"It is enough that the new president will know he could go to jail if he does something wrong," twenty-eight-year-old Mohamed Maher said assuredly, waiting to vote in the slum of Imbaba.

The generals boasted about their commitment to democracy. "If we wanted to commit fraud, we would have done it at the parliamentary elections," the general in charge of legal affairs said during a televised news conference, peering bookishly over his reading glasses. "A military coup, is this our plan? After all this?"

A journalist for the state media had a question for him. How could the military council possibly trust a new president chosen only by the voters and not known in advance?

"There is no worry," the general replied. Every Egyptian constitution since 1923, he said, had allowed the military to take power in a case of "catastrophe."

I had rolled my eyes at the Egyptian penchant for conspiracy theories, but the presidential race took so many bizarre turns that I began to wonder. The commission overseeing the election was composed of Mubarak-era judges appointed under the generals, and in the final weeks before the vote the judges unexpectedly disqualified on technicalities three of the strongest, most popular candidates. The hard-line Salafi was knocked out because his mother had become a U.S. citizen; she was registered to vote in Santa Monica, California, of all places. Shater, the Brotherhood's candidate, was eliminated on the basis of a politicized criminal conviction under Mubarak. A little-known understudy, Mohamed Morsi, stepped into his place.

Most intriguing to me was the case of Omar Suleiman, Mubarak's former spy chief and onetime American favorite. He had launched a presidential campaign from inside the intelligence service, run by his chief of staff. It had taken other campaigns months to collect the thirty thousand signatures from around the country required for a spot on the ballot; Suleiman's campaign pulled it off in forty-eight hours.

"Divine facilitation," Suleiman told a newspaper close to the intelligence services. (I saw no signs that anyone in the U.S. government was still hoping he would win, although I am sure some would have sighed with relief.)

Then the commission questioned a few of those signatures and disqualified him, too. Was the commission knocking out *all* the contenders it saw as strongest?

There was more weirdness. Borhami and the Salafi parties endorsed Aboul Fotouh—the equivalent of the Southern Baptist Convention backing Bernie Sanders. Salafi leaders told me Aboul Fotouh had the best chance of beating the Brotherhood. But he later told me that only one Salafi sheikh actually campaigned for him—an old friend from his student days who now lived in the Western desert province of Mersa Matruh. Aboul Fotouh concluded that the *mukhabarat* had orchestrated the Salafi endorsement to sabotage his campaign by driving away non-Islamist voters. Who knew? But the result was clear. He had started to build a movement transcending the old divides, and now I watched non-Islamist voters abandon him in droves.

"He uses double language," a rival candidate, the former diplomat Amr Moussa, declared in the only televised debate. "He's a Salafi with Salafis, he's a centrist with centrists, and he's a liberal with liberals."

The Coptic Church surprised me, too. The bishops put together a committee of laymen to pick a candidate, and until the final weeks all indications were that the Copts were rallying behind Amr Moussa—a popular civilian and former foreign minister who was not Islamist. Only seven months had passed since the Maspero massacre and the military cover-up. I thought surely the church could not back a military candidate.

But, to Moussa's surprise, the lay committee withdrew the church's support in the final days before the vote. "There were forces that shifted at the last moment for I-don't-know-why, but it was a plan," Moussa later told me. Instead, the church committee backed a former air force commander and Mubarak prime minister, seventy-year-old Ahmed Shafik, who was campaigning as a Mubarak-style strongman. He had told an audience of business executives that he was proud to call Mubarak "a role model." That was the kind of leader Egyptians needed. "The Egyptian people, contrary to the accusations, are obedient," he said, to a roar of applause.

To my amazement, Coptic support all across Egypt swung strongly behind him. How had the church thrown its weight behind Shafik so soon after the Maspero massacre? "Because of his military background," Youssef Sidhom, editor of the quasi-official Coptic newspaper and a member of the lay committee, told me at the time. "Copts are confident he will be strong enough to restore security and enforce the rule of law."

As for the Maspero massacre, Sidhom said he saw no "conspiracy." "There was a kind of chaos and panic among the small number of troops who were stationed there." Of the military, the church was forgiving.

Among the voters who cast their ballot for an Islamist, Morsi, with the Brotherhood machine behind him, beat Aboul Fotouh by a margin of about four to three. Aboul Fotouh formed a new party and started preparing for the next election.

A majority of Egyptian voters cast ballots for liberalism or moderation. A narrow majority of voters in the first round chose one of the many candidates in the more or less liberal middle, but those moderate voters were divided among ten different candidates. The two top vote getters were at the extremes: two conservatives, one religious and the other military. The runoff was Morsi, the Muslim Brother, versus Shafik, Mubarak's air marshal. That contest was a murkier story.

11

The Judges Club

June 17, 2012–June 30, 2012

The Rube Goldberg design of Egypt's transition—the election of a powerless Parliament followed by a misshapen presidential contest, all under military rule and with no progress toward a new constitution—was proving important. But as all this was being put together, the White House was focused on very different Egyptian issues. Instead of the architecture of the transition, the Obama administration was preoccupied by arguments with the generals over American aid to promote democracy, and especially with the case of Sam LaHood.

LaHood was thirty-six years old, slender, and boyish looking, with a head of thick, short dark hair and an easygoing drawl. His grandfather had emigrated from Lebanon to Illinois, and his father was former Republican congressman Ray LaHood, the secretary of transportation. I knew Sam as Egypt director of the International Republican Institute, one of two groups chartered and funded by the U.S. Congress to advance democracy abroad. The other was the National Democratic Institute. Both, if we are frank, were partly about dispensing patronage jobs to reward party operatives. The groups hired former congressional and campaign staff and sent them to interesting places all over the world. Some of those places were less safe than staying in Washington, but mostly working for IRI and NDI was a fun way to make a living. In Egypt, IRI and NDI used congressional funding to hold one- or two-day workshops to teach Egyptians about the basics of political campaigning—how to get to know your constituents, how to present your positions, and so forth. I naïvely thought Egyptians might appreciate the gesture. But it would never make much difference. How could a few workshops overcome networks and associations built up over decades?

IRI and NDI had operated on a small scale inside Egypt under Mubarak. They had never received any response to their requests for official authorization as nonprofits, so they were technically illegal, but they had never been expelled or prosecuted either. Now they had received $40 million of the $65 million that the State Department had allocated to foster Egyptian democracy. That was exactly the kind of direct funding of grassroots activity outside Egyptian government channels that Mubarak-era laws expressly prohibited. Nationalist Egyptian media outlets had been inveighing against such foreign subversion since the summer of 2011, and Egyptian generals had been complaining about it in Washington. A few National Security Council staffers working on Egypt had tried to placate the generals by proposing that future funding, after the initial $65 million, could go through official channels in Cairo. The staffers had surreptitiously persuaded Defense Secretary Panetta to suggest the compromise in a weekly meeting with Secretary of State Clinton. But the proposed walk-back leaked to the press. Denis McDonough, the deputy national security adviser, squashed it.

The stakes of that skirmish seemed small to me until December 29, 2011. That morning, hundreds of heavily armed riot police swooped in to raid the offices of IRI, NDI, and eight other organizations that took money from the West. Prosecutors barred Sam LaHood and a half dozen other American employees of the two groups from leaving Egypt. Fearing arrest, they soon moved into the U.S. embassy (the men initially slept in an auditorium, the women in a guest room at the ambassador's residence). The Egyptian employees of the groups were left at home on their own.

Egyptian prosecutors announced that they had ordered the surprise raids because the CIA had been using the NDI and IRI to weaken Egypt for the benefit of Israel. The official leading the case claimed that Freedom House, another congressionally funded group hit by the raids, was "founded by the Jewish lobby." And progovernment news media floated absurd conspiracy theories. LaHood had commissioned a poll with a question about religion; prosecutors called it a plot to sow sectarian strife. They cited IRI's wall maps of Egyptian voting districts as evidence of a plan to partition the country, like the carving up of the Levant after World War I. Street photographs were said to constitute spying on the army. Stacks of greenbacks proved the groups paid illiterate laborers to demonstrate against military rule.

Any trapped citizens were a problem for the White House. Americans working for groups close to Congress were a bigger issue. The captive son of a Cabinet member made this a full-blown crisis. In January and February 2012, as the Egyptian military was setting up the presidential election, the Obama administration convened weekly meetings of an intra-agency working group formed to deal exclusively with the funding crisis in Egypt. Tom Donilon had been forced to scratch a planned trip to Cairo. Leon Panetta and Hillary Clinton devoted virtually all of their discussions with their Egyptian counterparts to getting LaHood out. President Obama himself sent three letters and made two long phone calls to Field Marshal Tantawi (still acting as Egypt's head of state) about the funding case.

Panetta was stunned by the time it consumed. "You get involved in that stuff, you are going to find yourself missing the bigger issues," he told me later.

The Obama administration went all out: It threatened to withhold the $1.3 billion in annual military aid. It hinted it might block a multibillion-dollar aid package from the World Bank and the International Monetary Fund. All the critical policy questions about the structure and timetable of Egypt's transition—the questions that mattered to the outcome—had been set aside almost completely.

By late February, LaHood and the other Americans had spent five weeks inside the embassy, and the White House was up against a congressional deadline in March to renew or block the military aid. The trial finally opened, and LaHood and the other Americans never showed up—only the twenty Egyptians who had worked for IRI, NDI, and other American- or European-funded organizations. They sat through the hearing inside the metal cage used to hold criminal defendants. One, Nancy Okail, the Egypt director for Freedom House, read George Orwell's *Homage to Catalonia.*

The generals had told the Americans from the start that they could not possibly intervene in sacrosanct judicial deliberations. Now they elaborated further. They told the White House that their fidelity to the law had left them only one option: to put themselves above it. In exchange for $4 million in bail, the generals would smuggle the six Americans out of the country.

Some American officials felt that they had been baited into a trap, drawn into a pointless battle on the preferred terrain of the Egyptian bureaucracy—wrestling over the control of aid money. "We hugged the military council and let it drive our policy, and we waged the fight over democracy around funding," Ben Rhodes later told me ruefully. "Instead of arguing about things that really matter, like the sequence of elections, we were arguing about Sam LaHood."

On March 1, an aging propeller plane that the State Department had chartered to ferry diplomats to Libya took off from the Cairo airport with LaHood and the other Americans. One diplomat on board compared it with the last scene of *Casablanca*. Loudspeakers inside played the theme from *Raiders of the Lost Ark*.

The military aid to Egypt kept flowing. The United States later deducted the bail money from other nonmilitary aid to Egypt, and a Foreign Ministry spokesman complained about it angrily to me, as though Washington were depriving Egypt of its rightful *baksheesh*.

The military council was hardly the ally that some in the White House had expected; many in the administration thought the generals looked clownish. But even after the entrapment of the son of a Cabinet secretary (not to mention the avalanche of anti-American vitriol in the promilitary news media), the generals had suffered no repercussions.

If the generals concluded that American threats to cut the military aid were only bluffs, they were correct, Panetta later told me. "The Congress knew that in a part of the world where Israel does not have a lot of friends, it does not make a heck of a lot of sense to kick Egypt in the ass, because they are one of the few players in that area that are a friend to Israel," he said. The generals "knew that, when push comes to shove, little was going to happen."

Anwar Sadat, the nephew of the former president, told me the American relationship reminded him of an old Egyptian proverb: "I beg you for charity, but I am your master."

The LaHood case was my first encounter with the workings of the Egyptian judiciary, which played a pivotal role in the presidential runoff and everything that followed.

I passed the Supreme Constitutional Court every day on my way to the office. It was housed in a concave block of mirrored glass and beige concrete facing the Nile at the northern edge of Maadi. Its faux Pharaonic columns and totems might have been borrowed from a Disney movie about ancient Egypt. But the justices saw themselves as high priests of a holy tradition.

Their forebear, the great Egyptian jurist Abd al-Razzak al-Sanhuri, had laid the foundation of legal systems across the Arab world in the first half of the twentieth century. He grounded Western structures not only in natural law but also in Islamic tradition. He aspired to establish a distinctively Arab legal order that would constrain the powerful as well as the lowly—as any law must, and as Muslims believe that Islamic Sharia did in its early history. Iraq, Syria, Libya, Jordan, Kuwait, and other Arab states all recruited Sanhuri to help establish court systems on Egypt's model. Lawyers across the region still revere him.

Sanhuri's system, on a Napoleonic pattern, included no such thing as a Supreme Constitutional Court. But when Sanhuri and other liberal jurists were seeking to restrain the president's powers, Abdel Nasser bridled. He circumvented those jurists by grafting new courts and, in 1969, a "supreme" court, onto the preexisting judiciary. Sadat and Mubarak followed his example, adding special benches and emergency courts to get around uncooperative judges. Mubarak in particular became a master of court packing, especially in the run-up to his anticipated 2011 campaign for reelection.

In 2003, Mubarak installed onto the Supreme Constitutional Court the first woman in Egypt ever to serve at any level as either a judge or prosecutor: Judge Tahani el-Gebali. She was an outspoken Suzanne Mubarak–style feminist and a passionate admirer of Gamal Abdel Nasser. No fewer than six photographs of him adorned her chambers, like photographs of a rock star in the bedroom of a groupie.

"The military in Egypt is unlike in other countries," Gebali told me in our first interview, in July 2011. Because of the role Abdel Nasser and the

Free Officers had played in Egyptian history, "it is only normal that the military will share some of the responsibility" for governing, she said. She had sometimes argued that the uneducated or illiterate should be denied the right to vote altogether. And she hated Islamists.

After Mubarak's ouster, Gebali campaigned publicly to postpone any elections because Islamists might win. An Islamist Parliament would be "catastrophic," she declared in speeches and interviews, so the generals must forever retain some hold on power.

"I knew the elections would bring a majority from the movements of political Islam," Gebali told me in another interview.

She said she had begun advising the generals as early as May 2011, and by July, they had enlisted her to help prepare their aborted constitutional principles. But their plan to engrave their power into the new charter "was thwarted every time by all the noise, the popular mobilization, the 'million-man marches.'"

Gebali and the judges of Egypt saw themselves not just as a profession but as a caste. I once visited the downtown Cairo headquarters of the professional association for judges, known as the Judges Club. Men smoked cigars and read newspapers in battered leather chairs, or ate their lunches on a patio overlooking a well-tended garden. Obituaries posted on a notice board in the front hall read something like this: We mourn the passing of Judge So-and-so, who was the father of Judge So-and-so, brother of Judge So-and-so, and cousin of Judge So-and-so. The judiciary was one big clan. A seat on the bench was a birthright.

Judges defended their nepotism as a virtue. Mubarak, in 2007, tried to institute a minimum standard of law school results for new prosecutors and judges. The Judges Club rose in revolt and threatened to block it in court. Ahmed el-Zend, president of the club, argued that growing up "in a judicial environment," as the son of a judge, was more important than exam results. No "spiteful haters" would stop the "sacred march" of the sons and nephews onto the bench, he vowed, and he called judges "successors of God." (Three of his own sons were prosecutors or judges.) Zend won, and Mubarak backed down. I can only imagine how the uprising of 2011 must have frightened Zend, Gebali, and the rest of the judges.

In anticipation of the 2011 presidential election, Mubarak had appointed a chief to the Supreme Constitutional Court with virtually no experience as a judge or, for that matter, as a civilian lawyer. The new chief judge, Farouk Sultan, had spent his entire career prosecuting Islamists in special military or security courts.

Now, in 2012, Sultan was sixty-five, the mandatory retirement age. But the generals nonetheless made him chairman of the presidential election commission—the one that had knocked out so many candidates.

In June, a week before the presidential runoff, Zend and the other judges plunged into the campaign. "We won't leave matters for those who can't manage them, with the excuse that we're not people of politics," he said in a televised speech. He claimed that the Muslim Brotherhood had "a systematic plan meticulously designed to destroy this country: 'It is either us or no Egypt.'"

Ambassador Anne Patterson saw that a court challenge to the election of the Parliament was before the Supreme Constitutional Court, and she feared what the judges might do. She was a small woman with a blond bob and a slow Arkansas twang, but she brought with her a reputation for toughness from her previous assignment as ambassador to Pakistan. She had been deeply involved in the American drone campaign against Islamist militants, and I noticed that others in Foggy Bottom treated her with a deference bordering on trepidation.

Patterson implored the generals not to act against the Parliament at the very moment they were poised to fulfill their promise of a handover of power. She knew they were dictating the rules of the transition, so they controlled the implementation if not the substance of any court verdict. She reminded them how much they enjoyed the international praise they received for running fair elections, and how much they appreciated having an elected legislature for political cover.

Two days before the runoff, the generals moved anyway. The Supreme Constitutional Court had twice before dissolved Mubarak parliaments on election law technicalities, but in each case only after years of deliberations. Now the court announced after only a few weeks that it was nullifying Egypt's first freely elected legislature. The election scheme had always contained a "fatal poison," Gebali later told me, meaning that under Mubarak-era precedents it could have happened at any time.

I raced to the Parliament when the decision was announced, and military police in riot gear were standing guard outside. The soldiers had locked out the lawmakers and ringed the building in barbed wire.

Within twenty-four hours, the generals seized for themselves almost all the authority that had been expected to go to whomever was elected president. The military council, led by Mubarak's Defense Minister Tantawi, was evidently still afraid of a handover, no matter how gentle a transition Shafik or Morsi promised.

I thought Egyptians might object to the rollback of their first democratic election. In fact, the non-Islamist side of the political class—even those who had lost seats in the now-dissolved Parliament—welcomed it.

"Definitely it is a good," a leader of the Social Democratic Party, Emad Gad, told me. The Islamists, he said, were too popular. Liberals could demonstrate against a military strongman; "we cannot demonstrate against the Islamists."

I strained to understand how other Egyptians made sense of it. They dismissed specific decisions or judges as rigged or corrupt, but in the abstract they had an extraordinary regard for the judiciary. They revered the *idea* of their courts, which held the historic promise of fairness and justice. And since courts had dissolved parliaments before under Mubarak, invalidating one more seemed legal enough. In any case, the news media covered the decision as if the generals had no choice. This was the law. The public shrugged.

For the Muslim Brothers, the presidential runoff became a matter of life or death. The Brotherhood campaign headquarters was located across the street from the Interior Ministry. If former air marshal Shafik won, the staff joked, they would walk across the street to turn themselves in.

Voters went to the polls on June 16 and 17, and the ballots were counted in public inside the same polling place as soon as the voting ended: 52 percent for Morsi and 48 percent for Shafik. The difference was more than eight hundred thousand votes scattered across Egypt. It was impossible to fake.

Someone powerful had other ideas. Sultan and the electoral commission refused to certify the results and declare Morsi the winner. They postponed the announcement of any winner, they said, while they considered unspecified appeals.

The White House National Security Council was convening frantic, round-the-clock meetings in the Situation Room, worried that Egypt might explode again. American intelligence agencies were reporting that Farouk Sultan and others on the electoral commission wanted to invalidate the results and declare Shafik the winner. The generals were supportive. Saudi Arabia and the United Arab Emirates, which feared both Islamists and free elections, were pushing for it.

"It felt like the eighteen days all over again," Rhodes later told me, alluding to the eighteen days of protests that had removed Mubarak.

Many in the American military and intelligence agencies dreaded the prospect of an Islamist president of Egypt, too. But given the generals' performance so far, a rigged Shafik victory seemed to guarantee only continued chaos.

"You could tell a lot of the people in the room were sympathetic to the Shafik play," Rhodes recalled. "But even those people just could not sustain knowing that the other guy won a free election and we were acting against it."

The White House threw its weight behind the recognition of Morsi's victory. Clinton called it "imperative" for the generals to "turn over power to the legitimate winner." The administration again threatened to cancel the $1.3 billion in annual military aid. Diplomats told the Emiratis and Saudis to back off as well.

"The Gulfies did not appreciate it," Rhodes told me, "but I think it moderated their heavy-handedness."

In Cairo, a coalition of non-Islamist politicians (most of whom I had previously called liberal) held a televised press conference to urge the commission to declare Shafik president. "We have seen the United States forcing the military to hand power to the Muslim Brotherhood," claimed one, Osama el-Ghazali Harb.

"Real democracy," he told the Islamists without irony, "means the courage to accept defeat."

Khairat el-Shater, the Brotherhood's preeminent decision maker, warned the military council that if it called the election for Shafik, the Brotherhood would take over every public square in Egypt.

"The message was, if you steal this, we will be in the street in full force," an Islamist familiar with the conversations later told me. "We are going to stop holding back the antimilitary forces. You are on your own, and you are going to lose. Things have changed."

After a full week of delays, the electoral commission finally scheduled a news conference on Sunday, June 24, to declare a winner. Excitement had soured into anxiety. Another court had just ruled Mubarak's top security chiefs innocent of killing protesters, setting up Mubarak's own likely acquittal on appeal. By now anyone could guess that the commission was searching for an excuse not to call it for Morsi.

Cairo was nearly paralyzed. Banks, schools, and businesses closed. The streets were deserted. The army stationed tanks and armored vehicles at vital buildings, key intersections, and the airport. Soldiers in riot gear surrounded the square, and the military helicopters buzzed low again. The Health Ministry readied eighteen hundred ambulances.

By noon the temperature in Tahrir Square hovered around 90 degrees. It was virtually the only place downtown where people were out, and a crowd of Morsi supporters waiting there had swelled to tens of thousands. Finally, forty-five minutes late, a hush descended, and the rumbling voice of Sultan crackled from loudspeakers.

I strained to hear. He droned on about the hard work of the commission, the nobility of its purpose, and the calumny hurled against it. "Candidates' appeals came one after another, until the total number of appeals became 456. . . ."

Inside the American embassy, Ambassador Patterson was on a video call with Denis McDonough in the White House, and she was telling him it was over. The American pressure had failed. The generals had tipped the election, and Sultan was calling it for Shafik. It was time to plan for possible violence.

An aide interrupted their call. Sultan was forty-five minutes into his speech and he had just coughed up the full name of the winner: "Dr. Mohamed Mohamed Morsi."

American officials privy to intelligence reports later told me that the deciding factor was not the Brotherhood's threats or the White House's cajoling, although each took away an inflated sense of its own influence. Two honest members of the five-man commission had simply rejected the fix. One of them was the same son of a general who had helped draft the first transitional charter in 2011, the one who had earnestly turned to the Princeton University website for help: Hatem Bagato. (No Islamist himself, Bagato nonetheless publicly defended the inarguable evidence of Morsi's victory after its announcement at the price of enduring a campaign of slurs and conspiracy theories from Egyptians who wanted a different outcome. But when the political winds later turned, Bagato denied blocking a fix.)

The pavement around me in Tahrir Square turned into a giant trampoline. Tens of thousands of people jumped up and down in jubilation. Cars honked horns and people stopped traffic. "Freedom, freedom," they chanted, clapping their hands to give it rhythm. Revelers called out "Morsi, Morsi" and "God is great" in a kind of syncopation. Grown men wept in joy and relief. Putting down their weapons, soldiers embraced Islamists.

Some Egyptians had called the schemes of the generals to shape the constitution an unsuccessful military coup. Others described the dissolution of the Parliament as a "judicial coup." It looked that day like Egypt had beaten back its third coup d'état since the removal of Mubarak.

12

The Night of Power

June 30, 2012–November 19, 2012

I
n less than two months, Mohamed Morsi had stepped out of obscurity to win the first fair presidential election in millennia of Arab history. His victory was the greatest achievement in the eighty-five-year history of political Islam in the Sunni Muslim world. He now presided over eighty-five million citizens, in a nation of singular significance. Would he lead toward tolerance and democracy, or tyranny and extremism? Perhaps no one could be ready for his new job. Morsi certainly was not.

He was personally unimposing. He was short and stocky. He wore square wire-rimmed glasses that slid askew on his nose. He had grown up on a small farm in the Nile Delta and become engaged in 1978 at the age of twenty-six to a sixteen-year-old first cousin—a common arrangement in rural families. He moved to the United States the same year for a doctoral program in engineering at the University of Southern California. His wife joined him two years later. They made their first home in South Central Los Angeles, spent seven years in California, and give birth to a son there. It was in the Muslim community in Los Angeles that the couple decided to join the Muslim Brotherhood. Aside from a stint teaching in oil-rich Libya to support the family, he spent the rest of his career at the university in Zagazig, not far from his birthplace.

I first met Morsi in his presidential office. He slouched down in a Louis XIV desk chair, and I tried to warm him up with friendly questions like What did he think of his California sojourn?

Morsi looked worried. "The president is not quite sure if this is relevant to the interview, or is this socializing or something like that?" his official interpreter, a Mubarak-era holdover, said.

The new president was a stranger to such rituals. Panetta, a former congressman from California, also tried to break the ice by bringing up Morsi's history in the state. Morsi looked at him blankly. Later, he abruptly volunteered that his oldest son had been born there. "He could be president of the United States!" Morsi laughed. Panetta changed the subject.

Reassured by an adviser about my small talk, Morsi gushed with enthusiasm about his USC dissertation adviser. "Ferdinand A. Kroger—he writes it with a *u*, or with two dots over the *o*. He wrote a very big book, *The Chemistry of Imperfect Crystals*."

Morsi chuckled about USC campus culture—"Go, Trojans!"—and he reminisced about Barbara Walters in the morning and Walter Cronkite at night. "And that's the way it is!" he said, in a decent imitation.

Was there anything he admired about American culture? I expected him to pick an answer flattering to Americans and previously missing from Egypt, like freedom of conscience, equal protection under the law, or the peaceful rotation of power. No. Morsi admired American work habits and time management. "The people follow the advice of Abraham Lincoln: they go to sleep early and they wake early," Morsi said. (He was thinking of Benjamin Franklin.) "This is because the community has a firm and serious order."

He thought that a president should speak his national language, Arabic, but when he felt strongly about something, he switched into crisp English. When the interpreter said Morsi had "learned a lot" in the United States, Morsi quickly corrected her. "Scientifically!" Morsi interjected. What he had learned was science—just science. "I lived in America but I did not change a lot. I am Egyptian blood and flesh!"

Was there anything he disliked about life in the United States? Yes, the street gangs and violence of South Central Los Angeles. Cohabitation out of wedlock. The looser sexual mores. "I have seen a naked restaurant," he said. He meant Hooters, an adviser explained.

Sayyid Qutb, the radical Islamist thinker, had written of his disgust at the materialism and immorality he had seen when he was a student in

Washington, D.C., and Greeley, Colorado, in the middle of the twentieth century. Qutb saw a clash of civilizations. Morsi was more easygoing.

"They are living their way. I am not objecting." He shrugged. "This is the culture."

By then I was struggling to turn our talk back to Egypt.

In his one term in Parliament under Mubarak, Morsi had served as whip and enforcer for the Brotherhood bloc. He scolded young Brothers who wanted to ask questions or open debates. He lacked the charisma of either the power broker Shater or the liberal Aboul Fotouh. Nor had Morsi endured the long years in prison that made one a hero in an underground movement. He had done seven months in 2006, for demonstrating in support of judicial independence, and a few nights in 2011, at the start of the uprising. Morsi had turned sixty a few months later. He was ready to retire.

When the Brotherhood's governing board wanted to name him as an understudy to Shater in the presidential race, Morsi was dead set against it. Why not shoot me first? he asked. How could he possibly stand for president if his own party had marked him as its second choice? He thought the board was miserable at politics. But Morsi was obedient. The nickname "spare tire" dogged him through his presidency.

Internal Brotherhood polling showed that only 3 percent of the voters knew who Morsi was when he entered the race on April 20, a month before the first round of voting. Only two thirds of them approved of him. The disqualification of Shater had so demoralized his campaign personnel that many refused to work for Morsi. He was short-staffed, which is how he met Wael Haddara, an Egyptian Canadian physician.

The forty-two-year-old Haddara happened to be back in Egypt for the funeral of his mother. He was a bilingual polymath (he spoke Arabic and English, with some French and German). He had grown up around the Arab region and enrolled in a Canadian university at the age of fourteen. He helped patent a new form of gene therapy before he turned twenty-one and eventually earned degrees in pharmacology, medicine, and education. He now managed a large intensive care unit in a teaching hospital in London, Ontario, and on the side wrote scholarly articles applying the ideas of Michel Foucault to medical pedagogy.

Haddara had also served on the board of the Muslim Association of Canada in the years after September 11, 2001, and as its president in 2011. He was not a member of the Muslim Brotherhood but he had friends who were supporters, and in December 2011, he was asked to meet with a senior Brotherhood leader who would play a prominent role in Morsi's campaign and administration. Expecting to be leaving Cairo shortly, he saw nothing to lose. Haddara unloaded his unvarnished assessment of the Egyptian Brotherhood.

"You are patriarchal, paternalistic, anti-Semitic, full of ambiguity, and playing games with identity," Haddara told him. How could Egypt be an Islamic state with equal citizenship for non-Muslims? "If you really want to govern, these are the issues you have to face up to."

"This is great!" the Brotherhood leader, Essam el-Haddad, told Haddara. "Can you write all this down for me?"

Haddara was impressed. And when Morsi was nominated later that spring, Haddara's candid advice and experience with the news media convinced the campaign to try to enlist him. Haddara wondered why a candidate for president of Egypt might want his input.

"I have not lived in Egypt for thirty years," Haddara told an Egyptian Canadian friend who worked on the campaign.

"There is no one else who wants to work with him," his friend replied. "So anything you can provide would be helpful."

"Hold your nose and swallow the medicine" was the Brotherhood's attitude toward Morsi, Haddara later told me. "I felt sorry for him."

As a candidate, Morsi was long-winded and uninspiring. He was all but incapable of sticking to a prepared text without meandering into circular digressions. At an engagement party for a friend's daughter in early 2012, he mortified the non-Islamist groom by turning a toast into a political harangue.

Virtually all Egyptian politicians—Islamists, leftists, or ruling party— said things to local audiences that would appall Westerners, and Morsi was no exception. In a speech about Palestinians, he had once called Israelis "killers and vampires." In a 2005 interview with CNN, he doubted Al Qaeda's role in the September 11 attack on the World Trade Center.

"An airplane or a craft just going through it like a knife in butter?" he said. "Make a fair trial. They didn't do it. What's going on? There is some-thing fishy."

This was a doctor of engineering in materials science talking. But then I was astonished at how widespread such theories were in Cairo, perhaps because Egyptians are so skeptical of their own government's official sto-ries. Mubarak, too, insisted that Al Qaeda had not carried out the 9/11 at-tacks, according to the memoirs of his last foreign minister. Mubarak did not think Al Qaeda could be that sophisticated.

Inside the Brotherhood, Morsi had sided with the conservative faction against Aboul Fotouh. Morsi told me that scholars of Islam were split over the question of whether the president must be a Muslim male. But he drew a mosque and state distinction. Legal eligibility was one thing, and his personal religious views might be another.

"I would not stop a woman from nomination," he said. "Would I vote for her? That is something else entirely."

To prepare for the runoff, the Brotherhood was playing up its common front with liberals against the old regime. Morsi met with a group of liber-als at the Fairmont hotel in Cairo and pledged to bring in a diverse team of advisers in order to unite the "revolutionaries." But he could seldom resist throwing red meat to the Islamist base. He led a boycott of an Egyptian mobile phone service because its founder, the Coptic Christian tycoon Na-guib Sawiris, had retweeted a cartoon of Mickey Mouse in a long beard with Minnie in a full-face veil. An insult to Islam, Morsi said.

In practice, though, Morsi was more liberal than many Brotherhood leaders, possibly more liberal than most Egyptians. One young woman who worked for his campaign, Sondos Asem, told me she liked Morsi in part because he encouraged her parents to let her travel abroad alone—a step too permissive for most Egyptians, no matter how secular. He had socialized at USC in mixed-sex crowds, with uncovered Muslim women, and where al-cohol was served. His young wife had worked outside their home there, and the couple had encouraged their own daughter to earn at least a bachelor's degree in science (she married the son of another Brotherhood leader).

Haddara met Morsi as he was running out of his two-bedroom flat, in a distant suburb known as the Fifth Settlement, on the way to the first televi-sion interview of his campaign.

What would be the campaign message? Haddara asked. Morsi listed five priorities: food security, fuel security, public safety, traffic, and garbage collection; the bread-and-butter issues of common Egyptians. Rights and freedoms did not make the list, and neither did Islam nor morality.

But in front of the camera Morsi fell back on the old themes. "This is the old 'Islam is the solution' platform," he said, dusting off the venerable and ambiguous slogan. "It has been developed and crystallized so that God could bless society with it."

Moderating Morsi's sloganeering was "a constant battle for us on the campaign team," Haddara told me later. Morsi always asked his advisers for talking points about economics, corruption, and freedom. But during the runoff, hard-line Salafi firebrands were joining Morsi on the stump. "He would get up on the platform with these people and he was all fire and brimstone."

"The Quran is our constitution, and Sharia is our guide!" Morsi chanted with the crowd at his first rally, in a town in the Nile Delta. "Some want to stop our march to an Islamic future, where the grace of God's laws will be implemented and provide an honest life to all. . . . The Islamic front must unite so we can fulfill this vision!"

The night of Morsi's election, Mayy el-Sheikh called the former deputy general guide who had picked Morsi to head the Brotherhood parliamentary bloc, Mohamed Habib. He had left the group to start his own small political party, and Mayy asked him, Does Morsi have what it takes to lead Egypt?

"No," Habib said bluntly, "he doesn't."

I wondered if weakness was part of the reason the generals had allowed Morsi to win; they had disqualified so many strong contenders. Yet for a time he defied the odds.

I could hardly imagine a more humiliating inauguration. Morsi had vowed on election night to restore the disbanded Parliament and swear his oath before it. The military council forced him to take all that back. Two generals promised in a joint television interview before the inauguration that the military would remain "a trustworthy guardian," with sweeping powers over the rest of the government.

What kind of "guardian"?

"Interpret it any way you like," Major General Mohamed el-Assar answered.

Instead of a public ceremony, the generals made Morsi swear his oath at 11:00 A.M. on Saturday morning, June 30, 2012, deep inside the Supreme Constitutional Court. He was forced to pay homage to the same judges who had dissolved the Parliament and plotted to steal his election.

I watched on the small screen in my office as Chief Judge Farouk Sultan lectured Morsi about the importance of the Supreme Constitutional Court and the sovereignty of the law. Morsi sat in an upright chair in a curved alcove at the front of an empty courtroom, looking like a hostage. He glowered and stared. He muttered a few dutiful words about the separation of powers. I felt embarrassed for him.

Yet the trappings of the presidency seemed to enlarge him. He climbed into the same black Mercedes limousine that had ferried Mubarak, surrounded by the same retinue of bodyguards with earpieces and sunglasses who had encircled Mubarak. Field Marshal Tantawi was still defense minister and no one thought Morsi could remove him. But even the field marshal saluted the new president.

Morsi, it turned out, had his own ideas about his inauguration. He sped from the court to a lecture hall at Cairo University, where he recited the oath with new feeling before most of the disbanded Parliament and the international ambassadors to Egypt. And he had sworn his oath a third time, unofficially, in Tahrir Square the night before. The Muslim Brothers had erected an elevated stage, and tens of thousands—including more than a few non-Islamists—had turned out to hear him.

Few Egyptians had ever seen a president in the flesh. Mubarak, scared by the assassination of his predecessor and an attempt on his life during a 1995 visit to Ethiopia, had appeared almost exclusively on state television— always surrounded by that thick curtain of bodyguards.

Now an advance man climbed onto the stage. "God is great," he shouted, and it looked for a moment like a typical Islamist rally. Morsi, awkward as ever, clutched his prepared text in the same hand as his microphone. He paced the stage as if he were lecturing about high-temperature conductivity in aluminum oxide. He saluted a roll call of provinces, bureaucracies, and industries—the people of the media, the arts, tourism, and so on—as if he did not want to leave anyone out.

"O free world, Arabs, brothers and sisters, sons and daughters, Egyptian Muslims and Christians, all citizens wherever you are, inside Egypt and abroad. We are here today to tell the whole world: these are the Egyptians; these are the revolutionaries who made this epic, this revolution. . . ."

I thought I heard something new, a different earnestness in Morsi. His speech avoided any reference to Islam or Islamic law. He paraphrased Thomas Jefferson, about martyrs whose blood "watered the tree of liberty." He called out to political opponents, to Christians and secular Egyptians, and to resort workers or artists who feared Islamist moralizing. "Those who voted for me and those who did not—I'm for all of you, at the same distance from all."

"I come to *you* as the source of legitimacy," he said, again and again. "Everyone hears me, all the people and the Cabinet and government, army, police. There is no authority over this authority. *You* have the power! You grant power to whoever you choose, and you withdraw power from whomever you choose." He insisted that no "entity" or "institution"—every listener knew he meant the military—could gainsay the popular will.

He stretched out a hand like a linebacker, pushing two startled bodyguards out of the way until he stood at the front of the stage. A few feet from the crowd, he jerked open his sport coat, and, clutching his microphone to his lapel, he bared the front of his dress shirt.

"I have nothing to protect me from any bullets," he said. Unlike Mubarak, he wore no body armor. "I fear God almighty and after that I fear only you."

I thought unexpectedly of Gamal Abdel Nasser. He had been speaking in Mansheya Square in Alexandria in 1954 when bullets shattered a lightbulb over his head. Glass flew around him. Some later said a dark spot appeared on his chest.

"Let them kill Abdel Nasser. What is Abdel Nasser but one among many?" he continued, without any cringe or hesitation. "Men, stay where you are! I am not dead! I am alive! And even if I die, all of you are Gamal Abdel Nasser."

It was the greatest episode of political theater in Egypt since Antony and Cleopatra. Abdel Nasser was unharmed; legend has it that the dark spot on his chest was ink from a pen. Had Morsi meant to evoke Abdel Nasser, the nemesis of Islamists everywhere?

Morsi pushed back at the generals for their evisceration of his authority in office. "I have no right to give up presidential powers and functions," he said. "This is a contract between you and me. That is the concept of the modern state. . . . Are you ready? Will you stand by me to fully regain our rights?"

Yasmine El Rashidi, an Egyptian writer from an elite family, chronicled the period with eloquence for the *New York Review of Books,* and usually described the Muslim Brothers with a mixture of fear and disdain.

"Morsi won me over that day," Rashidi wrote of Morsi's speech in the square. "He won over my mother, too, although she's long been wary of the Islamists. He won over many who in those moments thought he deserved a chance."

Some of my most liberal or leftist Egyptian friends would look back on that hour in Tahrir Square as the moment when Morsi appeared to be, as he had promised, their president, too.

Washington saw a different picture. As Morsi pledged to free civilians convicted in military trials, he noticed signs in the square urging the humanitarian release of Omar Abdel Rahman, the blind Egyptian sheikh imprisoned in the United States for plotting related to the bombing in 1993 of the World Trade Center.

"I will make all efforts to free them," Morsi said, improvising again, "including Omar Abdel Rahman."

The *New York Times* headline the next day read EGYPT'S NEW LEADER TAKES OATH, PROMISING TO WORK FOR RELEASE OF JAILED TERRORIST. (I did not write it.)

Morsi's advisers cringed and clarified. He understood that the blind sheikh was a convicted criminal, not a political prisoner. No one expected his imminent release. But Americans wondered if Morsi was an amateur, an extremist, or both.

Al Ahram, the state media broadsheet, was known as the newspaper written for only one reader: the president—Abdel Nasser, Sadat, then Mubarak. Now that reader appeared to be Defense Minister Tantawi, not Morsi. Morsi tried to restore the Parliament, and *Al Ahram*'s front-page headline that day commended the generals for shutting it down: THE ARMED FORCES BELONG TO THE PEOPLE AND WILL REMAIN ON THE SIDE OF THE CONSTITUTION AND LEGITIMACY. A photograph depicted the defense minister towering over Morsi. A sidebar blamed Morsi for crashing the Egyptian stock market. State media ignored the lawmakers trying to reenter their offices; its television network rebroadcast a tribute to the heroics of the secret police. Speech-making aside, whoever was in charge, it was not Mohamed Morsi. I did not see how that could change.

F ive weeks after the inauguration, on August 5, 2012, sixteen Egyptian soldiers manning a checkpoint in the North Sinai desert gathered at sundown for a picnic to break the Ramadan fast. Three Land Rovers came speeding out of the hills. Islamist militants fired automatic rifles out of the windows, killing all sixteen soldiers. The attackers made off with an army truck and an armored vehicle. They belonged to an underground group calling itself Ansar Beit al-Maqdis—the Partisans of Jerusalem—and they drove hard toward Israel, their true target. It was the first I had heard of Ansar Beit al-Maqdis, which became important later.

Israeli air strikes made short work of the two vehicles, but the Egyptian army was humiliated. Its soldiers had failed to defend even themselves.

General Abdel Fattah el-Sisi arrived at the presidential palace a week later, on August 12, for a private meeting with Morsi. Some close to Morsi would later tell me that Sisi had won the trust of the president by warning him of an assassination attempt that awaited him at a military funeral for those killed in the attack. (Morsi skipped it.) These close Morsi allies also said that Sisi brought evidence of corruption by Tantawi's second in command, General Sami Anan.

Whatever they discussed, Morsi then called Tantawi and Anan into his office while Sisi returned to the Defense Ministry. Morsi aides in the hallways heard angry voices inside. Anan stormed out. And by that time, Sisi, back at the Defense Ministry, had finished locking down the support of the military council. (General Mahmoud Hegazy, related to Sisi through the marriage of their children, was surely a help.) A short, plump Morsi spokesman appeared on state television at 4:45 P.M. and read out a legalistic proclamation like some medieval herald. Its contents were stunning: the generals were relinquishing control of legislative authority and giving it to Morsi. Tantawi was seventy-six, Anan was sixty-four, and the spokesman announced their immediate retirement. The cameras cut to footage of Morsi swearing in a new defense minister, Sisi, aged fifty-seven, in a hasty ceremony at the presidential palace.

It was the holiest night of Ramadan, the night when the archangel Gabriel is said to have delivered the Quran to the Prophet Mohamed. Muslims celebrate it as *Laylat al Qadr*—the Night of Power. Morsi gave a sermonlike speech at Al Azhar and reveled in his victory.

"We go on to new horizons," he said, "with new generations, with new blood that we have long awaited."

No one in Washington had seen it coming, and a wave of anxiety swept the Pentagon. Some feared that Sisi was a closet Islamist. "There were worries that he was too close to Morsi," Derek Chollet, an assistant to the secretary of defense, wrote in a memoir. "Everyone was very suspicious of him," Chollet told me. The Pentagon, at least, still hoped Egypt's defense minister might check its president rather than report to him.

Israel, Saudi Arabia, and the United Arab Emirates rang more alarms. "Morsi never got it together with the Gulfies and the Israelis," as Chollet said, putting it mildly.

But Ambassador Patterson knew Sisi, and she sent Washington a different warning. He was ambitious, calculating, and ruthless, she wrote. "Morsi may have bitten off more than he can chew."

A few days later, I received a phone call from the same skinny bureaucrat who had welcomed me to Cairo. He was still in his job, and he was calling—as cheerful as ever—on behalf of President Morsi.

The president would be traveling to New York for the United Nations

General Assembly. Would the *New York Times* like an interview before the trip? Steven Erlanger, one of the paper's most seasoned correspondents, flew in to join me.

We met in the Ittihadiya Palace—the Unity Palace. It had been built before the First World War as a luxury hotel, designed by a Belgian architect in a combination of neo-Islamic style and Louis XIV decor. Abdel Nasser had commandeered it, and Mubarak kept it. Now Morsi, in a dark suit and a rep tie, met us in Mubarak's old office. The new president had changed almost nothing. Oil paintings of sailboats still adorned the walls. The only change was the addition of a small plaque on the gilded writing desk. The engraving was a verse from the Quran: "Be mindful of a day on which you will return to God."

Our conversation took place a few days after September 11, 2012. Vandals had hoisted a black jihadi flag over the U.S. embassy in Cairo during a demonstration against an American-made movie deriding the Prophet Mohamed, and their exploit in Cairo catalyzed a deadly assault the same night on the American mission in Benghazi, Libya.

Morsi had flown to Brussels that night for a meeting with the European Union. I later learned that he had videotaped a statement about the attack from the steps of his plane at the Cairo airport. He condemned the attack and pledged to secure all foreign embassies, then took off for Europe expecting the message to be broadcast on state television.

The presidential camera crew—Mubarak holdovers—had bungled the filming and failed to record his statement. Morsi did not find out until he landed the next morning. It might have been incompetence or sabotage on the part of the camera crew; that question came up often in the Morsi administration. Either way, the result was that Morsi had been strangely silent the night of the attack. He was determined to hide the screwup.

After the small talk about USC, I asked about that night: Why did he say nothing? "We needed to contain the situation and deal with it wisely," Morsi said. "At no point was anybody in the embassy under any threat."

Obama had recently been asked in an interview whether he considered Egypt under Morsi to be an American ally. "I don't think we would consider them an ally, but we don't consider them an enemy," Obama said, dodging the question. "A new government that is trying to find its way."

So we asked Morsi: Did he consider the United States an ally? "That depends on the definition of 'ally,'" he said, chuckling. "I am trying now, seriously, to look to the future and see that we are real friends."

The *New York Times* posted an audio recording of the interview on the internet, and the satirist Bassem Youssef—the self-described Jon Stewart of Egypt—replayed that answer on television as a punch line. The Islamist president was "real friends" with Washington.

I most wanted to know how Morsi had persuaded the generals to let him take real power. How did he remove Field Marshal Tantawi?

Wael Haddara had stepped in for the incompetent official interpreter, and he translated the answer: "The role of the armed forces is not a political role. Their role is to protect the borders and the institution of the state, and that is exactly what they decided to do."

"No," Morsi corrected, in English, "no, it is not what they decided to do."

Haddara tried again. "And that is what happened on August 12, the armed forces assumed their role . . ."

"No," Morsi interrupted again. They had not merely given up power; he had taken it, he insisted. "This is the will of the Egyptians through their elected president, right?

"And the armed forces are feeling very well," he continued. "The armed forces as a whole are living at peace with themselves. The president of the Arab Republic of Egypt is the commander of the armed forces. *Khalas.*" That's it.

"Egypt is now a real civic state. It is not theocratic. It is not military. It is a civic state, democratic, free, constitutional, lawful, modern," he said, still speaking emphatic English. "We are behaving according to the people's choices and will. Is this clear?"

I was dumbstruck. I knew the politician's playbook: thank the departing official (Tantawi) for his service, nod to his desire for time with family, and maybe call his retirement a mutual decision in the public interest. Was Morsi so confident that he could toss out the script? Or so insecure that he needed to boast?

We stood up to go. Morsi was almost swaggering now. "We are talking now about seventy percent popularity. That is what is going on! That is what they are telling me!" I saw his press aides wince and try to cut him off. Two rookie mistakes: admitting that he paid attention to his internal polls, then bragging about them.

Shaking hands to say goodbye, Erlanger gently touched Morsi's shoulder, fifty-nine-year-old journalist to sixty-one-year-old president. "You have a stressful job," he said. "Take care of your health."

I later learned that in Morsi's inner circle, the remark set off an uproar. Did these American journalists know about a danger to the president's life? Were they working with American intelligence? Could this be a threat?

13

A Day in Court

July 4, 2012–September 11, 2012

ven in the honking congestion of Ramses Street in downtown Cairo, the towering Italianate columns of Egypt's high court are impossible to miss. The double high doors were built to awe, and I felt it. But inside was bedlam.

People swirled like sand in a windstorm through the cavernous, dimly lit lobby. Men in the long black robes of lawyers and judges stepped briskly over families squatting on the stone floor surrounded by plastic containers of *kushari* and by a miscellaneous litter of plastic spoons, paper cups, and burned-out cigarettes. Some of the people looked like they had been camped there for days. Small men in grimy smocks hustled up to me selling sugary tea or Turkish coffee from dented metal trays. The air smelled heavily of smoke and, I thought, faintly of urine. I shuddered to think what the bathroom might be like—a question that would grow more pressing for me throughout that day.

My journey into the labyrinth of the Egyptian court system had begun with a newspaper article published a month and a half earlier, on July 4, 2012. I had quoted Judge Tahani el-Gebali of the Supreme Constitutional Court. She had described her advice to the generals about the danger of Islamists winning at the polls and, thus, about the wisdom of dissolving the Parliament.

Maybe Gebali had later thought better of a sitting judge bragging to a journalist about the political goals behind a court decision. Perhaps she had objected to my portrayal of the military council's shutdown of Parliament as a seizure of power. On the morning that the article was published, she had immediately called Mayy el-Sheikh to demand the audio recording of our interview at the court. Mayy said that we had only two sets of written notes, and Gebali's next call was to a television talk show. She publicly denied that she had ever spoken to us. She called the *New York Times* a hostile and offensive newspaper "under the control of the Zionist lobby."

She did not claim she was misquoted. She insisted that we had never spoken. "There was no interview at all and no statements. These statements are all made up. It is all lies and incorrect," she said in a phone interview broadcast on the talk show, "and they will pay a high price.

"I am being targeted. I am not accustomed to being blackmailed by anyone. I will sue the *New York Times* and demand compensation and it will be big," Gebali continued. She would collect $10 million from the *Times,* she announced, and give it to "the martyrs of this great revolution."

And why would the *Times* target her? The Central Intelligence Agency, she said, was punishing her for calling out Hillary Clinton's support for Morsi.

Gebali's complaint arrived at my office the next day, and it noted the special status of the plaintiff, "Her Excellency Judge Tahani el-Gebali, the first female Egyptian judge" and justice of the Supreme Constitutional Court. Our article was "the work of the writer's imagination, without re-gard to professional accuracy or journalistic ethics," the complaint said, asking "the harshest possible sentence for all those who dare to fabricate such things." In Egypt, that meant years in jail.

Few lawyers in Cairo were brave enough to face off against a sitting judge on the Supreme Constitutional Court. I was advised to find a lawyer with connections, but it was hard to know whose favors mattered most—the Muslim Brothers or the military council? In July 2012, the court and the generals had the upper hand over Morsi. No one knew yet who would come out on top.

Gebali's lawyer, Khaled Abu Bakr, was known for human rights cases, and he phoned me directly. "Really, I support you," he told me at the start, and I suspected he was trying to entrap me. "I really like your work," he continued in English. "I do not want to sue you.

"I said to Tahani el-Gebali, Why did you say those things? and she

denied everything. Then I talked to your assistant"—Mayy el-Sheikh—
"and she swore that Judge Gebali *did* say those things. So I don't know
what to think."

Was he more concerned about the opinion of the news media than he
was about Gebali? It was not a trick. Days later, he dropped her as a client.

The *New York Times* engaged the go-to lawyer for Egyptian news organizations in their libel cases—Negad el-Borai. He handled human rights
cases, too, and he was rumored to have nurtured contacts in the intelligence
services. (Those were the most valuable connections, if he was not trading
information.)

"Don't worry," he told me when I met him in his office. "This is a political case. It is not about the law."

Islamists were gleefully using our article to portray Gebali as the face of
the conspiracy against them. But she had often expressed similar sentiments
in the Egyptian news media. Thankfully, we had brought a photographer,
Tomás Munita, to the interview in her chambers. On Borai's advice, we sent
Gebali a date-stamped digital photograph as proof of the interview.

She dropped all her claims. Mayy and I sighed with relief. Then an Islamist lawmaker from the dissolved Parliament sued Gebali. The Islamist,
Mohamed el-Omda, said our article proved that the judges had conspired
with the generals against democracy. So in rebuttal, Gebali filed a new suit
against Mayy and me. This time Gebali no longer disputed anything we
had written. She asked the prosecutors to jail us for insulting a judge.

"Don't worry," Mayy assured me by email. "It seems it is part of
the job."

The prosecutors summoned Mayy and me for questioning on September 11, 2012, a long day. The generals had stepped back, Sisi had replaced
Tantawi, and Morsi was ascendant. More Islamists had filed legal complaints on the basis of our article. But our lawyer warned us that the prosecutors were still loyal to Gebali. Expect them to try to discredit us to
defend her.

The same courthouse handled most criminal charges or legal disputes
in Cairo. The vast tomb of a building included Egypt's highest appellate
court, the office of the chief public prosecutor, and the syndicate for lawyers. Disputes here had dragged on for decades. Of course, the worst that

might befall me was probably expulsion from Egypt. The general counsel of the *New York Times* had called the State Department on my behalf. The American consulate sent an observer. But Mayy el-Sheikh, an Egyptian, was not going anywhere. Our lawyer thought the prosecutors might pin it all on her, blaming her for some mistranslation of Gebali. Protecting Mayy was our special concern.

Our lawyer led us through a maze of hallways to the narrow and windowless office of the prosecutor assigned to our case. Two fat men were waiting at each end of the room. One was the prosecutor, and the other one was the Islamist lawmaker who had summoned us here. He smiled at me, patted my back, and called me a hero. I was mortified. I could see the prosecutor scowling.

The rules of procedure terrified me. Egyptian courts did not use electronic recording machines or even typewriters. A skinny young man sat at a small desk next to the fat prosecutor, writing fast in an enormous white notebook that must have been eighteen inches tall.

The prosecutor questioned me in Arabic. But when an interpreter conveyed my answer, the prosecutor very briefly summarized whatever I had said in a few of his own words, in Arabic, and those few words—the prosecutor's short summation of my testimony—were all the scrivener wrote down in the transcript. It hardly mattered what I actually said.

I had a lot to say. What, exactly, was Judge Gebali complaining about? She had never named any inaccuracies in the article. And what crime did the Islamists think she had committed? When I showed emotion, the prosecutor threatened to charge me with contempt—another jailable offense—for disrespecting him. Every time I crossed my legs, the prosecutor stopped the proceedings to tell me to uncross them. Mayy whispered to me that some in the Arab world considered leg crossing an insult. The day was dragging on. I badly needed the bathroom, and I was afraid to excuse myself.

The prosecutor, who spoke no English, was making his way through our 1,450-word article sentence by sentence, and after each one he asked me if Judge Gebali had said it. I tried to explain that only the words in quotation marks were her verbatim statements. It was a newspaper article, not a speech or transcript.

Was I admitting that she had not said those things? the prosecutor wanted to know.

He kept stepping out of the room for long stretches. Our lawyer thought that he might be consulting his superiors. He was caught between the new president, the Supreme Constitutional Court, the American embassy, and the international media. I suspected the real question was about who was in power; facts about guilt or innocence—mine or Judge Gebali's—were much less important.

Five o'clock came and went. "Your excellency," Negad el-Borai offered at last, perhaps we could consider the nature of this article? Egyptian newspapers favored interviews in a Q and A form, Borai noted, but Western papers like the *New York Times* published what he called "analysis," mixing verbatim quotes with the words of a journalist.

All the Egyptian papers had reported on our article in Arabic, and their translations were at best imprecise, especially about the quotation marks. Perhaps Judge Gebali and the Islamist plaintiffs had both read some of those translations? None of them read English. Maybe this was all a misunderstanding, the fault of poor translations by Egyptian newspapers.

The prosecutor jumped at it. He agreed to assemble a panel of academic experts in journalism, and a few weeks later our case was dismissed. Negad el-Borai had found the prosecutor a retreat with honor.

14

President and Mrs. Morsi

November 19, 2012–November 22, 2012

Naglaa Ali Mahmoud was surely as surprised as anyone to find herself, at the age of fifty, the First Lady of Egypt. Raised in a poor family in the Cairo neighborhood of Ain Shams, she was married at the age of sixteen to a cousin ten years her elder. She followed her new husband to Los Angeles. She volunteered at the Muslim Student House at the University of Southern California, translating sermons for women interested in converting to Islam. And she knew what she was doing when she joined the Muslim Brotherhood there with her husband, she told the organization's newspaper.

"The Brothers don't blindfold anyone," she said. "They told us that the path is long and full of dangers."

California suited her; she did not want to move back to Egypt. But she had given birth to a son and a daughter—the first two of five children—and her husband wanted them to grow up Egyptian. Naglaa was independent: she managed the household alone for four years while her husband taught in Libya to earn extra money. (Such temporary migrations to oil-rich neighbors are common for Egyptians.) His earnings enabled the couple to buy a modest apartment and a Mitsubishi Lancer.

Shaimaa Morsi, their daughter, got the education her mother had missed. After an undergraduate degree from the university in Benha, she had enrolled in a doctoral program in botany at the university in Zagazig. The mother and daughter both wore a *khimar*—a conservative form of head scarf that leaves the face uncovered but drapes over the shoulders and down to the waist. Both women kept their maiden names after marriage; taking a husband's family name, as Suzanne Mubarak and Jehan Sadat did, is a Western convention unusual in Egypt. In any case, Naglaa Ali Mahmoud preferred the customary nickname of an Egyptian homemaker, Um Ahmed—Ahmed's mom, after the name of her first son. She insisted that President Morsi stay in the suburban apartment that the couple shared with their youngest son, Abdullah, and commute to the presidential palace.

"A place like the presidential palace completely isolates you," she said in a rare interview with an Egyptian magazine. She told the magazine's photographer that he could take her picture, "only if your photos make me look younger and a little thinner."

Some saw Um Ahmed as an Egyptian Everywoman—socially conservative, jealous of her privacy, unashamed, and self-reliant. She could have been the mother of many young professional women in Egypt. But to the elite I lived among, she was everything they loathed about President Morsi. Jehan Sadat and Suzanne Mubarak were both half-British fashion plates with well-coifed hair and advanced degrees. How could Um Ahmed step into their high heels?

Mayy el-Sheikh and I stepped out for a latte near our office in Zamalek to sample the outrage. "If you travel to New York or wherever, people would make fun of you and say: 'Your First Lady wears the abaya, ha ha ha,'" lamented a mortified twenty-one-year-old female engineering student. "Previous first ladies used to be elegant."

"I cannot call her a First Lady under any circumstances," a twenty-nine-year-old male banker agreed. "She cannot be an image for the ladies of Egypt." I wondered what the Egyptians of Zamalek thought of Mayy, in her hijab and tennis shoes.

Egyptians joked about Um Ahmed calling Um Gamal—Gamal Mubarak's mom—to talk about housekeeping. An anti-Islamist newspaper moaned that her Islamic modesty would offend foreign leaders. "Do not look at her. Do not shake hands with her," an editorial imagined. "A comic scenario."

It was the symbolism of Um Ahmed—the *idea* of President Mohamed Morsi, what he *might* do rather than anything he had done—that most alarmed his critics. His style was so different. Like other educated people serious about Islam, Morsi spoke the classical Arabic of a religious scholar. Egyptians accustomed to street Arabic (or, in the elite, to English) struggled to understand him. His political speeches sometimes sounded like he was giving a Friday sermon at a mosque (he had had more practice at that). Even when he tried to set up a forum for citizen grievances, he reached for language from the early history of Islam—*diwan al mathalem*. After thirty years of Mubarak, it felt to some as though a pious hick had taken over the palace.

What did Morsi *do* in office? He had campaigned promising that a shadow government of Brotherhood experts would swoop in to remake the bureaucracy, like McKinsey consultants toting Qurans. Khairat el-Shater had worked for months on the plan, which the Brotherhood called the Renaissance Project. Members of the team expected an office in the presidential palace. I met a pair of experts working exclusively on fisheries.

Morsi pushed it all aside. His advisers told me he was waiting for a new Parliament. He also might have doubted that he had the juice. He issued only one law in his first five months as president: he barred the pretrial detention of journalists for crimes related to their work.

The Mubarak-era legal code still criminalized insults to the president. A team of lawyers working for Morsi filed lawsuits against a handful of journalists or talk show hosts. But Morsi said the suits had been filed without his knowledge and he withdrew them. No one was penalized. Anyone could tell that there was no censorship under Morsi. Criticism of the president saturated the newsstands and the airwaves. The newspapers were full of outrageous reports that Morsi was selling the Great Pyramids or the Suez Canal to Qatar, or that he was giving the Sinai to Hamas as a favor to Israel, or that some Morsi family member had enjoyed a fancy vacation. We chased all the rumors. They were all bogus.

Although the military council under Defense Minister Sisi now allowed Morsi to run the government and issue new laws, he did little to change Egypt. In December 2012, his Cabinet announced a package of tax increases—including sin taxes, such as on cigarettes and beer—but Morsi withdrew them within hours. He appointed Muslim Brothers to less than a third of his Cabinet (eleven positions out of thirty-five). He kept Mubarak-era veterans in charge of the big portfolios—defense, interior, foreign affairs, and finance. Mubarak's minister of irrigation became Morsi's prime minister. And he named Muslim Brothers as governors of only a minority of the provinces (ten out of twenty-seven). Former generals took most of the other seventeen, just like under Mubarak. Compared with the changes in administrations after an American election, Morsi tiptoed in slow motion.

His supporters said Morsi fulfilled the letter of his campaign promises about an inclusive government. He named a prime minister from outside the Muslim Brotherhood as well as a woman and a Christian as deputies. His critics said he failed to honor the spirit of his pledges. The most notable feature of his presidency may have been his determination to ingratiate himself with the military and the police. When an independent commission reported on the killing of civilian demonstrators under military rule, Morsi buried it. His advisers said its allegations were not yet substantiated and that it included inflammatory gossip about the American embassy. But it looked like he was protecting the generals. He repeatedly thanked and flattered the police (who had twice arrested him before he took office). He even commended the police on the anniversary of the 2011 uprising against them.

A columnist in the independent *El-Masry El-Youm* took stock: "For eighty years, hundreds of thousands of books and articles were published about what would happen if a Brotherhood president made it to power in Egypt. It was said that veils would be required, banks would be closed, a war would be declared, and bathing suits would be banned. Today we discovered what happens when a Brotherhood president holds power. Simply nothing."

President Obama was staying in the royal suite of the Raffles Hotel in Phnom Penh, Cambodia, on his way to an Asian summit. It was November 19, 2012, and Israel and Hamas had been at war for five days. Hamas rockets had killed three Israelis. Israeli air strikes had killed 150 Palestinians and devastated the cities of Gaza. Israel was calling up tens of thousands of reserve troops for a possible ground assault. I foresaw a repeat of the previous Gaza war, in 2009, which had lasted three weeks and killed 1,400 Palestinians.

But now a Muslim Brother was the president of Egypt. Morsi often pledged his commitment to the Camp David peace agreements. But in our interview he had also argued to me that Israel and the United States had failed to live up to their side. Camp David had envisioned a Palestinian state.

With Gaza under Israeli air strikes, Morsi pounded the table for Hamas and the Palestinians. "If a land invasion takes place—as Israelis have said it will—this would mean dire consequences in the region, and we could never accept that," he thundered at a news conference. "The free world could never accept that." Many in Washington wondered if Morsi would encourage, aid, or even arm Hamas.

Now, days later, on November 19, Obama had skipped dessert in Phnom Penh for an 11:30 P.M. phone call with Morsi; Morsi stepped out of a funeral service for his sister to take a call from Obama.

Before Morsi, Mubarak, too, had also blustered against Israel in public. But he kept an open line to his Israeli counterparts. Since the United States designated Hamas a terrorist group, the only way that Washington could negotiate with it was through Mubarak, who delegated the outreach exclusively to his spies.

Obama realized that Morsi changed the dynamic. Egypt's generals and diplomats were still talking to Israel. But Hamas was the Palestinian offshoot of the Egyptian Muslim Brotherhood, inspired by the ideas of its founder. Morsi himself was wired to Hamas.

"Morsi effectively had the Hamas guys on the other line. We were talking to people who were one degree removed from Hamas," Ben Rhodes, who was traveling with Obama, later told me. "This was a whole new world."

In his call with Obama that night, Morsi neither railed against Israel nor defended Hamas. He understood the Israeli perspective. He wanted only to end the fighting. Obama promised to send Clinton to Tel Aviv and get Israel to the negotiating table; Morsi pledged to bring Hamas. Obama fell asleep in the royal suite's four-poster bed and told Rhodes to wake him up at any hour if Morsi rang back.

At 3:00 A.M. in Cambodia, Morsi called to say that Hamas was on board. The two presidents spoke again later the same day, November 20, to fill in the details—their third call in twenty-four hours and their sixth call that week.

"The cease-fire talks had been going nowhere before Morsi stepped in," Rhodes said. "And he delivered. He kept his end of the bargain."

He surprised even the skeptics. "It was a litmus test for Morsi, and he passed with flying colors," Steven Simon of the National Security Council told me. "He was indispensable."

Clinton landed in Cairo on November 21. She and the Egyptian foreign minister announced the cease-fire a few hours later, at 7:00 P.M., and she thanked Morsi "for assuming the leadership that has long made this country a cornerstone of regional stability and peace." She made it home the next day for Thanksgiving dinner.

I expected weakness from Morsi on a critical question about Israel and the Palestinians: the tunnels used to smuggle goods and weapons into Gaza under the border from the North Sinai, past the Israeli embargo. Hamas and the residents of Gaza depended on the smuggling, and tunnel traffic had surged with the withdrawal of policing after Mubarak. Weapons from Qaddafi's looted arsenals traveled the same route.

But when I met him, Morsi had brought up the tunnels before I could ask. "There are radical and criminal elements, and they are using these tunnels sometimes," he told me sternly. "We destroy these tunnels these days as much as we can."

Morsi tried to deploy the army to crush the militants in the North Sinai. Sisi refused, he later told other officers. "My mission is not to combat terrorism," Sisi told them, and there would be "very grave dangers" of civilian casualties from an operation in the Sinai. "You would be creating an enemy against you and against your country, because there will have been bad blood between you and him." (A recording of his private statements later leaked to the public.)

My colleague Peter Baker was traveling with Obama during the Hamas talks, and we wrote an article together about the budding friendship between the two presidents. We quoted Rhodes anonymously, saying Obama had been impressed by Morsi's pragmatism and precision. "This was somebody focused on solving problems."

Morsi, too, was keen on Obama. "We felt there was a high level of sincerity in trying to find a solution," Morsi's foreign policy adviser Essam el-Haddad told me.

The *New York Times* published our article on the front page the next day, Thanksgiving 2012. Obama's national security advisers stepped up plans for Morsi to visit the White House.

"We really underestimated Morsi," a senior American diplomat in Cairo told reporters in a briefing.

I pictured Morsi looking into the mirror in the Ittihadiya Palace. Here he was, the unassuming engineering professor, believing he had indeed become the true president of Egypt.

15

Under the Cloak

November 22, 2012–December 3, 2012

Twenty months after the uprising began, calm in Cairo seemed to soothe the region. The Israel-Hamas truce held in Gaza. In Tunis, an assembly led by its Islamist party was drafting a new constitution with no reference to Sharia. The charter's guarantees of the rights of women, Jews, and other minorities made it the most liberal of any Arab state, Islamist or secular.

Libya, barely a functioning state during Qaddafi's bizarre forty-year rule, had held free parliamentary elections in July. I was in Benghazi, and the night before the vote a local militia demanding more power for the eastern province—they called themselves Federalists—shot down a helicopter delivering ballots. When the polls opened, I watched Federalists shoot up a polling place and dump out its ballot box. Then the fighters climbed back into their artillery-mounted pickup trucks to take out a second voting location. But unarmed civilians blocked the road.

A fifty-five-year-old woman in a designer head scarf marched into a voting center pockmarked with bullet holes. "We will vote for the fatherland whether there is shooting or not," she told me. "Whoever dies for their country is a martyr, and even if there are explosions, we are going to vote." Islamist fighters in long beards and mismatched fatigues started protecting polling places. The rest of the voting continued unmolested.

Ambassador J. Christopher Stevens and three other Americans were killed in Benghazi two months later, on September 11, 2012, when Islamist militants burned down the U.S. diplomatic mission. But on the Friday after the attack tens of thousands of Libyans filled the streets in tribute to the ambassador. When in the Arab world had that ever happened for a Western envoy?

By November 2012, the Western-friendly Free Syrian Army had liberated a broad, populous swath of northern Syria. Al Qaeda had not yet begun openly competing for Syrian fighters; it was still working under other names to infiltrate the uprising. No one anticipated the emergence of its vicious spinoff, the Islamic State, or ISIS. A few months later, in February, I crossed the Turkish border to a liberated Syrian village in the province of Aleppo; five bookish young university graduates had set up a local government and reopened the bakery. The bread made them the heroes of the town. Western journalists joked that we would soon ride into Damascus on the tanks of the Free Syrian Army.

In Cairo, the first, small demonstration against Morsi had started as early as August 24—just twelve days after he took power from the generals. An outspoken anti-Islamist lawmaker gathered a few hundred people outside the palace to demand a "second revolution" that would hand power to Farouk Sultan, Tahani el-Gebali, and the rest of the Supreme Constitutional Court. The anti-Islamist "second revolution" idea was tossed around even then, and it was no secret that the court was against Morsi.

But by November, those demonstrations, too, had dwindled. Morsi seemed right about his popularity. The few street protests that took place felt like echoes. On November 20, activists organized a demonstration to mark the anniversary of an earlier demonstration. The police still killed one more civilian. But by and large the strife had subsided.

So that Thanksgiving, November 22, Laura and I celebrated by inviting a group of British and Arab friends for an American-style dinner: an Egyptian turkey—*deek roomi*—with stuffing and cranberry sauce (imported by an upscale grocer, Gourmet Egypt). We set a table on the front porch for the kids. I uncorked some imported wine. With the pace of news slowing, I promised Laura that I would spend more time with our sons.

Mayy el-Sheikh called as our guests arrived. Hundreds of Muslim Brothers were protesting outside the Supreme Constitutional Court, presumably to pressure the judges about something. Just another demonstration, I told her.

Carving myself a second helping of turkey, I noticed other journalists at the table glancing down at vibrating mobile devices. The Cairo bureau chief for one of the Western news agencies did his best not to interrupt the meal. "I am sure it is nothing," he said. But we both pushed away our wineglasses.

When dessert was served, I opened my laptop and saw Morsi's spokesman on state television with another proclamation—his most stunning. In blunt language, with no speech or explanation, Morsi decreed that all of his own decisions were beyond any judicial review until the ratification of a new constitution.

"The president is authorized to take any measures he sees fit in order to face any threats posed to the January revolution," the spokesman intoned. "His decisions cannot be appealed or canceled. All pending lawsuits against them are void."

He listed lots of other provisions—a new trial for Mubarak, a new chief prosecutor, more benefits for the families of the "martyrs." But those were decoration. Just four months after freeing himself from the stranglehold of the generals, Morsi appeared to have decreed himself Pharaoh.

Even the leaders of the Brotherhood were surprised. "If I were not in my place, I would think he wants to be a dictator," Shater, their chief strategist, told his aides as they watched the declaration on television. But for Morsi and his advisers, the crux of the decree was one clause: "No judicial authority is entitled to dissolve the Constituent Assembly."

I learned the backstory later. Morsi's team had received reports that day that the Supreme Constitutional Court was poised within days to dissolve the committee drafting a new constitution. The military council's plan for the transition had been convoluted and ever changing to begin with, and the courts were reversing each tortured step. In April, another top court had struck down the first incarnation of a committee to draft a new constitution on technicalities, forcing a restart to the process. In June, the Supreme Constitutional Court had dissolved Egypt's first freely elected Parliament. Now, in November, a second drafting committee had almost completed a new charter, and the court was about to erase it. I had heard rumors (and so had Morsi) that the court was preparing to annul his election as president, too. The generals would be back in charge; no elected officials would be left standing. After nearly two years, Egypt would be no closer to building a new government than it was when Mubarak resigned.

Morsi and his aides spent hours that day in a frantic debate. Should he try to lower the mandatory retirement age of judges from seventy to sixty, which would force out the most vehement anti-Islamists (like Tahani el-Gebali)? Should he declare a national state of emergency, suspending all the laws? In either case, the court might try to overrule him.

"The decision was, we have to do something to get out of this cycle," his adviser Wael Haddara later told me.

The Canadian journalist Patrick Graham later asked Morsi if he felt protected by the gratitude he received from Hillary Clinton for the deal in Gaza.

"Oh, no, no. I don't do this. Never ever. Not then. Not now. Not in the future. Nothing like this has been discussed at all," he said. There had been no quid pro quo, he said.

Morsi must have worried, though. He returned to the subject moments later, to ask of Clinton, "She didn't say that, did she?"

The day after Thanksgiving, the cities of Egypt exploded. Thousands headed for Tahrir Square. Rocks and tear gas filled the air around the Interior Ministry. By late afternoon, vandals had either attacked or burned down Muslim Brotherhood offices in towns all over Egypt, including Alexandria, Suez, Ismailia, and Port Said.

A more astute politician might have made his case directly to his critics: his expanded powers were meant to protect the transition from imminent erasure. They would last only a few weeks. Instead, Morsi appeared that afternoon outside the palace, where he spoke at a televised rally of his core Islamist supporters calling for God's law. "We sacrifice our lives, our blood, to protect you, Islam!" they chanted.

Morsi rambled on about the Syrian uprising, the occupation of Gaza, martyrs' pensions, a recent train crash, and vague conspiracy theories—everything but his decree. "Illicit money earned under a criminal regime is being used to hire thugs to attack institutions," he said. Conspirators hid under the "respectable cloak" of the Egyptian judiciary. "I lie in wait for them and I will never let them go."

"Beware, do not imagine that I do not see you," he said, as though addressing the plotters. "I knew this morning that there were two, three, or four sitting somewhere that they thought might conceal them . . . in a narrow alley."

His "narrow alley" entered the vernacular of Egyptian humor loaded with sexual innuendo. But a short salute that he made to "my people and my tribe" became his most infamous line. His supporters said he meant all Egyptians. The Egyptian news media repeated the phrase as a confession that he cared only for Islamists. Egyptian DJs sampled his words into re-mixes. Morsi's "My people and my tribe" speech, we all called it.

The official state media encouraged the protests against the president. I had no idea who was controlling it now, or if its holdover editors just hated Morsi. On the front page of *Al Ahram,* a venerable Sadat- and Mubarak-era political analyst urged readers, "Take to the streets and die, because Egypt is lost. . . . Immunizing the decisions of the president with a constitutional declaration is a forgery and a fraud."

Morsi backpedaled furiously. He visited a council of judges to work out a compromise. His spokesman read out an "explanation" that sounded like a retraction. He limited the range of decisions that he said could not be overturned by the courts. His aides cited precedents set under Mubarak that would have justified his immunity without his decree. And he called for the constitution to be completed in only one or two weeks instead of two months. His time above the courts would be short, his spokesman said, because his decree specified that the courts would regain their full author-ity with the passage of the new charter. Then the court postponed indefi-nitely its ruling that might have struck down the constitutional committee. Morsi promptly rescinded the part of his decree about judicial review. His time as "Pharaoh" lasted less than a month.

The draft constitution he had been fighting for was released in Decem-ber. In an act of revenge, it shrank the Supreme Constitutional Court enough to kick off Judge Gebali. It was rushed and sloppy, a missed op-portunity. But it was still less authoritarian and more liberal than the Mubarak-era constitution. One clause, though, set the stage for a sensa-tional stunt by Yasser Borhami, the Salafi leader with the giant prayer bruise, and his stunt takes some explaining.

Arab constitutions for decades had had little consequence for actual governance. The texts became litanies of bombast about the people, their values, their Islam, and so on. The plebiscites that approved them were like mass loyalty oaths, as one American scholar put it.

The second article of the Mubarak-era constitution had for thirty years declared that its foundation was "the principles of Sharia." The courts had ensured the language was meaningless. Now the Muslim Brothers saw no need to change it. Liberals and Christians knew they had no chance of expunging it—the clause was too popular. But the Salafis had promised real Sharia, whatever that meant. They jammed up the process to demand something more.

To resolve the impasse, the Muslim Brothers leading the constitution-drafting committee put together a negotiating group of about three dozen—including Salafis and liberal intellectuals as well as representatives of the Coptic Church, Al Azhar, and the secular parties. All finally agreed on a compromise. An article (219) was added that spelled out the principles of Sharia in a standard, mainstream Sunni Muslim way. The compromise defined the principles of Sharia to include the four major schools of Sunni Muslim thought, leaving room for a wide variety of sometimes contradictory interpretations. Shiite Muslims—there were only a few in Egypt—had something to complain about. So did any liberals or Christians who hoped to strike from the text all reference to Islam. But the liberals and Christians on the committee believed they had won a victory. This was almost the loosest possible definition of Sharia, and it gave liberals and jurists room to maneuver. (The Supreme Constitutional Court decided only one related case while the clause was in effect, and it changed nothing.)

Salafi leaders, though, portrayed the compromise as a secret victory. "Secularists could not understand this point, just like the Christians also could not understand it," Sheikh Borhami bragged in a speech delivered to a Salafi audience that was recorded on video and posted online.

The new clause, he claimed, would secretly mandate a strict, literal-minded seventh-century Sharia: the stoning of adulterers, the amputations of thieves, the whole medieval package. "It was written and approved by thirty-six persons, Christians, liberals and Azharis! . . . This constitution imposes restrictions that have never been imposed by any Egyptian constitution before. . . . It restrains freedom of thought. It restrains freedom of religion. It restrains freedom of expression and creativity and this kind of thing."

Do not tell the news media, he said in the video. "Why? Because surely they were not aware of this point! They did not notice it!"

The video got out, of course, and the news media went wild. Every non-Islamist network and newspaper called Borhami's speech proof of the Brotherhood-Salafi conspiracy to take Egypt back to the Middle Ages. Khaled Dawoud, a liberal journalist and opposition party spokesman, summed up the reaction. "Hey, hey, hey, guys, we know each other!" he said. "This is where you start building an Iranian-style theocracy!"

Borhami had done more than any liberal or nationalist to energize the battle against the Muslim Brothers. The Saudis and the *mukhabarat* were surely delighted.

On Thanksgiving night at the White House, Prem Kumar, the Egypt director of the National Security Council, drafted a stern condemnation of Morsi's decree. But the voices who had wanted to stick with Mubarak for the sake of stability now wanted to stand by Morsi. He had secured the truce in Gaza. Tom Donilon told Kumar not to cut Morsi off at the knees.

The final statement ended up a puzzle of circumlocution. "The current constitutional vacuum in Egypt can only be resolved by the adoption of a constitution that includes checks and balances. . . ." But even that muted language enraged Donilon. He ordered a hunt to figure out who had revised the text and he demanded to know how it got through without his approval.

Morsi's decree was without a doubt the worst moment of his presidency, the nadir of his credibility as a democratic leader. For Egypt, it was a turning point. But in Washington almost nothing had changed. Morsi's foreign policy adviser, Essam el-Haddad, arrived a few days later for meetings at the State Department, the Pentagon, and the White House. Haddad was scheduled to meet Donilon, his American counterpart, on December 3. But after lunch at the White House mess, Haddad was surprised to find himself escorted all the way to the Oval Office.

Egypt's ambassador had accompanied Haddad to the White House. Now Obama's aides told the ambassador to wait outside the Oval Office, and as he sat there he fumed that no Egyptian president since Sadat had received such a welcome. Inside, Obama was warm and collegial. He made no effort to condemn Morsi's Thanksgiving decree. He talked politician to politician. He observed that he had just won reelection that fall by about the same margin Morsi had won in the spring—about 52 percent of the vote. Obama said his opponents could be frustrating, too. But negotiating with the Republicans in Congress provided political cover, he told Haddad.

"Our message was, you have to hug the opposition to give yourselves some space," Obama's adviser Rhodes later told me.

Obama and Haddad talked for forty minutes: an extraordinary allocation of time for a visitor who was neither a head of state nor even a foreign minister.

Haddad and Morsi, though, still thought Obama did not understand the dynamics on the ground. Their challenge was security, not politics. A wave of violence was rising against them. Vandals were burning Brotherhood offices, protesters menaced the presidential palace, and the police were letting it happen. None of that seemed to be under the control of their liberal opponents—and if it was, were they politicians or extortionists?

But the meeting itself sent another message: forty minutes with the president. Obama had their back, the Morsi team thought.

16

A Rumble at the Palace

December 3, 2012–December 7, 2012

Morsi's Thanksgiving decree conjured up a new alliance against him. An assortment of Mubarak-era politicians and businessmen gathered behind Mohamed ElBaradei, the liberal icon. Joined by one or two political newcomers, they demanded that Morsi cancel plans for a referendum on December 15 to approve the draft constitution (the rushed charter Morsi's decree had been intended to protect). And they organized demonstrations twice a week in Tahrir Square and outside the palace. The Judges Club, at war with Morsi since the presidential campaign, announced that its members would refuse to supervise the voting, a legal requirement. A judge speaking in the square compared Morsi with Caligula and Hitler.

The new alliance behind ElBaradei—calling itself the National Salvation Front—knew Morsi was unprotected. As demonstrations raged in Tahrir and the squares of other cities on the Friday after the Thanksgiving decree, Ahmed Said, a telecommunications mogul and anti-Islamist party leader, led a protest march to the presidential palace. The police and guards did nothing to stop him. His men scaled the palace walls and then strolled the grounds. No one lifted a finger.

"The army was not ready yet," Said told me later. "But the police were on our side. It was clear that the police and the army and the judiciary and all the institutions were not with Morsi. He had no control. His control was imaginary."

I had been requesting interviews at the Interior Ministry for two years.

I was always rejected. But when I called after the protests against Morsi started, a deputy interior minister invited me to his office.

It was a long, narrow room soaked in shadows. Closed blinds covered a row of picture windows. Clouds of cigarette smoke hovered in the air. I waited in silence through long pauses each time the deputy minister, Ahmed Helmy, took a drag.

I had asked for the meeting to discuss the suspicious death of an anti-Islamist demonstrator. Did Helmy have a response to the allegations that police killed him? Helmy seemed bored by the case. Before he would discuss it, he wanted to clarify "the lessons of the revolution," as seen through the eyes of the Egyptian police.

He solemnly admitted that the internal security forces had once protected Mubarak and punished his opponents. But those days were over. The police were now "away from politics," "independent," and working only for "the people." Most of all, he said, they did not work for Morsi.

Did I get that? The police did not work for Morsi, he said again, and he repeated it several ways.

I changed the subject. What were the ministry's ideas about police reform? That had been the signature goal of the Tahrir Square protests and it was a repeated promise from Morsi.

Helmy paused again to exhale. Did I mean geographic redeployments?

No, I said delicately. I was thinking of human rights.

More smoke. "Before I talk about human rights, I have to define, who is this human?" he told me. "Is it reasonable to ask me to be considerate of a citizen who has Molotov cocktails or a shotgun? And when I violate his rights, is it reasonable to accuse me of violating human rights?"

I see, I told him. In his view, it was not the police who needed reforming. It was the citizens. Some did not all deserve the rights of a human.

Khaled Amin, the police brigadier general, later told me that the younger officers felt "a lot of anger" toward Morsi. "The Muslim Brothers had been locked up before. The officers felt that they should not be in power."

Amin was stationed in the neighborhood near the palace that November. He said that by early that month, he had been starting to accept that Morsi was president. "I thought he was staying," Amin said. He started doing his job. But the Thanksgiving decree changed that. "He issued a lot of decrees and then went back on them. If he was really making these decisions, he would not reverse them so fast," he said. "That is when I decided Morsi was not in charge." He assumed that the Brotherhood's governing board was calling the shots.

Inside the palace, some of Morsi's advisers had urged him for months to move fast against the hostile institutions of the old regime like the Interior Ministry or the Supreme Constitutional Court. But others worried that he still did not have the clout. The first "second revolution" anti-Islamist demonstrators had started blocking roads outside the palace as early as August 24, and the police had repeatedly refused to disperse them. (A military spokesman would later tell my colleagues Mayy el-Sheikh and Kareem Fahim that Sisi, as defense minister, had also refused Morsi's requests to protect the palace.)

Morsi told advisers that the army and police would surely learn to accept "the new Egypt." But he could be darkly fatalistic. "Don't worry! Do you think this is the peak? No!" Morsi told his anxious advisers that December, grinning. "This is not the peak. The peak will be when you see my blood flowing on the floor."

Wael Haddara and other Morsi advisers met with Shater's staff in December to coordinate with the Brotherhood. But the meeting disintegrated into a shouting match. "It turned into one long venting session by Shater's people complaining that they were kept in the dark," Haddara later told me.

Shater's aides told me that he was becoming increasingly frustrated at Morsi's "stubbornness." The Brotherhood was forced to defend Morsi's unpopular decisions with its own money and manpower. He was cashing checks on the Brotherhood's bank account.

Voices all over the news media claimed Morsi was a puppet of Shater, but the tensions between them were an open secret in the political elite. "I had heard Shater was impatient with Morsi. I think everybody heard that," Said, the opposition party leader, later told me. Morsi was isolated even within the Brotherhood. But the Brothers were also his only reliable bastion of support. "That is who he can depend on," Haddara said at the time.

Essam el-Haddad returned from Washington on December 5, and the grounds of the presidential palace felt under siege. The drafting committee had released the new charter on November 30, and on December 4, virtually every privately owned newspaper in Egypt—eleven in all—had skipped publication for a day to protest its porous protections for freedom of expression. Even *Al Ahram* reported that sixty of its journalists were joining the protests (like the other Egyptian journalists, the staff of *Al Ahram* had discovered a new and short-lived passion for press freedom). The violence against the Brotherhood had continued, too. More than two dozen Brotherhood offices had been attacked or burned down.

The demonstrators around the palace were different from the mix in Tahrir Square. These looked like affluent urbanites, white-collar civil servants, and a large number of Coptic Christians. "This is not a revolt of the poor," Farid Beshay, a twenty-nine-year-old Copt, told me. "This is people coming to demand their rights."

"Shave your beard, show your disgrace, you will find that you have Mubarak's face!" they chanted.

One night they broke into a guardhouse, looted its contents, and sprayed the palace walls with anti-Morsi slogans. A favorite insult was to call the Muslim Brothers "sheep," brainwashed by their leaders. Some nights a Molotov cocktail might fly over the palace walls, and the guards inside extinguished the fire and let the protest continue. A Nasserite party provided tents and food for a sit-in, and some demonstrators spent nights there.

On December 5, the alliance around ElBaradei called for another "final warning" march on the palace, and Morsi's team turned in desperation back to the Muslim Brothers. Brotherhood media outlets rallied Islamists everywhere to defend the palace. "If state agencies are weak and still damaged by the wounds of the past, the people can impose their will," one Brotherhood leader exhorted. "Besiege those thugs! This is the opportunity to arrest them, and to reveal the third party which is behind the shooting of live ammunition and the killing of protesters."

Hard-line Salafis called it a holy war. One television sheikh, Safwat Hegazy, explicitly threatened Christians who protested against Morsi. "You're children of the homeland and partners in the homeland," he said, "but we will never let it go that sixty percent of those standing at Ittihadiya palace are *Nasara*"—Nazarenes, a derogatory term for Christians.

"May God insult them and quicken their destruction," another sheikh prayed on a Salafi television channel, and he claimed that the anti-Morsi demonstrators were drinking and fornicating in the tents outside the palace. "Grant victory to our religion and support to our president."

"The rule is well known," announced a third. "Their dead are in hell and our dead are in heaven."

Around 4:00 P.M., hundreds of young Islamists poured out of a nearby mosque and converged on the sit-in. "Strength, will, faith, Morsi's men are everywhere!" they chanted (it rhymes in Arabic), yanking up the tents and chasing away the few dozen demonstrators.

Mohamed Ismail, a twenty-eight-year-old coffee shop clerk, had been hanging around the tents. "They came from all sides and they punished us," he told me when I arrived moments later. "I got slapped on the face and the back of my head." (Others showed me video footage of the skirmish.)

Khaled Amin, the police general, had been stationed nearby. The Islamists "looked euphoric, high on their own power, like they were invincible," he later told me.

I slipped home for dinner, thinking the scuffle was over. But Morsi's opponents were rallying their troops. ElBaradei held a press conference to threaten a general strike. "We will not finish this battle for our freedom and dignity until we are victorious."

I was working with a versatile new interpreter—I will call him Ibrahim here. He was a Coptic Christian with a long beard. Islamists took him for one of their own; so did anti-Islamists when they saw the cross tattoo on his wrist.

After nightfall, Ibrahim called to tell me that thousands of Morsi's opponents were streaming back. We agreed to meet at the Roxy Cinema, a local landmark, but street fighting had closed off the roads. I got out of a taxi a few blocks away and tried to make my way among clusters of young men throwing rocks at one another. A tear gas canister landed at my feet. I joined a stampede, and when I got free of the gas I huddled with strangers by the fence around the Heliopolis Sporting Club.

A beefy, frat-boy-looking man with a crowbar crouched next to me and said he was with ElBaradei's Constitution Party. He shrugged at the fighting. "After a while, you kind of get to enjoy it."

When Ibrahim and I found each other, his Christian tattoo and Islamist beard enabled us to talk our way across the shifting battle lines. Both sides were using knives, clubs, chains, rocks, and Molotov cocktails. For the first time in Egypt, I heard gunfire from the ranks of civilians.

Gehad el-Haddad, Shater's aide, later said that a friend standing next to him had taken a bullet to the neck. He bled out so quickly that Gehad and other Muslim Brothers said his last prayer for him.

A thirty-three-year-old journalist, Al Husseini Abu Deif, plunged into battle against the Islamists. "To every true revolutionary, if you find yourself facing a Muslim Brother shooting bullets at you, or holding a knife saying you are an atheist, tell him God is great and the revolution is greater than your gang," he wrote that night on Twitter. "If I die there, I only ask you to continue the revolution!" He was shot and killed there.

Behind the Islamist lines, a boxy Lada cruised in circles with a loudspeaker roped to its roof. "This is not a fight for President Morsi," a staticky voice intoned. "We are fighting for God's law, against the secularists and liberals."

Squadrons of riot police fired tear gas in all directions but never held their ground. After about 9:30 P.M., the only police I saw seemed to be attempting to separate the combatants along the neighborhood's main commercial artery, El Khalifa el-Maamoun Street. The security forces were neither defending the palace nor dispersing the Islamists: they only added to the mayhem.

"The violence was unbelievable," Amin told me later. "We were ordered not to open fire. We set up blockades, and the protesters ran and gathered behind the police vans, or we set up blockades in front of them. But the Muslim Brothers thought we were on their side and we were protecting Morsi. They did not want to attack us." His twenty-three-year-old son was among the protesters fighting against Morsi and suffered a deep cut to his head.

I had seen plenty of clashes pitting protesters against police or paid thugs, and I knew about fights between Muslims and Christians; this was the first time I had ever seen so many ordinary Egyptians battle one another over politics. Dawoud, the ElBaradei spokesman, was horrified. "The Muslim Brotherhood in civilian clothes fighting against us in civilian clothes, and the central security—the people who used to beat me all the time—were standing by doing nothing! For the first time in my life I saw the seeds of civil war."

By dawn, the Islamists had captured, detained, and beaten dozens of their opponents, holding them in a small guardhouse that the police had abandoned. Yehia Negm, a forty-two-year-old former diplomat, was one of the prisoners. When I met him days later, bruises darkened both of his eyes and he had a bloody scab across the bridge of his nose. He pulled up a sleeve to show me red rope marks.

"They accused me of being a traitor, or conspiring against the country, of being paid to carry weapons and set fires," he told me. "I thought I would die."

Ola Shahba, a member of a socialist party, had worn a hood and a helmet to the fight, to hide her gender. She said her Islamist captors had groped her when they pulled off her hood and saw she was a woman. "What embassy do you meet in and receive money from?" her attackers demanded.

A Brotherhood official tried to persuade the Islamists to release her, but some were hard-liners from outside the movement. "If they were just Muslim Brotherhood, we would've gotten her out since the first moment," the official, Ahmed Sobei, said later.

"Did they beat people up? Yes, they did," he said. "Thugs infiltrated both sides. It was impossible to tell who was on which side."

The next morning, Islamists turned nearly 130 captives over to the district prosecutor, who—of course—immediately released them.

Hundreds had been injured in the fighting. At least eleven people died, mostly from gunshots. Aside from the journalist, all or almost all of the dead were Islamists, as far as I could tell. The Brotherhood insisted all the dead were Morsi supporters, and after great effort I was unable to confirm any non-Islamist deaths besides the journalist. Morsi's opponents were better armed. But no one was innocent.

The trauma of that night is hard to overstate. Westerners may expect chaos in the Middle East. But Egyptians think of themselves as citizens of the world's oldest nation, the cradle of civilization. Wild, amateur armies had stained the streets with the blood of their countrymen, in violence reminiscent of the last days of the monarchy. It felt like Syria, Libya, or Iraq, some failed state—not Egypt.

Walking away from the fighting, I met an Egyptian friend—Ahmed, a recent college graduate with an engineering degree and ambitions in solar energy. He said it reminded him of an American movie about the nineteenth-century slums of Manhattan—*"Gangs of New York."*

Morsi gave a televised address the next night and he invited all the non-Islamist factions to the palace on Saturday to negotiate a compromise. But he also claimed the detainees captured by the Islamists had, in fact, been thugs paid by a "fifth column" of Mubarak-era profiteers. They were passing out "black money," conspiring with foreign interests, and "giving out firearms." He sounded more than ever like a bearded Mubarak.

Morsi "closed the door to any dialogue," ElBaradei fired back on Twitter. Western diplomats often complained over the next months that Morsi refused to volunteer big concessions. But he made many invitations to negotiations and dialogue. The opposition always declined them.

Ibrahim and I met again the next day, Friday, December 7, near Al Azhar to join a funeral march for Islamists killed in the fighting. A parade of thousands snaked through the medieval city wailing, chanting, and seething. Ibrahim's beard fit right in. I felt safer having him with me.

Then an Islamist neighbor pointed him out to a friend. Moments later a tall man much bigger than either of us stepped out of nowhere, grabbed Ibrahim by the arm, and held up his wrist. The cross tattoo.

A small mob formed around us. They were sure Ibrahim was an infiltrator, a Christian spy. Why else would he disguise himself in a Salafi beard? Hands were all over him. A man slapped him hard on the ear. Ibrahim bent over in pain. I grabbed him and held up my press card.

Sahafi, sahafi—journalist, journalist—I said. The Islamists tried to pry me away. They meant me no harm, one of them told me. I was a guest in their country. Ibrahim was an Egyptian Copt. That was a different story.

Someone behind me lunged for Ibrahim, shoved into me, and knocked my eyeglasses off my face. They disappeared under the throng of marchers. I squinted and clutched at Ibrahim.

The mob parted for an older man with a graying beard and stern face. More trouble, I thought. The new authority figure took Ibrahim by an arm and pulled him through the crowd. I hung on to his other arm and bounced along behind like we were playing a game of Crack the Whip.

Trailed by a deferential posse, our captor dragged us past a chain-link fence into what appeared to be a schoolyard. The Islamists pulled up a pair of chairs and sat us down for an interrogation. We were journalists for the *New York Times*, I kept repeating, in English and Arabic. Ibrahim was murmuring in Arabic too fast and soft for me to follow, and a young man was using a mobile phone camera to film our interrogation. Was he hoping to record a confession? His video of my babbling, broken Arabic would turn up on the website of an anti-Islamist newspaper, *Youm el-Saba—7 Days*. The cameraman was the real spy.

The big man in charge grabbed Ibrahem and me by our elbows and we were on the move again. This time he found an Egyptian police officer and turned us both in. Moments later all three of us—Ibrahim, our Islamist captor, and I—were up several flights of stairs in the office of the chief of the local police precinct.

He had no interest in Ibrahim, but was *I* a spy? The chief peered intently at my Egyptian press card.

I breathed a sigh of relief. This happened all the time. Another policeman had taken my iPhone on the way in and, with typical professionalism, asked me if he could play games on it. So I borrowed back my phone and called the Egyptian government's foreign media director. I knew he would vouch for me. I emailed colleagues, and they notified the American embassy. Meanwhile, the police chief, in classic Egyptian fashion, served tea and made small talk. The Islamist, Ibrahim, and I shared a couch, sitting side by side.

I wanted to make sure that the umbrella of the *New York Times* would shelter Ibrahim, too. I went on and on about how he was working for us, what an excellent interpreter he was, what a valued part of our team he was. I repeated the words "the *New York Times*" as often I could. I barely knew Ibrahim, but I tried through my warm tone to imply that he had worked with us for years.

That is when Ibrahim whispered in my ear. "Save yourself and get out," he told me furtively. "I have a gun in my pocket."

Maybe he packed it after the bloodshed of the previous night. Maybe he had had it then, too. Either way, if the police found the illegal and unregistered handgun in his jacket pocket, we were both going to jail.

I grinned. I sipped my tea. I chatted about the weather. I pretended that there was no place in the world I would rather be right then than in the office of this police chief. He spouted the customary nonsense about the pluralistic tolerance of the "real Egypt," where Muslims and Christians always lived in harmony and never felt strife. And after a few hours, we all shook hands as friends. Thank God the Islamists had never searched us. The police—again, with their customary professionalism—never searched us either.

On our way down the stairs, our Islamist captor was feeling the spirit of the tolerant "real Egypt," too. He stopped to tell us that the building housing the police station had belonged to the Muslim Brotherhood in the days of its founder, Hassan el-Banna. Ibrahim and the Islamist exchanged phone numbers and promised to stay in touch. I squinted home without my glasses.

Attacked by an Islamist mob: this was what worried my mother when I moved to Cairo. But the paranoia of the Islamists no longer seemed so irrational. Ibrahim had been the one with a gun.

I could see why an Egyptian Copt might want to arm himself. But the Islamists turned out to be right to suspect a bearded Christian. Without the protection of the law, each of us falls back on the protection of his tribe.

17

Murder, Rape, Christians, and Spies

December 8, 2012–March 9, 2013

On January 26, 2013, two years and a day after the start of the uprising, hundreds of men, women, and children huddled around car stereos and transistor radios outside the main prison in the city of Port Said, at the Mediterranean end of the Suez Canal. Twenty-one local soccer fans, some of them inside the prison, stood charged with murder in the deaths of seventy-four people killed in a stadium riot a year earlier, on February 1, 2012, under the rule of the generals. The families of the accused had gathered to hear the verdict from a judge in Cairo.

The riot had been among the deadliest in the history of soccer. Ultras backing rival teams from Port Said and Cairo had smuggled knives, clubs, and fireworks into the stadium. Some victims were stabbed to death. Others fell from balconies. More were crushed in a stampede for the exits. In all, at least five hundred had been injured.

Outside the prison, a hush fell over the crowd. Then a whisper moved through it. "Execution." The judge, without explanation, had convicted and sentenced to death all twenty-one men.

Cell-phone videos of the next moment show a whiz of bullets. Someone in the crowd shot a guard outside the prison, and the police opened fire. Within a few hours, the police had killed at least twenty-one civilians. Someone had shot another deputy policeman. Violence engulfed the city. Hundreds of others were wounded. The hospitals were overwhelmed. Doctors were calling television and radio stations to plead for help from anyone with medical

training. Rioters started attacking television cameras, and the live broad-
casts ended.

Mayy el-Sheikh had grown up in Port Said. Her family there said the
police had fled the streets, falling back into besieged stations and prisons.
A police barracks was burning.

By 8:00 P.M., the Interior Ministry had declared, uncharacteristically,
that this time there could be no "security solution" to the Port Said chaos.
The army deployed troops to secure the canal and seaport. Egypt's third
largest city, with a population of about seven hundred thousand, had spun
out of government control.

When Mayy and I arrived the next morning, tens of thousands were
chanting for Port Said to secede from Egypt. An endless procession of
mourners carried over their heads two-dozen-odd coffins—the bodies of
those killed by the police. Chanting and wailing, the marchers snaked
along the Mediterranean toward the city's main cemetery, until the parade
passed the walls of the Grand Sky Resort—a beachfront club exclusively
for police officers.

Maybe a rock was thrown, maybe a taunt was shouted. However it
started, the police in guard towers began firing tear gas everywhere. Coffins dropped to the ground. The bodies of dead "martyrs" sprawled on the
sidewalk. I saw an angry mourner pull out a handgun, and we heard the
crackle of gunfire from automatic weapons. Police gunmen were crouching
and scurrying along the resort roof. Smoke rose from inside.

We pulled back toward the relative safety of the seaside cemetery,
caught our breath, and crept back to try to assess the damage. At about
4:00 P.M., we saw a row of policemen standing side by side on the pavement, firing straight ahead of them. That was enough. We fled for our lives.

When we reached our hotel, a spokesman for the Interior Ministry was
on television declaring that not a single policeman in the city had carried a
loaded weapon. "Infiltrating saboteurs" were the only ones shooting.
Among the police, "there is only a small group pushing back against in-
tense shooting." Even the tear gas, he insisted, had come from civilians.

Morsi declared a state of emergency with a curfew in Port Said and in
the neighboring canal cities. The rioting was "the ugly face of the

counterrevolution," he said, and then, to my astonishment, he thanked the police "for the great efforts they have exerted."

"I sent my orders to the Ministry of Interior's men, very clearly," he said. I could not figure out if he was trying to win them over, or if he was afraid to admit his lack of control.

General Sisi the next day warned for the first time against what he called a possible "collapse of the state." But he promised the military "will remain the hard, solid mass and the backbone" underneath that state.

When we left the next day, some stores were opening, carefully, but no representative of the central government dared show a face in the city. The state had pulled out of Port Said.

Cairo, too, felt increasingly lawless. That January, the *Times* had flown in a former commando with paramedic experience to train several of us in first aid for combat zones. He went for an evening walk by the Nile near our office, and two luckless thieves tried to mug him.

"One grabbed me and the other stabbed me with what could only be described as a sharpening steel," the trainer wrote to me in an email the next day. "I disarmed him after being stabbed and gave him his weapon back (straight into the upper shoulder). The other one I still had hold of and subsequently dislocated his left arm. Not much to tell really. . . . Oh, by the way, the police said 'they'll look into it.' LOL."

On January 25, 2013, Hania Moheeb, a forty-two-year-old Egyptian journalist, joined tens of thousands of revelers packed into Tahrir Square to celebrate the uprising's second anniversary. Not a policeman was in sight, of course, and some in the crowd saw a predatory opportunity. A gang of men cornered Moheeb, stripped off her clothes, and raped her for three quarters of an hour. Some of them shouted that they were coming to her rescue while they attacked her—"I'll help you! I'll help you!"

"My two hands were not enough to fight them all off," she later said.

At least eighteen women were sexually assaulted in the square that day, according to the most conservative tally verified by independent rights groups. The government's National Council of Women—still headed by Suzanne Mubarak's friend Mervat Tallawy—put the number much higher. Six women were hospitalized. One was stabbed in the genitals. Another was given a hysterectomy as part of her treatment (I cannot judge the medical necessity).

The police, under Mubarak, had almost never allowed a crowd to gather in public (except at houses of worship or soccer stadiums), and a combination of shame and censorship kept reports of rape out of the news. Now street demonstrations were a staple of public life. Men and women mixed in tight crowds, and the absence of the police invited aggression. But that was not all that had changed. An era of silence had broken. The collapse of the old authorities had given women like Hania Moheeb the courage and ability to speak out, with access to the recently free news media. Their accounts riveted the attention of the world on the scale of the crisis.

After Moheeb spoke out, Yasmine el-Baramawy came forward to describe her rape near Tahrir Square the previous November. A gang of men had separated her from a friend, used knives to cut off most of her clothes, and then pinned her half naked to the hood of a car like a trophy, for a slow, hour-long drive to another neighborhood.

Now, three months later, whenever she saw the corner where she was attacked, "my hand automatically grabs my pants," she said in a television interview. The *New York Times* stopped sending female journalists into Tahrir demonstrations, even accompanied by male colleagues.

Morsi condemned the attacks and defended the rights of women to join public events. Faulting the women in any way was "completely unacceptable," said Pakinam el-Sharkawy, Morsi's top political adviser and the highest-ranking woman in his administration.

But his opponents tried to pin the violence on Islamists, and prominent Islamists blamed the female victims. "Sometimes, a girl contributes one hundred percent to her own rape when she puts herself in these conditions," said Adel Abdel Maqsoud Afifi, a Salafi lawmaker in the almost powerless upper house of Parliament (he had been a police general under Mubarak before coming out as a Salafi).

"How do they ask the Ministry of Interior to protect a woman when she stands among men?" asked Reda Saleh al-Hefnawi, a Brotherhood lawmaker.

Sheikh Ahmed Abdullah, a Salafi television preacher also known as Sheikh Abu Islam, said it was the victims who were the monsters. "You see those women speaking like ogres, without shame, politeness, fear, or even femininity," he said. Such a woman was "like a demon," he said, who had gone to the square "naked" deliberately, "to get raped."

I came to suspect that the intelligence agencies were capitalizing on the chaos to move against the Muslim Brothers. One day a march of demonstrators against Morsi was snaking through the gauntlet of unlicensed peddlers along Talaat Harb Street—without police, the proliferation of peddlers had almost choked off the traffic—when I got a message about an attack on the nearby office of the Brotherhood's website, Ikhwan Online.

The doorman and a bystander told me a group of men in face masks had rushed through the front door, up several flights of stairs, and straight into the empty office. Someone had tried to break in a few days earlier with a firebomb. It had failed to break a metal door gate but left dark flame marks on the bars. This time the attackers returned with a vial of acid to pour into the padlock. That burned it open.

"They said, 'We are here to destroy this place,'" Ragab Abdel Hamid, a thirty-six-year-old printer for a liberal nonprofit in the same building, said. He had watched the attack. "It was planned."

Desks and chairs were upended. The floor was littered with broken glass and smashed computer screens. The television sets and other valuables were still there, but the attackers had scooped up all the computer hard drives. I could not prove they were *mukhabarat*, but they were unusual burglars.

Other clues about the role of the intelligence agencies became public only later. El Sayyid el-Badawi was a pharmaceuticals mogul with a private satellite television network who had run the largest of the several pseudo-opposition parties in Mubarak's rubber-stamp Parliament. He was recorded on a telephone call in early 2012 with someone who sounded like a senior intelligence official (based on his tone, his knowledge, and Badawi's deference). Badawi explained that he hoped to win the backing of the Muslim Brothers for a presidential run.

"Oh, Sayyid," the gravelly voice of the intelligence officer told him, "the upcoming period will be a dark one for the Brotherhood. . . . Armed militias will slaughter them in their own houses. Egypt will be full of orchestrated 'terrorism' to retaliate against the Brotherhood and seek revenge for the revolution that brought down the security apparatus." The recording leaked out too late to make a difference except to history, but he was promising a campaign of violence orchestrated by the intelligence services against the Muslim Brothers.

The National Salvation Front, the anti-Islamist alliance behind ElBaradei, often met in the headquarters of Badawi's political party, and members of the alliance later told me that they knew by early 2013 that the intelligence agencies were working covertly to bring Morsi down.

"We are not alone," businessmen and party leaders like Badawi would say at the meetings, using familiar Egyptian euphemisms for the *mukhabarat*. "The state institutions are with us."

"You would get people in the meetings who knew what the security agencies wanted, what the security agencies were pushing," Khaled Dawoud, the journalist acting as spokesman for the group, later said. "We were the nice civilian faces," but the spy agencies were "doing things to lay the groundwork."

Police officials refused to provide special protection for Brotherhood offices, explaining that they could not protect all political parties—although, of course, the Brotherhood was the only faction under assault. The spree of attacks on its offices around the country had continued unabated since November. The burglary at the website's office in Cairo took place on the second anniversary of the uprising, January 25, 2013, the same day other attackers burned or ransacked Brotherhood offices in Suez and Ismailia. In Suez, anti-Morsi protesters set fire to the government headquarters for the province. Seven civilians and two policemen were killed in fighting outside the building.

Brotherhood leaders looked pathetic. One night a rabble of the anti-Islamist protesters broke into the Brotherhood's main headquarters, and by the time I got there, small bonfires made from the books and papers of the Brotherhood's top leaders were burning in the streets.

"Be angry with us as you like, hate us as you like, but we're telling you to be reasonable," the Brotherhood's general guide, Mohamed Badie, pleaded in a press conference the next day. "Protect Egypt. The unity of Egypt cannot withstand what is happening now."

The intruders had ruined even his houseplants. "What did the plants ever do to be torn and cut apart?" he asked. He shook his head at the conspiracy theories about his power over the presidential palace. "Is this a man who's ruling Egypt, a man who can't protect his own office?"

Tensions flared between Muslims and Christians, too. Someone in the town of Khossous, just north of Cairo, painted a red swastika on the wall of a Muslim institute. Or maybe Muslim and Christian families had squabbled at a children's soccer match. The explanations varied. But on the afternoon of Friday, April 5, the town erupted in violence. The police arrived more than two hours late and did little to stop it. Four Christians and a Muslim were killed in the fighting.

Mubarak had always insisted that sectarian animus was alien to Egypt, blaming shadowy third parties for any such strife. Morsi at least acknowledged the problem. In the summer of 2012, clashes had broken out in Dahshur, about twenty-five miles south of Cairo, over the burning of a Muslim's shirt in a Christian-owned laundry. A mob of Muslims drove the Christian families from the town. Morsi sent his legal adviser to meet with the Christian families, directed the public prosecutor to investigate without bias, and ordered cash compensation to the Christian families affected. Almost all returned home.

The climate, nonetheless, had grown steadily more hostile to Christians since Mubarak's ouster. It went without saying that the dominant political party, sponsored by the Brotherhood, included only token Christians. Hardline Salafi satellite networks unleashed a torrent of anti-Christian rhetoric. In the polarized aftermath of Morsi's Thanksgiving decree, Islamists tarred their political foes as Christian "crusaders." The number of lawsuits accusing Christians of insulting Islam—a crime since before Mubarak—rose from three in 2011 to twelve in 2012 and thirteen in 2013. They were almost always initiated by complaints from individuals who might not have dared draw attention under Mubarak; their claims usually ended in dismissal, but only after legal ordeals for the defendants.

But some patterns were counterintuitive. The rate of anti-Christian violence—sectarian attacks on Christians, churches, or Christian-owned properties, whether by civilians or security forces—had declined under Morsi compared with the preceding eighteen months under military rule. "If you compare the number or scale of the attacks, for sure it was worse under the military council than it was under Morsi," Ishak Ibrahim, a researcher for the Egyptian Initiative for Personal Rights who tracked the incidents, told me.

The difference favored Morsi even more starkly if the tally included the massacre of two dozen Christians by soldiers outside the Maspero building—the deadliest episode of sectarian bloodshed anyone could remember. But the symbolism of the violence that followed the killing of the four Christians at Khossous, on April 5, overshadowed Maspero.

A funeral was held two days later, on Sunday afternoon, at the Cathedral of St. Mark in Abbasiya—the Coptic analog to the Basilica of St. Peter in Rome. Mourners walked out of the Mass chanting, "With our blood and our souls we will sacrifice for the cross."

A gang of men—apparently from the neighborhood—ambushed the procession, pelting the Christians with rocks and sticks. My colleague Kareem Fahim had attended the funeral and called me from the sanctuary. The mourners had retreated inside. The cathedral had come under siege.

When I arrived, I found the riot police, in black body armor, standing shoulder to shoulder with the civilian attackers. The officers were firing tear gas and birdshot *toward* the cathedral while the civilians standing with them flung rocks and Molotov cocktails in the same direction. Some made obscene hand gestures involving the sign of the cross.

Dozens of Christians were streaming in to defend the cathedral, pulling up their sleeves at the doorway to show cross tattoos on their wrists. Canisters of tear gas landed in the pews. Noxious fumes clouded the stained glass.

Young men on the rooftops returned fire with shards of brick or gas bombs. Kareem saw at least two of the Christians fire homemade handguns. At least two more Christians were killed in the fighting.

Yet the Interior Ministry blamed the Christians for all of it. "Some mourners vandalized a number of cars, which led to clashes and fights with the people of the area," the ministry said in a statement released during the fighting. The police were "separating the clashing parties."

Years later, I asked a Christian organizer who worked at the time with the anti-Morsi National Salvation Front if the Interior Ministry had ever helped their cause.

"Attacking the Coptic Cathedral was very helpful!" the organizer said. It was not that anyone in the ministry had orchestrated the initial attack or directed the police to join it; the locals and riot police were capable of that on their own. But Christians saw a clear warning, the organizer explained. "See what is going to happen if the minister of interior is aligned with the Muslim Brotherhood?"

Darkness had fallen by the time Morsi spoke. "I consider any aggression against the cathedral an aggression against me personally," he said. He called Pope Tawadros II and ordered an investigation.

The pope blamed Morsi. "Sentiments" from the president "are not at all enough," the pope said in a television interview two days later. "This inaction is humiliating for Egypt and for the image of the state."

The warm months in Cairo were just beginning. Peak summer air-conditioning season had brought occasional electricity blackouts every year since I had arrived. The lights were usually back on in less than an hour, at least in our affluent neighborhood. But in April 2013, the blackouts were getting worse by the week. The electricity went out several times a day, eventually for hours at a stretch, even in Maadi. Our sons did their homework by flashlight. We used iPhones to play the boys audiobooks in the dark as bedtime stories. I idled the car, plugged a laptop into the cigarette lighter, and filed articles from the passenger seat late into the night. We finally installed an industrial battery to keep a few lights on.

Fuel, though, was becoming an even bigger problem. Gas lines stretched for miles and clogged city squares. (The military owns its own commercial gas stations, which were always the last to run dry.) The *New York Times* authorized us to buy our own generator, like the bureaus in Baghdad and other war zones. But I wondered how we would obtain fuel to run it. Poor neighborhoods, of course, had it far worse.

Tourism, a critical source of hard currency, had collapsed with Mubarak's ouster. The central bank's reserves had fallen by half since 2010. The Egyptian pound dropped to almost seven pounds to the dollar that spring, down from about five in 2010. Inflation and unemployment were rising fast. Western diplomats worried privately about the wheat imports needed to provide the subsidized flatbread that sustained at least sixteen million families.

Newspapers reported (inaccurately) that Morsi planned to ration the bread. Dozens of bakers demonstrated downtown and blocked the traffic. The last time Egypt had cut bread subsidies was in 1977, under Sadat. Riots brought his government to its knees.

When I called, a new spokesman for the Ministry of Supply—a Muslim Brother named Naser el-Farash—invited me to his office in a Soviet-looking concrete pile not far from the Parliament. He said the government was rolling out a system of computerized "smart cards" to track the distribution of fuel and flour in order to cut down on black-market sales. The bakers were protesting because they were accustomed to reselling subsidized flour at a markup. "The bakers want to continue the old system because it is better for them, but it is illegal," he said.

The fuel shortage, though, was a quandary. Egypt was importing just as much fuel as it had in 2010 and the economy had hardly grown. So why such shortages? Farash claimed that scared farmers were filling their barns with hoarded fuel. "Did you hear about the donkey who drank diesel and died?" Those who say Egypt cannot afford enough fuel are "trying to make problems for Dr. Morsi," he insisted. "They are against the revolution."

I had seen tanker trucks pull off on the highway and sell their diesel before it ever reached a gas station. But I doubted that profiteering and paranoia could explain the crisis. The buck stopped with Morsi, I thought at the time.

The demonstrations against him continued all spring. Protesters and police were still tearing up city streets for bricks to throw at one another. Rights advocates complained that reports of police abuse and the deaths of prisoners in custody had resumed. Many of the street demonstrators told me the bad behavior of police was their main gripe with Morsi. Why did the police still attack demonstrations? Why did they fail to protect women or Christians, or to do something about the alleged corruption sapping fuel and flour supplies? And why had Morsi so publicly embraced the police unless he was in league with them?

"They are trying to build a new regime exactly like the old one, with all its disadvantages," Mohamed Mokbel, a thirty-year-old art student and veteran protester, told me that spring, sipping Turkish coffee in an arty café under an awning in an alley downtown.

"Police attacking protesters is what causes the chaos," he said, reminding me that riot police had the advantage of armor, helmets, and shields. "Even from the Molotov cocktails, not a single police officer has died. We do not want to burn down a place that we will end up paying to rebuild."

His mobile phone buzzed. Twitter reported another clash with police had broken out near the presidential palace. When we got out of a taxi there together, he pulled from his backpack a pair of charred fireproof gloves, a gas mask, and a thick, hooded sweatshirt. Hundreds of demonstrators were fleeing toward us ahead of an advancing pair of armored police vehicles. Mokbel ran against the fleeing crowds and straight toward the oncoming APCs. He grabbed the smoking canisters of tear gas and hurled them back into the ranks of the police. Throwing back tear gas was his vocation now, and he kept at it for hours. Whatever the intentions of the police, their thuggish but ineffectual tactics kept the protests at a simmer.

Another court ruling in the case of the Port Said soccer riot was set for March 9, and this time, an army general had arrived a day before the verdict. A cheering crowd urged the general to take over. "What are you waiting for, sir?" several shouted.

Handmade banners welcomed the army, and the soldiers hung their own, distancing themselves from the police. THE ARMED FORCES SHARE THE GRIEF OF THE PEOPLE FOR THE MARTYRS OF PORT SAID one read. The generals of the military council seemed to stand farther from the police than Morsi did.

The general in Port Said, Ahmed Wasfi, set civilian volunteers to work on a cleanup. "I want Port Said to look as beautiful as a bride tonight," he said to applause. "Shops must not close. People and weddings must come back. The normal work must return. People must see what Port Said is."

Mayy and I returned to Port Said in time for the March 9 ruling in the riot case, and the same Cairo court confirmed the original death penalties, sentencing two dozen others to jail. But this time the police had fled in advance, slipping off their uniforms and abandoning their stations. We found only a single policeman, Lieutenant Mohamed Gamal, hiding in civilian clothes inside his empty station.

"We are tired of confronting the people," he told us.

Soldiers watched passively as rioters burned tires near the empty port, and then, to my amazement, civilians linked hands to protect the soldiers from angry citizens. "The army and the people are one hand," they chanted.

"We are asking for a coup d'état!" one woman, Fatma el-Nabawy, a forty-year-old homemaker, told us. Others around her nodded.

"Military rule was bad, but they would be better," fifty-year-old Ahmed Abdel Fattah agreed. "Where is the state? Where is the Interior Ministry, the government?" He added, "The military should take over until the police are ready."

In Port Said, a military coup had already happened.

18

The View from the West

March 12, 2013–April 24, 2013

Not long after Morsi's inauguration, in the summer of 2012, Ambassador Yousef al-Otaiba of the United Arab Emirates met Ben Rhodes over lunch at Founding Farmers, a trendy restaurant not far from the State Department.

Otaiba was the son of a rich and well-connected businessman who served as the first oil minister of the United Arab Emirates. His father had four wives and numerous children, and Yousef's mother was an Egyptian who had raised him in Cairo. He was born in Egypt. He married an Egyptian. He often said that he understood Egyptians in a way that Americans or Europeans never could.

Otaiba looked and sounded American. He had attended the American high school in Egypt, in Maadi, and while there he attracted the mentorship of then U.S. ambassador to Egypt, Frank Wisner. Wisner encouraged Otaiba on to Georgetown. The UAE later sent him back to the National Defense University. Then he received further tutoring in the ways of Washington from Steven Simon of Obama's National Security Council staff; Simon had worked for a consulting company training Emirati officials during a break in his government service.

At thirty-eight, Otaiba shaved his beard and his head, worked out every day at the gym, and favored impeccable suits (although he sometimes pulled out a white *thobe* to look Emirati). He lived in a mansion on the Virginia banks of the Potomac, hired Wolfgang Puck to cook for his dinner parties, and maintained a legendary wine collection. "Bro-taiba," many in Washington called him, for his one-of-the-boys style.

Among foreign ambassadors in Washington, his connections were almost unrivaled. General Mattis would later call Otaiba "a friend and tremendous ally through some very difficult times." Michael Morrell, the acting CIA director, was close enough to Otaiba to casually stop by his mansion for a glass of wine from time to time. Richard Burr, the Republican chair of the Senate Intelligence Committee, once told the *Huffington Post*, "I've spent probably more time with Yousef than I have anybody."

Otaiba pushed the UAE's spending on Washington lobbying higher than any other country's, to as much as $14 million a year. He donated to think tanks like the Center for Strategic and International Studies and the Middle East Institute. He advertised heavily in influential venues like *Foreign Policy* magazine or *Politico* newsletters. He splashed money around high-profile charities, including giving $150 million for a pediatric surgery wing at the Children's National Medical Center in Washington and $3 million to the Clinton Foundation. A party he hosted for a New York cancer institute featured performances by Beyoncé, Alicia Keys, and Ludacris.

It was an open secret in Washington that an anonymous "Arab source" or "Arab diplomat" in a newspaper or magazine was almost always Otaiba (although he never agreed to speak to me). He and his Saudi counterpart, Ambassador Adel al-Jubeir—another suave and generous man-about-town—were singular fixtures in Washington who transcended the roles of mere envoys. "Adel was always one of my best advisers," General Mattis once said. And Otaiba, in particular, was one of the few foreign ambassadors invited to confidential meetings deep inside the Pentagon to discuss strategy in the region.

Ben Rhodes marveled at their effectiveness. "Youssef and Adel have gained this status in Washington where they aren't seen as representatives of foreign governments; they are seen as advisers on Middle East issues," he later told me. "They have a style that is very disarming, like they are telling you something you really need to know, for your own benefit."

Otaiba may have been the most energetic opponent in Washington of Morsi and the Muslim Brotherhood. The UAE and Saudi Arabia had fiercely opposed both the Arab Spring uprisings and the Muslim Brotherhood. The movement had adherents in both countries, and its idea that Islam could require elections was a unique threat to the Persian Gulf monarchies. With the help of Jubeir, Otaiba was pushing the line that the United States had betrayed its allies by forcing out Mubarak.

Otaiba argued to Rhodes that the Muslim Brotherhood was inherently antidemocratic, no matter what its leaders said and no matter how many elections they won. Its pan-Islamic ideology left no room for nation-states or borders. It posed an existential threat to the UAE and every other American ally in the region. Its rejection should be the bedrock of Washington's policy toward Egypt. You don't know these people, he insisted.

Maybe, Rhodes told him. But Egyptian voters could elect a new Parliament and throw out Morsi and the Muslim Brothers at the end of his term.

"I don't think they will even last that long," Otaiba predicted.

By April 2013, the Emirati-based satellite network Sky News Arabia, Saudi Arabia's Al Arabiya, and other Emirati-linked Egyptian media were all railing against a supposed American plot to bring the Brotherhood to power, with Ambassador Patterson as its ringleader. The Gulf-based satellite networks were full of accusations that she was a Brotherhood "lackey," "an old hag," or "an ogre." They claimed that she had pressured the Egyptian government to rig the election for Morsi and then pushed its institutions to bow down before him—all in the service of the larger American plot to weaken Egypt. It was a conspiracy to benefit Israel, of course.

"They essentially ran a plan to denigrate any nonmilitary Egyptian government, denigrate our ambassador, and denigrate our policy," Rhodes told me later. "Allies of the United States funded a denigration campaign against the United States ambassador in a country that is one of the largest recipients of U.S. assistance, to overturn the democratically elected government of that country. It was extraordinary, really. . . . Constant, incessant, and effective."

Patterson knew Morsi was politically inept, awkward in meetings, hopeless as an orator, and ill equipped for power. But, like Obama, she saw an elected president (Morsi) as the best chance for long-term stability: a more responsive government based on the nonviolent rotation of power. In a meeting at the presidential palace in March, Patterson warned two of

Morsi's foreign policy advisers that Mohammed bin Zayed of the Emirates—MBZ—was spearheading a campaign to lobby for a military takeover to remove Morsi. "But that is an era that has passed," she told them. Senior American diplomats in Cairo told Western journalists in a background briefing the same month, March, that a military intervention was "extraordinarily unlikely."

The continual conversations between Egyptian and American military officers, though, were fast becoming mutual "bitch sessions" about the Morsi government, as several of the Americans involved later told me.

General Mattis of Central Command—who still believed that the Brotherhood and Al Qaeda were "swimming in the same sea"—had flown to Cairo in February to meet with Sisi and underscore Washington's commitment to the Egyptian military alliance.

Mattis later explained his view of the crisis in Egypt in the spring of 2013 to an audience of journalists, intellectuals, and policy makers in Aspen, Colorado: "What happened was Morsi."

Morsi had fomented "divisiveness," Mattis said, and he claimed, incorrectly, that the 2012 constitution that Morsi backed had been "rejected immediately by over sixty percent of the people. [In fact, about two thirds of the voters had approved it.] We have a people there who are not very patient with imperious leadership. . . . The Muslim Brotherhood made their own problems."

General Michael Flynn was the director of the U.S. Defense Intelligence Agency that spring, and he was as outspoken as Mattis about his conviction that the Brotherhood was, in effect, Al Qaeda. (Obama later fired Flynn over his management of the agency, and he earned notoriety in a brief tenure as national security adviser to President Donald J. Trump, alongside Mattis as secretary of defense.) "It is all the same ideology," Flynn told me when I met him in 2016.

Flynn had publicly called Islam "a cancer" and "a political ideology" rather than a religion. The only ornament in his Arlington, Virginia, office in mid-2016 was a foot-high wooden cross on his desk that looked useful for fighting vampires, and he warned me gravely that Muslim Brothers had infiltrated Washington. Both President Obama and Ambassador Patterson, he suggested to me, were dangerously close to the Islamists.

"I would ask the leader of the Muslim Brotherhood today—whoever that person is and wherever that person is—why don't you disavow the Islamic State and these attacks? And if they do disavow these radical ideas, where are they and why aren't they saying it?"

I was stunned at his misinformation. For all its faults, the Muslim Brotherhood had consistently and loudly condemned terrorist violence for decades; Al Qaeda and the Islamic State never tired of excoriating the Brotherhood for the naïvete of its faith in elections.

Flynn had been an intelligence officer in Central Command and worked closely with General Sisi. "I had an excellent relationship with Sisi," Flynn said. "I found Sisi to be, one, a very good guy; two, a strong leader; and three, very secular, if you will."

By 2013, Flynn was also bonding with Sisi's successor as chief of military intelligence, General Mahmoud Hegazy (the one who was related to Sisi through the marriage of their children). Hegazy "was a tough guy, another secular-type Muslim, very effective," Flynn said. He talked at least once a week with Egypt's military attaché in Washington, General Mohamed el-Keshky, who was close to both Sisi and Hegazy (I later knew Keshky as assistant minister of defense in Cairo, where he once half-jokingly threatened to have me and Mayy arrested for our reporting).

When Flynn returned to Cairo that spring, the Egyptian generals welcomed him as an old friend, organizing a "cultural day" for him to visit the Pyramids. At lunch, Flynn and his Egyptian counterpart scrawled out a map of the Islamist threats they saw around Egypt.

Flynn told me that he had foreseen only trouble from Morsi. "I thought that what we were going to see was a takeover of the country by the Muslim Brotherhood," creating "a radical Islamic state in Egypt." He said that he had left his meeting with the Egyptian generals convinced that the Muslim Brotherhood was taking over the Interior Ministry. After that, "in a country like Egypt, it is very hard to get them out, because then they have their hands in every part of the government."

All this was a fantasy, of course. But what did Flynn advise the Egyptian generals to do about the problem of Mohamed Morsi?

Flynn sidestepped, saying only that he had sought information. "Was the Muslim Brotherhood going to last? Were they consolidating? What other things were they doing in other facets of their government? What was the military doing? How was the military responding?"

I asked again what he advised them. "I have to be cautious here," Flynn said, more slowly. "I will just say that tensions existed."

The splits within the American government were becoming obvious to diplomats and soldiers around the region. Obama and part of the White House hoped Morsi would succeed; many in the Pentagon, like Mattis and Flynn, agreed with their Egyptian and Emirati counterparts that Morsi was a danger. The American schizophrenia was so open that Egyptian generals complained about it to their Pentagon contacts.

"It was very clear to the Egyptians that we had a divided policy and we would hear it from them," Matt Spence, then deputy assistant secretary of defense for Middle East policy, later told me. "We were hearing from our Egyptian interlocutors that they were frustrated with the White House and the State Department, and the Egyptians would call them out by name."

But he was stunned when I told him that Flynn had also been visiting Cairo and meeting with the generals. "There were a lot of actors and agencies in the U.S. government talking to the Egyptians in ways we were not even aware of," Spence said, shaking his head.

John Kerry arrived in Cairo for his first visit as secretary of state on March 2, at what appears to have been a turning point.

Kerry prided himself on friendships around the Middle East that he had built up over his years in the Senate. In Egypt, he was especially close with ElBaradei, often visiting his house in Giza, and with Amr Moussa, the former foreign minister and presidential candidate who had also become a leader of the alliance against Morsi. And the new secretary of state had socialized for years with the diplomats and princes of the Persian Gulf monarchies, including Ambassador Otaiba and Crown Prince Mohammed bin Zayed. "I am friends with the whole gang," Kerry told me later in a conversation in the parlor of his Beacon Hill mansion in Boston. "I like my relationship with them and I think they are very smart."

Kerry had come to Cairo to push Morsi toward economic reforms like cutting back food and fuel subsidies and reducing the bloated public pay-roll. (One reason for the shortages, hoarding, and black market in fuel was that the government subsidized the official price so heavily that I could fill up our SUV for less than twelve dollars, while nine out of ten Egyptians could not afford a car.) The cuts were all part of a proposed deal for a badly needed $4.8 billion loan from the International Monetary Fund.

Slashing jobs and subsidies looked to Morsi like political suicide, with so much unrest in the streets and no Parliament to share responsibility. After Mubarak's ouster, the Muslim Brotherhood had hired the prize-winning Peruvian economist Hernando de Soto as a consultant, and he had told the Brothers that Egypt could grow by regularizing more of its vast off-the-books informal economy. But Kerry could not understand why Morsi kept talking about Egypt's "two economies" as if he did not grasp the severity of the problems.

"He is the dumbest cluck I ever met," Kerry told his chief of staff as they left Morsi's office. "This isn't going to work. These guys are wacko."

Morsi and the Brotherhood had "started to strip away the veneer of democracy," Kerry told me later, mentioning Morsi's Thanksgiving decree. "That is where we just said, 'This stinks, these guys aren't doing anything constructive and ultimately they are going to be antidemocratic.'"

Morsi, for his part, was put off that Kerry wanted him to meet with his friend Tim Collins, a billionaire who ran the private equity firm Ripple-wood Holdings and did extensive business with the Emiratis. Kerry sug-gested that Collins could give economic advice and bring in investments. Morsi thought that sounded like Mubarak-style crony capitalism. He had a foreign policy adviser take the meeting.

Then Kerry met separately, one on one, with General Sisi. He sounded deeply worried.

"I will not let my country go down the drain," Sisi told Kerry.

"What do you mean?" Kerry asked.

"Just take my word," Sisi replied.

"This is a dangerous time," Kerry told Sisi, without pressing further.

He knew then that "Morsi was cooked," as Kerry later told me: Sisi was prepared to intervene. And Kerry felt partly relieved.

"It was reassuring that Egypt would not fall into a civil war or a complete massacre of the public or an implosion," he said. "But it was worrisome in terms of how things were going to unfold. I did not sit back and think, 'Great, our problems are going to be solved.'"

Sisi later recounted in a public speech that he had met in March with a senior American official visiting Cairo—presumably Kerry. "He said to me, 'Please, they say you know the reality here, what would you advise?'" Sisi recalled.

"The time is up" for Morsi, Sisi said he had responded. "I have no more advice for you."

When Kerry returned to Washington, he testified on Capitol Hill and his prognosis was grim. Morsi was leaning away from "inclusion" and instead seeking "to consolidate and to leave people out," Kerry said. "It's a question mark whether they're going to make the right choices, and I can't frame it any other way." But he called the nearly $80 billion in United States aid to the Egyptian military over the previous decades "the best investment America has made for years in that region."

British Ambassador James Watt had been an early optimist about Morsi, impressed by the competence of his cabinet. But Watt was close to many in the Egyptian elite hostile to Morsi, including the anti-Islamist political leaders Ahmed Said and Amr Moussa. By the spring of 2013, Watt's Egyptian friends and staff had changed his opinion. He began describing the Muslim Brothers as corrupt, dangerous, and even deranged. "They were in fairy land," he told a friend. Watt met with Morsi's advisers for the last time that April. The conversation degenerated to a shouting match over the billions of dollars that Egypt owed British oil and gas companies—a longstanding issue that had grown steadily worse since 2011.

Watt's new views were at odds with his government's. He tried in vain to persuade Prime Minister David Cameron to cancel an invitation to Morsi for a state visit to London planned for that summer, and Watt spoke to many around Cairo about his disagreement with Cameron. "I am seriously concerned about mismanagement" under Morsi, Watt told contacts in the Egyptian military and the opposition, and he worried aloud that Morsi might be "beyond rescue."

"If you do move," Watt told one general that spring, "try not to be violent."

Secretary of Defense Chuck Hagel landed in Cairo on April 24, and he formed a very different assessment of Morsi. "He was Americanized. He had taught in California," Hagel said. "He was well informed."

Unlike Kerry, Hagel brought Ambassador Patterson to sit in on his meeting with Sisi, and she noticed a change in his tone: Sisi signaled for the first time in her hearing that the military was considering intervening to oust Morsi. Another general, Assar, had also begun hinting that if the Americans could not control Morsi, the military might need to step in. Now, in an encrypted email to a select readership, Patterson warned the White House in explicit terms.

"She was pretty definitive," one White House official who read her email later told me. "She said that, if not imminent, a coup was a high likelihood within a few months. She knew his tones and his body language, and she could tell from his responses that a coup was likely to happen."

Any military intervention, Patterson warned, could only be brutal.

19

A New Front

April 24, 2013–May 1, 2013

Mohamed ElBaradei had insisted to his new allies in the anti-Morsi opposition for months that a military takeover was out of the question: the West would never accept it. His reputation for liberalism was crucial to the credibility of the National Salvation Front. Almost all the other members had compromising ties to the intelligence agencies or the Mubarak government. And no one else had his high-level contacts in every Western capital. He was the Front's liaison to Washington and Europe. He had met at his home with Brotherhood party leaders as late as February to negotiate plans for new parliamentary elections, and when his allies in the Front complained, ElBaradei explained to them that he had to take the meeting for the sake of Western opinion. Appearing to obstruct democracy would alienate the West.

But by April, ElBaradei and the Front had committed to boycotting the elections. The courts had repeatedly rejected the Morsi government's electoral plans, always citing technical flaws, and it became impossible to elect a new Parliament before Ramadan that summer in any event. And for some reason ElBaradei's worries about Western objections to a military takeover also seemed to go away in April, others in the National Salvation Front later told me.

The change was "remarkable," said Amr Hamzawy, a liberal political scientist and former parliamentarian who was one of the few in the group who had entered politics since 2011. When ElBaradei stopped worrying about the West, Hamzawy told me, "I guess it was a signal."

After April, "the plan was spelled out quite clearly—popular mobilization, followed by tanks, followed by early presidential elections. I sensed that the National Salvation Front was dead set on its decision to call on the army to intervene."

Hamzawy was a lone voice of dissent. He argued in a series of newspaper columns that military intervention would throw Egypt back into dictatorship, and he caught hell for it from others in the National Salvation Front.

"They would say, 'Why are you telling people to be afraid of calling on the army to interfere in a case of popular mobilization or state failure?' This was an argument in the meeting!" Hamzawy said.

By May, ElBaradei himself finally told Hamzawy to get out of the way. "Without the army, we stand no chance!" ElBaradei told the group.

Sisi, though, held the key. No one imagined any removal of Morsi without the go-ahead of the defense minister, and until May the leaders of the National Salvation Front did not know whether Sisi was with them or against them. Two other senior generals on the Supreme Council of the Armed Forces had been in contact with the Front since December. But after an abortive offer that month to try to broker negotiations between Morsi and his opponents, Sisi seemed to yield to Morsi or even side with him. Sisi had urged voters to ratify the Brotherhood-backed constitution. Even at the end of April, his allegiance was a mystery.

That was when three twentysomething journalists showed up out of nowhere to propose a new plan for the anti-Morsi movement. All three were unaccomplished freelancers who took on fifteen-dollar assignments from Nasserite or nationalist tabloids, and none of them had experience at political organizing. But they knew the Front's spokesman, Dawoud, and over coffee at a café near the state media building they told him that they intended to collect fifteen million signatures demanding that Morsi step aside on the one-year anniversary of his inauguration, June 30. "Tamarrod"—Rebellion—the three newcomers called themselves.

"We are in a state of stagnation," Dawoud told the others in the Front. "We have to stir the waters."

ElBaradei posed for a picture with them in the garden of his villa. Anti-Islamist political parties printed petition forms and put their offices to work collecting signatures around the country. The billionaire communications mogul and party leader Naguib Sawiris secretly paid to produce a soaring music video promoting the Tamarrod petition. A popular satellite network he owned broadcast the video constantly. ("Tamarrod did not even know it was me!" he told me later. "I am not ashamed of it.")

The news media and opposition parties rallied around the three young men before they produced a single signature. Tamarrod supporters were immediately deluged with invitations to appear as guests on talk shows across the private networks. Tahani el-Gebali provided legal and strategic advice: she told the organizers that an unwritten "constitutional tradition" would allow the defense minister to replace the elected president with the chief of the Supreme Constitutional Court (a personal friend of hers).

Mohamed Hassanein Heikal, the ghostwriter who had advised Abdel Nasser in the run-up to his 1952 coup, coached Tamarrod, too. "Heikal is a genius," Hassan Shahin, one of the three journalists who founded Tamarrod, told me later. "He told us that on June 30 we would be creating 'a new history' for generations to come."

Heikal was a nexus. ElBaradei visited the book-lined office in Heikal's apartment overlooking the Nile to vent his impatience at Sisi's diffidence about intervention. "Where is Sisi? What is he waiting for?" ElBaradei asked.

Heikal and Sisi were so close that the defense minister later personally delivered Heikal a cake for his birthday when he turned ninety, in September 2013. Heikal advised Sisi on the themes of his speeches and even political slogans. Sisi, ElBaradei, and Tamarrod—each party knew that conversations with Heikal reached all the others.

Volunteers and others in the Front later told me that they saw suspicious older men who appeared to be *mukhabarat* hanging around Tamarrod offices. "We got to hear names around the campaign who were associated with general intelligence—people known as interlocutors or businessmen close to the intelligence services," Hamzawy told me.

Others said piles of cash turned up around Tamarrod headquarters after someone returned from a trip to Dubai. I dismissed such talk as a conspiracy theory until I later heard a leaked recording of a telephone call sometime that spring from General Sisi's office.

"Sir, we will need two hundred tomorrow from Tamarrod's account—you know, the part from the UAE, which they transferred," Sisi's office manager told the military's chief of staff.

"What do you mean by *mukhabarat*, sir? The *mukhabarat* guys?" the office manager asked a moment later. "Do you remember the account that came for Tamarrod? . . . We only need two hundred from it—yes, two hundred thousand."

We were entering a time of shadowy battles between unseen antagonists when mysteriously leaked audio recordings became an indispensable source of information about events behind the scenes. In the case of the leak about Tamarrod, American diplomats with access to intelligence reports later told me that they, too, confirmed after the fact that the United Arab Emirates had provided millions of dollars through the Egyptian Defense Ministry. In the spring of 2013, I believed Tamarrod was a campaign to push Sisi to act. In fact, Sisi was behind it.

20

A Dutiful Son

May 1, 2013–June 23, 2013

General Abdel Fattah el-Sisi grew up in the medieval district known as Islamic Cairo. His family's apartment was a fifteen-minute walk from the closest road wide enough for a car, through a maze of low stone buildings right out of Naguib Mahfouz novels. Middle-class traders and tradesmen had populated the area during Sisi's childhood, and his father was one of the richest. The family owned a shop selling arabesque woodwork and other handicrafts in the storied Khan el-Khalili bazaar—the second stop after the Pyramids for many Western tourists. The Sisi family employed many of their neighbors.

Hussein Abdel Naby was a boyhood friend of Abdel Fattah el-Sisi and lived in a rented room downstairs in the same building, which was owned by Sisi's father. "He always dressed in a suit and tie, and all the others wore galabiyas," Abdel Naby, now a lawyer, said. "He was the only one who drove a Mercedes."

The Sisi family was religious and conservative, and Sisi's father was polygamous. He had married a second wife and had a second family. He was also ambitious. He once campaigned unsuccessfully for a seat in the rubber-stamp Parliament under Sadat—a position more about prestige and patronage than politics or policy. Another son, Ahmed, became a senior judge.

Neighbors saw Sisi's father as stern and intimidating. Abdel Fattah was desperate to please his old man, in part by devoting himself to physical exercise. While other boys played in the street, the young Sisi hopped up and down stairs to develop his calves, or he interrupted his schoolwork to do sets of push-ups.

"He used to punish himself," Abdel Naby remembered.

Sisi's father once looked askance at his teenage son for the vanity of a necklace and open-collared shirt, so the young Sisi shaved his own head in atonement. "Because I know I did something wrong," he told his friends.

If he felt any impulse to rebel, he hid it well. But he had grand dreams, as he later confided in private conversations with a trusted Egyptian journalist (audio recordings leaked to the public). Sisi had dreamed "that I was holding up a sword inscribed in red with the words 'There is no God but God'"—the rallying cry of the Prophet Mohamed and the essential creed of Islam. A voice in another dream told him, "We will give you what we have given to no other." And in a third, Sisi sat with former president Anwar Sadat to discuss their shared premonitions.

"I said to him: and I know I will be the president of the republic," Sisi later recounted.

He never saw combat. He specialized instead in diplomacy and intelligence. He served as a military attaché in Riyadh, trained at the Joint Services Command and Staff College in Britain, and studied at the United States Army War College, in Carlisle, Pennsylvania.

Sisi arrived at the War College in 2005. The local mosque lacked a full-time imam, and Sisi himself sometimes led Friday prayers. (So did one of his sons, who enrolled at Dickinson College.) Sisi joined campus debates about the American-led occupation of Iraq, and he bridled at arguments that political Islam was inconsistent with democracy. Any Arab democracy must incorporate Islamists, "including radical ones," Sisi argued in his final paper.

Sisi was "keen that the Muslim Brotherhood, the Islamist option, be given a chance" in Egypt, Mohamed Hassanein Heikal told me. Sisi told other friends and American diplomats that he would be happy to serve an elected president who happened to come from the Muslim Brotherhood.

He and Morsi started working together almost as soon as Mubarak was gone. Sisi, as head of military intelligence, was the army's liaison to the Brothers; Morsi, as head of the Brotherhood's political arm, was its point of contact with the generals. They had piety in common. Sisi and other generals would turn up for meetings with the Muslim Brothers with rolled-up sleeves and wet hands, as though from the ablutions before prayers, Brotherhood leaders told me.

"I can't believe they fell for it," a young Muslim Brother who was the son of one of the leaders said. "That is just what I would do when I was growing up if I wanted my parents to think I had been praying."

Sisi also went out of his way to cultivate Ambassador Patterson, a sign of his ambition. In addition to avowing his comfort with an elected president from the Brotherhood, Sisi emphasized to her that he prized his close relationships with the Israelis. He also hinted at rivalries with other generals—especially General Sami Anan, the American favorite, and former air marshal Ahmed Shafik, who had lost the election to Morsi. (Sisi told Patterson that the other officers saw both as corrupt, although the Americans knew that self-enrichment among the generals was pervasive.)

Looking back, one might have noticed a pattern in Sisi's advancement. He praised Mubarak like a father but told the military council to push him aside. And Sisi had been a favorite protégé of Field Marshal Tantawi. But Sisi had surprised Tantawi, too, and replaced him (while eliminating a rival, Anan).

Several of Morsi's Islamist advisers began to suspect in February that military officers were plotting against them. A friendly customs official at the Cairo airport tipped them off that a plane en route from the United Arab Emirates to Malta had stopped to refuel and started unloading crates of money and narcotics (tramadol, an opiate sold on the black market, with presumed facilitation from inside the police). But an army officer had told the customs police to ignore everything. It all disappeared.

About a half dozen Morsi advisers began meeting in random, unlikely rooms of the palace to avoid surveillance. They left their mobile phones outside and sometimes communicated in written notes that they immediately destroyed. They studied the staging of photographs of the president meeting with the generals for hints of their intentions. They implored Morsi to include one of them during his meetings with Sisi.

The president rebuffed them. He told them that Sisi preferred to meet onc on one, without those *shabab*—young people—as the general called the advisers. Morsi said he would manage Sisi.

Sisi, outwardly, appeared almost obsequious. News photographs and videos invariably showed him walking a few paces behind Morsi with his head bowed, or sitting with hands together between his thighs, smiling at the president. Newspapers quoted anonymous military officials disparaging Morsi, but Sisi brushed off the reports. "Newspapers and media exaggerate," Sisi would tell the president. Yes, there were "tensions toward the president inside the military," Sisi would acknowledge. But he presented himself as the ally who would control the discontent.

"Morsi trusted him," Mourad Aly, a senior Brotherhood spokesman, later told me.

At least until April 24, Ambassador Patterson was hearing and believing the same things from Sisi: that he intended to stay out of Morsi's way. Many thought as much—even former president Mubarak, then being held in a military hospital. In an audio recording made in his doctor's office that spring and later leaked to the public (the leaks were everywhere in those days), Mubarak insisted that the military would stay out of politics. Sisi was with the Islamists.

"The defense minister, I think, is to their liking," Mubarak said.

The most authoritative poll that spring, from the Pew Research Center, had put Morsi's approval rating at 53 percent and the Brotherhood's at 63 percent. A strong majority of Egyptians favored democracy over stability. So even the most nervous Morsi advisers did not see a military coup coming; for one thing, it would inevitably set off a violent backlash and undo any progress toward restarting the Egyptian economy. "We didn't think they were that stupid," Wael Haddara said.

"No one is going to remove anyone," Sisi said on May 11 to a select handful of Egyptian journalists and intellectuals he had invited to a military exercise in Dahshur. Military intervention "is extremely dangerous. It could turn Egypt into another Afghanistan or Somalia." It would set Egypt back "for the next thirty or forty years."

Privately, Sisi presented Morsi a written memorandum of broad suggestions about how to strengthen his position by reaching out to his opponents. Morsi felt reassured; Sisi was still with him. He later proposed, in another memorandum in June, nine specific steps, including a mechanism for amending the constitution, the incorporation of more young people in government, and either a reshuffling of the Cabinet or an early presidential election.

But by late May, senior Egyptian military officers openly told an American lobbyist who worked with them that they supported Tamarrod's project and hoped it would succeed. "They did not make a big secret of it," the lobbyist later told me.

The two generals from the Supreme Council of the Armed Forces began calling members of ElBaradei's National Salvation Front at around the same time with a new message. Do not fear, they said. The army would "protect" their demonstrations to demand Morsi's resignation. On June 30, his one-year anniversary in office, the army would be with them.

El Sayyid el-Badawi, the business mogul who had been recorded talking to the *mukhabarat* about the Brotherhood and its fate, was so excited that he summoned the members of the Front to an emergency meeting in the garden of his mansion in the suburbs. The military was now on their side, Badawi told them with enthusiasm. "It was understood as 'we are now good to go,'" Hamzawy later told me.

By June 5, leaders of the Front were confident enough to tell the State Department about their plans. A Washington emissary, Ramy Yaacoub, an Egyptian who had previously worked on Capitol Hill, delivered a memorandum with the cryptic title "Operation 6" that spelled out the steps Tamarrod would follow if Morsi did not immediately resign in response to the June 30 protests.

Tamarrod, leading the Egyptian people toward their liberation, will issue a constitutional declaration to include the following:

The current Egyptian president will step down, ending the authority of the current constitution. . . .

The Council of National Defense will continue to practice its powers . . .

In a small meeting with another Egyptian, Yaacoub handed the memorandum to Thomas Melia, then deputy assistant secretary of state, in the

Bureau for Democracy, Human Rights, and Labor. Melia was incredulous. "So, you guys are going to make a little coup?" Melia asked.

"Mr. Melia," Yaacoub told him, "don't say 'you guys.'"

But with no clear authority behind it, the memo was set aside and forgotten. Melia told me he has no memory of the meeting.

21

June 30

May 25, 2013–July 3, 2013

Kerry and Morsi were both scheduled to attend an African Union summit on May 25, 2013, in Addis Ababa, Ethiopia. Neither wanted to meet. "He is not going to listen," Kerry told the aides who briefed him. "This guy is completely hopeless."

They met nonetheless. Kerry prodded Morsi to make concessions to ElBaradei. "You are going to end up like Mubarak," Kerry warned Morsi. "You are going to have people back in the streets."

Morsi thought Kerry was exploiting Egypt's economic crisis to try to bully or topple its new democracy. "We don't need you to tell us what to do," Morsi angrily told Kerry. "We see your pressure."

After that, Kerry turned instead to the rulers of Qatar, a financial supporter of Egypt under Morsi and an ally of the Egyptian Muslim Brotherhood (Qatar's Al Jazeera network flattered Morsi almost as assiduously as Saudi Arabia's Al Arabiya or the UAE's Sky News Arabia insulted him). Kerry asked the Qatari diplomats to persuade Morsi to yield power without the disruption of a forced ouster.

"Some sort of acquiescence to the needs of the country," as Kerry later explained to me. "It was an effort to avoid implosion, not an effort to avoid change in reality, but an adjustment to what had already happened with Morsi."

Obama had given stirring speeches about Egypt and its chance to build a new democracy. In 2011, his advisers had called the success of the Egyptian transition a top priority. But in 2013, he had detached from day-to-day policy.

The White House discouraged staff from criticizing Cabinet members in writing to avoid leaks, and lower-ranking aides who noticed the discrepancy in messages had difficulty communicating about it. It is unclear to me how much Obama knew. But while Kerry was trying to finesse "acquiescence," Obama and his closest national security advisers were doing their best to keep Morsi—the bumbling but fairly elected president—in office.

The NSC sent Chuck Hagel tough talking points to warn Sisi that the United States would punish the Egyptian military for a military takeover. A so-called coup law mandated a cutoff of American aid to any military that removed an elected government.

Hagel, though, saw his priority as winning over Sisi. "The talking points from the White House are not what you would say to someone you have an ongoing relationship with, so you have to adjust them," one Hagel adviser later told me. "But with Hagel," the adviser said, "it was just really difficult to get him to deliver the hard message."

The White House received reports on the calls and saw that Hagel had coddled instead of scolded. "It was totally, totally different," a senior official on the National Security Council told me. "The White House wanted the message to be, 'Democracy is important,' and Hagel wanted it to be, 'We want to have a good relationship.' We never could get him to deliver stern talking points."

In one conversation, Hagel set aside the talking points to tell Sisi flatly: "Don't do a coup."

Don't worry, Sisi responded calmly. We won't.

Great, then, Hagel told him, as though that settled the question.

When I met him in early 2016, Hagel recalled that he had been besieged by complaints about Morsi from the defense ministers in Israel, Saudi Arabia, and the United Arab Emirates—especially from Mohammed bin Zayed, the crown prince of Abu Dhabi and the de facto ruler and military chief of the UAE.

"MBZ and other leaders in the Middle East were warning me then that the Muslim Brotherhood is the most dangerous element afoot in the Middle East today," Hagel said, and he had always agreed. "I said, yes, it is dangerous. We recognize that. I am not contesting that. You are right."

"I said the same thing I said to Sisi. 'We have got to deal with this in a smart way, in a wise way,'" Hagel said. "The Gulf States were focused on

'Let's just hammer them and extinguish them now. Let's just get rid of them now and if anybody gets in the way, well, you don't understand how ruthless these people are. They will destroy us. It is not in your interests. Why can't you Americans understand that?' And they would go back to their old refrain, 'You let Mubarak go down.'"

The Israelis made clear that they were backing Sisi, too. "Sisi and the generals have a very close relationship with the Israelis. The Israelis were letting us know very clearly that Sisi was the only guy protecting everything here, and they were concerned."

Hagel agreed with them. "We get that," Hagel said he told Israeli Defense Minister Moshe "Bogie" Ya'alon and Prime Minister Benjamin Netanyahu. "The security arrangement is in our interest, too."

Hagel said he cautioned Sisi gently: "You have to give it some time, because you don't want the world against you."

"Yes," Sisi responded, according to Hagel, "but you know there are some very evil, very bad forces afoot. You cannot understand it like we can understand it here. These are revolutionaries who want to change our way of life, who want to bring back centuries-old practices."

"I don't live in Cairo, you do," Hagel said he conceded. "So I will never tell you how to run your government or run your country. You've got to figure that out. I would never put myself in your shoes. . . . You do have to protect your security, protect your country."

After the calls, Hagel stunned his aides by telling them to learn from his example: Did they see how he was building up Sisi's trust and confidence? It was only later—after the question was moot—that Obama paid closer attention and felt irked over the distorted message.

Ambassador Patterson, on the ground in Cairo, urged Egyptians to stick to the democratic process they had started. "This is the government that you and your fellow citizens elected," Patterson told a gathering of non-Islamist intellectuals and activists on June 18 in a speech at a Cairo think tank.

Beat the Brotherhood at the ballot box, she urged, not in street protests. "More violence on the streets will do little more than add new names to the lists of martyrs." She explicitly disavowed support for Morsi. The Egyptian, Emirati, and Saudi news media all denounced her speech as a confession of just that.

She met Khairat el-Shater at his office the next day, June 19, hoping that he could convince Morsi to make concessions that would placate his opponents. Shater told her that he, too, was exasperated with Morsi. But he was more frustrated with the Emirati and Saudi conspiracies to undermine him.

How would the Brotherhood handle the June 30 protests? Patterson asked. Shater told her the turnout would be big, but Morsi could survive it.

"I have my doubts," she told him, "but I hope you are right."

Obama was trying to help Morsi. Patterson was warning the Muslim Brothers. Kerry had given up on Morsi. Hagel was reassuring Sisi.

O n Sunday, June 23, Sisi lectured the military's Department of Moral Affairs about the protests expected seven days later, and his words were carried over the state media. Widening divisions in society were "a danger to the Egyptian state." If necessary, the military had a duty "to intervene to keep Egypt from sliding into a dark tunnel."

He gave political factions one week—"during which much can be achieved"—to find "a formula of real understanding, agreement, and reconciliation to protect Egypt and its people."

Morsi's opponents heard a promise. If their June 30 protests were big enough, Sisi would remove the president. But on a visit to the palace after the speech, Sisi was reassuring. He insisted his comments were meant only "to satisfy some of his men," according to several Morsi advisers. It was "an attempt to absorb their anger." A military spokesman told journalists that Sisi's intent was "supportive" of the political process. Morsi again believed him.

On June 26, Morsi advisers drafted a forty-minute speech announcing several concessions that Sisi had recommended. Among other things, Morsi would bring more political opponents into the Cabinet and create a new panel to propose constitutional amendments.

Morsi delivered it, but kept talking. He rambled on for two and a half hours. He railed again against "enemies of the revolution" at home and abroad. He blamed his opponents for refusing to negotiate. He claimed media moguls were trying to bring him down to dodge their back taxes. He threatened to investigate his former opponent, Ahmed Shafik, for corruption. He accused judges of electoral fraud against the Muslim Brothers eight years earlier, in 2005, when Morsi lost his own seat in the Parliament.

"A disaster," one senior adviser later called the speech.

Morsi promised to take legal action against anyone who claimed he lacked the full support of the armed forces. Television cameras panned to Sisi in the front row, frowning and stone-faced.

Morsi blundered many things that June. He named a member of a political party linked to a former Islamist militant group as governor of Luxor, where a faction of the same group had massacred more than sixty people at a tourist site in 1997. Protests blocked the governor from his office, and he quickly resigned.

Then Morsi attended a conference full of Saudi and Salafi clerics, calling the Syrian uprising a holy war against Shiite Iran. When it was his turn to speak, Morsi surprised his advisers by blurting out that Cairo was cutting off diplomatic ties with Damascus. (Ten days later, a mob in a village near Cairo killed four members of Egypt's small Shia minority as police did nothing. Foes blamed Morsi for condoning sectarianism at the conference.)

Morsi invited representatives of all political factions to discuss the threat of a proposed dam up the Nile in Ethiopia. Morsi lectured briefly about engineering. The other attendees mused aloud about Israeli and American conspiracies, sabotaging the construction, sending spies to Ethiopia, or manipulating its politics. Then someone slipped in a note telling the participants that their discussion was being broadcast live on state television (a frequent opposition demand, used as a pretext to refuse any dialogue). Morsi looked as shocked as anyone. But his missteps only added momentum to the movement against him.

By the last week of June, the intelligence agencies no longer hid their objectives. Egypt had one celebrity spy: the silent, burly figure who had stood behind former vice president Omar Suleiman when he had announced Mubarak's resignation. Egyptians had dubbed the anonymous figure "the man behind Omar Suleiman." His face popped up all over the internet in the background of historic photographs with Abdel Nasser, Sadat, Saddam Hussein, Obama, Carter, Hitler, the Sphinx, Pharaohs, and Darth Vader. His real name was Hussein Kamal Sharif, an intelligence officer and Suleiman's chief of staff in the spy agency. In the run-up to June 30, he gave a televised

press conference full of unsubstantiated allegations of Islamist intrigue under Morsi. Kamal claimed secret intelligence and urged Egyptians to turn
out against the president. "We will consider it a referendum" on "the utter
failure of the leadership of the Muslim Brotherhood."

The state-sponsored police association released a video of an internal
meeting in which officers bellowed about their "betrayal" in 2011 and the
"catastrophe" of their humiliation since then.

"People who were in prison are now presidents," an officer complained,
and he vowed to kill any policeman who tried to protect a Brotherhood
office. "I swear to God almighty he will be shot."

He got no argument. General Salah Zeyada, a senior ministry official,
reassured the boisterous officers, "We all agree, brothers, that there will be
no security provided for the headquarters of the Muslim Brotherhood."

Over three days, unknown gunmen around the Nile Delta had killed at
least five Muslim Brothers during assaults on their local offices. The Brothers had fortified their headquarters, in the Muqattam cliffs overlooking
Cairo, with iron gates and sandbags. The grand imam of Al Azhar warned
of impending "civil war."

I could not sit still on the night of June 29. I did not believe Egyptians would
march to remove a president they had so recently elected. Confused, I called
some of the original organizers of the Tahrir Square sit-in. Islam Lotfy, expelled from the Brotherhood for starting an independent political party, called
his former Islamist leaders "a bunch of losers." But the people driving the anti-
Morsi protests were "the people who killed my friends and tried to kill me"—
the Mubarak security services, Lotfy said. He felt like leaving Egypt.

Some of his former friends from Tahrir Square were marching again
and this time arming themselves. "The Islamists, well, most of them are
basically terrorists," Shady el-Ghazaly Harb, the British-trained surgeon,
told me. "Molotov cocktails or whatever, but people have to have a way to
protect themselves."

Ambassador Patterson had sent another message earlier that week
warning that after meeting with Sisi she believed a coup was imminent. On
the night of June 29, American intelligence reports showed Egyptian army
troops moving to positions surrounding the palace, the state media building, and other strategic locations around the capital. At least some on the

staff of the National Security Council believed that night that a coup was in motion. "It was coup 101," a staff member on duty at the time later told me.

But no one in the Pentagon, the State Department, or the White House told Sisi to stop moving. No one told Morsi that Sisi had turned against him, or that a coup had begun.

The next morning, on June 30, hundreds of thousands swarmed through the streets of the capital. At least hundreds of thousands more came out in cities across the country. It had taken courage to march against Mubarak in 2011. But now the army, police, most television stations, many big employers, movie stars, and the most visible liberals and leftists were all urging Egyptians to join in the protests.

Foes of the Muslim Brothers had mocked them for months as "sheep" because of their vows of obedience. Now someone brought out real sheep, scrawled the names of Brotherhood leaders in black on their wool, and slaughtered them outside the palace.

Uniformed police officers applauded, cheered, and egged on the crowds. Some handed out bottles of water, and one passed out roses. Another tore open his uniform, Clark Kent style, to reveal a Tamarrod T-shirt. Demonstrators carried him on their shoulders. Footage of his stunt filled the newscasts. Military helicopters dropped Egyptian flags fluttering to the ground, and the crowds whooped in gratitude.

"Come on, Sisi, make a decision!" they chanted.

Liberal activists who had marched against Mubarak on January 25, 2011, were startled at the embrace of their old foes. "On the twenty-fifth of January the police were shooting at us; on the thirtieth of June they were giving us flowers," one of those liberals, Mustafa el-Naggar, a thirty-three-year-old dentist, later told me.

Khaled Youssef was the filmmaker whose movie *This Is Chaos* culminated in the revolt against the bullying policeman Hatem and prefigured the uprising against Mubarak. A Nasserite who despised Islamists, Youssef had predicted in television interviews that the army would remove Morsi before the end of his first term in office.

On the afternoon of June 30, Youssef called a friend in the military's propaganda arm, and the army rushed him to a helicopter so that he could film the demonstrations. And a few hours later, a military spokesman called the *New York Times* bureau with a similar proposal: would I like a ride in a military helicopter to see the crowds from above? I agreed, but the spokesman never called back. Youssef's footage must have been enough.

The Brotherhood had held its own competing counterdemonstrations at a public square not far from the presidential palace. At least tens of thousands of its supporters had rallied there the previous Friday, and some were still demonstrating there now. I visited that morning. Battalions of middle-aged men in polo shirts and button-down collars were marching back and forth in rows, kicking up their knees and singing Islamist anthems. Some carried wooden sticks or baseball bats as weapons, or they made shields out of trash can lids and kitchen woks.

"We will sacrifice our lives for our religion," they chanted. "Morsi's men are everywhere." They looked like overgrown Boy Scouts playacting as soldiers. I could not decide if they were frightening or pathetic.

Would Morsi respond to the massive crowds? I asked Gehad el-Haddad of the Muslim Brotherhood over the phone. He made no effort to hide his shock at the scale of the protests.

"You would think he would have to," he said, shaken. "The president is headstrong."

By midnight, I was outside the Brotherhood's headquarters. Six decades earlier, on October 27, 1954, the day Abdel Nasser survived the attempted assassination in Alexandria, a government-orchestrated mob attack on the Brotherhood's headquarters in Cairo marked the beginning of the most severe crackdown in the history of the movement. Now a thinner but more methodical crowd had surrounded the Brotherhood's gleaming new offices. Dozens of young men hurled rocks and Molotov cocktails. A few fired shotguns loaded with birdshot, and others were shining green laser pointers toward the upper floors.

Why the light show? I asked discreetly. They were hunting for a few remaining Muslim Brothers hiding inside, one of the attackers said. "Their leaders have left them like sheep for the slaughter."

I later saw video footage of Muslim Brothers hiding behind sandbags inside the windows and firing shotguns at the attackers. But while I was there the crowd outside was hurling their gas bombs with businesslike efficiency. There was no cheering or chanting, no street demonstration. A fire engulfed the entrance. Two middle-aged men watched from folding chairs at the edge of some open ground abutting the headquarters, like football fans at a tailgate party. Were they spectators, or supervisors? I suspected intelligence agents.

Two uniformed policemen were talking on handheld radios outside a patrol car about a block away from the fire, doing nothing. Then two armored police vehicles pulled up. The attackers taunted the policemen to arrest the remaining Muslim Brothers inside. But the police drove away and let the arson continue.

After I left, one of the Brothers tried to escape but was beaten, dragged along the ground, and turned over to the police. That, too, was recorded on video. Eight others were killed at the scene, according to the Health Ministry, presumably shot by Muslim Brothers defending their headquarters. It was still burning in the morning, on July 1. Two looters were carrying out a porcelain toilet.

I wondered how it must feel to be the elected leader of eighty million people—the first democratically elected leader in the history of your country—hunkered down to fight your last stand. Crowds outside are baying for your blood. Your security forces have turned against you. You believe that you are defending nothing less than the chance to build a new democracy after millennia of tyranny. But everything I imagined was wrong. Morsi still did not see it.

Fifteen people had been killed around the country. Several governors appointed by Morsi were locked out of their offices, but the ones who had come from the military or the police were all well protected. Almost everyone who was not a Muslim Brother had resigned from his administration—including the Salafis. Now, on July 1, Egyptian Air Force F-16s with colored contrails were painting hearts in the sky over Tahrir Square. Five military helicopters circled downtown with giant Egyptian flags hanging below them.

The military's presidential guard unit had relocated Morsi to a work spacc inside its own complex, ostensibly for his own protection during the protests. He was isolated there with his top advisers, who monitored the demonstrations through the media, intelligence reports, the provincial governors, and the Muslim Brotherhood. They saw the slaughtered sheep and they heard the Sisi chants. But Morsi thought he had survived.

A British political scientist who studied the crowd sizes, Neil Ketchley, later put the "plausible upper threshold" of the turnout against Morsi on June 30 at around one million people across the country. But on July 1, the Brotherhood, the news media, the military, and the intelligence agencies all gave Morsi widely varying estimates. The military's estimate was highest and put the number around 650,000 in Cairo. Morsi and his aides collected data from the mobile phone companies about how many phones were in Tahrir Square and other places, and his advisers had turned to Google Earth to try to compare crowds. The demonstrations in their support had continued in Cairo and elsewhere, and they concluded that the crowds for Morsi had been as big as the ones against them. Why not? For two and a half years, the Islamist crowds had always been bigger.

Now that the opposition had shown its full strength, Morsi was ready to negotiate. He had discussed a package of compromises with Sisi over the last week, and now Morsi expected to share control of the government by working out the details of a new prime minister and Cabinet.

Obama was traveling in Africa and called Morsi from Tanzania. It was their second conversation in two weeks, and Obama warned for a second time that Washington could not control the Egyptian army.

"We conveyed our interest in avoiding military intervention in the political system," Obama told him, according to a record of the call made by the staff of the White House. "The fact is, if the Egyptian military thinks the country's stability is at risk, they are going to make their own decision. They are not taking direction from the United States."

Perhaps the military should take direction from Egypt's democratically elected government, Morsi replied.

Obama knew by then that the military and intelligence agencies were spurring on the protests. But he and some advisers still believed that Morsi might salvage his presidency and with it a political process. Obama again urged Morsi to seek reconciliation as a way to hang on to his office.

"I have made calls for dialogue," Morsi told him. "I am trying to reach out to Christians, the youth . . . I will take what they are saying very seriously. . . . I don't like to see my country divided. I am interested in making changes to the government. If we finish the law and start elections for the Parliament . . ."

Morsi was still talking about a long term. "I am doing my best to write history for a new Egypt that is really democratic, and what I want to see in my life is that power is transferred in elections to another candidate. I will be very happy if that happens."

Obama underscored the urgency of crisis. "If you just treat this as another routine problem, I am afraid it won't be enough to break the fever," Obama told him. "You started with fifty-one percent of the vote and a lot of people who weren't sure about the Muslim Brotherhood, so you need structures that you are bringing them into, so it is almost a unity government."

Then Obama set aside his talking points.

"I just left South Africa, where Nelson Mandela is in the hospital and is very sick. When he came to power he could have gone to the white minority and said, 'We are the majority and we are going to do what we want.' But he did not do this. He went out of his way to reach out to the minority. He even put his former prison guard—the man who had been the warden at the prison where he had been held—and he put him in charge of the security services. It was because of those gestures that he showed he was about bringing the country together and sending a message that everyone is a part of this thing."

Morsi seemed to grasp Obama's earnestness. "I agree with all of what you have said," he said. "I consider this very good advice, from a sincere friend of Egypt and to myself."

Morsi pledged to meet the next day with his opponents to discuss drastic actions, "about building a civil, democratic state."

"Be bold," Obama told him. "History is waiting for you but you have to meet it, not just with legalism, not just with following the rules on the page, but you have to make some bold gestures."

Ambassador Patterson arrived at the presidential guard complex after Obama's call. "I hate to say it," she told them, "but it is going to be over, you have got to do something. You are going to end up in jail."

Haddad, Morsi's national security adviser, asked what the U.S. presi
dent meant by "bold gestures." Patterson replied that changing the prime
minister might have been enough a few weeks ago, but now it could require
Morsi's resignation. She wanted to be sure Morsi knew that it was not his
civilian opponents who were making the decisions. "Your audience is Sisi."

Haddad told her that Sisi had agreed days before to support Morsi's
compromises, and Patterson looked stunned. As one Morsi adviser later
described it, "It was as close to her jaw dropping as you can get from a
diplomat." The team showed her a list of candidates whom Morsi proposed
to name as prime minister—perhaps one of the Western-friendly current or
former central bank governors, or perhaps a third time around for a geriatric premier who had served first under Mubarak and then under the generals. Patterson approved of any of them, if it would resolve the impasse.

"Are you sure you are safe?" she asked as she left. "Take care," she said.

Everyone around Morsi believed Washington could control the generals
(despite what Obama had said). They pestered Haddad about what Patterson had told him.

"She said, 'Take care,'" Haddad answered. Morsi's advisers adopted it
as a nickname. "Ambassador Take Care," they called her.

Sisi arrived moments later. In a photograph released to the news media,
the two men looked like nothing had changed. Morsi leaned back in a
gilded armchair and smiled confidently. Sisi sat on the edge of a couch,
slightly hunched, with his hands together between his knees and a briefcase
beside him, looking at Morsi.

But while they were discussing potential Cabinet shake-ups, Morsi's
office manager interrupted them to hand the president a message. State
television had broadcast a communiqué from the Supreme Council of the
Armed Forces.

"If the demands of the people have not been met" within "forty-eight
hours," the military council would "enforce" its own "road map," the communiqué read. "The armed forces will not be party to the circle of politics
or ruling" but "the wasting of more time will only create more division and
conflict."

What did this mean? Morsi demanded.

Sisi again tried to explain it away. The armed forces were encouraging all sides to compromise, not planning a coup, he told Morsi. Sisi promised that a new statement would clarify his intentions.

But the statement released a few hours later was a puzzle of double meanings. It pledged that the Egyptian armed forces would never carry out a "military coup," but it defined "coup" in a way that excluded the military takeovers of 1952 (deposing the king) or of 2011 (deposing Mubarak). The army had gone into the streets only "to stand with the will of the great Egyptian people."

Morsi was the last in his circle to realize that Sisi had turned on him, but now even Morsi saw it. "We understand it as a military coup," Wael Haddara told me. "What form that will take remains to be seen."

The capital and country were quiet. The June 30 crowds went home that night and stayed out of the streets. Only a small demonstration of promilitary nationalists were still waiving Egyptian flags in Tahrir Square when Sisi visited Morsi in the Republican Guard complex again on Tuesday, July 2.

Morsi had a new gambit, a "bold gesture," in Obama's words: Morsi offered Sisi the added role of prime minister. No one could doubt the authority or independence of Egypt's minister of defense. No one could say that Morsi was hogging control.

Sisi presented himself as a mere intermediary. He promised to carry Morsi's ideas to the opposition, and he said he would report back as soon as possible. But no one in the opposition heard from him. It is unclear if he consulted any civilian. He never again spoke to Morsi.

The answer came at 9:00 P.M. in a call from a different member of the military council, General Mohamed el-Assar, one of the two who had been talking to ElBaradei's group all along.

"*El basha yemshy,*" Assar told Haddad. The pasha goes.

Morsi turned to the public. Convinced Egyptians would not stand for a military takeover so soon after rising up against Mubarak, Morsi delivered his final address as president from a small television studio in the guard complex. "The people empowered me, the people chose me, through a free and fair election," he said. "Legitimacy is the only way to protect our country and prevent bloodshed."

The Arab word for legitimacy, *shareia*, comes from the same root as Sharia. Morsi repeated *shareia* more than fifty times in the space of a few minutes. "If the price of protecting legitimacy is my blood," he said, "I am willing to pay the price."

The first draft of the official history was rolling off the presses. REMOVAL OR RESIGNATION was the banner headline on the front page of *Al Ahram* as the first copies hit the newsstands around midnight. The newspaper reported that the generals were already arresting leaders of the Muslim Brotherhood. Soldiers would detain "anyone who resists these decisions." Television networks displayed "Morsi timers" counting down Sisi's forty-eight-hour deadline like the minutes to the New Year.

The Qatari foreign minister, Khalid al-Attiyah, called Haddad with a final proposal from Kerry. Morsi could remain a figurehead while delegating all of his powers to a new prime minister, presumably ElBaradei. "A polite way of stepping down," one Morsi adviser later told me.

The advisers knew Morsi would never accept. He had often pointed to his own neck and told them, "This before that." I will die before capitulating to a military takeover.

So Haddad called Patterson with Morsi's counteroffer. He was willing to step down after the election of a new Parliament.

Too late, Patterson said. Sisi was finalizing the road map, with ElBaradei and others.

Now Haddad was thinking about history. On his laptop, he wrote a warning to the West in English and posted it to Facebook.

> As I write these lines I am fully aware that these may be the last lines I get to post on this page. For the sake of Egypt and for historical accuracy, let's call what is happening by its real name: Military coup. . . .
>
> On January 25 [2011] I stood in Tahrir square. My children stood in protest in Cairo and Alexandria. We stood ready to sacrifice for this revolution. When we did that, we did not support a revolution of elites. And we did not support a conditional democracy. We stood, and we still stand, for a very simple idea: given freedom, we Egyptians can build institutions that allow us to promote and choose among all the different visions for the country.

We quickly discovered that almost none of the other actors were willing to extend that idea to include us.

You have heard much during the past thirty months about *Ikhwan* excluding all others. I will not try to convince you otherwise today. Perhaps there will come a day when honest academics have the courage to examine the record.

Today only one thing matters. In this day and age no military coup can succeed in the face of sizeable popular force without considerable bloodshed. Who among you is ready to shoulder that blame?

I am fully aware of the Egyptian media that has already attempted to frame *Ikhwan* for every act of violence that has taken place in Egypt since January 2011. I am sure that you are tempted to believe this. But it will not be easy.

There are still people in Egypt who believe in their right to make a democratic choice. Hundreds of thousands of them have gathered in support of democracy and the Presidency. And they will not leave in the face of this attack. To move them, there will have to be violence. It will either come from the army, the police, or the hired mercenaries. Either way there will be considerable bloodshed. And the message will resonate throughout the Muslim World loud and clear: democracy is not for Muslims.

I do not need to explain in detail the worldwide catastrophic ramifications of this message. . . .

In the last year we have been castigated by foreign governments, foreign media, and rights groups whenever our reforms in the areas of rights and freedoms did not keep pace with the ambitions of some or adhere exactly to the forms used in other cultures. The silence of all of those voices with an impending military coup is hypocritical and that hypocrisy will not be lost on a large swath of Egyptians, Arabs, and Muslims.

Many have seen fit in these last months to lecture us on how democracy is more than just the ballot box. That may indeed be true. But what is definitely true is that there is no democracy without the ballot box.

Haddad delivered a version of the same warning in a last phone call to the White House. He spoke with Susan Rice, Obama's new national security adviser, who had taken over on July 1. Rice had been ambassador to the United Nations in 2011 and she had been among the early advocates of breaking with Mubarak and siding with those in Tahrir Square. But the tumult under Morsi had dampened her enthusiasm about the hope for a democratic Egypt. She told Haddad that Morsi should accept his ouster, for the sake of stability. When he hung up, Haddad told the others around Morsi to expect no help from Washington.

"Mother just told us that we will stop playing in one hour," one of Morsi's advisers wrote in a text message to a relative outside Egypt. Mother America, Egypt's international patron.

Only one woman was in the guard complex with Morsi and his inner circle—Pakinam el-Sharkawy, his chief policy adviser. Morsi ordered her out for her safety. He expected that soldiers would kill him that night, his advisers later told me. But he seemed oddly at peace. He told stories and laughed about the politicians of his youth, under President Sadat.

As the last aide walked out of the complex, he heard a general order the guards: "Lock the gates."

S isi, looking boyish in short sleeves and a black beret, appeared on television standing at a podium with an all-star cast seated behind him: Mohamed ElBaradei, the Coptic pope, the grand imam of Al Azhar, and a Salafi party leader.

Egyptians "are not calling on us to assume power," Sisi said, only "to secure essential protection for the demands of the revolution."

I raced back toward the place where Morsi's supporters had gathered, to look for signs of violence, but military vehicles blocked the way. A column of tanks and armored personnel carriers churned through the streets. They had encircled both the presidential palace and the guard complex as well.

I had seen several almost–coups d'état in Egypt: generals removing a president because they feared public unrest, generals scheming for behind-the-scenes control, generals dissolving a Parliament, and generals trying to overturn a vote. In each case, politics went on, full of suspense and surprises. But there is no mistaking a real coup when you see one.

22
Coup d'État

July 4, 2013

Obama summoned his National Security Council to the White House the next day, on July 4. Only a few days earlier, traveling in Africa, Obama had reminded journalists that unlike Mubarak, Morsi was "democratically elected." So his opponents should follow "legal, legitimate processes." But now Obama surprised the room. Of course, we cannot call Morsi's ouster a coup d'état, Obama announced at the outset of the meeting.

Everyone else had come prepared to argue over the application of the "coup law": the statute that required cutting off aid to any military that toppled an elected government.

Puzzled about the apparent turn in the president's thinking, Philip Gordon, the White House coordinator for the Middle East, observed aloud that calling the takeover a coup would not necessarily require demanding Morsi's reinstatement. Aid could flow again after a restoration of democracy.

Obama, newly engaged, pointed to General Martin Dempsey, the chairman of the Joint Chiefs of Staff. "If Marty deposed me and then another country cut off relations, Marty would not have to restore me before the other country restored relations?" Obama asked.

Dempsey also defied expectations. Soldiers are taught not to remove an elected government, he said. Isn't that what happened? Wouldn't the White House risk its credibility if it did not call the coup what it was? Rhodes made the same case.

But others wanted to back Morsi's ouster. Some in the administration welcomed a return to military rule, several present later told me. The return of a military government "did represent some degree of familiarity and predictability that you could not entirely discount as having some benefit," one senior official involved acknowledged.

A top intelligence official had already conveyed his approval of the takeover to one of Sisi's supporters in the region. Michael Morrell, deputy director of the CIA, had received a call hours after the takeover from a senior Arab ambassador to Washington. "Michael, what do you think about Egypt?" the ambassador had asked.

"This is a good thing," Morrell had replied. "Morsi was leading the country to ruin, to instability, and to extremism. Now Egypt has a chance again."

Morrell knew that answer was "inconsistent with U.S. policy," as he later wrote in his memoir. But the ambassador concurred.

"You are right," the ambassador replied. (I later asked Morrell in an email if the ambassador was his friend Yousef al-Otaiba. Morrell declined to name his sources and added a smiley face emoticon.)

Otaiba, for his part, had celebrated the night of the takeover with cocktails at the Hamilton, a trendy Washington bar and restaurant, joined by Ramy Yaacoub, the Egyptian who had delivered to the State Department the "Operation 6" memo about the planned military takeover. Otaiba had also fired off a threatening email to the White House.

"My friendly advice here, the U.S. needs to somehow bless this move, even if it is a subtle and private wink-nod," he wrote to two senior administration officials, Jake Sullivan and Antony Blinken. "If this blessing is not given, the perception will be the U.S. is defending Morsi and the anger in the streets that is currently directed toward Morsi will be redirected toward you and your embassy."

Some National Security Council staff told me that they also worried about the safety of the embassy personnel if Washington came out against the takeover. But Kerry argued in the July 4 meeting at the White House that Morsi's removal was not, in fact, a coup. Sisi was bowing to the public will and acting to save Egypt, Kerry asserted with passion. "The generals said they removed Morsi for the purpose of avoiding an implosion and establishing the rule of law, not for the purpose of governing. They said they were going to put a road map back to elections in place. There was a clear schedule for the elections," Kerry later told me he had argued.

The military was not asking to run the country, he insisted. They said they were ready to let the voters decide. "We had to test that," Kerry told me, and he added more pragmatic arguments. "If we called it a coup and walked away, we would lose any leverage and other countries would have happily filled the void."

Hagel, the intelligence directors, and ultimately Dempsey all sided with Kerry: the alliance with Egypt was too important to jeopardize, and the aid would give Washington pull to sway Sisi toward democracy and away from violence.

"Why would you take away every instrument of influence that we have?" Hagel asked in the meeting. "If you cut Sisi and Egypt loose, Sisi will be on a plane to Moscow in forty-eight hours, and to China, and he will get funding." The Saudis and the Emirates "will pour millions in, and the Israelis will be very upset, which we will have to deal with."

Years later, Kerry told me that the Americans who had opposed Morsi's ouster were naïve about the region. "Everybody sits back and makes a judgment on a place like Egypt or the Middle East right now based on such a classic American mistake: they make suppositions about what it ought to be and what Egyptians ought to do based on our situation, our view of life, and our view of the world," Kerry said. "But the problem is, that is usually completely divorced from the reality on the ground and what other actors are doing. We see things only through our own lens and our own ideals.

"In Egypt, what was the alternative?" he continued. "It wasn't Jeffersonian democracy. Was it Morsi? Or the Salafists? Or was it Sisi and company, and the establishment that has been there awhile? Are they democratic? No. Are they something to brag about at home? No. But over whatever number of years we have put about eighty billion dollars into Egypt. Most of the time, this is the kind of government they had—almost all of the time. And the reality is, no matter how much I wish it was different, it ain't going to be different tomorrow."

To defend Morsi at the expense of alienating Israel and the Persian Gulf monarchies made no sense to Kerry. He needed those allies for higher priorities. He was focusing on the nuclear deal with Iran, the Syrian civil war, and a Palestinian peace agreement. He did not want to "get into a fight with them over something as historically clear as how Egypt works," Kerry told me.

"If we just say, 'Hey, you guys, we are washing our hands, you are done,' then guess what? Saudi Arabia and Kuwait and all the other countries, including Israel, will be right there, one hundred percent. They are all, at heart, in the same frame of mind."

In their customary roles, a secretary of state lobbies for concerns like rights, democracy, and long-term stability while the secretary of defense speaks for immediate security interests. But in this debate both Cabinet members lined up on the same side. The loudest voice in the White House for rights and democracy, Samantha Power, was absent, preparing for her confirmation as ambassador to the United Nations. It was a one-sided debate, in favor of Sisi.

"We were isolated in our own government," Ben Rhodes later told me. "The people who wanted to have a different kind of relationship with the Egyptian people, including the president, were on an island in our own government. It was hard enough to take the position that we took at the height of the Tahrir Square protests, and now it was much harder. There was a sense of inevitability about the military resuming control."

Obama did not fight it. He decided not to disclose any decision. The administration made no determination about whether what had happened on July 3 in Cairo was or was not a military coup, thus sidestepping the coup law. Privately, some White House staff came to call Morsi's ouster "the couplike event."

23

Killing Themselves

July 3, 2013–July 24, 2013

abaa al-Adawiya was a slave girl in the eighth century in the city of Basra, in what is now southern Iraq. Her father, a poor man, had named her *rabaa*—fourth—because she was his fourth daughter. One day her owner-master found her kneeling in prayer and surrounded by light.

"If I were free I would pass the whole day and night in prayers," she prayed aloud. "But what should I do when You have made me the slave of a human being?"

Moved by her faith, her master granted Rabaa her freedom. She ran into the desert, slept with a brick for a pillow, and wrote poetry. She became the first in a long line of female Sufi mystics and saints. Then 1960s Egyptian cinema, in its Nasser-era golden age, got hold of her story. Rabaa was reborn in celluloid as the most glamorous scribbling ascetic in history. An Egyptian-made film portrayed her in her slave days as a dazzling beauty in gold hoop earrings and flowing silk. She danced in and out of love affairs to the songs of the great Egyptian diva Om Kalthoum. It may have been the film as much as the legend that had inspired a group of Cairo businessmen in the 1990s to build a mosque named for Rabaa al-Adawiya in the middle-class neighborhood of Nasr City.

Rabaa was still twirling through late-night television around the Arab world when I lived in Cairo, and I thought of her as the patron saint of the city's special blend of piety and hustle. Cairo is the capital of a transnational Arab culture that defies stereotypes and generalities, where the same people might revere the saint, enjoy the movie, and laugh off the contradiction. The *New York Times* banned the use of the word "secular" to describe any Egyptian. Even the most ardent anti-Islamist so often turned out to be fervently religious (albeit in different ways), and even the most secular Egyptians spoke and acted in ways that struck Americans as pious. Never trust anyone who tries to generalize about "the Egyptian people" and their religion, especially anyone who tells you that "the people" either chose or rejected political Islam.

The open pavement around the mosque named for Rabaa al-Adawiya was the place that Morsi's supporters chose as their rallying point before the June 30 protests. It was walking distance from the presidential palace, but far enough away to avoid another clash there like the rumble in December. By the time Sisi's forty-eight-hour ultimatum expired on Wednesday, July 3, the crowds around Rabaa al-Adawiya Square had grown to tens of thousands.

The security forces started rounding up Morsi advisers and Brotherhood leaders while Sisi was still talking. Soldiers and police shut down all Islamist television networks and Al Jazeera's Cairo office. Every Egyptian news outlet still operating was celebrating the takeover. One talk show host wrapped himself in an Egyptian flag. Another danced around his studio as balloons fell from the ceiling. A female newscaster wept into her handkerchief and then sang the national anthem.

"Welcome back, Egypt," they all said. Egypt has "returned."

Television screens showed bearded men led away in handcuffs through crowds of jeering soldiers. Then the cameras cut to middle-aged women in abayas waving flags and ululating. Newscasters argued about whether they were celebrating a second revolution or the completion of the first one.

There was no turning back. Some percentage of Egyptians believed that day that Sisi was committing a crime. Was that 15 percent, as his supporters might say? Or was it 30 percent, or 50 percent, or perhaps even more, and where was it? Support for the Muslim Brotherhood had always run much higher outside of Cairo, so anecdotal evidence from the capital had limited value. In any case, Sisi risked a prison sentence if he ever allowed a democratic election.

Mayy el-Sheikh had stayed at Rabaa to monitor the scene, and she reported that the numbers continued to swell after Sisi announced Morsi's ouster. Nervous energy amped up the chants. Grown men wept. Soldiers had been keeping watch around the perimeter. Now some of the Islamists hugged the sentries, wrapping arms around their body armor. Confidence or denial?

At the edge of the crowd, Mayy struck up a conversation with a Muslim Sister named Esraa el-Berry, a thirty-year-old wife and mother who covered her hair but wore a Western-style skirt and a blouse. "We're staying until our votes mean something," she shouted to be heard over the din. "We didn't defend our votes the first time when we went to the ballot boxes and elected a Parliament and then watched as they shattered it. But from now on, we will cast our votes and we will stand behind them with our blood. . . . I will not give up my freedom."

But it is all over, Mayy told her. Morsi's gone. The constitution is gone.

"We thought the military was at our backs," the woman answered. "God wanted to teach us that no one has our back in this world, that He and He alone is our refuge."

Tens of thousands marched through the streets that Friday carrying pictures of Morsi and demanding his return. Hundreds of thousands were rallying for the same cause in other cities and towns (where the Islamists were stronger). The police shut down all train service and blocked the highways into Cairo, to prevent an invasion.

News reports said that Mohamed Badie, the Brotherhood's general guide, had been arrested. But he appeared at Rabaa to declare his defiance: "Our peacefulness is stronger than their bullets." That became the slogan of the sit-in.

A gunfight had taken place the night before the coup at a smaller, parallel Islamist sit-in that had been taking place at Nahda Square, near Cairo University in Giza, and in the morning, Mayy and I counted the smoldering remains of seven cars and a motorcycle. Islamists said that unknown gunmen had killed a dozen of their number. But the bullet holes had gone in two directions and extended deep into the side streets. At Nahda Square, both the Islamists and their opponents must have had weapons.

Neither I nor any other Western journalist I know ever saw weapons at Rabaa during the sit-in, and I visited often. Rabaa was the place to find all the Brotherhood leaders not yet in jail; it was the only place they were safe from arrest. They had set up a headquarters and media center inside the mosque. All of them told me with great confidence that the Egyptian public would never stand for a coup. The soldiers and police would never turn on their fellow Egyptians. Every soldier had a cousin who was a Muslim Brother.

"I think the military has to yield; they won't have any choice," Gehad el-Haddad, the Brotherhood spokesman, told me. "We are stepping it up every few days, with protests around the country. We are logistically capable of carrying this on for months." His father, Essam el-Haddad, had disappeared with Morsi.

The crisis revived the unity of the movement. Within about a week, more than a hundred thousand people—men, women, and children—were spending the night at the Rabaa sit-in. A little town extended over several blocks and intersections. Some left for work each day but returned to sleep there. The organizers stacked bags of sand or pried stones from the pavement, and they built low walls and improvised gates at the perimeter. Bearded men in orange vests checked my identification and patted me down. Some kept sticks or clubs handy in case of attack. But they were always very welcoming to Western journalists like me. We were their best hope of getting a message to the world. Although the Qatari-owned Al Jazeera network was on their side, every Egyptian news organization still in business was against them.

Footpaths led through rows of makeshift tents or wooden structures, some of which grew to two stories. Residents camped on cots, pads, or blankets. During Ramadan many napped on the ground through the heat of midday. They strung wires from lampposts to pirate electricity for lights, fans, televisions, or internet access. They used small, portable gas stoves to make tea or coffee, or to cook plates of beans.

The Brotherhood organized four large communal kitchens making simple meals like *kushari* or macaroni. Some served more than twenty thousand meals a night. Men and women formed separate lines, segregated by gender, to pick up their dinner. Trucks hauled in clean water, and men carried jugs of it back to campsites within the sit-in. Cleaning crews passed through the sit-in twice a day to collect trash, but litter was accumulating, and you could smell the humanity.

Much of the time the camp atmosphere was oddly festive. Maybe it was the feeling of community, or a nervous excitement, or a willful denial. When Ramadan began on July 8, families and friends broke the fast there together. Islamic anthems blared over loudspeakers. Stalls sold grilled chicken, roasted corn on the cob, or Egyptian flags. A barber was giving out trims on a chair near his tent (free, but donations were welcome). A few couples held weddings. Children fired plastic water guns or jumped on trampolines and inflatable slides. Someone set up a small swimming pool.

My colleague Ben Hubbard spent twenty-four hours wandering the sit-in with a video camera, and he concluded that it was Woodstock for Islamists. Some giggling families were snapping photos by a pen of a dozen ducklings under a sign that read DUCKS AGAINST THE COUP.

"The duck comes out of an egg and cannot go back in, just as we got our freedom and will not go back," their owner, forty-nine-year-old Ahmed Abdel-Rahman, told Hubbard.

Sometimes it felt like a reenactment of the original Tahrir Square protests, the way middle-aged Americans march with bayonets to relive Gettysburg. This time, though, there were no bushy-haired hipsters, no curious matrons from the Egyptian elite, no "Gucci corner" of rich kids from the American University, and no Copts. These were almost all Islamists. Five times a day, every man in the sit-in was down on his knees.

As time went on, an undercurrent of anxiety grew more palpable. Men and women at Rabaa talked about the bad old days when a loud knock on the door before dawn meant that the police had come to haul an Islamist out of his bed and lock him away. Some recalled their torture—beatings, suspensions in the air, electrical shocks to the genitals. A MILLION MARTYRS! signs at Rabaa declared, all but daring Sisi to try to kill them all. But no one wanted to die.

I knew by then that the leaders of the Muslim Brotherhood privately blamed Morsi for getting them into this mess. But in public they lionized him. His picture covered every tent, wall, lamppost, and picket. Vendors sold Morsi face masks and demonstrators wore them around. Speakers on the soundstage repeated his name like a prophet of God.

The Brotherhood organizers were welcoming any ally now. Hard-line Islamists raged from a soundstage about Islamic law and legitimacy—*Sharia* and *shareia*. A local affiliate of Al Jazeera was broadcasting live from Rabaa, and the other networks replayed sound bites about martyrdom, jihad, or retribution—terrifying many Egyptians who never came near the square.

"These people dare to mock our religion!" roared Safwat Hegazy, the fire-and-brimstone TV preacher. "God will punish them!"

"The people want the trial of the serial killer," the crowd chanted against Sisi.

Some blamed Christians or called the soldiers the "thugs of the church." "Have you seen the crosses in Tahrir Square?" one asked from the stage. "Is this a crusade?"

Mohamed Soltan was appalled by the rhetoric. His father was one of the Islamists giving those fiery speeches. But Mohamed was a twenty-five-year-old Egyptian American who had grown up mainly in the midwestern United States. Everyone around the sit-in knew him as the fat kid in Michael Jordan shorts and flip-flops. One of Mohamed's uncles was a senior Brotherhood leader and (in classic Egyptian fashion) another uncle was a general in the army. Soltan himself was much more liberal than most Muslim Brothers. He had headed the thousand-strong Muslim Students Association at Ohio State University, volunteered for the Obama presidential campaign in Ohio in 2008, and returned to Egypt just in time to join the Tahrir Square protests in 2011. He did not consider himself an Islamist. He thought Morsi was too conservative and a lousy president. But Soltan opposed the military ouster of any democratically elected leader. So on the night of the coup he moved to Rabaa.

"That Sharia and legitimacy thing—that does not represent me and people like me!" he told the Brotherhood leaders. He persuaded them to "rebrand" the sit-in. He switched the color of the backdrop behind the stage from green, the color of the flag of the Prophet Mohamed, to black, the color of mourning. Soon there were PRODEMOCRACY and ANTICOUP signs and T-shirts everywhere, beginning with the guards who patted me down at the gates. Soltan made sure that no television camera could zoom in on any sign with the written word JIHAD without also taking in at least one logo that said PRODEMOCRACY ANTICOUP. Banners spread everywhere that read CHILDREN AGAINST THE COUP, PHARMACISTS AGAINST THE COUP, LAWYERS AGAINST THE COUP, and so on. One sign proclaimed CHRISTIANS

AGAINST THE COUP, though I doubted that many Egyptians flocked to that one.

Beyond the sit-in, I met a few storekeepers, taxi drivers, service people, or strangers in elevators who probed my allegiance with careful questions. Is the *New York Times* controlled by the American government, like *Al Ahram* in Egypt? What did I think of Rabaa? If convinced that I was not a spy, the questioner might whisper that he stood with Morsi or loathed Sisi. But I must not tell anyone!

O utside of Rabaa, Cairo felt transformed overnight, as though the Morsi era were already a distant memory. By July 4, smiling policemen appeared on the corners. The Interior Ministry took down the concrete barriers erected to block the streets around its headquarters. The minister—a Mubarak-era official appointed by Morsi and now an enthusiastic supporter of the coup—announced that the police at last stood "with the people." Police posters sprang up around the city with a picture of children beaming up at a uniformed officer.

The police were now open about their relief. "You had officers and individuals who were working under a specific policy that was against Islamic extremists and Islamists in general," said Ihab Youssef, a former police official who acted as an informal spokesman to Westerners. "Then all of a sudden the regime flips and there is an Islamic regime ruling. They could never psychologically accept that."

Day-to-day life immediately improved. The gas lines and blackouts ended the day after the coup. Had some player—the military, for example—been holding back fuel reserves?

"This was preparing for the coup," Naser el-Farash, the Morsi-appointed ministry spokesman, now told me. "Different circles in the state—from the storage facilities to the cars that transport petrol products to the gas stations—all participated in creating the crisis."

Giddy newscasters and politicians wildly inflated the number of demonstrators who had turned out against Morsi on June 30. Where the military had initially told Morsi the demonstrators against him numbered

650,000 in Cairo, talk show hosts now said the turnout had been ten million. Then the Interior Ministry said seventeen million. Soon all the newscasts insisted that it must have been at least thirty million. "Fifty million Egyptians," the tycoon and party leader Naguib Sawiris proclaimed in an interview on American television—virtually every Egyptian adult. "We are the ones who told the army to come!"

Fireworks exploded over Tahrir Square every night for weeks. Egyptian flags covered the city. Roadside entrepreneurs rushed to my car window with buckets of little flags to try to sell me. Strangers in expensive latte shops heard me speak English and pulled me aside to tell me what a triumph had occurred. Egypt had reemerged from darkness! Why did Obama support the Brotherhood? Didn't I fear the militants at Rabaa? Why did the Brothers refuse to disperse?

Sawiris had predicted to me before the takeover that removing Morsi would bring in so much money from the oil-rich Persian Gulf that Egypt would no longer need a $4.8 billion IMF loan. His forecast was well informed: Saudi Arabia, the UAE, and Kuwait immediately gave Egypt a total of $12 billion—three times as much as the proposed IMF loan and eight times the annual American aid. Sisi "managed to save Egypt," King Abdullah of Saudi Arabia declared in a statement issued within two hours of the coup. (Qatar, the lone Gulf state that supported the Brotherhood, did not join the donations.)

"That will take us for twelve months with no problem," Sawiris told me. In fact, Saudi Arabia and the Persian Gulf monarchs gave the post-Morsi government more than $2 billion a month for more than two years. On June 20, 2014, nearly a year afer the takeover, King Abdullah landed his executive jumbo jet at the Cairo airport long enough for Sisi, the onetime military attaché to Riyadh, to come aboard and pay homage in a half-hour meeting. One scholar called it "a victory lap" for the king. The Saudi press emphasized that the king had brought along his intelligence chief, Prince Bandar. It was a "thank you gesture" for helping to orchestrate the coup.

The Egyptian foreign minister, Mohamed Kamel Amr, had resigned in the run-up to the takeover on July 3. But the next morning, he was back on the job and summoned me to his office. A thirty-four-story skyscraper among the luxury hotels along the Nile, the Egyptian Foreign Ministry contained nearly as much floor space as the State Department's Foggy Bottom headquarters—a towering symbol of bureaucratic authority. Amr was a veteran Mubarak-era diplomat appointed by the generals and retained by Morsi. He welcomed me to his palatial office overlooking the river with a handshake and a grin, and he told me Morsi's ouster was a great day for Egypt.

Had I not noticed, at all those press conferences with visiting Americans, that he had always hung back, never smiling? That he had left the talking to others? Yes, he had stayed in the job under the new president. But he had always opposed Morsi, Amr said, including to Western diplomats. "I was presenting the true picture of this country to the outside world," he told me. "I don't mean to be blowing my own horn, but I believe that was respected by my counterparts." Morsi's own minister had been poisoning other foreign governments against him.

I received a phone call from Mohamed ElBaradei while I was still in the building. I had admired ElBaradei since he had predicted in December 2010 that Mubarak's time was up. He had defended the Muslim Brotherhood against false charges of terrorism. He was honest about the military massacre of Christians outside Maspero.

But for three years he had repeatedly offered himself as a candidate for high office only to back out before elections. He never found the playing field clean or fair enough. His favorite strategy appeared to be a boycott. The only available polls confirmed what was obvious inside Egypt: ElBaradei was far more popular among Western journalists and diplomats than he was among Egyptians.

Now, the day after the coup, he told me that he had just gotten off long phone calls with John Kerry and Catherine Ashton, the top diplomat for the European Union. ElBaradei had talked extensively to each of them all year, and he referred to them by their first names, like old friends.

He said he had worked hard to convince them that Morsi's removal would "restart" a transition to democracy, and now he tried to convince me, too. "As Yogi Berra said, 'it's déjà vu all over again,'" ElBaradei said. He meant that the "revolution" in Tahrir Square had a second chance, an opportunity to begin again and get it right this time. "I would be the first one to shout loud and clearly if I see any sign of regression in terms of democracy."

This time, he was sure the generals would respect the rule of law and yield to elected civilians. "The security people obviously are worried—there was an earthquake and we have to make sure that the tremors are predicted and controlled," he said. "They are taking some precautionary measures to avoid violence; well, this is something that I guess they have to do as a security measure."

Still, he expressed surprising confidence in the chief prosecutor—a Mubarak loyalist whom he had previously panned. "Everybody who is being rounded up or detained, it is by order of the attorney general—and being a member of the Muslim Brotherhood is no crime," ElBaradei said.

He was talking as if he held some personal power in the new government to guarantee his promises. "I have emphasized to all the security authorities here that everything has to be done in due process," he told me.

About the Muslim Brothers, he said, "I was told that there are a number of accusations and they need to be investigated." But President Morsi "was treated with dignity and respect—and that is important." ElBaradei said he hoped the Muslim Brotherhood would compete in parliamentary elections.

I felt sorry for him. He was a Nobel laureate, and he believed everything the generals were telling him.

The next day, on Friday, July 5, a soldier outside the presidential guard complex tore up a Morsi poster hung on the barbed wire. A group of Morsi supporters had camped outside in the belief that the president was still held inside (which was correct, as I later learned from someone with him), and they grew angry. The soldiers shot and killed at least four of them. Around Egypt that day, at least thirty civilians were killed at demonstrations against the coup. No Egyptian television network covered any of it.

Ebrahim el-Sheikh, Mayy's younger brother, lived with another sister in an apartment tower just a few blocks from the presidential guard complex. He had been apathetic about politics before 2011 but filled with hope after the uprising. After the presidential election, he blamed Morsi for the continued police abuse and thought he hogged too much power. So Ebrahim joined the Tamarrod petition and the June 30 protests.

He was up before dawn on the morning of July 8—he had stayed out most of the night, as Egyptians sometimes do during Ramadan—when he heard the sound of gunfire outside. He ran to the window with a video camera and saw a group of unarmed men running up the street. Soldiers fired their weapons after them. The regular policeman stationed near the corner was a friend of Ebrahim, and the officer got into his patrol car to hide until it was over. The bullets blasted the doors and shattered the windows.

A few hours later, Ebrahim and another neighbor pulled the policeman's body out of the bullet-strewn car. "He did not have a head anymore," Ebrahim told Mayy.

The killing of the policeman was the tail end of an outburst of violence that morning. The guards outside the guard complex had started shooting again at dawn, for reasons I could never understand. By the time I reached the scene, T-shirts, scarves, and scraps of clothing were soaking in pools of blood on the street. Moataz Abu al-Shakra, a twenty-five-year-old electrical engineer, was holding up a sheet of corrugated metal that the demonstrators had tried to use as a shield. It was riddled with bullet holes. He and other witnesses—including opponents of Morsi—said soldiers inside guard towers had inexplicably started shooting during the prostrations for dawn prayer.

"It is like they were fighting a war between two countries, not like our army or police," he said.

Bullet casings and bloodstains were spread over hundreds of yards. The soldiers had gunned down fleeing men as they ran, and they kept chasing demonstrators through the side streets for hours.

An Egyptian American professor visiting from New York was staying in a thirteenth-floor apartment nearby, and he emailed me an account of what he had seen out of his window around 4:00 A.M. (He asked that I keep his name private for the safety of his family in Egypt.)

"I saw hundreds of army and police soldiers firing bullets at unarmed protesters who were running frantically east-south direction into Al Tayaran street away from the soldiers and the bullets. . . . The protesters were running, there was no battle or exchange of fire."

The soldiers killed more than sixty and wounded more than four hundred. Officials said later that a soldier and two policemen were also killed.

One was presumably the policeman-bystander killed by police bullets whose dead body Ebrahim helped to pull from his patrol car.

I posted on Twitter from the street, amid the bullet casings and bloodstains. "Egyptian massacre . . . Dozens of witnesses, including bystanders who hate the Brotherhood, say the protesters were unarmed when the shooting began."

I thought I was reporting the news. My dispatch was received like an act of war, and from unexpected quarters. My tweet caught the eye of Nagla Rizk, an Egyptian economics professor affiliated with Harvard, Yale, and the American University of Cairo, and, as it happened, a friend of my wife, Laura.

I thought Rizk was as liberal as could be. She wore her hair down, favored catlike red eyeglasses, and lived back and forth between New York and Zamalek. Her academic work was skeptical of property rights. She had marched against Mubarak on the Day of Rage, and a can of tear gas had torn her jeans.

"Unfortunate that your coverage shows 1 side/part of story," she fired back at me on Twitter after I used the word "massacre." "Extremely unprofessional."

Dozens of others piled on.

"I thought you were professional. Shame on you."

"Those are terrorists."

"They provoked the army."

"Why not gather a mob of 500 thugs & attack a US army facility with bricks, Molotov, and AK47? I bet they will be throwing roses."

"They were sneaking weapons into the mosque."

I called Rizk to ask, was she not worried about the dangers of the military retaking control?

"It is not ideal" for the army to oust the president, she said, "but this is the best thing that can happen. . . . We know that this is the will of the people, and I am cautiously optimistic."

What she feared was the Muslim Brotherhood. "I am worried about safety. I am worried about terrorism. I am worried about somebody trying to bomb himself in a jihad move in the name of Morsi. I don't want my kids to get bombed in the streets by some Morsi supporter who wants to defend Islam. That is my worry. This is a movement for an Islamic caliphate, so for them Egypt is just a detail." The Brothers "were taking us back to the Dark Ages, at all levels," and violence was "the only language that they know how to speak."

As for the mass shooting, "the evidence is mixed," Rizk said. "I think that the pro-Morsi protesters are provoking counteractions that will get sympathy—global sympathy," she said. "They are very good at portraying an image that appeals to the Western world, using Western terminology like 'legitimacy' and 'democracy.' They are very good at playing this game!"

It was almost as if she believed the protesters had gotten themselves killed on purpose, as a performance for the West. (Years later, she acknowledged that she had been swept up in the moment, and in fact had communicated with me that day from New York. "What happened in 2013 . . ." she said, trailing off. "I mean, we are not happy. I am not as politically active as I was.")

I was beginning to feel the anti-Islamist mania gripping the liberals of Egypt. The National Salvation Front—so critical of police abuse under Morsi—defended the killings. The Front called a news conference and held up a banner: MUSLIM BROTHERHOOD-AMERICAN CONSPIRACY AGAINST THE REVOLUTION.

"We expect violent actions from the side of the Muslim Brotherhood," its spokesman declared.

Talk show hosts who had crowed about their liberation from the *mukhabarat* in 2011 fell back into line as the Greek chorus of the crackdown. "Do you know what it means for Egyptians to take themselves to stand and shoot their military?" one host lamented, as though the demonstrators had been shooting at the guards.

"Forget ideas. Forget the ideology they are saturated with. Only remember that it is Egyptian blood," he declaimed solemnly, warning listeners that Brotherhood leaders had the minds of "wild beasts."

I felt a personal connection to one host: Lamees el-Hadidi. She had started her career as an assistant reporter for the Cairo bureau of the *New York Times* (in 1998, right after she had graduated from the American University in Cairo). She had gone on to become one of the most influential voices in the Egyptian media. Her face, with her trademark bangs swinging down over her forehead, was on billboards all over the highways. When we met for coffee at the Four Seasons, we were interrupted by fans seeking autographs. But she was still "a *New York Times* girl," Hadidi told me whenever we talked.

When Morsi had won the election, she "blacked out" from crying, Hadidi told me. "I closed the door behind me for half an hour, crying."

An old mentor had consoled her: Mohamed Hassanein Heikal, the same adviser to Abdel Nasser who was now advising Sisi, conferring with El-Baradei, and guiding Tamarrod. "Heikal used to tell me, 'Don't worry, they will fail, give them one year and they will fail.'"

After the killings outside the presidential guard complex, Hadidi was bold. She insisted that the Muslim Brothers had deliberately killed one another in order to generate sympathy. "They found themselves being killed by their friends—some of them, and investigations will show that," Hadidi asserted on her broadcast that night. The theory was spreading on social media, too.

The government's spokesmen and their talk show chorus began offering a new reason for Morsi's removal: the Muslim Brothers always had been "terrorists." "What human rights are there for an armed person who terrorizes citizens and attacks military establishments?" a military spokesman, Colonel Ahmed Ali, asked a group of Western correspondents around a conference table the day of the shooting.

Egypt, he explained, had been facing "fourth generation warfare," a new "information warfare," which had spread across the region since the start of the Arab Spring.

"They're all wars against the state by its own citizens, and the main weapon in these wars is the circulation of strife, rumors, and lies." Sisi's spokesman was repudiating the same "revolution" that Sisi, just five days before, had vowed to protect. ("Fourth generation warfare" became a favorite theme of Sisi's.)

Every television network affixed a new motto in the corner of its screen: Egypt Fighting Terrorism, in English as well as in Arabic, presumably for the benefit of Western journalists and diplomats. Talk show hosts now spun tales of weapons stockpiles at Rabaa or torture under the speakers' platform. (We checked and found nothing.) Every voice on television argued that the Islamists were never real Egyptians. Syrians, Palestinians, and other infiltrators paid by Qatar filled the tents at Rabaa. America and Israel had brought the Muslim Brothers to power as part of a plot to weaken and destabilize Egypt. Its transnational ideology would destroy the state. Morsi's presidency had been a foreign occupation. The Interior Ministry paid to produce its own patriotic pop song about the Islamists: "Not from Our Country."

No longer merely "sheep," the Muslim Brothers were now described on the talk shows as cockroaches or vermin. Some said that the Rabaa sit-in festered with disease. Others (including Al Arabiya) spread rumors of "sexual jihad": Islamist women were giving themselves to the men of Rabaa to keep up morale. A year ago, the Muslim Brothers had won Egypt's free elections. Now they were dangerous, foreign, alien, even subhuman.

An Interior Ministry spokesman claimed at a press conference that the Brotherhood's alleged violence that morning had somehow proven that the police were innocent of killing civilians during the uprising against Mubarak. "Policemen never thought history would speak so quickly," he proclaimed.

The journalists booed an Al Jazeera crew out of the room because of the network's critical reporting on the killings. "We are in Egypt, the country of democracy," the spokesman crowed after the fleeing crew.

The liberal intelligentsia was almost entirely silent or cheering. One of Egypt's most prominent human rights lawyers, Malek Adly, blamed the predawn killings on the Brotherhood's own "filthy" leaders. The columnist Khaled Montaser called the Islamists worse than "criminals and psychopaths," because they were incapable of change. "Their treason, terrorism, and conspiracies are an indelible tattoo."

Ahmed Maher, the leader of the April 6 group who had spearheaded the uprising against Mubarak, was one of the few liberals to publicly question trusting the generals. "When they screw us again like they did in 2011, what would I tell people?" he tweeted.

Other liberals turned on him, calling him an Islamist and trying to drive him out of his own movement. A cofounder of the April 6 group, Esraa Abdel Fattah, wrote in a newspaper column attacking him: "It is inevitable for the great Egyptian people to side with its armed forces against the foreign danger."

Only one prominent intellectual spoke out clearly against both the military takeover and the anti-Islamist hysteria that went along with it: Amr Hamzawy, the political scientist in the National Salvation Front. In newspaper columns, he decried "fascism under the false pretense of democracy and liberalism" and called intellectuals who remained silent "the birds of darkness of this phase."

The news media and his fellow liberals vilified him as a traitor. "He was the Cassandra," one human rights advocate, Dalia Abdel Hamid, told me years later, after passions had cooled. "We were the Trojan Horse—the 'popular mobilization' that let the military in to take over."

History had seen it all before: The collapse of a political process, the revenge of an entrenched bureaucracy, the hypernationalist hysteria, the glorification of the military, the scapegoating and demonization. Weimar Germany, for example. But I had fallen in love with the young liberals of Egypt. It broke my heart to see them like this.

24

A Lion

July 24, 2013–August 6, 2013

A new song hit Egypt's airwaves just days after the coup. *"Teslam el-Ayadi"* ran the refrain. "Bless the hands, Bless the army of my country." It was everywhere. It saturated the television coverage. It pumped from every taxi stereo. It thumped out of the windows of boats along the Nile. You could not take a walk around the block without hearing it. The president of the state-sponsored musician's syndicate had recorded it. He lifted a catchy melody from a decades-old Egyptian pop song (its chorus, "The moon is full too soon," was about the joys of Ramadan). He enlisted an ensemble of seasoned Egyptian pop stars to sing verses in turn, in the style of "We Are the World."

The lyrics began "This is the hero who gave up his life, who raised the name of my country and sacrificed himself for it," and the music video cut to Sisi wearing dark glasses and a black beret. Clips of him alternated with military footage of soldiers rappelling down walls, somersaulting over moving vehicles, or firing cannons into the desert. In one clip, Sisi led a morning jog with hundreds of soldiers in fatigues running in rows behind him.

"A real man, son of a real man," a smiling man sang. "He told Egypt, 'it does not matter if I live or I die,' and he never agreed to forgive and forget." A blond starlet belted out, "Egypt, you order us and we obey."

By late July, posters of Sisi hung from shop windows everywhere outside the Rabaa sit-in. Everyone knew who was in charge now. Some taped up the posters in enthusiasm, others for protection. Islamists hung Sisi's posters to help keep away the police. I kept one as a souvenir: Sisi, with his clean cheeks and military cap, juxtaposed against a roaring lion.

State newspapers published long, florid tributes in verse to Sisi's "flawless appearance" and "Herculean strength." Stores in Zamalek sold Sisi cupcakes. A lingerie store downtown sold Sisi panties—"for the woman who really wants to show her man who's boss," one journalist quipped on social media. The maker of "Bless the Hands" produced a second song saluting Sisi for taking on the "terrorists"; this one concluded with the chorus "June thirtieth was not a coup." (A third song thanked the United Arab Emirates and Saudi Arabia for their role in the takeover.)

When he announced Morsi's ouster, Sisi grabbed his lectern with both hands and insisted that he had tried to help the president. Sisi said then that he had given up on Morsi only after his last speech, on July 2, because it "failed to meet the full demands of the people."

In truth, the generals had signaled to ElBaradei's National Salvation Front and others by the beginning of June that they backed Morsi's ouster. A general had told Morsi's team "the pasha must go" hours before the July 2 speech. Yet Sisi sounded almost regretful about ousting Morsi.

American officials reading intelligence reports about conversations among the top generals would later tell me that Sisi was indeed more reluctant than some of the other generals about removing Morsi (the military council had never relished recognizing Morsi's election in the first place). But the police, the spies, the judges, Al Azhar, the Coptic Church, the owners of the private news media, the Western-style "liberals," the monarchs of the Persian Gulf—all of them were pushing for Sisi to replace Morsi. Washington did not speak with a single, credible voice on the question.

Sisi acceded to that push, and it transformed him. In his first speeches and interviews, Sisi had cooed to his audience in colloquial Arabic: you are "the light of my eyes." His honeyed speaking style was so sentimental that it almost seemed romantic, and some compared him with Abdel Halim Hafez, the Egyptian Sinatra.

"Sisi is soft and sweet, as if he is flirting with a beautiful woman," the political scientist Hassan Nafaa told me. Some on social media dubbed Sisi "the pimp."

"People think I'm a soft man," Sisi told his journalist-confidant in another private conversation that was later leaked to the public. But they were wrong, Sisi warned. He would be firm. A Sisi presidency would be "torture and suffering."

He stayed out of the limelight at first, having installed a civilian figurehead as acting president: Adly Mansour, the chief of the Supreme Constitutional Court. (ElBaradei was named vice president, in charge of relations with the West.) Mansour's main job was the promulgation of an interim charter, and its preamble based its legitimacy on the words of Defense Minister Sisi. The coup was official.

Sisi reemerged three weeks after the coup for a televised speech on July 24, and he was a changed man. He no longer looked up with his hands between his thighs, or wore his boyish beret and short sleeves. Now he wore dark aviator sunglasses and gilded epaulets, like an Arab Pinochet.

Yet he seemed to fall a step behind his propagandists. The state and private media—all presumably guided by the same intelligence agencies—were denouncing the Muslim Brothers as dangerous, alien terrorists. Sisi still defended the sincerity of his efforts to help Morsi.

Speaking before an audience of military cadets, he told Egyptians to trust him as cubs trust a lion. "Do lions eat their cubs?" he asked. "The Egyptian army is truly like a lion."

"We did not betray or conspire," he insisted, again and again. "I did not deceive the president. . . . Do not think I misled the former president!"

"To whom could I lie?" he interjected a few moments later. "To my family of Egyptians?"

He counted out the times that he said he had tried to save Morsi—"once, twice, thrice." At one point, he cliamed that he had told Morsi as early as January to abandon his whole "project"—"this form of religion." But then Sisi insisted that he had not given up on Morsi until March or even the last week of June. He recounted advising Morsi on details as small as the wording of speeches. When I read it again later, Sisi's repetition that he had not betrayed the president seemed compulsive, like compensation for a feeling of guilt.

But his tone grew sterner at last. The Muslim Brotherhood was now out to destroy Egypt, "to bring down the country or to rule it."

"If anyone imagines that through violence or terrorism! Terrorism! . . ," he said, trailing off. He called on "all honorable and trustworthy Egyptians" to go to the streets that Friday "to give me a mandate to combat potential violence and terrorism."

"Show the world," he said. "Shoulder the burden with me."

The news media alarms of foreigners, militants, weapons, and disease had primed Sisi's audience to fear the camp at Rabaa. A kind of nationalist rush surged again through Cairo. We have removed another tyrant! Liberal Egyptian friends who privately dreaded the military's return to power told me that their own families complained that Sisi was waiting too long to empty Rabaa by force. "We were animals," the rights advocate and journalist Hossam Bahgat told me later. "We were horrific."

Egyptians normally spend sleepy afternoons in Ramadan watching television serials made for the season. On the Friday that Sisi had called for a demonstration, eight popular satellite television networks all canceled their programming to push viewers off their couches. Helicopters buzzed low over the city, armored military vehicles patrolled the streets, and soldiers and police turned out to cheer. Tens of thousands marched, just as Sisi had requested, to give him his "mandate." Posters of his face floated over the throngs.

"Grind away, Sisi," some chanted. Eviscerate the Islamists. Eight more were killed that day during clashes near Rabaa.

Then, around 10:30 P.M., when the crowds had gone home, an Islamist countermarch set off from Rabaa through the neighborhood of Nasr City. When they reached the open plaza around Egypt's version of the Tomb of the Unknown Soldier, the soldiers and police opened fire, gunning down more than eighty demonstrators. A second mass killing.

One of Mayy el-Sheikh's best friends worked in our office. Mayy's friend had marched with her mother, as Sisi had asked. "If you can live with the blood, you should live with its weight," Mayy told her. They did not talk for weeks, and never again about politics.

The State Department had urged on the day after the coup that any Americans living in Egypt "depart at this time." Laura and our sons had left for the summer. Americans who stayed in Cairo might have been forgiven for thinking we had woken up in Tehran or Pyongyang. Posters and banners sprang up all over the city, putting a black *X* over the face of the American ambassador, or superimposing Obama's face with Osama bin Laden's. Former judge Tahani el-Gebali claimed on television that Obama's Kenyan half brother was financing the Brotherhood.

The same wildly counterfactual line was pushed all over the news media: Obama and Patterson (the "Brotherhood Ambassador") had conspired with Israel, Turkey, and Qatar to bring the Islamists to power in a plot to divide and cripple Egypt. The White House knew that the Saudis and Emiratis were driving the propaganda campaign, and Ben Rhodes marveled that such vitriol was coming from allies. "They celebrated the military takeover, and yet there was no questioning of that in Washington," he told me.

The White House made gestures. On July 24, the day of Sisi's "mandate speech," the administration delayed delivery to Egypt of four new F-16s. But all in all the United States was remarkably nonchalant about the anti-American invective from its Egyptian client.

Hagel talked to Sisi nearly every other day that summer, for a total of seventeen calls over five weeks, sometimes for as long as ninety minutes. Hagel told me he warned Sisi, "This is what is coming. We are going to pull down a lot of the support. We are going to put on hold the weapons systems. . . . We don't want to be there either. Hold elections. Let the people out of jail. Let them organize protests." But Hagel's tone was still conciliatory. He sent Sisi a biography of George Washington, as a role model, and they laughed together at the vanity of leaders who think they can never leave office.

Sisi ran him in circles, Hagel said. "The excuse that he would always use is 'These are the courts,' 'We are a democracy,' and all this bullshit. 'The rule of law! I can't override the courts.' He would get me trapped back in the same kind of web."

Hagel "still just wanted to build a relationship," a senior White House official told me. Obama, now more focused on Egypt, grew annoyed. Hagel resigned in November 2014, after conflicts with the president over other policies in the region.

Israel was lobbying hard for Washington to support the coup, and Sisi knew it, Hagel said. Sisi "would intimate that to me, too."

"The Israelis were telling me, 'This is our security, and this is the best relationship we have ever had with the Egyptians,'" Hagel told me. "And they were working Capitol Hill, as they do. It was all about Israeli security. 'You can't let us down here.'"

Senator Rand Paul, the Kentucky Republican, introduced a bill to end Egypt's military aid because of the coup. The American Israel Public Affairs Committee, better known as AIPAC, wrote to every senator arguing that any cuts "could increase instability in Egypt and undermine important U.S. interests and negatively impact our Israeli ally." The Senate voted 86–13 to protect the aid.

I had long ago stopped thinking of Egypt and Israel as hostile neighbors who needed American payoffs to maintain their peace. Now the Egyptian and Israeli military leaders were teaming up with one another against the White House to keep the money flowing.

Kerry was traveling in Islamabad at the time of the "mandate" massacre, when Egyptian soldiers killed more than eighty demonstrators. Susan Rice, the national security adviser, called him more than once and personally reminded him to stay on message: the United States wanted a return to democracy. A crackdown would destabilize Egypt. The American aid was at stake.

Kerry ignored her. The generals "were restoring democracy," Kerry told a Pakistani television network. "The military was asked to intervene by millions and millions of people."

In the White House, "it was a WTF moment," a senior national security official later told me. Obama's advisers complained to Kerry's staff, but on a visit to Cairo a few weeks later he again commended Sisi's government for following its road map to democracy. As late as the next June, almost a year after the coup, Kerry publicly thanked Egyptians "for their hard work in transitioning to a democracy."

But the massacre of July 26, 2013, alarmed the White House enough that it sent one of the State Department's most senior diplomats, William Burns, to try to broker some agreement that might stop the killing. The European Union dispatched Bernardino León, a Spanish diplomat, to join Burns.

Sisi's transitional government allowed them to meet Shater at the Tora prison complex near Maadi—at 1:00 A.M., accompanied by a warden. Shater, cool and matter of fact, made clear he had little regard for Morsi but refused to negotiate for him. Only Morsi had been elected president.

"I am sixty-five years old, I have spent fourteen years in prison," Shater told them. "Maybe I will spend another fourteen."

When they met with Sisi, he was long-winded and self-justifying. He told the diplomats that the Muslim Brotherhood had threatened to destroy Egypt. "The people called me," Sisi insisted. "As the military, we had an obligation to save Egypt."

For Sisi, "everything was existential," Burns later told me.

Two Arab foreign ministers had showed up unexpectedly to join them for their meetings: Prince Abdullah bin Zayed—known as ABZ—of the United Arab Emirates and Sheikh Khalid al-Attiyah of Qatar. Burns and León had not asked either of them to come. Each alluded to private conversations with Kerry. The diplomats hoped each foreign minister could work on his country's client in Egypt. Qatar could persuade the Muslim Brothers to bend. The Emiratis could soften up Sisi.

But ABZ, it turned out, was double-dealing. As soon as he left Burns and León, ABZ goaded the Egyptian generals to do whatever it took to break the Islamists, with as much force as needed. We have your back in Washington, he assured them.

American intelligence agencies reported ABZ's undermining to Burns, Kerry, and the White House. But ABZ hardly hid his support for the coup. Before leaving Cairo, he grinned for a newspaper photograph with his arms around the shoulders of two Tamarrod founders, embracing them with pride as protégés of the Emiratis.

Kerry, years later, told me that his friends in the Persian Gulf had actively worked against Obama's policy in Egypt right through that summer. "That is one of the realities of the region," he said. "They will all look you in the eye, and they don't want to say 'no'—they don't want to displease you to your face—but they will always pursue their bottom-line interest." Unlike Washington, he said, the petroleum-rich Gulf monarchs "had a free-flowing spigot to back up their interests."

The month-old sit-in at Rabaa was still growing, but, on August 6, after nearly a week in Cairo, Burns and León believed they had a deal for first steps to build trust between the Brothers and the generals. Sisi's government would release from jail two notably moderate Islamist politicians; the Brotherhood would begin to dismantle the sit-in at Rabaa. León told the Brotherhood's lead negotiator, Amr Darrag, that the two Islamists would be released within two hours. Then he called back the next day to tell Darrag to be patient—the releases were coming.

Instead, Sisi's government announced that negotiations were over. The security forces were preparing to clear Rabaa. Burns and León left Cairo. Two years later, León accepted a lucrative job from ABZ as head of a new diplomatic training center in Abu Dhabi, for the United Arab Emirates.

25

Clearing the Square

August 14, 2013–August 15, 2013

woke up every morning at the first light that summer wondering, Had
the police moved in during the night? Had they started to clear Rabaa?

Waiting for a massacre is a singular feeling. In early 2011, I visited
the Libyan city of Zawiya, west of Tripoli, after its residents had liberated themselves in the first moments of the uprising against Qaddafi. "Free
Zawiya" was celebrating in the town square, and I handed out business
cards.

Three weeks later, I was woken up before dawn in my Tripoli hotel
room, my phone buzzing with repeat calls from Zawiya. Qaddafi's troops
were retaking the city. Soldiers were shooting everywhere. They will kill
everyone. Please do something, my callers implored. Tell Washington.
Won't somebody help us?

I posted a short article on the *New York Times* website. Zawiya was a
ghost town when I made it back. The minaret of the mosque had been destroyed by mortar shells and newly dug graves filled a corner of the square.
July and August 2013 in Cairo felt like a slow-motion replay. I felt just as
powerless.

On August 11, an Egyptian official tipped us off that the assault on Rabaa would begin the next morning at dawn. Mayy and I watched the sunrise
from outside a gate of the sit-in. Anxious sentries paced back and forth with
wooden sticks in their hands.

Nothing happened. The Egyptian interior minister called it off at the
last minute; American diplomats following the process told me that he

was afraid to take the fall alone. He insisted that army troops join the operation, too.

Two nights later, on August 13, our driver got another tip from his *mukhabarat* handler (of course he had a handler—I always assumed that). Don't come to work the next day, stay out of the crossfire. So the driver split the difference, as he later confessed to Laura and others. He waited to pick me up until after the assault had begun. He dropped Mayy el-Sheikh and me blocks from the shooting, in Nasr City.

Mohamed Soltan, the Ohio State grad in flip-flops and basketball shorts who had tried to broaden the message of the sit-in, had spent the night running errands around the sprawling tent city, and he paused at dawn near the corner of Nasr Road and Yousef Abbas Street to take a picture with about a dozen friends. Two were sons of Brotherhood leaders.

They were smiling for the camera when the bullets started flying from all sides. Soltan grabbed his gas mask, ran to a sandbag barricade, and held up his iPhone to try to film the assault. But gunfire was coming from above and behind him, from the top of an abandoned building. He counted seven army bulldozers rolling toward the sit-in. Hundreds of riot police with Kalashnikovs were coming on foot. One of the Islamist demonstrators jumped onto a bulldozer to try to climb into the cabin. A rifle blew him to pieces.

Soltan remembered that his father was inside the sit-in and ran off to find him. He turned out to be huddling with a group of Brotherhood leaders under a table on the soundstage, hiding from the bullets. Each leader took turns holding up a sheet of wood as a shield, running to the microphone, and exhorting the frantic crowd to keep faith in God. Then each retreated back below the table. Soltan hid with them.

Al Jazeera's Egyptian affiliate had stationed a freelance cameraman on the stage. But at 11:30 A.M. a bullet hit the cameraman in the head and he fell to the ground. So another freelancer grabbed a bicycle helmet and stepped behind the same camera, until about thirty minutes later another bullet took him down, too. The bicycle helmet fell upside down on the stage, full of brains and blood, and Soltan took a picture of it.

A young woman—Marwa Saad, a pharmacist—lunged past the cowering Brotherhood leaders and grabbed the microphone. "Where are you? Where are the men of the world?" she screamed. "You are letting us die!"

Soltan was still filming the violence with his iPhone camera. When he leaned down to plug it into a generator, a bullet whizzed past his head. He pulled back, and a second shot hit his tricep. A doctor among the Brotherhood leaders made a tourniquet out of a keffiyeh Soltan had worn around his neck.

Soltan was built like a midwestern American frat boy, five eleven and 272 pounds. It took four friends to carry him to a field clinic near the Rabaa al-Adawiya Mosque, where doctors gave him painkillers and bandaged his wound. The adjacent room had been converted into a morgue. Bodies were stacked one on top of the other.

Mayy and I made our way on foot through the apartment blocks of the neighborhood, Nasr City, "the City of Victory." The Interior Ministry had promised for weeks that the police "dispersing" the sit-in (their clinical phrase) would leave "a safe exit" for any demonstrators willing to go, especially for the women and children living inside. We heard the reassurances repeated again on state radio that morning on the way to the scene. But as hard as we looked, we could find no way in or out. The soldiers and police had the sit-in surrounded. There was no safe exit.

The side streets were a swirl of hate and anger. A middle-aged woman was patrolling her block in her sleeping gown, with a long head scarf covering her shoulders. She waved a small Taser at us as though she were ready to lend a hand to the police and soldiers. "Finally, they are clearing the square," she told us.

A block away, a man who had managed to escape the sit-in held up his hands to show the bloodstains on his palms. "You let him kill us, you traitors," he screamed toward the balconies. "You gave him a mandate."

A few blocks from the sit-in, a group of young men was crouched over a plastic milk crate filled with bottles. They were pouring gasoline and dipping scraps of torn T-shirts into the neck of each bottle: Molotov cocktails. Then one looked up. He saw me watching, with my pen in my notebook. I averted my eyes and we turned to flee.

Before we could, an armored personnel carrier rumbled around a corner behind us. A handful of masked riot policemen in black body armor were approaching with raised rifles. Standing near the Molotov makers made us obvious targets, so Mayy and I hustled across the street.

Glass shattered around us; shards hit Mayy's jeans. A bullet had smashed a bus window two yards away. I remember soldiers and police shooting from both sides; Mayy remembered protesters throwing gas bombs from one side and police shooting from the other. Either way, we were stuck in the middle.

We ducked together into the shelter of an alley perpendicular to the street. A dead end. Gunshots cracked in volleys through the street behind us outside the alley. Canisters of tear gas streaked past and clouds obscured the view.

"Don't worry, Mayy," I said, trying to sound like I meant it.

I looked in vain at the walls and fences, hoping for something to climb, like a drainpipe or a ladder, or for a window to knock on. I remembered that at Mayy's job interview she told me she had learned English rereading *Jane Eyre*. Now she was twenty-seven years old. She had just gotten married the previous September. She had already risked her life more than once doing this job. I imagined telling her parents that she had died at Rabaa.

Mayy was murmuring her last prayers. She gasped and jumped, and I thought for an instant that a bullet had hit her. Then I glimpsed a cat's tail disappear between bins. For a novice journalist, Mayy was remarkably cool in perilous situations—in tear gas in Cairo, in gunfire in Port Said, inside the offices of the Egyptian Defense Ministry. But she was terrified of small animals, even the tiny lizards that crawled the walls of my office. One of the ratlike cats that swarm over Cairo had sprinted across our alley hiding place and brushed against her ankle.

At least four journalists were killed that day in and around Rabaa. At least one, the photographer Mahmoud Abou Zeid, known as Shawkan, was detained that day and imprisoned for more than four and a half years without any conviction. But all I could think about was Mayy, and all Mayy could think about was a street cat. I would look back on our moment in the alley as a parable about the way Egyptians managed, or displaced, their feelings about the horror of that day.

Tear gas, dust, bullhorns and screams, the dull thud of gas cannons, and the cracking of gunfire: smells and sounds are what I remember. We crouched close to the walls for what seemed like another twenty minutes. The battle had moved on; the tear gas had mostly cleared from the street outside the alley. Mayy and I peeked around the corner to make sure it was clear enough, then sprinted out. A man in a red T-shirt lay dead on the stoop.

We found ourselves across a plaza from the entrance to the Rabaa al-Adawiya Medical Center. We huddled near a corner. Snipers fired down from nearby rooftops. A handful of Islamist protesters near us held up garbage can lids or Styrofoam kickboards to try to shield themselves.

We had stumbled onto a kind of makeshift gateway in and out of the sit-in that the protesters had created, although it was hardly a safe passage. They had managed to haul Dumpsters, debris, and overturned cars to partially shelter a path in and out of the medical center, from which a second entrance opened on the opposite side into the Rabaa sit-in.

"There is no safe passage," said Mohamed Abdel Azeem, a twenty-five-year-old storekeeper. He had escaped the besieged camp and was now trying to get back in through the hospital. We watched as he sprinted and crawled in bursts over the twenty yards of partially protected pavement to the door of the building. I held my breath until I saw that he had made it.

Mayy and I dashed forward behind him, dropping to the ground at the beginning of a low stone ledge along a path toward the door. It seemed to offer some shelter, and we crept along on all fours.

"Come over here, there are bullets holes just over your head!" Mayy yelled to me.

"There are bullet holes over your head, too!" I shouted back defensively, and for some reason we both laughed.

We inched along the dirt, with our heads close to the ground and the seats of our jeans in the air. I felt a pang of guilt for the cost to Mayy's dignity. "I feel like a coward," she called out.

"You are the opposite of a coward! Just stay down," I snapped at her, suddenly furious that some sense of honor might compel her to lift her head.

We sprinted up the steps of the medical center—the last meter to safety—and I looked around me. The marble floor of the lobby was covered in blood. Women walked through the room, trying to help the wounded, and blood stained the hems of their abayas.

A young woman sat cross-legged on the floor, a baby cradled in one arm. Her name was Hayam Hussein, and she had been sleeping in a tent with her daughter, Sarah, eighteen months old, when they were awoken at dawn by the sound of gunfire, sirens, and screams. She grabbed her daughter and ran, forgetting her shoes. Holding Sarah tight to keep her out of the blood on the tiles, Hayam redialed her mobile phone again and again trying to reach her husband. "I just can't stand all the blood I have seen," she sobbed.

"Martyrs, this way!" a medic called out. Men rushed by in groups of four, carrying more corpses in their linked arms to a makeshift morgue in the basement. Dead men, women, teenagers. Asmaa Beltagy, the seventeen-year-old daughter of a Muslim Brotherhood parliamentarian I knew, was killed there that day. One rights group counted at least thirty children under the age of eighteen killed at Rabaa. At least nineteen women were killed there that day, most with bullets to the head or the chest, according to Mozn Hassan's Nazra for Feminist Studies. Many mothers with small children had taken them to beds elsewhere or there might have been more.

Downstairs in the morgue dead bodies filled the shelves and tables. Volunteers were spreading them out on the floor. I could not possibly count them all. If I was a better journalist, I would have been studying details like the location of the wounds on the bodies. Had the security forces been shooting to kill? All I could think about was the volume of blood. There was no way to convey the magnitude of the gore in the few hundred words of a newspaper dispatch.

I decided to try to measure its velocity. How fast were the newly dead coming into this room? I made a mark in my notebook as each corpse was brought through the door. Nine bodies in fifteen minutes. Another dead every hundred seconds, with no end in sight. Of course, the medical center was not the only repository of fresh corpses at Rabaa. I still had no way of knowing how fast people were dying. I was fooling myself, or distracting myself. When I later looked back at that page of my notebook, I saw only hash marks and numbers.

We tried to make our way out of the medical center and across to the mosque. Mayy overheard a young man on his phone. "Safe exit? I'll ask," he said into the phone. Another man in bloodstained clothes told him there was no such exit, and the younger man punched the air in anger. Then he feigned calm and reassured the caller. "I am heading for the safe exit right now. . . ." Mayy guessed he was talking to his mother.

Afraid of the gunfire, we retreated to the safety of the medical center and tried climbing its stairs. From a sixth-floor window, we saw thousands of demonstrators crammed into the square, and they seemed to ebb and flow in unison, first in one direction and then in the other. Waves of police were advancing from both sides, squeezing the crowd back against itself.

A crouching hospital orderly pulled us back from the window. Snipers, he said, and he showed us where a bullet shot from a nearby rooftop had shattered a window near us.

I later saw amateur video footage taken that day of army bulldozers flattening open-sided tents with rows of dead bodies in white shrouds lying inside. In the background a police officer yelled through a megaphone, "The Interior Ministry is very keen on the safety of the citizens." Riot police doused other tents with fuel to set them on fire.

A journalist I trust later told me that he saw two demonstrators in the sit-in fighting back with firearms. One had a homemade handgun that fired a single shotgun cartridge at a time and the other had what looked like a small submachine gun. I would have been surprised if no one had smuggled in a gun. The police later said eight of their own were killed there. The interior minister announced that the police had recovered fifteen firearms used by the demonstrators, who numbered in the thousands. Rocks and Molotov cocktails were the only weapons I saw in the hands of civilians. Who has a gun but instead throws a stone or a gas bomb?

Mohamed Soltan was in the field hospital at the mosque, waiting for a letup in the violence. By 5:00 P.M., his painkillers were wearing off and his arm was throbbing. A senior Brotherhood leader—Mohamed Beltagy, whose daughter had just died—announced to the room that the army had agreed to provide a safe exit for any injured who could walk on their own.

"If you can get away with your skin, get away," he said. Leave behind any possessions.

Soltan filed out with the others, staring at the ground, through a gauntlet of riot police. He heard an elderly man in front of him mutter, "From God we seek refuge and to him we return."

Putting a gun to the head of the old man, a riot policeman told him, "What we are doing is for the sake of God. We are killing you hypocrites."

The interim prime minister later said that "close to a thousand" civilians had died that day at Rabaa. A yearlong study by Human Rights Watch released in 2014 determined that the deaths almost certainly exceeded that number and confirmed the names of at least 817 of the dead. "The indiscriminate and deliberate use of lethal force resulted in one of the world's largest killings of demonstrators in a single day in recent history," the study concluded. Rabaa surpassed the Tiananmen Square massacre in China in 1989 and the Andijan massacre in Uzbekistan in 2005.

Families and human rights groups told me that government coroners were forcing families to accept falsified death certificates to hide the real death toll (a common practice to lower riot statistics in many Arab autocracies).

"About three hundred deaths were written off as suicides," Khaled Amin, the former brigadier general in the police, later told me. "As though everyone just decided to kill themselves that day! Hospitals and morgues were pressured to do it. They told the families, 'Call it a suicide or you don't get your kids.'"

I tried for years to find a soldier or policeman who participated in the operation and would tell his side of the events. Each one refused or backed out. Some told intermediaries that members of the security forces were afraid to be caught talking about it to a Westerner.

The official story was a variation of the one that the Egyptian police have told many times to explain excessive violence: The demonstrators fired the first shot. The security forces, enraged by a noble zeal, avenged their fallen comrades. "They started shooting and three martyrs fell from our side in less than forty-five minutes," a police general insisted in a television interview a few days later. "So how can we deal with gunfire? We can't just say, 'Be quiet.'" He maintained that the police had restrained themselves as best they could. "If we had kept firing shots, everyone there would have died."

Then he added, even less plausibly, that most of the dead civilians were killed by "friendly fire" from other Islamists anyway.

None of this, of course, was ever remotely corroborated.

Amin later told me that the security forces had used their standard procedure for any major operation. The senior officers "charged up" the rank and file before the clearing of Rabaa ever began. The commanders reminded the troops about their friends and colleagues who had been killed in the past by violent Islamists and warned that the Rabaa sit-in was heavily armed. Prepare for fierce, violent resistance, the commanders instructed. The Islamists inside wanted the blood of the police.

"They really pump them up," Amin said. "The message is, 'They killed your friends, they have guns, they will kill you, they are scary.' The officers manipulate you emotionally and charge you up, so you can fire on others."

Amin had retired at the beginning of that summer, but he stayed in touch with his colleagues. "No one talks about it because it is unforgivable," he told me years later. "Those who regret it are too scared to talk, and those who don't regret it are quiet."

Sisi's government decreed a 7:00 P.M. curfew. Military checkpoints sprang into place across the city. Cairenes had scoffed at curfews during Mubarak's last days. Activists and intellectuals had defiantly headed out at night as if it were a matter of high principle. But on the night of August 14, 2013, Cairo was as still as a graveyard. Laura and our sons had recently returned from the United States to Cairo, and they spent the day within a few blocks of home for fear of the violence. I fell asleep at 4:00 A.M. at a cheap hotel near the *New York Times* bureau, and the next morning I headed to another mosque a few blocks from Rabaa.

The Muslim Brotherhood had turned the gymnasium-size sanctuary of the mosque into another improvised morgue. Hundreds of corpses wrapped in white sheets were laid out in neat rows on the floor in the midday August heat. Men walked among them spraying antiseptic into the air. Others wheeled coolers containing large blocks of ice and put one on each dead chest to reduce the smell. They had been at it all night. Water from the melting ice had soaked the carpet.

I moved through the room, counting corpses—I got to 240 even though the removal process had been going on for many hours, and this was only one of many repositories of the dead killed at Rabaa. Many of the bodies were charred beyond recognition, incinerated in their tents.

Tables in a corner displayed rows of identification cards taken from the dead to help families claim them. A small boy about the size of my four-year-old son, Emmett, was asleep on a dry patch of carpet between the tables.

Outside, a cluster of men ignored pleas from the mosque loudspeaker to disperse in order to avoid attracting the security services. "Shoot anyone in uniform," one man said. "It doesn't matter if the good is taken with the bad, because that is what happened to us last night."

Others reassured him that the bloodbath would turn the Egyptian public against the army. "It is already happening," one insisted.

But at the site of the massacre, I found a scene of jubilation. Workers in orange jumpsuits were removing rubble and washing away the bloodstains from the charred ground outside the Rabaa al-Adawiya Mosque. Soldiers and riot police stuck their chests out like heroes. Civilians stopped to congratulate them. A group of young men was dancing to music blasting from the stereo of a nearby parked car. It was the summer's omnipresent hit: "Bless the Hands" of the soldiers.

> As life took us for a turn
> A voice filled with kindness said,
> "May our hands be severed from our bodies
> If they ever touch Egyptians."
> The vow of a real man, son of a real man
> We swear you kept your promise.

26

Jihadis in the White House

August 15, 2013

President Obama, on vacation in Martha's Vineyard, convened a meeting of his National Security Council by teleconference, and now he was no longer so detached or pragmatic. The massacre was hardly unexpected. Essam el-Haddad warned that bloodshed was inevitable. Of course, only violence could break the opposition to the ouster of Egypt's first elected president. Indeed, Sisi's ministers had vowed repeatedly to use all necessary force to eradicate the demonstrators, and everyone knew that the police worked at two speeds: lazy or lethal. The security forces had already carried out two mass shootings in July, killing dozens at a time. But Obama, the Pentagon, and others in the White House were somehow surprised. The president was furious now.

"That is not what we were expecting after we had not reacted as harshly as we might have to the unconstitutional change of power," one senior official, who spoke with Obama that day, later told me. "We were surprised that they would be so ruthless, brutal, and public in their brutality."

Samantha Power, by then UN ambassador, was on the conference call with national security staff.

"He said, 'They just mowed down hundreds of unarmed people. We are allied with a government that is just shooting people in the street,'" Power recalled.

"He was more angry and more horrified than anyone in the Situation Room."

But again Kerry, Hagel, and the Pentagon argued that punishing the Egyptian military would diminish American influence.

Obama delivered a televised address at 10:30 A.M. "Our traditional cooperation cannot continue as usual when civilians are being killed in the streets and rights are being rolled back," he said. He announced the cancellation for the year of a biannual joint military exercise, known as Bright Star. Two months later, in October, the White House suspended the $1.3 billion in annual military aid to Egypt, "pending credible progress toward an inclusive, democratically elected civilian government through free and fair elections."

Egypt was America's closest Arab ally. We may never know if the Arab Spring might have turned out differently had the United States taken a more consistent position toward events in Cairo, or if Washington had pressed its Persian Gulf allies harder to respect the elections in Egypt. Now the administration was more deeply divided than ever: Kerry, Hagel, and others argued that resuming the aid was the only way to retain any sway with Egypt. Power and Rhodes argued that capitulating completely relinquished Washington's influence and credibility.

"It was a surreal experience," Philip Gordon, the White House coordinator for the Middle East, said, looking back. "Neither side believed their policy was going to have any effect on Egypt."

Vexed by the aid suspension, Pentagon officials called Rhodes, Power, and others on the National Security Council staff "the Muslim Brotherhood caucus" or "the jihadis in the White House."

27

Retribution

August 14, 2013–June 1, 2017

A violent backlash broke out across the country as soon as the assault on the sit-in began. As the soldiers and policemen moved into Rabaa al-Adawiya Square, mobs of Muslims in other towns attacked dozens of churches, blaming Christians for supporting the coup. Kerdasa, a town west of Cairo, had been a hub of Islamist militancy for decades. Gunmen stormed its police station, executed fourteen officers, and left their bodies strewn on the floor.

Graffiti calling Sisi a murderer sprang up all over Cairo, even in the affluent blocks surrounding our villa. *CC qatil.* Sisi is a killer, written using the two English *C*s to stand for his name.

The streets were deserted on Friday morning, August 16, two days after the massacre. The army stationed soldiers and a tank at the entrance to our neighborhood. Laura and the boys planned to spend the day in the safety of Maadi House, the club run by the American embassy. They were virtually the only Western family who had returned to Cairo after the summer. They had the place all to themselves. Work crews were raising the exterior walls and adding barbed wire.

I picked up Mayy, for safety in numbers, and we drove downtown together. We did not get far. A dozen men in civilian clothes carrying Kalashnikovs had closed the elevated highway over Bassetine, just northeast of Maadi. At first I thought that they might be Islamists, or maybe carjackers.

Then I saw some lean over the edge of the roadway and point their guns at the Bassetine police station. No one was shooting back, so these were the police, or at least working for them. But that was no relief. The police had already detained several journalists. With an American in the car, they might take us for spies. Our driver made a U-turn and drove back against the direction of traffic—if there had been any traffic. That day, we had the whole road.

Mayy and I got out on the Nile corniche, planning to catch up with an Islamist march protesting against the coup and the massacre. We heard nearby gunfire almost as soon as the driver pulled away. Two men with bandanna masks over their beards came running around a corner, carrying long guns. One berated passersby to join the Islamist protest. Had the "Brotherhood militias" we had heard so much about finally appeared?

We hid behind a sycamore tree near the river. Two women in head scarves and a bearded man holding a Morsi poster were hiding behind another tree next to us, and one of the women called to Mayy. "Who are these men? Are they with us or with them?"

"We are journalists!" Mayy told her. "We should be asking you!"

One of the two masked gunmen appeared out of nowhere from the other side of the tree and moved his gun barrel across the five of us, like an outlaw at a holdup.

"They are journalists!" the woman spat out. She was throwing us in to protect herself.

The gunman aimed at Mayy. After a long moment he appealed for sympathy. "They have been shooting at us all day," he said. I had no idea who he meant.

"We were trying to cover the demonstration. We are just trying to leave!" Mayy pleaded.

The gunmen would let us escape if we walked south by the Nile, away from the Islamist march we had planned to cover. Mayy and I were convinced that the men were police provocateurs in disguise. It was becoming hard to know who was who.

As we walked, we followed reports and videos on social media of gunfire all around Cairo. In one video, a Morsi supporter was firing a rifle near the entrance to the Four Seasons Hotel opposite the zoo. In others, pedestrians fleeing gunshots jumped or fell from bridges over the Nile. We saw an empty office tower burn unchecked and unattended.

The Muslim Brothers were still trying to organize street demonstrations, and all came under withering assault by the military and police. Amr Darrag had handled the eleventh-hour negotiations with Western diplomats to try to avert the massacre. He walked with his wife and three daughters that Friday in a protest march across a bridge from Zamalek toward down-town. Gunmen started shooting from the top of a hotel. Plainclothes thugs cornered them on the roadway, and the police smothered the march in tear gas. (There were non-Islamist witnesses, too.)

"We are dealing with vampires," Darrag told me when I caught up with him that afternoon. "My analysis is that they would like to force people to go to violence." (Darrag was among the lucky few Brotherhood leaders who eventually managed to escape Egypt—mainly to Istanbul, Doha, or London.)

By afternoon, thousands of Islamist demonstrators gathered in Ramses Square, the open plaza about a half hour's walk northeast of the Tahrir traffic circle. Ramses Square was where the founder of the Muslim Brother-hood had been assassinated decades earlier by agents of the king. Young Islamists hurled rocks and Molotov cocktails at a police station, and the police shot back. A thirty-year-old grandson of the Brotherhood's founder was killed. So was the thirty-eight-year-old son of the Brotherhood's gen-eral guide, Mohamed Badie (who coined the slogan "Our peacefulness is stronger than their bullets").

The official reports concluded that more than a hundred civilians had been killed, but my colleague Kareem Fahim counted at least thirty dead bodies in another makeshift morgue inside a mosque near the square. I doubted the Health Ministry counted them in its total.

I wondered if this was how Algeria felt as its civil war started. Laura and the boys evacuated the next day, Saturday, to Tel Aviv, but she brought them back a few weeks later, with some trepidation. We did not want to miss the start of the school year. Many expats stayed away. Our sons' classes at the Maadi British International School shrank to half the size they used to be.

Michael Morrell of the CIA and other American intelligence officials had worried under Morsi that Al Qaeda might find a foothold in the North Sinai—the loosely governed strip of rocky desert between the Suez

Canal and Israel, about 120 miles east of Cairo and 200 miles north of the biblical mountain. Now the backlash against the takeover expanded that initial foothold into a nascent insurgency. Within hours of Morsi's arrest, militants released an online video of a crowd of thousands in the North Sinai rallying under the black flag of jihad. "The age of 'peacefulness' is over, no more peacefulness after today," the speaker declared, mocking the Brotherhood slogan.

"No more elections after today," the crowd chanted back.

The jihadist group Ansar Beit al-Maqdis—whose murder of sixteen Egyptian soldiers in the summer of 2012 had scandalized the country— was reborn as the main armed opposition to Sisi. After the Rabaa massacre, Ansar Beit al-Maqdis shifted from attacking Israel to attacking the Egyptian security forces. It claimed responsibility for near-daily attacks on police and soldiers. The militants shot one or two here and there, executed them by the busload, or set off bombs that killed dozens at a time. Killing sixteen soldiers at once became almost routine.

Within weeks, the militants started carrying out bombings and assassinations inside Cairo. A car bomb blew a crater in a Nasr City street but failed to kill the interior minister. An improvised explosive device took out the top prosecutor. On the third anniversary of the uprising—January 25, 2014—an explosion demolished a security headquarters and damaged an Islamic art museum. And so on. By the spring of 2017, thousands of members of the security forces had died and the numbers were still growing.

Ansar Beit al-Maqdis was almost as hostile to the Muslim Brothers as it was to Sisi. Jihadists everywhere had long faulted the Muslim Brothers for eschewing violence, for demanding democracy, for befriending Washington, and most of all for trusting the generals. Ayman al-Zawahiri of Al Qaeda compared the Brotherhood to "a poultry farm" that "breeds happy chickens pleased with what they are given and ignorant of the thieves and monsters around it."

In a video taking responsibility for a bombing in Cairo that October, a narrator for Ansar Beit al-Maqdis mocked "this farce called 'democratic Islam.'" The voiceover told the Muslim Brotherhood it would have lost nothing by joining a puritanical jihad. "Would they have prevented you from reaching power? Now they have ousted you. Would America have been upset with you? Now it is upset. Would they have detained you? Now they are detaining you. Would they have shed your blood? Now they are shedding your blood and burning your headquarters and assaulting mosques." Sisi's battalions "found only chants and shouts and bare chests. So you were easy prey for him—to be murdered, captured, tortured, and harassed."

"Armed confrontation" was the only response, the narrator concluded. "Iron must be fought with iron and fire by fire." Jihadists across the region proclaimed their vindication.

Egypt was the pivot. Until the coup of July 3, 2013, journalists, scholars, and diplomats all talked without apology about an Arab Spring, a democratic opening. Tunisia's Islamist party had won parliamentary elections, then formed the region's first Islamist-liberal coalition government. The Syrian uprising was still more or less centered on democracy—not revenge or theocracy. Only a small faction of the rebels had pledged allegiance to Al Qaeda, and they dared do so in public only as recently as April. Libya had held credible parliamentary elections and chosen a liberal prime minister. The State Department held up Yemen as a model transition to democracy.

But after the Rabaa massacre, Al Qaeda's Iraqi arm could declare that "two idols have fallen: democracy and the Muslim Brotherhood—bankrupt." The choice now was clear: "ammunition boxes over ballot boxes."

A renegade Libyan general, Khalifa Hifter, took his cue from Sisi. He announced in early 2014 that the imaginary Libyan Supreme Council of the Armed Forces would dissolve its Parliament, arrest its Islamists, and eradicate their movement. Hifter repeated parts of Sisi's coup speech almost verbatim, like his promise of a transitional road map.

The prime minister laughed it off. At his base near Benghazi, though, Hifter received weapons and other support from the UAE and Egypt in violation of a United Nations embargo (first confirmed in a leaked recording from Sisi's office and in hacked emails among UAE diplomats, and later common knowledge). Soon armed groups for and against Hifter were bullying the Parliament. The political process broke down. Libya burst into a civil war that continued for years.

The Iraqi arm of Al Qaeda broke away a few months after the massacre in Cairo to become the Islamic State in Iraq and Syria, also known as ISIS or ISIL. By June of the next year, ISIS had declared a "caliphate" stretching deep into Syria. And by the summer of 2015, it had capitalized on the chaos of the Libyan civil war to seize control of a hundred miles of its Mediterranean coastline around the city of Sirte.

I often heard people in the Arab world and in the West cite the mayhem that broke out across Syria, Iraq, Libya, and Yemen to justify Sisi's takeover. Look at the mess the Arab Spring made! But the hope soured only after Sisi took power, with the resurgence of the old order and the vindication of the jihadists. What Tahrir ignited, Rabaa extinguished.

E gyptian military spokesmen began predicting the imminent defeat of the North Sinai jihadists almost immediately after Rabaa. As more and more soldiers were killed there, month after month, the spokesmen repeated the same predictions. The army was just mopping up. The generals barred foreigners and journalists from the area. Then the military police arrested the local stringer we had relied on. A military press release had boasted of killing four militants in his village, and his crime was writing on Facebook that the soldiers had instead killed four unarmed civilians. He was let out after a few weeks but was scared away from reporting.

So Mayy el-Sheikh—always brave—went undercover: an Egyptian woman in a head scarf in the passenger seat next to a Bedouin driver in a small, beat-up car with North Sinai license plates. At checkpoints, the police talked only to the male driver, assuming she was his female relation.

The army had walled off the center of the provincial capital, Arish, like a miniature version of the American Green Zone in occupied Baghdad. The Egyptian authorities had shut down all mobile phone or internet service during daylight hours, in part because militants used phone signals to detonate roadside bombs. And at dusk the soldiers enforced a strict nighttime curfew. Residents and doctors reported dozens of innocent civilians killed by gunshots from jumpy soldiers at checkpoints. Helicopters hunting militants had turned whole towns into rubble. Locals in Arish ducked behind closed doors to speak to Mayy, and they whispered nervously about Brigade 101—a military detention facility inside the walled security zone and notorious for torture.

"The slaughterhouse," several residents called it. "The people who get taken to Brigade 101 don't get out," a doctor at the local hospital told Mayy. I thought of Room 101, the interrogation chamber in George Orwell's *1984*.

Some referred to Ansar Beit al-Maqdis as "Brigade 102"—the rival gang that terrorized their villages. Brigade 102 owned the night, when the soldiers retreated inside their walled compounds. But even by day the jihadists put up checkpoints and controlled the roads in some areas of the North Sinai.

Ansar Beit al-Maqdis swiftly grew in sophistication, staging coordinated attacks with waves of assailants, and striking ever farther from the Sinai—especially in the western desert, close to Libya. No longer an Al Qaeda foothold, Ansar Beit al-Maqdis pledged its allegiance to ISIS in 2015 and tested the tactics of its new caliph. The renamed Sinai Province of the Islamic State captured and briefly held the major North Sinai town of Sheikh Zuwaid. The Egyptian air force attacked the town in order to drive the militants out before sundown.

The militants beheaded suspected informers and, in one case, a Westerner: a Croatian working for a French petroleum company whom they had abducted on a highway. They put out slick, gory videos in the Islamic State style. Then they tried their hands at bombing airplanes. In the fall of 2015, the jihadists brought down a Russian charter jet taking off near Sharm el-Sheikh in the South Sinai. Two hundred twenty-four people were killed. After that the militants shifted to attacking Christians, too.

Over the next eighteen months, the Islamic State fighters assassinated more than a half dozen local Copts, burned homes, destroyed churches, and forced more than a hundred families to flee for their lives. On Palm Sunday 2017, two Islamic State church bombings far from the Sinai, in the cities of Tanta and Alexandria, killed at least forty-five people.

Western officials had told me privately in 2014 and 2015 that they believed there might have been at most 2,000 Ansar Beit al-Maqdis fighters in the North Sinai; some American diplomats put the number at half that. The Egyptian authorities said only a few hundred. But by April 2017, Egypt had lost more than 3,000 soldiers and police fighting what, by its own count, were only a few hundred "terrorists." If you added up the body counts in its press releases, the Sisi government claimed its security forces had killed a total of more than 6,200 militants—more than three times the highest estimate of the number of fighters in Ansar Beit al-Maqdis at any time. The official numbers did not add up.

American diplomats griped to one another about how little fighting power that $1.3 billion a year in military aid had bought. Even after four years, the Egyptian army could not defeat the rabble of militants in the Sinai. Were new fighters replacing the fallen so quickly? Who was Egypt killing?

The story of two Bedouin brothers shed some light on the puzzle. The episode began in Rafah, a town of about 80,000 people near the Gaza border. By the summer of 2015, Sisi's government had demolished thousands of buildings there, displacing more than 3,200 families and razing acres of their farmland. The idea was to create a buffer zone with Gaza to prevent militants from hopscotching the border. But leveling a whole city won few friends among the displaced.

On July 18, 2016, two teenage brothers—Daoud Sabri al-Awabdah and Abd al-Hadi Sabri al-Awabdah, both of the Rumailat clan—were arrested in the wreckage. It is impossible to know why, because the police brought no charges and conducted no trial. The brothers disappeared. Their families assumed Brigade 101 had swallowed them up.

But the two brothers turned up a few months later, in a leaked video recorded that fall in a patch of rocky desert. Soldiers, intelligence officers, and progovernment militiamen in military uniforms and body armor were milling around near an American-made Humvee. The militiamen were leading around some captives, bound and blindfolded. Daoud, who was sixteen, was lying on the ground in a red shirt, with his hands and feet tied together.

"Just not in the head, not in the head," a commander was heard shouting. A militiaman fired four shots from his Kalashnikov into Daoud. "That is enough," the commander said.

Daoud's nineteen-year-old brother, Abd al-Hadi, was wearing blue jeans and standing, with his arms tied and eyes covered. "Boy, are you from the Abu Shanana family?" a militiaman demanded, grabbing him by the hair. Sporadic gunshots went off in the background. Abd al-Hadi and his captor traded tribal names and village locations until they had pinpointed where Abd al-Hadi's family had lived, like two people from the same hometown meeting in a faraway place.

"Okay, come then," the soldier or militiaman said at last, and he led away the prisoner.

Militiamen tossed Abd al-Hadi to the ground. "Get on with it, come on!" someone shouted. Two progovernment gunmen stood over Abd al-Hadi. One pulled off his white blindfold. Another shot him five times, lowered his Kalashnikov, and walked calmly away. Six other dead bodies in civilian clothes were lying nearby.

After the killings, militiamen and soldiers placed weapons on the ground around the corpses, as if they had been armed when they died. This bit of staging, too, was all recorded on video.

"Should I change the position of the weapon?" a voice asks. "Finish, finish!" the cameraman tells him.

On November 5 and again on December 6, the Egyptian Defense Ministry released official propaganda footage showing the two dead brothers and six other bodies. "Eight armed terrorist elements" eliminated in a gun battle, the ministry said.

Footage from the same scene also appeared on a promilitary website. "This is the revenge for those who died," a soldier standing near the bodies proclaimed in this video. The Department of Moral Affairs, the military's propaganda arm, was in on the frame-up, and the satisfied officers had shared their home movies.

Human Rights Watch and Amnesty International called the videos evidence of war crimes, part of a pattern of arbitrary and extrajudicial killings by a military that received more from American taxpayers than any country but Israel.

Egyptian officials shrugged off the complaints. An army general said on a television talk show that the scenes filmed were Brotherhood fabrications. Sisi was unbothered. But I better understood where some of those dead "jihadists" came from. Western diplomats told me they believed that the Egyptian security forces were using the Sinai as a dumping ground for the bodies of prisoners killed under torture in the prisons of the mainland. The torture victims were added to the "terrorists" body count.

I did not see how the Egyptian military's haphazard tactics would get anywhere, but I was surprised again. By 2017, British and American diplomats were telling me that the Islamic State no longer set up checkpoints on the highways. Soldiers no longer cowered in their barracks at night, afraid for their lives.

What was the secret, after four years of fighting? It was not the Egyptian military. It was Israel.

Egypt and Israel had fought four wars on their Sinai border, if we count the skirmishing around the Suez Canal crisis. On April 25 of each year, Egypt celebrates Sinai Liberation Day, commemorating the final withdrawal of the last Israeli troops in 1982. But the two militaries cooperated closely through their four decades of peace, I knew. Sisi's government and its news media still ceasely vilified the Jewish state as a loathsome enemy. Collaborating with the "Zionists" was as damnable as treason.

A few weeks after Sisi took power, in August 2013, two mysterious explosions killed five suspected militants in a district of the North Sinai not far from the Israeli border. When an Associated Press report suggested Israeli drones had killed the militants, Sisi's spokesman vigorously denied it. "There is no truth in form or in substance to the existence of any Israeli attacks inside Egyptian territory," Colonel Ahmed Ali said, promising an investigation that never happened. "The claims of coordination between the Egyptian and Israeli sides in this matter are totally lacking in truth and go against sense and logic." The Israeli armed forces declined to comment. The event was almost forgotten.

But by late 2015—when the Islamic State had planted its flag in Sinai, begun aspiring for territory, and brought down the Russian jet—Israel's leaders lost patience. The continued failure of the Egyptian army to secure the peninsula was getting dangerous. The Israeli air force began a secret campaign of air strikes against suspected militants inside Egypt, often hitting them as frequently as twice a week or more, all with the blessing of President Sisi.

Israel flew unmarked drones, jets, and helicopters. The jets and helicopters covered up their markings and flew circuitous routes to give the impression they took off from the Egyptian mainland. Sisi hid the strikes from all but a small circle of senior military and intelligence officers. No journalists were allowed in the area, and the state-dominated news media never asked questions. Israeli military censors restricted public reports of the strikes there as well.

But by the end of 2017, Israel had carried out far more than a hundred secret strikes inside Egypt: a covert air war.

Amazed British and American government officials had hinted to me for two years about the growing scale of the attacks that Israel had carried out over the Egyptian Sinai with Sisi's blessing. By 2017, several American officials told me that Israel deserved much of the credit for the Egyptian government's limited success in containing the Islamic State (even though more vicious jihadists sprang up to replace each leader killed, one diplomat noted). Israeli military officials griped to the Americans that Egyptians were not doing enough on their end, sometimes failing to send in ground forces after an air strike when the Israelis had asked for a coordinated sequence of operations. But for more than two years, under two American administrations, all sides kept it quiet, afraid of the potential for unrest in Egypt if Israel's role became known.

Egypt's reliance on Israel, though, altered the dynamics of the region. On February 21, 2016, Secretary of State Kerry convened a secret summit in Aqaba, Jordan, with Sisi, King Abdullah, and Israeli prime minister Benjamin Netanyahu. Part of Kerry's agenda was a regional agreement for Egypt to guarantee Israel's security as part of a deal for a Palestinian state.

Netanyahu scoffed. What could Sisi offer Israel? Netanyahu asked, according to two Americans involved in the talks. Sisi depended on Israel to control his own territory, for his own survival. Sisi needed Netanyahu; Netanyahu did not need Sisi. And Sisi, for his part, told American officials directly that he would do nothing to pressure Netanyahu.

In 2017, President Trump announced that the United States was recognizing Jerusalem as the capital of Israel. Washington was no longer waiting for an Israeli agreement with the Palestinians to make the Holy City the shared capital of two states. Egyptian diplomats publicly denounced Trump's decision, even initiating a United Nations resolution to condemn it. But a leaked audio recording captured an Egyptian intelligence officer coaching talk show hosts about how to persuade the public to accept the Jerusalem decision in the interests of stability.

The officer, identifying himself as Ashraf el-Kholi, told the hosts that the Palestinians could make do with their current headquarters in the West

Bank city of Ramallah. "How is Jerusalem different from Ramallah, really?" Kholi repeated.

Because "Rabaa" means fourth in Arabic, Brotherhood-style Islamists from Istanbul to Manila adapted a four-fingered salute as a symbol of solidarity. A logo of a black hand holding up four fingers against a bright yellow background became the new icon of the Muslim Brotherhood, and the Sisi government criminalized the gesture. Anyone caught making it could be punished. A professional soccer star was suspended from his team, students were expelled from schools, vacationers were arrested for taking selfies at a train station. We told our sons never to hold up four fingers in school or on the streets, even as a joke—a hard lesson for a four-year-old.

Gehad el-Haddad, the Brotherhood spokesman and the son of Morsi's foreign policy adviser, was thirty-two years old. He had been educated in Britain and previously worked for the Clinton Foundation on Middle Eastern and energy issues. Members of his family told me that he was a personal friend of Chelsea's. Haddad had met Prime Minister David Cameron at 10 Downing Street, and he became a liaison to Western diplomats and journalists. I knew Haddad as a flak: he did public relations for the Brothers. But he was bright and well read. I enjoyed his company.

After the Rabaa massacre, that history made him a wanted man, and he escaped underground. I reached him six days later by Skype. He was staying off phones or email, sneaking from apartment to apartment, hiding his face in public, and spending no more than one night in any one place. "State security is very aggressive and I'm a recognizable face."

The Brothers had stopped calling for street protests or "martyrs." Too many were dying. Islamists "joke about 'the good old days of Mubarak,'" Haddad said. "We came close to annihilation once under Nasser, but this is worse," he told me. "This is the worst ever."

He was captured on September 17. Both Gehad and his father, Essam, were sentenced to life for inciting violence. Soon, almost every Muslim Brother I knew was in jail or exile. In 2017, American officials would put the number of political prisoners still behind bars in Egypt at more than thirty thousand. Some said as many as sixty thousand. The Interior Ministry built new jails to hold them. But there were nearly half a million dues-paying Muslim Brothers in Egypt. The ministry could not jail them all.

Would young Muslim Brothers accept the logic of violence, as the jihadists argued? On May 27, 2015, more than a hundred Muslim scholars signed an open letter, "The Egypt Call."

"The aggrieved party has the right to fight back against the aggressor," the letter declared. "A murderous regime" ruled Egypt, and its collaborators—"rulers, judges, officers, soldiers, muftis, media professionals, and politicians"—should be punished as "murderers" under Islamic law. A death sentence.

A spokesman for the Brotherhood's leadership-in-hiding—now writing online under a pseudonym—endorsed the Call the next day. The Egyptian government had executed a handful of Brothers, and the spokesman proclaimed that "retribution" was the only response to such "murderers"—"a revolution that reaps heads from atop rotten bodies."

Satellite television networks linked to the Egyptian Brotherhood and broadcasting from Istanbul seethed with demands for revenge. "Now, it's not 'Our peacefulness is stronger than bullets,'" a man on the edge of a riot in greater Cairo told an interviewer in a phone call to one of the networks. "Our peacefulness is stronger *with* bullets.... Their women for our women. Their girls for our girls. Blood for blood."

"That is what I was just saying!" the interviewer, Mohamed Nasser, agreed. "I sent a message to the wives of the officers and told them that revolutionaries will kill their husbands!"

The Egypt Call was too much for some elders of the movement. Sticking to nonviolence may feel like "grasping a burning coal," one elder, Mahmoud Ghozlan, wrote in an open letter posted on the internet from an undisclosed location. But Brotherhood history had proven that "violence is the reason for defeat and demise."

A revered senior scholar sometimes referred to as the mufti of the Brotherhood, Abdel Rahman al-Barr, seconded the reprimand. "Peacefulness is not a tactic or a maneuver," he wrote in his open letter from a hidden location. "It is a fundamental choice based on religious jurisprudence" and "a correct reading of history."

Online messages from angry young Brothers drowned out their warnings.

"What you're describing isn't called 'peacefulness,' it's called 'shame and humiliation.'" "Bloodshed has overrun the meaning of prone 'peacefulness.'"

Within days, the police arrested both elders. A court had already convicted them in absentia of inciting violence despite their public efforts to stop it. Their death sentences were waiting.

The Brotherhood, the grandfather of Islamist movements, had presented itself for decades as a bulwark against violence and extremism. Now it was too internally confused and divided to play any such role. By 2017, the Brotherhood had collapsed into endless debates about what went wrong, how to move forward, and most of all about who should take over. Had they moved too fast or too slow? Should they retreat into separatism or embrace confrontation? Could there be such a thing as "defensive violence"? Individual cells were split by loyalties to rival leadership teams.

For two years after 2011, Western journalists in the Middle East wrote about debates over the compatibility of Islam and democracy. After the summer of 2013, we wrote about whether Islam was inherently violent.

For the first few months after Rabaa, the army deployed heavily around the city each Friday morning to crush any protest before it got going. Occasionally supporters of the Brotherhood would hold Friday marches in or near our neighborhood, Maadi, and we had a couple of close calls. But most marches were quickly scattered by police. We always managed to keep our sons away. Then the pattern of street protests gradually faded.

The months of demonstrations were followed by an unnerving period of nocturnal explosions, sometimes in earshot of our bedroom. One night in October, a bomb destroyed a satellite dish that we passed each day driving our sons to their school. But over time it became clear that, unlike the jihadists, these attackers were targeting infrastructure or empty shops, not trying to kill civilians. Laura commended their restraint and breathed a little easier. The boys' lives were now circumscribed by the few blocks between our home, their school, and the pool club, but they did not seem to mind. There were school plays and swim meets. Laura was working at the American University in Cairo. Most of her elite, Anglophone Egyptian colleagues were delighted to be rid of the Muslim Brothers.

One day a few weeks after Rabaa, my phone rang as I was ducking into a restaurant in Zamalek for dinner. "Hey, David, this is Mohamed Soltan . . ."

It was the Egyptian American Ohio State grad who took a bullet in his arm at the Rabaa sit-in. He was calling me from a lightless, overcrowded dungeon in the Tora prison complex.

The police had arrested him in a raid on his apartment a few days after the massacre. He had been inducted into prison with a ritual initiation known as the *tashreefa*, or honoring ceremony. He and the other new inmates were stripped to their underwear, then forced for two hours to run between two rows of guards beating them with whips, belts, and batons.

Provided no medical attention, Soltan relied on a prisoner with a medical degree to remove two thirteen-inch pins from his injured arm, using pliers and a straight razor, without anesthetic or sterilization. Then Soltan's jailers threw him into an underground cell. Prisoners screamed and begged to get running water turned on for a few hours a day. Soltan had paid the equivalent of forty dollars to a street criminal for an hour's use of a smuggled mobile phone. He called me and Abigail Hauslohner, my counterpart at the *Washington Post*.

I was terrified that he would be caught talking to me (was my phone under surveillance?) and endure more beatings. But Soltan knew his only hope was his American passport. He wanted to tell Americans that a fellow citizen was in jail for defending democracy. He bet that his midwestern accent would stir in me a feeling of connection, and in that he was right.

Egyptian prisons make the harshest American supermax look like the Four Seasons. The tens of thousands rounded up after the coup were deprived of decent food, sanitation, health care, or bedding. They slept on crowded floors infested with bugs. They were beaten and occasionally tortured. None of that was a surprise.

It was difficult, in a perverse way, to empathize. Their stories blurred together: a regional marketing executive for a Danish pharmaceutical company who was arrested at the airport on his way to a sales conference; the genial physician-turned-parliamentarian paraded before cameras still in his bedclothes; the septuagenarian general guide led off without his dentures. How could Egyptians do that to one another?

One memorable day two years after Rabaa I received three separate phone calls about three other friends who were all locked away in Egyptian jails—two Islamists and a liberal. The brother of one, the son of another, and the fiancé of the third all wanted to know: was there anything I could do to call attention to their cases?

No, I gently told them, there was nothing I could do. One more Egyptian political prisoner was hardly newsworthy.

Soltan was charged with inciting violence, just like so many others. But he knew his Americanness made him different. It was his slang, his profanity, his zeal for the Ohio State Buckeyes, his work knocking on doors for the 2008 Obama campaign. When he turned twenty-six on November 16, 2013, I helped arrange for the website of the *New York Times* to publish an open letter to Obama that Soltan had written that day and smuggled out of prison.

"Mr. President, all I long for is the opportunity to get together this Thanksgiving with family and friends and enjoy some turkey and pie. I keep dreaming about watching my Buckeyes winning it all this year after beating Michigan. Counting down the clocks on New Years. Watching the Super Bowl in my Tom Brady jersey (hopefully he isn't a disappointment this past season!) and eating a good ol' cheeseburger with a side of fries . . ."

On his twenty-seventh birthday, he smuggled out of prison a letter to his mother. He was surviving, he told her, on the lessons in determination and perseverance he learned playing high school basketball, from a coach he called Slappy.

Soltan had entered prison at five eleven and weighing 272 pounds. Over three months that fall, he gradually stopped eating protein or meat (what little there was in prison), then carbohydrates, and then dairy products. On January 26, 2014, he began a hunger strike, consuming only water, salt, and vitamins provided by his family.

After about fifteen days, he began losing consciousness occasionally. Sometimes he was taken to a prison hospital for intravenous infusions of glucose and saline. He was locked in solitary confinement and briefly broke down, banging his head against the door until he bled and needed a bandage. He later told me that guards had slipped razors under the door and exposed electrical wire inside his cell, to tempt him with suicide. "Relieve us and you of this headache," one told him.

He was kept awake by screams of pain from other cells. He was put under a twenty-four-hour-a day spotlight and then a blinking strobe. When he refused to let prison doctors take his vital signs, he was handcuffed to a wheelchair and beaten into submission.

Then an ailing prisoner named Rida was wheeled into Soltan's hospital room. His new roommate screamed in agony and died in front of him. But no one answered Soltan's cries for help. When someone finally came in at 3:00 P.M. the next day, Soltan had spent half a day alone with the corpse.

After eleven months on water and vitamins, Soltan had lost one hundred sixty pounds. United States diplomats in Cairo pleaded with the Egyptians to deport him. In September 2014, Obama met Sisi for the first time, during the United Nations General Assembly, and made a face-to-face push for Soltan's release. Sisi murmured about the independence of the Egyptian judiciary. Soltan stayed in jail.

In January 2015, Soltan acceded to his family's wishes and began accepting milk and yogurt, to keep his organs intact. They said Obama's intervention might win his freedom. On May 30, 2015—after twenty-one months in prison and sixteen months on a hunger strike—he was finally deported to the United States.

I met Soltan at his sister's home in northern Virginia the next winter, and he told me that the three friends arrested with him were all still in prison. So was his aging father. Unlike him, they were only Egyptians.

Islamic State jihadists, he said, had been recruiting avidly in the prison. "They say, 'These apostates will never respect anything but violent resistance. They only understand the language of weapons,'" Soltan said. "The one thing that everybody in the prison had in common—the ISIS guys, the Muslim Brotherhood guys, the liberals, the guards, the officers—is that they all hated America."

28

Deep State

August 14, 2013–June 1, 2017

Laura and I often bought our groceries at a chain store called Seoudi Market. Laura could walk there without leaving the safety of our neighborhood. Friendly deliverymen dropped off our purchases at our door, and Laura got to know them all. Then one day in late 2013 she went shopping and found a crowd of policemen outside the store. All the staff had been fired. The military had taken over the chain. Its owner was a Muslim Brother. The owner of its competitor, Metro, had connections.

On a drive to Alexandria that fall, we noticed that uniformed soldiers were running the toll road, too. The military, in the interest of security, had taken over the management and construction of all roads and bridges. The Alexandria highway tollbooth soon moved next to a military-owned gas station and rest stop, devastating the privately owned businesses at the old location. Over six months in 2014, military-owned firms received more than $1.5 billion in contracts to build apartment blocks, tunnels, roads, and many other things. These were boom times for Egyptian Army Inc.

The generals "consider Egypt a battlefield," Mounir Fakhry Abdel Nour, Sisi's trade minister, told Abigail Hauslohner of the *Washington Post*. "That gives the military the right of first refusal on every piece of land."

A British friend was developing a shopping mall in Cairo, and over drinks one night he explained the system. There had been bureaucracy and *baksheesh* under Mubarak, of course. But now the developer was required to hire the military to build all roads, sewage or water networks, and other infrastucture. The military subcontracted the jobs to a company whose principal shareholders had heavily backed the coup (the Sawiris family). That company passed contracts on to the son of Sisi's then–prime minister, Ibrahim Mehleb. Everyone in the chain got a cut. And it was dangerous to bring up such official corruption in public.

Mehleb, who had headed the state construction company under Mubarak, brought a long record of corruption to the prime minister's job. Court records introduced after Mubarak's ouster showed that Mehleb had inflated government contracts to allow the president and his family to embezzle millions for lavish purchases like five German-made refrigerators, a private office for the First Lady in a five-star hotel, several villas by the Red Sea, and a farm outside Cairo. Mehleb fled to Saudi Arabia in 2012 to avoid prosecution for corruption. He returned only when Sisi's government named him housing minister in 2013. Sisi made Mehleb prime minister eight months later, in February 2014, his past forgotten.

Was Mehleb now brazenly steering contracts to his son? I rushed to investigate, but there was no need. His son's firm—Rawad Construction, founded by Mohamed Mehleb—listed its government contracts and subcontracts in a prominent place on its website: a terminal for the Cairo airport; sewage and water facilities in Cairo and on the Mediterranean coast; infrastructure for a new university in Giza; a power plant in the city of Bani Suef; a wind farm near the Red Sea; and roads for a new administrative center. In a downbeat economy, the Mehlebs were soaring.

Executives of the company assured me that it was all based on merit. But Sisi had suspended the competitive bidding rules, so it was impossible to know. And there was no independent prosecutor, Parliament, or Egyptian press to investigate.

"It's not only Mehleb's son," Anwar Sadat, a lawmaker and the nephew of the former president, told me. "The whole military economic empire needs oversight." (I assumed his famous name would protect Sadat, but in 2017, the rubber-stamp Parliament voted almost unanimously to expel him, for the crime of defending the independence of nonprofits. "We saw that Sadat was working against the Parliament and against the state," one lawmaker said, suggesting treason.)

Corruption was the price of autocracy. The Egyptian government for decades has boasted an exceptionally powerful anticorruption watchdog—the Administrative Oversight Authority. It is a military-run domestic spy agency, conducting electronic surveillance, running its own jails, and detaining suspects or even witnesses without warrants or trials. Created by Abdel Nasser to help control the civilian bureaucracy, the authority reports directly to the president. That is the catch: it makes no pretense of autonomy.

In practice, the Adminstrative Oversight Authority often charges the president's enemies with venality while covering up for the self-dealing of his friends and family. The watchdog, in other words, is itself an instrument of corruption. Other Arab autocracies run similar systems.

The uprising of 2011 once promised an end to impunity for self-dealing. In the heady days after Mubarak's ouster, a police officer working for the agency came forward to expose its corruption. In formal complaints and, later, in television interviews, the whistle-blower presented evidence that the agency's chief, General Mohamed Farid el-Tohamy, was still covering up for Mubarak even after his ouster. "He is protecting the former regime" by locking the evidence in "a secret safe," the whistle-blower, Lieutenant Colonel Moatassem Fathi, charged.

He said Tohamy had pocketed millions of dollars in gifts—really, protection money—from state-owned companies and government agencies. In return Tohamy spent as much as sixteen thousand dollars a year of the agency's budget on presents for the defense minister and still more on gifts for Mubarak's sons. The allegations filled the newspapers. Prosecutors opened a case. A parliamentary committee started an investigation. And Morsi replaced the sixty-six-year-old Tohamy with another general from inside the authority.

Tohamy, though, was also a mentor to Sisi. Tohamy had promoted Sisi at military intelligence and then hired one of Sisi's sons at the Administrative Oversight Authority. The day after Sisi took over—on July 4, 2013—Tohamy made a comeback. Sisi named his old friend as the new chief of the Egyptian General Intelligence Service, one of the most powerful positions in the state. With Sisi's ear, Tohamy became one of the most influential advocates of a scorched-earth eradication of the Muslim Brotherhood. "He was the most hard-line, the most absolutely unreformed," one Western diplomat told me. "He talked as if the revolution of 2011 had never even happened."

The allegations against Tohamy vanished. The whistle-blower was exiled to a desk job far from Cairo. "They have got him locked in the basement," Mohamed Ibrahim Soliman, a former housing minister incriminated by Fathi's disclosures, told me with glee. Several politicians like Soliman who had been jailed for corruption after the uprising were soon back in business—including Ahmed Ezz, the most infamous face of the late Mubarak era. I found him back to work at an office inside the Four Seasons.

How much did corruption cost Egypt? Archaeologists had fretted after the 2011 uprising that the withdrawal of the police allowed looters to pillage ruins and excavations. But corruption continued to eat away at Egypt's ancient patrimony after the police returned under Sisi. Western and Egyptian archaeologists spoke of the theft or mistreatment of ancient artifacts as an unreported tragedy. In 2014, Egyptian Museum workers were fixing a light fixture around the 3,300-year-old burial mask of King Tutankhamen when they accidentally snapped off his beard. Curators hastily reattached it with a form of superglue in order to cover up their error and keep the museum's biggest draw open. A visitor noticed a sloppy ring of epoxy around the repair job, and it is unclear if King Tut's beard will ever be the same.

A government auditor, Hisham Geneina, estimated in early 2016 that graft had cost the country $76 billion over the previous three years, mostly through the corrupt sales of government land. That was about three quarters of the annual government budget, and his estimate was surely low if you factored in the bribery, nepotism, and self-dealing at every level of the bureaucracy. Transparency International, the corruption monitor, ranked Egypt near the bottom of the Arab world, on a par with war zones like Yemen and Iraq.

Sisi took the assessment personally. He promptly fired Geneina. A court convicted Geneina of spreading false news. He was fined $2,200, sentenced to jail, and falsely attacked across the progovermment media as a secret Muslim Brother. (His sentence was suspended, stirring speculation that his conviction had been devised to snuff out political ambitions. In the run-up to Sisi's reelection in 2018, a gang of unidentified men beat up Geneina and a few days later the police again arrested him.)

Kerry and other American officials had lost patience with Morsi for moving too slowly to reach a deal with the International Monetary Fund during his first and only year in office. Sisi openly opposed the deal and sent the IMF packing.

Why reform? The Persian Gulf monarchs could not let Sisi fail and thereby give another chance to the Muslim Brothers. The Gulf rulers appeared willing to pay anything to keep propping up their man in Cairo.

Another secretly recorded conversation captured Sisi conferring with other generals in early 2014 about how to handle one of his Persian Gulf patrons. "You tell him that we need ten to be put into the army's account. Those ten, when God makes us successful, we will put to work for the state," Sisi said, rattling off his demands for more cash. "We need another ten from the UAE, and an additional two cents to be put in the Central Bank, to complete the accounting for the year 2014."

His office manager, who was another general, chuckled out loud. "Why are you laughing?" Sisi asked. "They have money like rice, man!"

Sisi sometimes lost count of it all. "No, no, no! Not eight billion dollars in six months—no!" he exclaimed in another recording. So the generals tallied it all up with him. A few billion here, a few billion there, and they realized that they had received far more—more than $30 billion.

"May God continue providing!" Sisi said.

"Amen, sir," another general answered.

Sisi held his hand out to Washington, too. In a private meeting, he told Kerry to send "an aircraft carrier full of money," according to several Americans present or briefed on the meeting.

But by late 2016, after his first three years in power—three times as long as Morsi held office—Sisi had made only token reforms to the economy. He continued a program begun under Morsi to use "smart cards" to track subsidized goods like fuel and flour. But without accountability or oversight, it ended up as riddled with corruption as the rest of the bureaucracy. So the military took it over, naturally.

By then, with oil prices and revenue down, even the Persian Gulf monarchs lost patience. They tempered their generosity. Dependent on their donations, Egypt's reserves dipped dangerously. The value of the pound started to fall, and Sisi tried to prop it up through coercion alone. He decreed an artificially high exchange rate and jailed money changers who undercut it. The authorities restricted bank transfers out of the country, limited the use of Egyptian credit cards abroad, and searched luggage at the airport for any large wads of cash.

It was no use. Dollars grew scarce. Stores and factories ran short on imported goods and materials. Manufacturers laid off workers. Imports vanished from store shelves. For me, that meant doing without my preferred brands of cereal and peanut butter. For Egyptians it meant serious shortages of medicines, including antibiotics. Mothers who needed imported infant formula demonstrated in the street over a shortage, and the army brought in a supply to start handing it out. The real value of the pound fell to half the official rate and a black market in dollars flourished despite the police.

Finally, in November 2016, Sisi was forced to go back to the International Monetary Fund. The $4.8 billion bailout discussed under Morsi was no longer nearly sufficient. Egypt needed $12 billion now.

The IMF mandated a free float of the currency that cut the value of the Egyptian pound by more than half overnight. It hung at around 18 or 20 pounds to the dollar, down from about 7.5 under Morsi. In 2017, food prices were rising at a rate of more than 30 percent a year. Wages were stagnant. Unemployment was soaring. With my wallet full of dollars, I could live like a king. My Egyptian friends shook their heads in misery.

S isi rewrote his own history. In the thirty months before the Rabaa massacre, he had often told Egyptian confidants and American officials that he was happy to be serving under a democratically elected president from the Muslim Brotherhood (as several of those confidants and officials told me at the time). After Rabaa, he insisted that he had warned all along against allowing Islamists a chance to take power.

"I always told you, Anne, that political Islam would fail," he told Ambassador Patterson, who wrote to Washington that Sisi had never said anything of the kind.

No longer defending the earnestness of his efforts to help Morsi, Sisi hinted that he had duped the president from the start. "He underestimated me," Sisi told the visiting American scholar Shibley Telhami in early 2014.

Mubarak, in another leaked recording of a conversation with his doctor, reassessed Sisi. "He turned out to be devious."

Sisi spoke of himself in the third person, like a historical figure. "Sisi would never do a coop," he told Hagel and Obama—pronouncing the *p* in coup d'état.

He always returned to the classic authoritarian's refrain, that the alternative was chaos. I heard the same thing constantly from supporters of his takeover. Sisi's first prime minister was Hazem el-Beblawi, an internationally recognized economist who had been among Egypt's most prominent liberals. When I visited his home less than a year after the Rabaa massacre, Beblawi was sitting in an armchair by a window of his grand apartment overlooking Nasr City. A book of economics and a tobacco pipe sat on a small, round side table.

Beblawi had spoken out against the Maspero massacre and he had at least acknowledged that the death toll at Rabaa approached a thousand. I was ready to like him, and I tried to warm him up with easy questions. In your tenure as prime minister, I asked, what were you most proud of?

Clearing the Rabaa sit-in, he volunteered, without hesitation.

Really? I asked, delicately. He was proudest of the bloodshed?

Of course he knew many would die, he told me. So did Sisi. "This is the police of a country like Egypt," Beblawi said. "I cannot say this is Denmark."

"It is a matter of the prestige of the state," Beblawi continued. "We are talking about a country where the state is central, and if there is a doubt about the state everything will disintegrate." The Rabaa sit-in "was a test of whether we could have a state or not."

Beblawi had distilled for me the ideology of the Arab deep state. Turks and Arabs have been using the term for years to describe the machinery of the permanent government—the bureaucracy, the military, the police and judges, the media, and religious establishments, and so on—long before the phrase "deep state" came into vogue under Trump in Washington. The deep state is a machine that can churn on regardless of who is supposed to be driving. As Morsi discovered.

The institutions of the Egyptian deep state seemed to me remarkably sturdy. They had survived revolutions, elections, parliaments, and presidents. The same functionaries who had welcomed me to Egypt under Mubarak had set up my meeting with Morsi, and they were still in place under Sisi. Everywhere, the same bureaucrats occupied the same desks that they had when I first arrived in Egypt.

But the philosophy of the deep state—the ideology of Arab authoritarianism—depended on the opposite premise: that the state itself is as fragile and precious as a sarcophagus under glass in the Egyptian Museum. At the slightest jolt, savagery would prevail. The prestige of the state—the awe of the state, as it was sometimes translated—was the only bulwark against chaos.

We learn in American civics class that stability rests on the rule of law, and that the law, by definition, must constrain even a president. The ideology of the deep state turned that axiom on its head. The social order was so tenuous that its guardians—the generals, the police, and the *mukhabarat*, the "state institutions," in the Egyptian euphemism—must wield power without constraint. They must put themselves above the law in order to save it.

Sisi embraced the paradox the moment he removed Morsi, on July 3, 2013. He was forced to act to prevent "the collapse of the state," he declared, and to do that he suspended a newly ratified constitution, removed a recently elected president, and ordered a blitz of extralegal arrests and censorship. He vowed to preserve the rule of law and in the process shredded it completely.

In meetings with Kerry or Obama, Sisi smiled, nodded, and seemed to agree with them. He said yes in body language, but no with his words. No, he would not free jailed Americans, or Egyptian journalists, or Brotherhood leaders. No, he would not loosen the restrictions on rights groups or political parties. He could not interfere with the sacrosanct independence of the judiciary, he insisted, convincing no one.

He acted as if the bloodshed at Rabaa had been out of his hands. "He said, 'Yes, it is terrible. We are investigating. The police got out of control,'" Kerry later recalled. "Sometimes I thought he was genuinely trying to work through problems. . . . Other times, he was making excuses."

Sisi, in de facto power since the coup, stood in a pro-forma presidential election in 2014. He scheduled it at the last minute, and he campaigned for only three weeks. He never bothered to attend his own rallies, nor did he spell out a platform. He was "the candidate of necessity," as Heikal put it.

Sisi's only opponent was a Nasserite civilian. He mostly agreed with Sisi, especially about his ouster of Morsi. But when the polls opened on May 26, 2014, a panic seized the deep state. Almost no one was voting!

At the last moment, election officials opened the polls for an extraordinary third, additional day. The prime minister declared a national holiday, canceled public transit fares, and threatened fines for nonvoters. Talk show hosts flew into hysterics. "Anybody who does not vote is giving the kiss of life to the terrorists," one host, Mustafa Bakry, screamed. "Those who do not come out are traitors! Traitors! Traitors! They are selling out this country."

Sisi was declared the winner with 98 percent of the vote. But the independent monitors had pulled out over the irregularities, so who could be sure? A coalition led by a former intelligence officer dominated the parliamentary elections a few months later, with a platform consisting only of support, in all things, for President Abdel Fattah el-Sisi. (He was reelected by a similar margin in 2015 after the arrests of several possible challengers.)

What was Sisi's vision for Egypt? At the center of the square where the Rabaa sit-in took place, Sisi erected a singular monument. Two towers of granite each angled toward the other, and in the center a flimsy-looking white ball hung suspended in the air. A plaque explained that the taller stone was the military and its shorter sibling was the police. They were two hands. The fragile white orb cupped in them was the Egyptian people.

Sisi had once told fellow military officers to think of Egyptians as children. The army is "the very big brother, the very big father who has a son who is a bit of a failure and does not understand the facts," he told a group of senior officers, in another leaked recording. "Does the father kill the son? Or does he always shelter him and say, 'I'll be patient until my son understands'?"

"You want to be a first class nation?" he asked Egyptians in another conversation, this time with his journalist-confidant. "Will you bear it if I make you walk on your feet? Will you bear it when I wake you up at five in the morning every day? Will you bear cutting back on food, cutting back on air conditioners? Will you bear me removing the subsidies all at once? Will you bear this from me?"

Instead of faulting government policies, Sisi always blamed Egyptians—
for their supposed lack of industry and enterprise, for their moral laxity,
and for their prodigious birth rate. On the campaign trail, he complained
to doctors that his government could not possibly afford to provide all
Egyptians with the same standard of health care that the army provided
soldiers. "Why? Because there is nothing, there is nothing!" he shouted.
The doctors, he said, must work harder for less.

But if the people were the problem, government power was always his
answer. Inflation? He proposed mandatory price controls and state-run factories. Energy shortages? He would force Egyptians to install energy-
efficient lightbulbs in every home socket, even if he had to send government
employees to screw in each one. "Sisi bulbs," the hardware store clerk told
me when I bought one (voluntarily).

"I'm not leaving a chance for people to act on their own," Sisi explained
in the only television interview of his short campaign. "My program will
be mandatory."

In the economy, "the state has to be in control here," he added, so his
government would plan, choose, "and execute."

The centerpiece of his economic program was a "new" Suez Canal—
his answer to Abdel Nasser's High Dam. Twenty thousand conscripts a year
had worked for ten years to dig the original canal, completed in 1869. Sisi
promised to finish his new one in a single year, no matter how much the
rush cost. In September 2014, he sold $8 billion of special government
bonds to the public to pay for it (with no foreign funding).

EGYPT REJOICES, EGYPT'S GIFT TO THE WORLD newspaper headlines
declared when construction was finished on time in 2015. The government
ordered every imam to preach a sermon comparing the new canal with a
battle trench dug by the Prophet Mohamed himself. "An additional artery
of prosperity for the world," Sisi declared to an audience of ambassadors
and dignitaries at the opening. Its official $8 billion price tag was roughly
as much as Egypt spent that year to subsidize bread.

This "new canal," though, was actually a parallel bypass that ran alongside only about a third of the original. It eliminated some potential bottle-
necks, but not all of them. And it was unnecessary. The Suez Canal had
been operating far below capacity for years. Changing trade patterns meant

shipping volumes were falling. But no matter. When canal revenue continued to decline, the Egyptian news media forgot the embarrassment of Sisi's rosy forecasts of future windfalls.

In 2016—three years after he took power, two years after his inauguration, and one year after the seating of his rubber-stamp Parliament—Sisi delivered a speech about his plan for Egypt over the next two decades. But he was still talking, now sometimes manically, about the same existential threat he had used to justify his takeover.

"Our goal is to preserve the Egyptian state," Sisi declared, and he repeated the phrase another dozen times. "Any country's main goal is preserving the state, preserving the state, preserving the state," he insisted. "There are still efforts and conspiracies being carried out to bring Egypt down," he said. "I am still talking about the national goal of preserving the state."

Everyone knew he depended on the backing of the military council, but Sisi now warned his listeners that only he could save Egypt. "Do not listen to anyone but me," Sisi said. "I am a man who does not lie, who does not beat around the bush, and who cares only for his country!"

He would eradicate all enemies, he repeated again. "I will wipe off the face of the earth anyone who threatens this country," he promised. "I am telling every Egyptian listening to me now, What do you think is going on? Who are you?"

An echo: Colonel Muammar el-Qaddafi, Egypt's crazy neighbor, had used the same words to challenge the Libyans rising against him in the Arab Spring revolt. *Man antoum?* Who are you? When revolutions were in style, I bought *Man antoum* T-shirts for my sons. Did Sisi intend to quote Qaddafi?

Sisi bluntly acknowledged he had no time for the democracy he once pledged to restore. "It's still early to start practicing democracy in an open sense, where we criticize this or that, and this guy is kicked out. It's still early days."

Stop complaining, he told Egyptians. He would be the judge. "Will you know better than I do if this government is good or not?" he asked. Why should his ministers tolerate criticism from the public? "What do they get in return for tolerating you? What do they get in return for your attacks all day and night?"

Yet a few months later, at a youth conference in Suez in April 2017, Sisi blamed those ministers for his government's failings. "His excellency the minister of agriculture is talking about creating 'synergistic communities,'" Sisi said sarcastically. "Why didn't we create them three years ago? There have been three ministers of agriculture. Why didn't we do it?"

"People," Sisi chided, "saying things here is one thing, but turning this talk into action is a completely different story—or else Egypt would not be so backward."

He reminded the audience of his own unfulfilled promise to develop a million and a half acres of desert as farmland, and he again blamed his ministers. "The ministries of irrigation and agriculture would allocate the lands, allocate the water, and then retreat." He could hardly fire them, though. "Will I let someone go who has only worked with me for five or six months? Where would my credibility be if I removed everyone who comes to work with me?" Where indeed! The crowd at the conference roared with applause.

Plenty of Egyptians told me that they were grateful for Sisi. They felt lucky not to live in the chaos of Libya, Syria, Iraq, or Yemen. That idea was a running theme of the progovernment news media. Even my former Arabic tutor, who once ranted at Mubarak's "gang of thieves" and his brutal police, told me in 2016 that he had changed his mind. The "revolution" taught him to appreciate the police and to appreciate Sisi.

Other Egyptians, though, could only laugh at their leader. Sisi boasted of his love for Egypt at the end of one speech. "I swear to God, if I could sell myself, I would."

An eBay listing was up within minutes: "One Egyptian president slightly used . . . May not ship to Qatar." Bids surpassed $100,301 before eBay shut down the auction. (The author of the listing remained anonymous and presumably abroad; insulting the president is once again a jailable crime inside Egypt.)

To some Egyptians, Sisi called to mind a comic film made in Cairo in the 1980s. Its cab driver hero happened to resemble a delusional mental patient named Balaha—which is also the Arabic word for a date, as in the fruit on palm trees.

Why did you try to escape again, Balaha? an asylum guard mistakenly asked the cab driver, forcing him into the hospital. "I am not *balaha*!" he sputters. I am not a date!

The *balaha* scene lasted only minutes and contributed nothing to the plot. But Egyptians found a new nickname for their president—Balaha. By 2017, an Arab speaker searching Google for information about date fruit—"*balaha*"—would find only a long list of satiric web postings and videos about Sisi.

"Did you escape again, Balaha?" interviewers asked him in dubbed dialogue. "I am not Balaha!" he protested again and again. "I am not Balaha!"

W hen somebody comes who tries to divide you, then kill them, whoever they are," a gray-bearded sheikh was saying. In his customary tall red fez wrapped in white—the uniform of a religious scholar trained at the Al Azhar Institute—the former Grand Mufti Ali Gomaa had come to a Defense Ministry auditorium after the Rabaa massacre to give the soldiers a religious pep talk.

Sheikh Gomaa was appointed by Mubarak in 2003, served for a decade as Egypt's highest Muslim religious authority, and carried on a tradition of hostility to the Muslim Brotherhood that has shaped the clerical establishment since Abdel Nasser's takeover. Now, in August 2013, Gomaa told the soldiers that the Muslim Brothers were heretics—like Kharijites, a sect notorious for its rebellion against the early Muslim caliphs. "Even with the sanctity and greatness of blood, the prophet permits us to fight this."

"Shoot to kill," he said, again, at these "rotten and stinking people."

A senior scholar in the ministry of mosques took the stage and backed up Gomaa. The protesters at Rabaa were "aggressors who have to repent" and "not honorable Egyptians." Using deadly force against them was a military duty. "The heart is at ease about this."

Then a celebrity televangelist, Amr Khaled, reminded the soldiers that Islam obliged them to obey the orders of their commanders. "You, you conscript in the Egyptian military, you are performing a task for God Almighty!"

The military's Department of Moral Affairs showed a video of the lectures on Islam to soldiers and riot police stationed across the country, presumably to help put to rest any moral or ethical qualms about killing their fellow Egyptians. Gomaa became an informal religious adviser to Sisi and often preached the same bloody sermon. At a Friday prayer service in early 2014, for example, he again sanctified the soldiers and police who fought that "faction of hypocrites" and "terrorists," the Muslim Brothers. "Blessed are those who kill them, as well as those whom they kill," he proclaimed. State television broadcast the sermon, and its cameras panned to Sisi listening attentively from the floor. This was the Islam of the deep state, and its clerics were as adept as jihadists at justifying bloodshed.

Abdel Nasser had been the first to nationalize Egypt's Muslim religious establishment—Al Azhar, the Grand Mufti, and the ministry of mosques. It was under his rule that Egypt's clerics had set the template for demonizing the Muslim Brothers. "Brothers of the Devil," his sheikhs called them.

In 2011, all the highest religious authorities in Egypt had urged Muslims to shun the Tahrir Square protests against Mubarak, and in 2012, Grand Mufti Gomaa had endorsed the general running against Morsi. Air Marshal Shafik was "closer to God," Gomaa announced. Now, after 2013, the voices of the religious establishment sometimes hailed Sisi as "a messenger of God" or "God's shadow on earth."

Sisi embraced the role. He pledged several times in his short campaign that part of his job would be to "present God" in the correct way to the public. He vowed to remain "alert and responsible," to fix the errors of others about Islam. "I lead the people, so there cannot be a leadership that speaks and presents while I am sitting on the sidelines watching," he said on the subject of preaching. The new constitution approved under Sisi at the start of 2014 was scarcely more secular than either the one passed under Morsi in 2012 or the one in place under Mubarak. The principles of Islamic Sharia were still its foundation.

After terrorist attacks against the West in 2015, Sisi made headlines around the world by calling for a "revolution" in Islam. "It is unbelievable that the thought we hold holy pushes the Muslim community to be a source of worry, fear, danger, murder, and destruction to all the world," he told the clerics of Al Azhar in a televised speech. "You need to stand sternly."

American commentators heralded the speech as a sign that Sisi was the long-awaited Muslim Martin Luther. George Will recommended him for a Nobel Peace Prize. Many, to my bewilderment, called him secular.

An Egyptian lawyer and television host tried to answer Sisi's call for reform by opening a debate about the sayings attributed to the Prophet Mohamed. Misunderstandings of the sayings had justified violence, the host, Islam Beheri, contended.

The sheikhs of Al Azhar accused him of insulting Islam and insulting them, too—both crimes under Sisi's constitution. And Sisi backed Al Azhar against the free thinker. Only Al Azhar could guide any "reform," Sisi said, and no one could contradict it. Sisi's government imprisoned Beheri in Tora a year for his heresy, before he was released by a presidential pardon.

When it comes to our own religion or politics, Americans and Western Europeans usually say we believe that independent reasoning and open debate are the way to reform. (Sheik Muhammad Abduh thought so as well.) But Sisi's idea of "reform" was the Islam of the deep state: dictated from above. He banned heterodox books about Islam and imposed tight controls over Islamic teaching. He closed down twenty-seven thousand independent mosques. He forbade preaching by unlicensed imams. His government issued mandatory sermon guidelines for those still at their minbars.

"To avoid evil and please God, a person shall obey the rulers" read an official 3,100-word sermon issued for the 2016 anniversary of the Arab Spring protests. Rising up brought only "ruin and chaos," the sermon text warned.

American Christians would riot if our government tried to control our churches. But Arab authoritarians have pushed that same top-down approach to religious "reform" for more than half a century. It has so far succeeded only in driving dissent underground, where radicalism has flourished. Will the outcome be different under Sisi?

In time I came to suspect Sisi and his supporters believed the fundamental problem was not behind the minbar at all. The problem was the people on the prayer mats. The elite distrusted Egyptian Muslims too much to allow them to consider or reject reforms for themselves.

"Religious thought, or religious discourse, is afflicted with backwardness," Sisi's first minister of culture, Gaber Asfour, declared in a morning television interview, throwing up his hands, as he often did, at the failings of his fellow Egyptians. "We now live in an age of backwardness."

Tawadros II, who ascended to the Coptic papacy in 2012, preached a parallel gospel. He not only endorsed Sisi for president; Tawadros absolved the military of the Maspero massacre. The pope usually maintained that no one knew who had killed those two dozen Christians. Sometimes, though, he went as far as to blame the Muslim Brothers: he claimed that they had somehow duped the Christians into clashing with the army and then fled the scene.

"We can pray in a nation without a church," Tawadros II said in June 2014, "but we can't pray in a church without a nation." It was the psalm of the deep state, trumpeted the next day on the front page of *Al Ahram.*

Sisi brought some boons to the church. He silenced the sectarian invective of the Salafi television preachers. After his inauguration as president, he paid a surprise visit to Mass for Coptic Christmas Eve, on January 6, 2015. Mubarak and Morsi had wished the pope Merry Christmas over the telephone and sent envoys to the service, and Morsi had attended the Mass in his capacity as a Brotherhood leader before his election. But Sisi was the first president to show up at the service.

"Let no one say, 'What kind of Egyptian are you?'" Sisi told the worshippers. "We must only be Egyptians!" Then he left with his retinue of bodyguards before the first prayers.

In some ways, though, Christians fared worse under Sisi than they had under Morsi, in part because they became scapegoats for anger at the coup. I visited the Father Moses Church in Minya, 140 miles south of Cairo, a month after Rabaa. Its soaring sanctuary had been stripped of stained glass, icons, iron light fixtures, copper wires, and anything else the looters could steal. Attackers had built a bonfire of the pews. The high stone dome was blackened; ashes and debris covered the floor. So I joined hundreds of parishioners gathered in folding chairs in a low concrete basement. It was lit by bare lightbulbs hanging from the ceiling, and I felt like I was praying in the Roman catacombs.

Sixty-eight-year-old Father Samuel Aziz, with a long white beard and glasses, told me he was trapped in a church office during the attack. A police commander called to offer an escort to safety, but none ever showed up. "They were too weak and outnumbered," the priest said. A month later, he was still waiting for any police officer to visit the scene.

In the nearby town of Dalga, a mob attacked a 1,650-year-old monastery and stole icons and relics older than Islam along with a medieval baptismal font. Arsonists set fire to thirty-five homes belonging to Christians. One Christian had defended his home with a gun, and he was killed and dragged through the streets.

But the police had not shown up yet in Dalga either. Forty-seven-year-old Father Abraam Tenesa told me that "thugs" were trying to shake Christians down for protection money, like the medieval tax on Christians, *jizya*.

Christians complained of the same bias against them. Three months after Sisi took power, a court convicted three Christians of murdering a Muslim in the outbreak of violence that had led to the assault on the cathedral under Morsi. Each Christian was sentenced to fifteen years in prison. No Muslims were found guilty of killing any of the five Christians who had died during the fight.

Prosecutors still jailed Christians for blasphemy against Islam. A committee of Muslim scholars still censored the screening of movies. Despite a promise from Sisi, church building still required special permission from security agencies, which frequently denied it.

Worst of all, police failed to protect Christians from the rising violence against them. In May 2016, a rumor spread through the village of Karm, Minya, about a love affair between a Christian man and a Muslim woman. A mob of forty Muslims burned the Christian's home to the ground, beat up the family, and dragged the seventy-year-old matriarch, Suad Thabet, naked through the streets. Prosecutors found insufficient evidence to charge anyone for the crimes. No wonder the Islamic State saw an easy target, declaring Christians its "favorite prey," and started bombing churches.

When I found Father Matthias, who led the march that ended in the Maspero massacre in 2011, he told me that the soldier who had kicked and beaten him—then major Ibrahim el-Damaty—had been elevated the next year to chief of the military police under Defense Minister Sisi. "Under Sisi, pushing a priest gets you promoted right away," Father Matthias said ruefully.

Father Filopateer, the other priest at the head of that march, told me he could no longer return to Cairo without fear of arrest for his activism.

"Life for Copts under the Muslim Brotherhood was a lot better," Father

Filopateer told me. At least then Copts had the freedom to organize and protest. "We are dealing with a dictator and he is ready to do anything to maintain his power," he went on. "In economics, in politics, in freedom—everything is going in the wrong direction."

The standard coup playbook calls for special tribunals to dispense with the old regime. Sisi did not bother. He designated only a circuit of existing courts where quick-ruling, anti-Islamist judges handled "terrorism" cases. No need for special rules or panels. Judges everywhere were eager to lock up anyone the police or *mukhabarat* hauled into the docket.

On March 24, 2014, a three-judge panel in Minya had sentenced 529 alleged members of the Muslim Brotherhood to death, all for the killing of a single police officer during an antigovernment riot on the day of the Rabaa massacre. The trial took only two sessions, each less than an hour. More than 400 defendants were sentenced in absentia.

A month later, the same panel sentenced to death another 680 alleged Muslim Brothers, after an equally swift trial, again for the murder of a single policeman. One of the condemned was the seventy-year-old general guide of the Muslim Brotherhood, Mohamed Badie; he had been in Cairo on the day of the crime and no specific evidence was presented to link him to the killing. Another alleged culprit was a feeble sixty-year-old high school principal, Mohamed Abdel Wahab.

Sitting at home in his living room surrounded by several grown children, the principal said he had just returned from his retirement party when he heard the news of his conviction in absentia. "We are living in absurdity," he said, and his children all nodded.

He had survived multiple heart surgeries. He could not walk up stairs or breathe near smoke. He pulled up his galabiya to show me surgical scars on both calves. "I am the one who broke into the police station and killed the police officer?" he asked. "Everything is a whim. There is no rule of law."

In December, a court in Giza sentenced to death another 188 alleged Muslim Brothers (one of them a minor). The *Times* barely covered it. Preposterous mass death sentences had become so common they were not news anymore. The appeals process dragged out for years.

Morsi, who the military had quietly transferred to a prison in Alexandria, was sentenced to life for walking out of his brief detention during the Tahrir Square uprising. Prosecutors said Hamas, the Sunni militants in Gaza, and Hezbollah, the Shiites in Lebanon, had improbably conspired together to bust him out of prison in Cairo.

Another court convicted Morsi of committing espionage while in office as president, allegedly by sharing secrets with Qatar. A third court sentenced him to death for the killings in the brawl outside the presidential palace in December 2012, when he was far from the scene.

I assumed the appeals process would keep him from the gallows, but I wondered how a judge could keep a straight face about such ludicrous rulings. The Egyptian judiciary had prided itself for decades on its independence.

Judge Mahmoud Sherif, the general secretary of the judges club at the time of the coup, had been promoted to an office high in the justice ministry when I met him in early 2017. Sherif wore French cuffs and a European suit, and he acknowledged candidly that Morsi never controlled much—certainly not the army, police, judges, state media, the religious establishment, or the rest of the bureaucracy. But why take the chance that he might? "I don't have to wait until he becomes a tyrant!" Sherif said.

Egypt had now cycled through three constitutions in three years—the charter in place under Mubarak, the charter approved under Morsi, and a third ratified under Sisi. Was it difficult, I asked, for the judges of Egypt to adjust so quickly to new legal frameworks? Not at all, he said. "The people chose several different constitutions. We have to obey, because we rule in their name."

How did all the judges know that a constitution ratified only six months earlier had lost all legitimacy overnight? "When people take to the streets," he fired back, grinning at his own rousing populism. "The power comes from the people!"

So how many of "the people" does it take? Would a few million do it? I asked, probing gently.

"We need thirty million exactly!" he answered instantly: the obviously inflated figure that government propagandists had settled on as the size of the June 30 protests against Morsi. "Not twenty-nine million, not twenty-nine and a half million!" he said, slapping his desk. "It must be *exactly* thirty million!"

We both burst out laughing.

Controlling the news media was a priority for the generals. After Mubarak's ouster, "people and the media rode roughshod over us in a way that isn't normal," one senior military office had groused to Sisi in a private meeting before he took power. (An audio recording later leaked out.)

"Correct," agreed Sisi, but he urged patience. "It takes a very long time until you possess an appropriate share of influence over the media," but "we are working on this, for sure."

Within months after his takeover, Sisi's levers of influence were locked into place. A new law prescribed a jail sentence for any journalist who contradicted the military's official statements about its war against "terrorism." The owners of all the major newspapers pledged in writing not to criticize Sisi's government during the time of crisis. Television networks suspended talk show hosts who came too close to the line. Soldiers confiscated newspaper print runs. Four years after the takeover, Egypt had become one of the world's most aggressive jailers of journalists. More than twenty-five were behind bars.

Sisi used the media to build his own cult of personality, too. In another leaked recording, he told his office manager to be sure the news media portrayed him as a hero "on a nearly impossible mission" and "carrying the responsibility of a country in an existential crisis." Another recording caught the office manager ensuring just that. "There is a point we want all of our media personalities on TV to debate," he told an unnamed intermediary: questioning Sisi was a "shame" to the nation.

Criticizing Sisi—"this brave, special, free and patriotic Egyptian"— would be "slandering this beautiful thing we have found in our lives," the office manager said, and he listed a half dozen talk show hosts who should deliver that message.

"Our dear Egyptian people, do you like this being done to the man who labored and sacrificed?" the office manager suggested. "Are you listening? Are you writing this down or not?" he interjected several times. "Stir up the people with it!"

The distortions could be mind bending. Sisi spoke at the United Nations General Assembly in October 2014, and ended his speech by chanting his campaign slogan, in Arabic, *"Tahya Masr!"* Long Live Egypt! Most delegates looked on in bemused silence.

But Sisi's entourage and some Arab allies leaped to their feet chanting and applauding. Egyptian networks showed only narrowly cropped shots of the cheering. The anchors reported that the whole general assembly was acclaiming Sisi.

"LONG LIVE EGYPT" ROCKS THE ASSEMBLY! *Al Ahram* declared in its front-page headline.

"Abdel Fattah el-Sisi was the groom of the United Nations, and Egypt was the bride," said Amir Adeeb, a nationalist talk show host. "A thing of genius."

When I wrote about that misrepresentation, *Al Ahram* published an article saying that I, too, was applauding for Sisi. "In Kirkpatrick's view, Sisi was able to erase the image that was in the minds of some people, that what happened in Egypt in June 2013 was a 'coup,' not a revolution. . . . Kirkpatrick pointed out that all the diplomats were in a state of silence and enjoyment throughout Sisi's speech."

So the *New York Times* published on its website an English translation of *Al Ahram*'s article about "Kirkpatrick's view," side by side with my original.

Al Ahram's editors did not see the humor. Kirkpatrick "fervently defends the terrorist organization"—the Muslim Brotherhood—"and always promotes the idea that there is oppression of freedoms," *Al Ahram* wrote the next day in an unusual nonretraction of its original claims.

By 2015, progovernment talk show hosts were denouncing me on air, by name, as an enemy of Egypt. One host, Osama Kamal, put up my photograph and insisted on referring to me as Kirk Douglas. Did he know that my middle name is Douglas? I worried the attention might make me a target for harassment or mob violence, and I kept my head down. (Prosecutors opened a formal case against me in 2018.)

Female foreign correspondents told me that the intelligence agencies targeted them for other abuse. A British journalist told me that while she was reporting on the first massacre after the coup, a group of men broke into her apartment. She hid in the bedroom and listened as they searched the living room and desks. But the intruders stole nothing. (Her male roommate, another journalist, was away that night.)

A few days later, a group of men sprang on her outside her apartment and grabbed her from behind. One dragged a knife over her chest and her crotch. "Do you want me to cut your breasts?" he threatened in English. "Do you want me to cut your clitoris?" Then the men ran away, without stealing anything.

A few weeks later, after the Rabaa massacre, she received an anonymous email from an account under the name "Military Military." In broken English, it accused her of sleeping with her housemate, called him a spy, and warned that she had drawn "the people rage" by joining the "terrorist" of the Muslim Brotherhood.

"We are watching all of you, counting your breath, 24/7," the message read. "We are guardian angels. We can turn in a minute into kill devils."

She moved in with another friend for safety. Then, on a Friday afternoon a few weeks later, a mob of a dozen men assaulted her not far from where she had been accosted with the knife. They shoved their hands inside her, and she screamed, struggled, and ran. At an army checkpoint up the street, she told me, soldiers watched and did nothing. She soon relocated out of Egypt.

I thought that the return of the police might at least better protect Egyptian women. But during the four days of demonstrations from June 30 through Morsi's ouster, mobs had sexually assaulted at least ninety-one, according to a tally by Human Rights Watch and Nazra for Feminist Studies. At Sisi's inauguration, in June 2014, female television correspondents covering the celebrations in Tahrir Square tried to report another wave of assaults. In at least two cases their anchors cut them off.

"They are happy," the anchor Maha Bahnasy giggled to her correspondent. "They are having fun."

A mobile phone video made one assault that day impossible to ignore. It showed a woman in the square naked except for a black shirt covering her shoulders. Her bottom was bruised purple and black, and men's hands were all over her. A policeman waved his handgun, the camera moved away, and she reappeared. She was fully naked and faceup, her body limp and reddened. The hands of strangers laid her in a car.

Sisi had campaigned for president promising to restore Egypt's "gallantry" and "manhood." After two days of uproar over the video, state television cameras followed him into a hospital as he delivered a bouquet of red flowers to the victim. (Her face was pixilated.) "I apologize to you, and, as a state, we will not allow this to happen again," he told her, placing his hand over his chest.

"Shame on you to let this happen," he told Egyptians, speaking into the camera.

That apology was the extent of Sisi's defense of women's participation in public life. The state-sponsored National Council of Women resumed its official monopoly on women's organizing. Mozn Hassan, the young feminist who tried to build a movement, was charged with the crime of accepting foreign donations to her nonprofit. Prosecutors froze her assets and banned her from travel. The last time I saw her, in early 2017, she was waiting to go to jail.

The new president of the National Council for Women, Maya Morsi (no relation to the former president), had no sympathy for Mozn and defended the prosecution. "Let us not judge the law!" Morsi told me. "If you know that there is a law saying 'Don't do this,' would you?"

She insisted Sisi was "a savior" to the women of Egypt. She said she saw no problems at all with the way that the army and police treated women. When I asked about the virginity tests, she offered excuses. The soldiers had to follow procedure. The abuse of the Blue Bra Girl had misrepresented the true character of the noble Egyptian army.

"We saw the real Egyptian army afterward, in the second wave of the revolution, on the thirtieth of June," she volunteered. "No one touched any woman, right?"

I was incredulous. Independent rights groups had collected the testimony of dozens of women sexually assaulted in the demonstrations that day.

Did she think there were any problems at all with the treatment of women by the army and police?

"I don't see it." She paused to consider. "No, I don't see it," she told me again.

Laura wondered at her own receding standards. She would never have agreed to move to an Arab capital on the brink of a revolution. Now bombs were going off in Cairo. The police had started arresting Western journalists. I had been labeled a terrorist sympathizer in the news media.

Egyptian mothers she met at the playground took a step back at the mention of my name. But here we still were.

Maadi was shaken in the spring of 2015 by the news that an online message board used by jihadists had posted detailed instructions about how to hit a local international school. Security consultants for the international petroleum companies were buzzing about a wave of carjackings targeting SUVs (like ours). The consultants thought the militants wanted four-wheel-drive vehicles to run guns in the desert. A major energy company pulled its fleet of Land Rovers and required all employees to drive smaller cars. We canceled plans to visit the Siwa Oasis, in the western desert, and Mount Sinai, in the South Sinai. We no longer felt safe on the roads. The American embassy barred its employees from driving outside of Cairo or Sharm el-Sheikh.

When the Islamic State militants beheaded the Croatian employee of the French oil company that August, we took it as an ominous sign that they might target Westerners. The militants brought down the Russian charter jet a few months later, and they were testing attacks on tourist sites. But those worries were abstract.

More pressing was the day in early 2015 when my son Thomas stepped on a nail. He was nine years old. A flare-up of street protests had closed off the roads again, and there were reports of more shooting. Laura was afraid to take him to a hospital. She made do with a trip to a local pharmacist, who mishandled the wound. Thomas needed surgery on his foot when we got back to the States.

Most Western journalists who had covered Tahrir Square were long gone by then. Some rotated out. Others decamped for Istanbul or Beirut—cosmopolitan cities closer to the action in Syria and Iraq. We met again when I was on assignments in Baghdad or Tunis, and the conversations over drinks always turned back to the tragedy in Egypt. But Laura and I stayed.

President Obama had decided not to call Sisi's takeover a coup to avoid a cutoff of the $1.3 billion in annual military aid. Now he may have been the last one in his administration to accept the idea of resuming it. His face-to-face meeting with Sisi on the sidelines of the United Nations General Assembly in September 2014 was a turning point. Advisers had warned Obama that Sisi could be long-winded and grandiose, even talking over former president Bill Clinton during a meeting at his foundation. So Obama tried to put Sisi on the defensive with specific demands about rights and freedoms. That is one reason he asked for the release of Mohamed Soltan, the American citizen then on a hunger strike in prison.

Officials who sat in on the meeting remember Obama as forceful and tough. But Sisi smiled, nodded, and stonewalled. He wanted to remove any irritant to their relationship, he said, but Soltan's fate was up to the judges. Sisi kept pushing for more military aid, to fight the war on "terrorism" inside of Egypt.

"Well, that guy is never going to change," Obama murmured to his advisers as they were leaving the room.

Intelligence agencies reported back that Sisi barely noticed the criticism. He was delighted with the attention.

Obama met with his National Security Council in the spring of 2015 about the suspended military aid. Almost all the principals now were pushing for a restart, but Obama was still against it. "I have read all the papers and I am still not convinced," Obama told one adviser before the meeting.

The White House, too, had been lowering its standards. First it had demanded a full restoration of democracy, then the loosening of restrictions on nonprofit groups, or greater access to the North Sinai. Now Obama was asking only for the release of some political prisoners, even one American citizen. Sisi still gave nothing. (Sisi had named as his national security adviser the same Mubarak loyalist who had led the raids on the American-backed International Republican Institute and National Democratic Institute, the one who had trapped Sam LaHood in the U.S. embassy—Fayza Aboulnaga.)

Ambassador Robert S. Beecroft, the new envoy to Cairo, weighed in by teleconference. He emphasized the reactionary forces within Sisi's own government—the judiciary, the religious establishment, the police, the intelligence agencies, his fellow generals, and so on. Sisi did not control the deep state, in other words. He was its instrument. Another general could replace him.

Obama was persuaded that continued pressure would gain nothing, and he called Sisi that March to announce the restoration of aid. The Egyptian military suffered almost no penalty.

Between the beheading of the Croatian and the nail in Thomas's foot, Laura and I decided in the fall of 2015 that it was time to leave Egypt. Laura and the boys moved to London, my next posting. I filed from Cairo and Libya until a new bureau chief, Declan Walsh, took over in 2016. But unanswered questions kept pulling me back. What had come over Egypt in the summer of the coup? What happened to the young people who had filled Tahrir Square in 2011, the liberal intelligentsia that I had so admired? Some were once again bravely standing up for human rights under Sisi. But how could so many have celebrated the coup and the crackdown?

Even if liberal intellectuals did not win elections, their voices resonated in Egypt and beyond. If more had spoken out against the massacres, the military could not have claimed so successfully that its takeover was a liberal revolution or a national consensus. Washington, especially, listened to the liberals.

Mohamed ElBaradei, Egypt's most famous liberal, quit during the storming of the Rabaa sit-in. "Violence only begets violence," he wrote in a public letter of resignation. "The beneficiaries of what happened today are the preachers of violence and terrorism, the most extremist groups." He fled the country that day.

If ElBaradei ever took responsibility for his own role in the coup, I never heard it. Prosecutors opened a case against him for betraying the country. The news media denounced him as a traitor.

Amr Hamzawy had been virtually the lone liberal to publicly oppose the takeover as it happened. After Rabaa, prosecutors charged him with insulting the judiciary on the basis of a tweet he had written under Morsi. (It was about a court decision against the American employees of NDI and IRI.) First the authorities barred him from leaving Egypt (forcing him to cancel a lecture at Yale). Then he was threatened with jail and forced into exile.

Other "liberals" soon felt the same boot. Sisi promptly banned unauthorized street demonstrations—the tactic that had brought him to power. A crackdown on organizing threatened to extinguish every independent human rights group.

Human Rights Watch was expelled from the country. Heba Morayef, who had dined with me at the embassy *iftar* when I first arrived in Egypt, relocated to Tunis. Police imprisoned several of the most prominent activists linked to the Tahrir Square sit-in. The left-leaning April 6 Youth Movement was declared a terrorist organization and membership became a crime. Sisi also eventually jailed Abdel Moneim Aboul Fotouh—the liberal Islamist who had taken on the Muslim Brotherhood.

Private conversations no longer felt safe. A website and television show called *The Black Box* specialized in broadcasting telephone surveillance of liberal activists, Islamist lawyers, and others. It was almost never damning but always creepy. (Its host was elected to Parliament under Sisi.) Egyptian friends started insisting that we put our smartphones in a refrigerator whenever we talked, because even in the "off" mode they can be used as listening devices. By 2017, the Egyptian government blocked encrypted communications apps like Signal or WhatsApp. It blocked dozens of liberal or left-leaning publications and websites. An Egyptian essayist, Sara Khorshid, was briefly detained for the crime of sitting in a café with a foreigner; another patron had taken her for a spy and called the police. A member of the April 6 group was turned in by his mother.

A highly regarded liberal journalist, Ahmed Nagy, was jailed for ten months for obscenity in a literary novel. Sisi's government cracked down on homosexuality and arrested dozens after rainbow flags were displayed at a rock concert; secret police flirted with gay men through online dating services to try to entrap them. Parliament debated criminalizing atheism. At the beginning of 2018, the scholar and former American diplomat Michele Dunne asked on Twitter, "For the umpteenth time, what would the international community have said had this happened during Morsi's presidency?" It was a running joke in Egypt: Thank God we got rid of the Islamists.

Shaimaa el-Sabbagh was a leftist who had supported the protests against Morsi and celebrated Sisi's takeover. She had grown up in Alexandria as the daughter of a conservative Muslim preacher and chafed against his traditionalism. "For the likes of you, wearing pants is 'covering,'" he told her in resignation. Keeping her pants on was all the modesty he could hope for. She wore her wavy dark hair uncovered and cut above her shoulders.

By the time of the takeover, she was about thirty, married to an artist, the mother of a four-year-old son, and an accomplished poet. Most serious Egyptian poets write in formal Arabic; Sabbagh was one of the few published poets who wrote in the avant-garde style of free verse but using the colloquial Arabic of everyday life. Her poem called "A Letter in My Purse" begins:

I am not sure
Truly, she was nothing more than just a purse
But when lost, there was a problem
How to face the world without her
Especially
Because the streets remember us together
The shops know her more than me
Because she is the one who pays
She knows the smell of my sweat and she loves it. . . .

Anyway, she has the house keys
And I am waiting for her.

Sabbagh was active in a small socialist party that had backed Sisi's take-over, imagining a more progressive Egypt. The party then endorsed Sisi on the principle that he was better than an Islamist. But on the fourth anniversary of the original uprising, January 25, 2015, Sabbagh and her friends wanted to commemorate the "martyrs" who died protesting Mubarak.

Because police would be out in force that day to ensure against any repeat, Sabbagh and about two dozen others gathered on the afternoon of January 24. They met a few blocks from Tahrir Square, armed only with flowers that they planned to lay there. They saw no reason to fear the squad of masked riot police a few feet away.

The tear gas hit them almost before they took a step. Gunshots cracked through the smoke. Sabbagh's head tilted back. Blood streaked her cheeks. As she started to collapse, a kneeling friend grabbed her by the waist to hold her upright, his head pressed against her abdomen. He cradled her and slowly lowered her to the ground.

Dozens of people drinking coffee in nearby sidewalk cafés watched her die in the street. Photojournalists captured her killing second by second, frame by frame. The pictures spread across Facebook within hours.

Yet her friends who went to the police were detained as suspects and held overnight. An Interior Ministry spokesman declared the next day that the police could not possibly have killed her; they would never shoot at such a small crowd. The photographs and videos were "no proof at all," General Gamal Mokhtar insisted.

"There is a faction of the Muslim Brotherhood whose entire job and concern is to fabricate photos and videos that tell people that the police are assaulting protesters—that this one is bleeding, that one is injured," he said.

A few days later, the police arrested the deputy chairman of her political party—he had been a personal friend of Sabbagh's—on suspicion that he had fired a concealed weapon through his jacket pocket to murder her. Progovernment newscasts were saying it was a setup to blame the police. Then a judge ordered a media blackout on news, and we heard little more about it.

I was so inured to the deaths that I barely reacted. I was at a swimming pool with my sons when I first heard of Sabbagh's killing. I did not think it was worth interrupting a day with my family to write about the death of one more protester. Police killed at least a few almost every week—mostly Islamists, but also leftists or liberals. They killed a seventeen-year-old girl at an Islamist rally in Alexandria the same day Sabbagh died. They killed twenty more the next day, January 25, on the anniversary of the uprising. They killed a student five days later in clashes after a demonstration in the province of Sharqiya, a short drive north of Cairo. It went on and on.

But those pictures. The expression on Sabbagh's face during her last seconds was unforgettable. So startled, so naïve.

For three years, whenever I asked an Egyptian liberal or leftist about the repression under Sisi, their answers always began the same way: with a long prologue about the culpability of the Muslim Brotherhood. The Brothers should have shared more power. They should have taken on the generals. They should have governed better. They should have exited the stage before they were pushed. Sisi was the Brotherhood's fault. Every Western diplomat and journalist in Cairo from 2013 through 2016 heard the same argument over and over. But time attenuated that explanation. No Muslim Brother held the gun that killed Shaimaa el-Sabbagh.

After four years, the answers started to change. Sisi surprised Egypt in 2016 by announcing the transfer of two empty Red Sea islands to his patron, the king of Saudi Arabia. Sisi's fellow blood-and-soil nationalists demonstrated against the surrender of Egyptian territory, and the police started arresting and shooting them as if they had been Islamists. He had turned on his nationalist allies. I thought of the pigs in *Animal Farm* crushing a strike by the hens.

New evidence emerged of disorder in the regime. While an Italian trade delegation was visiting Cairo in early 2016, the body of an Italian graduate student who had been studying in Egypt, Giulio Regeni, was disovered half naked and covered in blood by the side of the Alexandria highway. One of his front teeth was missing and others were chipped or broken. His skin was pocked with cigarette burns. His back was lacerated with deep cuts. His right earlobe had been sliced off, and the bones of his wrists, shoulders, and feet were shattered. An Italian autopsy later confirmed that he had been beaten, burned, stabbed, and probably flogged on the soles of his feet over a period of four days. A broken neck finally killed him.

The police tried to put over a series of explanations. First they made up false allegations of homosexuality. Then they invented a gang that impersonated police in order to steal foreign passports. Their implausible scenarios all crumbled away. Debating which branch of the military or security services killed him and why became a gruesome parlor game among Egyptian intellectuals.

American officials in Washington and Cairo later told me that they had concluded that the intelligence service that killed Regeni did not do it on Sisi's order. Nor did it kill Regeni to undermine Sisi. It had tortured and killed Regeni on its own authority, without asking permission. And the killers had deliberately left his body to be discovered while the Italian delegation was in Cairo, to send some kind of message.

A Western passport was no longer protection. Units of the security services believed they could kill whomever they liked. More than a year later, in 2018, the Egyptian government had not identified the unit responsible, and two American officials told me that they thought they knew a reason. Sisi's son Mahmoud was one of three officers in the general intelligence service who might have directed the operation.

Dalia Abdel Hamid was a thirty-five-year-old researcher for a human rights group. She wore little wire glasses and had long, wavy hair, and she worked on issues that would be considered forward thinking even in New York and London, like the rights of Egyptian transsexuals.

Like most Egyptians I knew, Abdel Hamid had relatives on both sides of the culture wars. Her parents were left-leaning teachers in the state schools, and her brother was a prominent organizer of the Tahrir Square uprising in 2011. But her uncle was a midlevel Brotherhood leader. After the street fighting outside the presidential palace in December 2012, Abdel Hamid refused to talk to him.

"I was so angry. I felt like they were dragging us to some kind of civil war," she told me.

In early 2017, Abdel Hamid decided to compose a reflection for an online journal about the psychological state of her milieu—the Cairo intelligentsia, the liberals, leftists, and artists who were her community. I invited her to dinner at a Japanese restaurant popular with Egyptian liberals and Western journalists, expecting to hear the customary Brotherhood blaming.

For her, she said, the massacre at Rabaa had erased that. "It all seemed so meaningless." Her uncle in the Brotherhood fled underground but snuck furtive visits to his sister—Abdel Hamid's mother. Her uncle had planned to attend a secret meeting in June 2015 of fugitive Brotherhood leaders and defense lawyers at an apartment in the October 6 suburb. The police broke into the apartment and executed everyone present—at least nine people in all. Abdel Hamid's uncle survived because he had been caught and arrested before he got there.

"So I guess I am glad he is a prisoner," she told me. He sometimes called her from inside, and she was glad to hear from him.

She divorced her husband in the summer of 2013, and two of her close friends got divorced that year as well. She thought it was related to the depression hanging over her circle. Facebook, once the signature tool of the Tahrir Square organizers, had become a receptacle of their agony.

"My Facebook timeline starts each morning with people narrating the nightmares that they had the previous night," she said. "'I was running from the army,' 'I was in the middle of a mob sexual attack in my nightmare,' 'I dreamed of my imprisoned husband.'

"As the day progresses, people complain of panic attacks, anxiety attacks. 'I am so depressed I cannot get out of the bed today.' 'I am so depressed I cannot move a muscle today.' By night, they are talking about insomnia, and it starts all over again.

"All our Facebook postings now are about 'Please free this person,' 'Get this prisoner to a hospital, he needs to be treated,' 'Allow this person out to see his dying parent and bury his dead,' or 'This person is eighty years old, let him out to die in dignity.' These are now the demands of everyday Egypt."

What were her friends doing about it? "We have all turned to personal projects. The obsessions we have developed. Cooking, children, the gym, yoga, learning a musical instrument, learning a new language, alcohol, eating disorders, anorexia, bulimia—you name it, we have it all. You want to feel that you are in control of something, if only your own body. But we are failing at this as well.

"The trauma we went through, the dead people we saw, the morgue scenes, the sexual attacks, the massacres . . ." Abdel Hamid trailed off. "On the anniversary of each incident in the revolution, Facebook turns into a war zone. 'You did this,' 'You did that,' 'You did not join this march,' or 'You did not sign that petition.' People accuse each other of stuff that happened six years ago. It is absolute madness, a manifestation of helplessness and utter defeat. We are all turning against each other, like when cocks are fighting. We are becoming so vicious to each other."

She paused. "Everybody wants to find the point where it all went wrong," she said, "and nobody wants to discuss Rabaa."

I had seldom heard a Cairo liberal acknowledge that reticence. Abdel Hamid immediately changed the subject. She turned back to the feelings of her fellow activists. "We were so full of ourselves," she said. "I think that some of us, maybe not consciously, hated that a different revolutionary faction than us"—the Muslim Brothers—"made it to power."

She rushed through the obligatory disclaimers. "Of course, the record of the Muslim Brothers in power was so miserable. Of course, I am not defending them by any means. But we need to stop our obsession with what *they* did wrong. We need to look at what *we* did wrong.

"We forgot that these people also participated in this revolution, and they paid a price. In the early days of the revolution, in Tahrir Square, it was the Muslim Brothers who slept under the wheels of the tanks to prevent them from moving. They were there, and they were courageous. . . . I think we hated the Muslim Brothers so much that some of us thought regaining the old regime would be better than having them in power."

Ethics, she said, was what activists and intellectuals stood for. "That summer, in 2013, we did not abide by our ethics," she said slowly. "Consciously or not, we were so blinded by hatred . . ." She trailed off again, and tears welled up in her eyes. "See how I struggle talking about it?"

"We did not want to believe it was a coup. We thought that we would have another chance. We overestimated our power. We hated the Brothers so much. We were brainwashed by the media . . ." Another long pause.

"The defeat is so heavy, you don't want to be accountable. It is difficult to imagine that you have something to do with this," she acknowledged at last.

"We were non-Jews in Nazi Germany," she continued. "We failed the test. We failed to bear witness. Ethics is our capital. When that is lost, you have nothing. You forget who you are. You can drown yourself in alcohol or Xanax or whatever you want. But this thing will keep haunting you. And sooner or later, we all arrive there."

I left Cairo early the next morning with no plans to return.

Epilogue

I watched much of the 2016 presidential race from Cairo, and that vantage point made the discussion of the Middle East especially bracing. Candidate Donald J. Trump's hostility to Islam was blunt and unmistakable. He made a point of saying "radical Islam" instead of "Islamic radicalism" to underscore that the creed itself was the problem. He promised to bar all Muslims from entering the United States. He claimed Muslims in Jersey City had cheered for the destruction of the World Trade Center on 9/11. He told apocryphal stories glorifying the killing of Muslim fighters with bullets soaked in pig fat. He even insinuated that Obama himself was a crypto-Muslim. So how would Trump get along with Sisi, who had pledged as president of Egypt to teach and defend Islam?

They adored each other. Sisi leaped to excuse the candidate's promise to ban Muslims. It was just campaign talk, Sisi told CNN. He was the first foreign leader to congratulate Trump on election night, and when they met at the White House, Sisi seized the new president's outstretched hand with the awkward eagerness of a teenager meeting his idol. "I have had a deep appreciation and admiration of your unique personality," Sisi told Trump.

"A fantastic guy," Trump called Sisi when they first met, in September 2016, and again during Sisi's official visit to the White House the following April. "He took control of Egypt, and he really took control of it," Trump raved, explaining that Egypt had "tremendous problems" with "terrorists" before Sisi had "wiped them out."

The facts were less flattering. The number of Egyptians killed each year from bombings or shootings by Islamist militants had escalated sharply under Sisi—whether compared with Morsi's sole year in office or with Mubarak's last years. By "terrorists," Trump presumably meant the Muslim Brothers, whom Sisi had indeed driven underground (although not eradicated). But Trump was clear enough. Sisi was a strongman, just the kind he admired.

"We are going to be friends for a long, long period of time," Trump concluded after their White House meeting.

The rulers of Saudi Arabia and the United Arab Emirates were just as delighted with Trump as Sisi was. The Saudi royals hosted him in Riyadh, handed him a sword, and danced arm in arm. King Salman, Sisi, and Trump posed together at a Saudi counterterrorism center with their hands on a surreal, glowing white orb of no clear purpose. Prince Mohammed bin Salman, the king's favorite son and dominant adviser, visited the White House and pronounced Trump "a true friend of Muslims."

Why did Trump and the Arab autocrats get along? Trump had chosen General James Mattis as his defense secretary and General Mike Flynn as his first national security adviser, both eager supporters of General Sisi and relentless foes of the Muslim Brotherhood. Ambassador Otaiba of the UAE—Bro-taiba—became a kind of tutor in regional affairs to Jared Kushner, Trump's son-in-law and Middle East adviser. Perhaps Trump and the Arab autocrats both found reasons to overlook his fear of Muslims.

I wondered, though, if Trump's fear of Muslims was not an impediment at all. It was part of the bond. Flynn had admired Sisi precisely because he was a "very secular" or "moderate" Muslim. He was one of the good ones, not like the others. In some ways, Sisi and the Arab autocrats appeared to agree that their Muslim citizens were too "backward" to govern themselves. Egyptians lagged Western Europeans by a "civilizational gap," Sisi told a German magazine in 2015, trying to explain the necessity of the killings at Rabaa. Egyptian friends took the prejudice for granted: Arab dictators like Sisi always appealed to a kind of Western bigotry. The rights that Westerners considered universal at home could not apply to Arabs, because the people and culture were fundamentally different.

By 2016, the hope for democratic change in the Arab world felt like a cruel hoax. It was easy to forget that the revolts of 2011 had created a real opening, that for a time Egypt's generals had feared public disapproval, or that Tunisia had completed a peaceful rotation of power. The uprisings had spread more chaos and violence across the region than at any time since the end of World War I. Libya, Yemen, Syria, and Iraq were riven by civil war; Bahrain was held together only by Saudi military force. Struggles for democracy had degenerated into sectarian feuds. Local antagonists were enlisted as pawns in cynical proxy wars between Saudi Arabia and Iran, or between the UAE and Qatar—two rich little American allies in a bizarre family feud.

The leaders of Al Qaeda had worried in 2011 that movements for democracy were upstaging their jihad, offering Muslims what Osama Bin Laden called "half-measures." But the jihadists came roaring back after the turn again to authoritarianism. America was pulled back into war in Iraq for the third time in a quarter century. Refugees from Arab conflicts flooded westward and triggered a nationalist backlash. It was scarcely an exaggeration to say that the tumult across the Arab world had helped to elect Trump as president and to scare Britain out of the European Union.

I happened to be in Washington on the fifth anniversary of the Egyptian uprising, January 25, 2016. Tom Donilon, Obama's national security adviser from the start of the uprising until the weekend of the coup, spoke at a public forum hosted by *Politico* magazine. What happened to the Arab Spring? was the first question put to him.

"It has been a negative for the people of the Middle East, and it has been a negative for the security of the United States," Donilon said, with I-told-you-so resignation. "You have seen a collapse of the state system in the Muslim Arab world." I thought of Sisi's warnings about "the collapse of the state," and I saw heads nodding around me.

The conclusion that settled over Washington was that the people of the region would have been better off if they had never risen up. Arabs had failed at democracy; maybe they preferred strongmen. We should thank Sisi for restoring order. We should coax him to open the Egyptian economy (Washington's perennial recommendation). And we should keep sending $1.3 billion a year in Apaches and F-16s to fight the Islamic State in the Sinai (as if Sisi's takeover itself had not ignited the insurgency). Political Islam—whether ISIS or the Muslim Brotherhood—was a threat to the West, and Sisi was a bulwark against it. He was a "natural partner," Dennis Ross, the veteran Middle East diplomat who stood with Obama during his last call to Mubarak, argued in his *New York Times* op-ed, "Islamists Are Not Our Friends."

"The only way to support Egypt's maturation as a country with civil society, with democracy, is to support President el-Sisi," General Mattis argued in April 2016, in a speech at the Center for Strategic and International Studies (which received major funding from the Emiratis). Three years earlier, Mattis had said Egyptians removed Morsi because of his "imperious leadership." Now Mattis said that with Sisi trying "to reduce the amount of negatives about the Muslim religion, I think it's time for us to support him and take our own side in this."

Six years in Egypt, though, convinced me that the uprisings were hardly the source of the chaos. The old order was crumbling, visibly, from the moment I landed in Cairo, long before the first demonstrator set foot in Tahrir Square. It felt obvious in 2011—and even clearer in 2018—that the failure of that Arab state system was the cause of the uprising, not its consequence. The old autocracies were as fragile as their rulers had feared, but that was because their dependence on corruption and coercion had hollowed them out. So nothing could be more naïve than to think that putting the face of a different soldier in front of a refurbished autocracy would yield a more stable result. The thirty months of imperfect steps toward democracy in Egypt had offered at least a chance of an alternative.

Plenty of Egyptians now say that their struggle was doomed from the start. Oddly, living through the utter, calamitous failure of the uprising has convinced me of the opposite: Egyptians have as much potential as any people to fulfill the promises of freedom and democracy that brought Tahrir Square to life. I watched thousands give their lives to build a more just and free Egypt. Their sacrifices are no less inspiring because they were defeated. They labored under the burden of more than six decades of unresolved fears and resentments, against powerful cliques like the judges and generals still deeply invested in the old status quo. And for those thirty months, longer than anyone had a right to expect, Egyptians nonetheless beat back repeated attempts to restore that old order.

Egyptians elected a president from the Muslim Brotherhood, and the dreaded theocratic takeover did not come to pass. Morsi may have been a second-rate amateur of a president, yet for a time he looked like he might hang on long enough to be voted out of office, like the Islamists of Tunisia. Morsi was not wrong to suspect enmity from the deep state. Nor was he wrong to worry that the Saudis and Emiratis were out to undermine him, or that many in Washington would be glad to see him gone. Morsi was wrong to trust Sisi.

Nor were liberals like ElBaradei wrong to fear that Muslim Brotherhood leaders might be tempted to cling to power. The demonstrators outside Morsi's palace were not wrong to worry that the Interior Ministry was still intact, abusive, and menacing. But ElBaradei and the demonstrators made the same mistake. They trusted Sisi. They lent their credibility to a coup that destroyed the very thing that they said they stood for: the chance to build a liberal democracy. The civilians let their fears divide them, and the generals were ready and waiting.

On the morning of Trump's election, I met my friend Hossam Bahgat for coffee in Zamalek. He was thirty-seven years old but still looked like a graduate student. He was clean-shaven, with close-cropped hair and oval-shaped glasses, and he hauled around a leather satchel of books and newspapers slung over his shoulder.

Fifteen years earlier, at the age of twenty-two, Bahgat had founded what became Egypt's most important human rights organization, the Egyptian Initiative for Personal Rights. He had done more than anyone to document the dark sides of authoritarianism—torture, police abuse, sexism, homophobia, sectarianism, and corruption. To a generation of Western journalists and diplomats, Bahgat was an indispensable resource. Whenever a big shot from the home office came to Cairo, the first thing we all did was to set up a meeting with Bahgat. Then Mubarak fell, the news media opened up, and Bahgat reinvented himself as Egypt's most important investigative journalist. He wrote for and then edited the left-leaning online publication *Mada Masr* (The Scope of Egypt, though *mada* can also mean the setting of a precious stone). I thought Bahgat was one of the smartest people I have ever met, and one of the bravest.

He had narrowly evaded arrest at least twice since Sisi took power. In October 2014, he was tipped off that the police were coming for him. He caught the next flight to New York, where he accepted a fellowship at the Columbia School of Journalism. But Bahgat loved Egypt. Also, he hated cold weather. So a year later he convinced himself that Cairo was safe enough to return.

Military intelligence called him in for questioning in November 2015 about something he had written. The officers detained him in their head-quarters, and as soon as I found out, I wrote an article for the website of the *New York Times* as quickly as I could. The State Department expressed alarm about the rule of law and freedom of expression. Secretary General Ban Ki-moon of the United Nations issued a personal appeal. And after two nights Bahgat was out. "Mama Amreeka" still had some clout, I thought.

But the *mukhabarat* was only biding its time. In early 2016, prosecutors opened a criminal case against Bahgat for accepting unauthorized foreign contributions to the rights group he had founded. He was banned from travel and his assets were frozen (along with those of several others). A long series of hearings began.

Then Trump won the election. "Now I am definitely going to jail," Bah-gat joked to me in a text message that morning.

He had no great love for Hillary Clinton; Bahgat preferred Bernie San-ders. But we both knew that Trump had shown no patience for human rights at home, much less in Egypt. He was not about to pressure Sisi to free someone like Bahgat.

Bahgat's trial ground on through 2017, and he kept a brave face. He told me that over time he had found something to like about Trump. Bahgat thought: Here was an American president who made his family members top White House advisers. He pushed conspiracy theories, called critics treason-ous, and bullied the news media. He lied with impunity. He disdained legal customs and parliamentary process. He fired a top law enforcement official whose investigations threatened him. And Americans on both the left and the right had started speaking of a "deep state" of their own—a permanent gov-ernment that had either stymied Obama or thwarted Trump, depending on who was talking.

Washington had puzzled about why Egyptians behaved so differently than we did. Bahgat thought we were starting to act a little Egyptian. "America," Bahgat wrote on Twitter in the spring of 2017. "So deliciously third world."

Acknowledgments

Mayy el-Sheikh risked her life, braved threats and insults from her fellow Egyptians, and worked around the clock for more than two years—all to try to tell the truth about what was happening in her country. I was an incidental beneficiary of her efforts, and so were the readers of the *New York Times*. During the writing of this book, she consulted on its planning, filled in gaps in the reporting, and provided valuable comments on early drafts of the chapters. My gratitude to her is undying, and I hope some day she writes her own book about all that she witnessed.

Anthony Shadid was the *Times* bureau chief in Beirut in 2011. He raced to Cairo to help cover the Tahrir Square sit-in, and I knew him only for the next thirteen months, until he died on February 16, 2012, covering the uprising in Syria. He was the greatest international correspondent of our generation working in the region, and he taught me a great deal. Anthony had a special gift for translating the poetry in the voices of everyday Arabs, and I have tried my best to follow the example of his exceptional empathy. I wish I could read the book he would have written.

The unrivaled commitment to international reporting by the *New York Times* and the Sulzberger family made this book possible. I am especially grateful for the support, insight, and friendship of Michael Slackman—my predecessor in Cairo, my editor during the Arab Spring, and head of the international desk by 2018. I also owe thanks to many others: Dean Baquet, Joe Kahn, Susan Chira, Bill Keller, Jill Abramson (who I suspect helped

persuade the international desk to send me to Cairo), and Jim Yardley. Bill
Schmidt arranged for my family during its first evacuation; Janet Elder,
who died last year, took care of the second. I benefited from the wisdom
and patience of more editors and copy editors on the desk than I can possibly name here.

I am grateful for the collaboration and camaraderie of many *New York
Times* colleagues in the field, including Kareem Fahim, Ben Hubbard, Declan Walsh, Anne Bernard, Neil MacFarquhar, Rod Nordland, Robert
Worth, Liam Stack, Mona el-Naggar, Nour Youssef, Robert Mackey, and
others. Outside the *Times,* I am thankful for the friendship in Cairo of the
journalists Patrick Kingsley, Edmund Blair, Amina Ismail, Leila Fadel,
Abigail Hauslohner, Heba Saleh, Max Rodenbeck, Maggie Michaels, Lou-
isa Loveluck, Matt Bradley, Thanassis Cambanis, and others. I also owe
deep thanks to the Egyptian staff of the *Times* Cairo bureau. They asked
not to be named, for their safety.

Nour Youssef made valuable introductions and provided insightful con-
sultations during the writing of this book. Two interpreters who worked
with me also asked not to be named, to avoid retaliation.

I owe thanks to many for places to stay during the research and writing:
Simon Kitchen and Karima Zein el-Abedeen, Andre and Annie Houston,
Jared and Shaye Hardner, Kathy Bradford, Susan and Peter Bradford, and
my parents, Nancy and Douglas Kirkpatrick.

The Royal United Services Institute provided a base in London and the
Woodrow Wilson Center provided office space in Washington. Steven
Cook, Hazem Kandil, Khaled Fahmy, Michele Dunne, Nathan Brown, Mi-
chael Hanna, Amy Hawthorne, Andrew Miller, Daniel Benaim, Tamara
Cofman Wittes, Samuel Tadros, Moktar Awad, Brian Katulis, and Jon Al-
terman all shared their time and consultation.

My agent, Elyse Cheney, coaxed out of me a book-length proposal that
remained the blueprint for this book. Wendy Wolf at Viking was brilliant,
committed, and merciless—all that any author could hope for. Jane Cavo-
lina copyedited with the eyes of an eagle.

Rebecca Corbett read early drafts of each chapter (as well as some that
died along the way) and advised me on their structure. I am not sure I could
have finished the book without her. Ruth Feycech gave it an extra line edit

at the end. My father, Douglas Kirkpatrick, interrupted his retirement to mark up the pages in process. Ariel Kaminer, my friend and editor for more than a quarter century, provided valuable suggestions in several places and sustained me with her enthusiasm. Patrick Kingsley, who covered Cairo for the *Guardian* in 2013 and now works for the *Times,* read the near-finished manuscript and helped fix many details. Mietek Boduszyński, a political scientist who was an American diplomat in the region during the Arab Spring, offered helpful comments as well.

Many others who lived through the events provided advice or corrections on parts of the text: Hossam Bahgat, the founder of the Egyptian Initiative for Personal Rights, and Emad Shahin, editor of the *Oxford Encyclopedia of Political Islam,* each read large sections. Wael Eskandar, Mina Thabet, Wael Haddara, Shadi Hamid, Nour Youssef, Mozn Hassan, Mohamed Soltan, Suliman Ali Zway, and Moises Salman read portions.

None of them bear any responsibility for any defects of this work. Any conclusions, faults, or errors are mine alone.

My sons Thomas, now twelve, and Emmett, now nine, are heroes: marvels of resilience and determination. They not only inspired me; they also nagged me to get back to the keyboard. "Dad, you have got to finish the book!"

My greatest debt is to Laura Bradford. I am thankful that she married me fifteen years ago, thankful that she moved with me to Cairo, and thankful for her insights and contributions as a partner in all that went into the writing this book. I forced her to shoulder the burden of parenting alone all too often. Who could forget my weekend trip to Libya that went on for two months, or the year I spent your birthday covering a riot in Cairo? But it is as true today as it was the day we met: I would rather look at you than all the portraits in the world.

Notes

The main sources of information for this book were my personal experiences and interviews. Many of those I interviewed speak for themselves in the text, so I have not noted them here. Others—mainly current and former officials in Washington or political dissenters in Egypt—spoke on condition of anonymity to avoid reprisals of one kind or another. When I have relied on undisclosed sources, I have confirmed their accounts with one or more others wherever possible.

I wrote this book in part to answer questions that troubled me at the end of my time as the bureau chief in Cairo, and to do that I pursued additional reporting in both Egypt and Washington. But I have also made extensive use of my reporting in the *New York Times*: published articles, crates of notebooks, megabytes of digital files, and hours of audio recordings produced during my work for the paper. Where I have relied on specific reporting by other journalists, I have tried to acknowledge that in the text.

These notes are for readers with a special interest in Egypt, the Arab world, or American foreign policy. I have listed selected books or articles that I relied on for historical background or context, and I have provided names or details that I removed from the text to avoid overburdening a general reader. In a few places, I have also addressed debates of concern primarily to those who have lived through or studied these events. In transliterating Arab names, I followed no consistent rule. I tried to use the preferred spelling of the subject, the most common English spelling, or the spelling in the *New York Times*, for easy reference to its archives.

1: Whoever Drinks the Water

I first encountered the truism that rivers shaped the cultures of Egypt and Iraq in *Night Draws Near* by Anthony Shadid (New York: Henry Holt & Company, 2005). A great book about the city is *Cairo: The City Victorious* by Max Rodenbeck (London: Picador, 1998).

I relied on two firsthand accounts of the Aswan Dam and the Suez Crisis from an Egyptian perspective: *The Cairo Documents* (Garden City, NY: Doubleday, 1971) and *Cutting the Lion's Tale* (New York: Arbor House, 1987), both by Mohamed Heikal. I used *Eisenhower 1956* by David A. Nichols (New York: Simon & Schuster, 2011) as a reference for the American role. I also benefited from *Economic Aid and American Policy Toward Egypt, 1955–1981* by William J. Burns (Albany: State University of New York Press, 1985), who appears in these pages as a diplomat.

In 2017, the import of new Western-made drugs had recently begun to lower the prevalence of hepatitis C.

2: City of Contradictions

The blogger at the American embassy *iftar* was Wael Abbas; the political scientist was Maye Kassem. The newspaper columnist sentenced to jail, Ibrahim Eissa, was saved from incarceration by a presidential pardon.

Some of the background about Ahmed Ezz comes from my conversations with him after his release from prison.

Two excellent and very different histories of modern Egypt that I have consulted are *The Struggle for Egypt* by Steven A. Cook (New York: Oxford University Press, 2012) and *Soldiers, Spies, and Statesmen* by Hazem Kandil (London: Verso, 2012).

For background on the Obama administration's approach to the Arab world before the Arab Spring, a useful starting point is *The Obamians* by James Mann (New York: Viking Penguin, 2012).

Three different people with very different agendas and ideologies but all with firsthand knowledge told me independently about Sisi's warnings to the generals in 2010: Mohamed Heikal, Abdel Nasser's propagandist and the dean of Egyptian political commentators; Hassan Nafaa, a liberal professor of political science at Cairo University; and Yasser Rizk, an Egyptian journalist close to Sisi. Nafaa is especially credible about this because he is sharply critical of Sisi. Heikal and Nafaa heard the account of Sisi's assessment from groups of generals, including Sisi himself, in 2011, as I recount later in the book.

Heikal, who became an adviser to Sisi, told me that Sisi had asked the generals: "'Are we ready? How do we respond to this question?' . . . He was the one who proposed to the army that they should not back Mubarak."

I heard the memorable phrase "irreversible decline" from Parag Khanna, a scholar of international relations.

The Egypt Human Development Report 2010, sponsored in part by the United Nations Development Programme, provided statistics on poverty in Egypt. Some official Egyptian statistics were assembled by the journalist Mohamed Aboul Gheit in the newspaper *El-Masry El-Youm*.

The Naguib Mahfouz novel here is *Palace of Desire*, the second volume of his Cairo trilogy, first published in Arabic in 1957. I read the English translation published in 1991 by the American University in Cairo.

I drew on *Counting Islam* by Tarek Masoud (New York: Cambridge University Press, 2014) for its excellent reflection on Egypt in 2010, including Ezz's assessments. I am following the general usage of "the Washington consensus" to mean a set of prescriptions for free markets and privatizations—what critics call neoliberalism.

Sisi disclosed details about the size of the public payroll in speeches, and some of the comparisons here first appeared in "Egypt's Failed Revolution" by Peter Hessler, in the January 2, 2017, issue of the *New Yorker*.

For the history of the United States and Egypt, important sources were *The Cairo Documents, Cutting the Lion's Tale*, and *Secret Channels* (London: Harper-Collins, 1996), also by Heikal; *Egypt's Liberation: The Philosophy of the Revolution* by Gamal Abdel Nasser (Washington, D.C.: Public Affairs Press, 1956); *In Search of Identity* by Anwar Sadat (New York: Harper & Row, 1977); *Thirteen Days in September* by Lawrence Wright (New York: Alfred A. Knopf, 2014); *Eisenhower 1956* by Nichols; *The Struggle for Egypt* by Cook; and most of all, *Soldiers, Spies, and Statesmen* by Kandil. I drew heavily on Kandil.

There are conflicting accounts about the details of the Free Officers' communications with the Americans before the launch of the 1952 coup, but there is no doubt that the outreach took place, and the Free Officers correctly believed that they could enlist the United States on their side. Kandil's *Soldiers, Spies, and Statesmen* documented Sadat's courtship of Henry Kissinger. Sadat said that the United States "holds 99 percent of the cards" during a March 1977 interview on CBS television and he often repeated the phrase, as the *Washington Post* noted in its obituary on October 7, 1981. The "God help us" comment was recounted to me by Mietek Boduszyński, a diplomat who heard it.

Hisham Talaat Moustapha was removed from prison to a hospital for health reasons after three years. He received a full pardon from President Sisi in 2017.

3: Police Day

The best account of the suicide of the fruit peddler, "Slap to a Man's Pride Set Off Tumult in Tunisia," was published in the January 22, 2011, issue of the *New York Times* by Kareem Fahim.

The organizer who told me "we always start from the elite" was Islam Lotfy. In addition to Fahim's real-time reports, this account of January 25 is based on interviews with many of the organizers and others who marched that day. Sondos Asem was one of the Brotherhood women who believed they were first to reach the square, along with her mother, a former Brotherhood lawmaker. I was back in Cairo by the morning of January 26.

Waleed Rashed, who had predicted a revolution on the morning of January 28, gave up politics to found and sell an internet-based messenger business. The last time we talked, over coffee in 2016, he was a mentor at an "incubator" for start-ups and was founding a second company.

The number of police stations and cars burned on January 28, 2011, and the inside account of the state media, comes from *Tahrir: The Last 18 Days of Mubarak* by Abdel Latif el-Menawy (London: Gilgamesh Publishing, 2012). Menawy was president of the news division of the state media at the time.

Michael Morrell, the former acting director of the Central Intelligence Agency, reflected on the period in his memoir, *The Great War of Our Time* (New York: Twelve, 2015). *Duty: Memoirs of a Secretary at War* by Robert M. Gates (New York: Alfred A. Knopf, 2014) set the conventionally accepted narrative of the White House debates over the uprising. His opponents in that debate say he misstated their argument. They argued in part that Mubarak's rule was untenable regardless of the American position. The account here reflects interviews with more than a dozen people involved in all sides of that debate.

The journalist who decorated her apartment with revolutionary graffiti was Wendell Steavenson of the *New Yorker*. I relied on *Revolution 2.0* by Wael Ghonim (New York: Houghton Mifflin Harcourt, 2012) and a March 21, 2018, reflection he wrote on the website Medium. I also interviewed him in 2011 as well. "Orientalising the Egyptian Uprising" by Rabab el-Mahdi, published April 11, 2011, in the online journal *Jadaliyya*, dissects Western views of the Egyptian uprising.

Edward Walker was quoted in *The Ghost Plane* by Stephen Grey (London: C. Hurst & Co, 2006). I have also relied on *Alter Egos: Hillary Clinton, Barack Obama, and the Twilight Struggle over American Power* by my colleague Mark Landler (New York: Random House, 2016) and *Hard Choices* by Hillary Clinton (New York: Simon & Schuster, 2014). Morrell describes his own back channels with Suleiman in *The Great War of Our Time*.

4: "We Don't Do That Anymore"

The dinners with intellectuals and journalists were organized by General Mohamed el-Assar. Among the subjects discussed was General Sisi's advice to the military council in 2010 about the likelihood of an uprising against a Gamal Mubarak succession in 2011; as noted previously, Hassan Nafaa, a liberal critical of the military, and Yasser Rizk, a promilitary nationalist close to Sisi, each independently described to me the dinners and the message about Sisi.

Tantawi's nickname, "Mubarak's Poodle," was reported by American diplomats in a 2008 cable released by WikiLeaks.

I learned about the improvisation of the constitutional drafting committee and its reliance on the Princeton website from a committee member who spoke on condition of anonymity. Nathan J. Brown, a political scientist at George Washington University who studies the Egyptian judiciary, has reported the reliance on the website as well. Other members of the panel, notably Tarek el-Bishry, have written about its goals. The general in charge of legal affairs who announced the rule change was General Mamdouh Shahin.

Some Egyptian liberals or leftists consider the moment of the referendum to have been the beginning of the end for the uprising because it turned Islamists and non-Islamists against one another, dividing those seeking a civilian government. Islamists campaigned for the military-backed interim charter in the hope of an early transition from military rule; some non-Islamists opposed the referendum and sought delayed elections because they believed the Islamists had a head start in organizing. The fiercest liberal critics of the Muslim Brotherhood argue that supporting the referendum amounted to collaboration with the military, swapping the Brotherhood's support for political advantage. But it was clear to me even then that the Islamists feared the generals. The Brotherhood sought early elections to get the military out of power as soon as possible, not to collaborate with it. And the Muslim Brothers were all too confident of their long-term popularity. They did not see any electoral advantage in early elections, because they did not fear that delaying elections might allow others to catch up. Most diplomats and analysts I spoke with concur.

Some Muslim Brothers, on the other hand, argue that at least some of the liberals were not merely afraid of early elections; they dreaded any elections because they knew they would lose. But it is easy enough to understand why non-Islamists preferred a delay without resorting to such theories, and many of the people who campaigned against the referendum went on to demonstrate for a swift end to military rule. Although the referendum was the first split in the unity of the uprising; I do not credit the conspiracy theories from either side.

About the "Thursdays of concessions," Menawy wrote in *Tahrir: The Last 18 Days of Mubarak* that "the tactic of announcing concessions to the public like this, the day before a protest, was widely adopted throughout the following months in Egypt, in order to mitigate the size and aggression of the coming demonstrations."

The young woman I quote brushing back the bribe-seeking officer was Lara el-Gibaly.

The Egyptians: A Radical History of Egypt's Unfinished Revolution by Jack Shenker (New York: New Press, 2016) focuses on labor and working-class activism during the years of the uprising.

The blogger Hossam el-Hamalawy once worked as a reporting assistant for the *New York Times* in Cairo, long before I got there.

In the high-level American courtship of Egyptian military leaders, Secretary of State Clinton and National Security Adviser Donilon each met in Washington with the military general who had been appointed to succeed Suleiman as spy chief, Murad Muwafi.

About the attack on the Israeli embassy, I interviewed many American officials, including Steve Simon, Leon Panetta, and Daniel Shapiro, then U.S. ambassador to Israel. The Egyptian journalist Heba Afify reported with me for the *New York Times* from outside the embassy.

The number of jihadists released by the generals appeared in "Who Let the Jihadis Out?" by Hossam Bahgat, published in the online publication *Mada Masr* on February 16, 2014. Supporters of the military takeover in 2013 falsely blamed Morsi for the release.

5: The First Lady and the Blue Bra

This chapter has benefited greatly from the insights and guidance of Nour Youssef and Mayy el-Sheikh. In *Orientalism* (New York: Pantheon, 1978), Edward W. Said wrote at length about the Western preoccupation with Arab sexuality and a Western impulse to explain Arab politics in sexual terms (anticipating the "blue balls theory" of jihad). Said famously accused the scholar Bernard Lewis of belittling the idea of an Arab "revolution" by comparing it, in sexual language, to the "rising up" of a camel.

Among other sources, I have relied here on two important biographies. One is *Doria Shafik: Egyptian Feminist* by Cynthia Nelson (Cairo and New York: American University in Cairo Press, 1996). The other is *Casting Off the Veil: The Life of Huda Shaarawi, Egypt's First Feminist* by Sania Sharawi Lanfranchi (London: I. B. Tauris & Co., 2015).

The United Nations survey that assessed the prevalence of female genital mutilation was taken in 2015. It is safe to say that the rate was at least as high in 2011. More background is in *Sex and the Citadel: Intimate Life in a Changing Arab World* by Shereen El Feki (London: Chatto & Windus, 2013).

The "summer bride" deposit law was implemented by Justice Minister Ahmed el-Zind under President Sisi. It updated a seldom-enforced law that had previously required only a small token sum.

I learned about Tawfik Hamid from his book *Inside Jihad: How Radical Islam Works, Why It Should Terrify Us, and How to Defeat It* (Mountain Lake Park, MD: Mountain Lake Press, 2015). The cover features a blurb from Senator John McCain.

Merna Thomas later worked for a time as a journalist for the *New York Times*.

The columnist Lamees Gaber was writing in the *Wafd* newspaper, and Khaled Abdullah spoke on television.

6: The Theban Legion

I am grateful to Mina Thabet, a former spokesman for the Maspero Youth Union, and Wael Eskandar, a liberal activist and writer, for their help and comments on this chapter. The account of the Maspero massacre here is the product of my own reporting from the scene that night, interviews with more than a dozen witnesses to the killings or participants in the march, and a review of the voluminous video footage.

Samuel Tadros, a scholar in Washington who writes about Egypt, helped put me in touch with Awad Basseet, a former editor of the *Theban Legion*. Basseet provided valuable perspective, helped me track down the two priests, and volunteered the conclusion that life for Egyptian Christians was better under Morsi than it was under Sisi.

Another useful account of the night of the Maspero massacre, including the allegations against Father Filopateer, is in *Once Upon a Revolution* by Thanassis Cambanis (New York: Simon & Schuster, 2015).

The generals who held the press conference were Adel Emara and Mahmoud Hegazy. Hegazy, related to General Sisi through a marriage of their children, later succeeded him as chief of military intelligence and then became military chief of staff.

7: "How the Downfall of a State Can Happen"

Many Egyptian liberals argue that the Muslim Brotherhood effectively collaborated with the generals by discouraging direct confrontations against military rule while the uprising still had momentum. But it is unclear if a direct confrontation in 2011 would have produced a different outcome. The Brothers' nonconfrontational approach was an outgrowth of the group's traditional gradualism. It may also have reflected a credible—even correct—assessment of the military's power. In any case, the end of the story here turned out to be about conflict between the military and the Muslim Brotherhood, not conspiracy or collaboration between them. In the West, I have more often heard the contention that the Muslim Brothers moved *too* quickly to challenge the generals, and that is certainly wrong.

General Mohamed el-Assar led a delegation to Washington in the summer of 2011, and on July 25, he told an audience at the United States Institute of Peace that "the Muslim Brothers and Salafis are components of the Egyptian people" and thus "cannot be ignored." He added: "They have the willingness to share in the political life . . . they are sharing in good ways."

As for the Muslim Brotherhood's thinking during this period, Khairat el-Shater, the Brotherhood's chief financier and strategist, had talked publicly for months about the fear of "the Algeria scenario"—an Islamist landslide in parliamentary elections in Algeria in 1991 had triggered a Western-backed coup and a decade-long civil war that killed more than two hundred thousand Algerians. The fighting gave birth to the group that later became Al Qaeda in the Islamic Maghreb.

I visited Shater's office around the time of those street clashes, and one of his advisers told me that during the fighting the generals had been on the phone every day with Shater, all but baiting the Brotherhood into the streets: Are you going down yet? Are you going down now?

Arguing Islam After the Revival of Arab Politics by Nathan J. Brown (New York: Oxford University Press, 2017) provides an excellent analysis of the public debate in Egypt during this period. Freedom and social media made it easier than ever to argue and demonize, but the absence of a political process made resolution impossible. Division and polarization were the result. "It should be no surprise that rhetoric spins out of control if it finds no traction in policy outcomes."

The Supreme Council of the Armed Forces issued its Communiqué #69 on July 22, 2011. Fayza Aboulnaga, a holdover Cabinet member, had been leading an investigation of the Western funding of Egyptian nonprofits since early spring.

The military council's "principles" for the constitution appeared under the name of one of the civilian deputy prime ministers working under them in the government, Ali el-Selmi; the principles were known as the Selmi document.

The Brotherhood leader who was jeered out of the square was Mohamed Beltagy, the one who wryly brought a bouquet of flowers to the Police Day protest on

January 25, 2011. In the first days of the clashes, he apologized for the fact that the rest of the Brotherhood leadership was staying away. "You have a right to be angry," he wrote on Twitter. "We have to reconsider our positions."

I caught up with him as he sat in a folding chair in the dusty anteroom of the Brotherhood's old headquarters two days after he was chased out of the square. "I thought that we should go to the square in great numbers to protect the protesters, secure the entrances, ensure the peacefulness—that we should not keep a distance," he told me, but Shater and the other leaders saw the fighting "as an attempt to draw the Brotherhood into a made-up crisis."

Ben Rhodes recalled writing the Thanksgiving statement and Tom Donilon's anger. Steven Simon, the senior director for North Africa and the Middle East, described his call with Donilon; Donilon did not respond to repeated requests for comment. Several others in the Obama administration said it was not uncommon for the tone or content of White House statements to reflect differences depending on who was on duty at the time.

8: Forefathers

I am grateful to the scholar Emad Shahin for his consultation and comments on the chapters about political Islam.

This chapter is based primarily on my reporting among Egyptian Salafis in Cairo, Alexandria, Giza, and Port Said. For background, I have consulted *Islam and Modernism in Egypt* by Charles C. Adams (London: Russell & Russell, 1933) and *Muhammad Abduh* by Mark Sedgwick (London: Oneworld Publications, 2010), which are among the few good English-language biographies of Abduh.

For the context of contemporary Salafism, I relied on *Global Salafism: Islam's New Religious Movement* edited by Roel Meijer (London: C. Hurst & Co., 2009) and, in that volume, "On the Nature of Salafi Thought and Action" by Bernard Haykel.

Islam and Politics by Peter Mandaville (London: Routledge, 2014) is a terrific overview of Islamist political movements, and its author appears in these pages as an adviser to the State Department. Another useful book by someone who was in the White House during this period is *The Age of Sacred Terror: Radical Islam's War Against America* by Daniel Benjamin and Steven Simon (New York: Random House, 2012).

The title "khedive" was used by the heirs of Mohamed Ali Pasha, the founder of the modern Egyptian state, who in 1805 had established himself as the independent ruler of the Ottoman province of Egypt.

The claim that the Prophet Mohamed invented constitutional democracy is a reference to the Charter of Medina. Promulgated there by the Prophet Mohamed when he arrived from Mecca in 622, the charter guaranteed equal religious freedom and political rights to Jews and pagans as well as Muslims living in the city. Some scholars reckon it a social contract establishing a pluralist ministate, even if the Prophet Mohamed later deprecated other faiths or preached religious war.

9: Parliament Grows a Beard

In addition to Emad Shahin, Shadi Hamid read and commented on an earlier version of the short history of the Muslim Brotherhood presented here.

The most important source of history and background for this chapter is the landmark *The Society of the Muslim Brothers* by Richard P. Mitchell (New York: Oxford University Press, 1969). I have relied significantly on two more contemporary articles about the recent history: "The Metamorphosis of the Egyptian Muslim Brothers" by Mona El-Ghobashy, in the *International Journal of Middle East Studies* (vol. 37, no. 3, August 2005) and "The Brotherhood Goes to Parliament" by Samer Shehata and Joshua Stacher, in *Middle East Report* (no. 240, fall 2006). I also drew on "U.S. Policy and the Muslim Brotherhood" by Steven Brooke, in *The West and the Muslim Brotherhood After the Arab Spring* (Washington, D.C.: Foreign Policy Research Institute, 2013), which quoted Condoleezza Rice at the American University in Cairo. Mandaville's book *Islam and Politics* is indispensable.

In discussions of the Muslim Brotherhood in this chapter and throughout, I also drew on *Hasan el-Banna* by Gudrun Krämer (London: Oneworld Publications, 2010); *Sayyid Qutb and the Origins of Radical Islam* by John Calvert (Cairo and New York: American University in Cairo Press, 2011); *A Mosque in Munich* by Ian Johnson (New York: Houghton Mifflin, 2010); *A Portrait of Egypt* by Mary Anne Weaver (New York: Farrar, Straus & Giroux, 1999); *Temptations of Power: Islamists & Illiberal Democracy in a New Middle East* (New York: Oxford University Press, 2014) and *Islamic Exceptionalism: How the Struggle over Islam Is Reshaping the World* (New York: St. Martin's Press, 2016), both by Shadi Hamid; *Counting Islam: Religion, Class and Elections in Egypt* by Tarek Masoud (New York: Cambridge University Press, 2014); *Inside the Brotherhood* by Hazim Kandil (Cambridge, UK: Polity Press, 2014); and *Arab Fall: How the Muslim Brotherhood Won and Lost Egypt in 891 Days* by Eric Trager (Washington, D.C.: Georgetown University Press, 2016), among others.

Two non-Islamists whose incarceration President George W. Bush made a fuss about were Ayman Nour, a liberal politician, and Saad Eddin Ibrahim, an intellectual.

In 2007, Representative Steny Hoyer, a Maryland Democrat, bumped into Saad el-Katatni at the home of the United States ambassador.

General James Mattis described the Muslim Brotherhood and Al Qaeda as "swimming in the same sea" on May 14, 2015, in a speech at the Heritage Foundation. He has said similar things many times. Dennis Ross's op-ed was published in the *New York Times* on September 11, 2014.

The intercepted phone call between Abdel Nasser and the king of Jordan was recounted vividly in Lawrence Wright's *Thirteen Days in September*.

Aboul Fotouh's meeting in the shoe store was with Kamal al-Sananiri, a brother-in-law of the thinker Sayyid Qutb. It was described in *Abdel Moneim Aboul Fotouh: A Witness to the History of Egypt's Islamic Movement, 1970–1984* (Cairo: Dar el-Shorouk, 2010), his memoirs as told to Hossam Tammam. It is available only in Arabic, and I relied on Deena Adel and Mayy el-Sheikh for translation.

The best source in English for personal background of Banna is Krämer, cited above. The quotes from Banna used here come from Mitchell's definitive early work. The main intellectual successor to Muhammad Abduh was Rashid Rida, who was a pivotal intermediary in the evolution of Islamic modernism from Abduh to Banna.

The quote about the head scarf appears in "The Metamorphosis of the Egyptian Muslim Brothers" by Ghobashy, attributed to the guidance council members Essam el-Erian and Aboul Fotouh. *Legacy of the Prophet: Despots, Democrats, and the New Politics of Islam* by Anthony Shadid (London: Westview Press, 2002) is about post-Islamist politics and tells the story of the Center Party in Egypt. That was the Brotherhood breakaway party that included Essam Sultan.

10: Thug Versus Thug

The general in charge of legal affairs was Mamdouh Shahin. Youssef Sidhom was the editor of the Coptic newspaper *Watani* and an unofficial spokesman for the church. Outside relatively liberal areas, Aboul Fotouh performed well at the polls in only two districts: Mersa Matruh, where his old friend helped, and the North Sinai, where he told me he was the only candidate who visited. I doubt the Salafis brought him many votes.

11: The Judges Club

The Rule of Law in the Arab World: Courts in Egypt and the Gulf by Nathan J. Brown (Cambridge, UK: Cambridge University Press, 1997) is an excellent and sympathetic account of the Egyptian judiciary. This chapter has also benefited from "Independence Without Accountability: The Judicial Paradox of Egypt's Failed Transition to Democracy" by Sahar F. Aziz, in the *Penn State Law Review* 101 (2016).

The account of the American side of these events is based on interviews with more than a dozen officials involved, but most spoke on condition of anonymity.

The paradigmatic example of the kind of hawkish Egyptian nationalist outraged by American democracy funding is Fayza Aboulnaga. She was the official driving the prosecution against the International Republican Institute and the National Democratic Institute. When I called her office in early 2012, the military council had assigned a general to answer her phone. President Sisi named her as national security adviser and in 2017 she was still involved in the American aid.

Steven Simon and Sergio Aguirre were the National Security Council staffers who tried unsuccessfully to work through Leon Panetta and Hillary Clinton to shape a compromise with the generals about the American aid. The Foreign Ministry spokesman who complained to me that the United States had deducted the bail money from the aid payments was Ambassador Badr Abdelatty.

I heard the same account of Shater's message to the generals from several senior figures in the Morsi campaign, some of whom spoke on condition of anonymity. The words I am quoting here are from Wael Haddara, a Morsi adviser.

I encountered the term "judicial coup," describing the dissolution of the Parliament, in an analysis by Nathan Brown in *Foreign Policy* magazine on June 14, 2012.

12: The Night of Power

Haddara's first contact on the Morsi campaign was Khaled al-Qazzaz, a permanent resident of Canada who was married to a Canadian. His background is in education, but he worked on Morsi's foreign policy team.

The general who spoke about the military's role as "trustworthy guardian" was Mahmoud Hegazy, who appeared with General Mohamed el-Assar.

To clarify the chronology, Morsi's inaugural rally in Tahrir Square was the night before his official inauguration. I described it last because it was the speech that was remembered.

The assassination attempt on Abdel Nasser in 1954 was carried out by Mahmoud Abdel Latif, a member of the Muslim Brotherhood from Imbaba, in Cairo. Some believed (and some still suspect) that Abdel Nasser staged the episode as a pretext to crush the Muslim Brothers. The scene is described in many places, including Richard P. Mitchell's *The Society of the Muslim Brothers* (New York: Oxford University Press, 1969) and *The Looming Tower: Al Qaeda and the Road to 9/11* by Lawrence Wright (New York: Alfred A. Knopf, 2006).

This account of Morsi's meeting with Sisi in August 2012 is based on interviews with two people who worked in the palace at the time and on the account of a senior Muslim Brother with knowledge of the details.

The Long Game by Derek Chollet (New York: Public Affairs, 2016) recounts the Obama administration's worries that Sisi was "too close to Morsi."

13: A Day in Court

Another Islamist who sued Tahani el-Gebali on the basis of our article was Essam Sultan, who had also helped start the post-Islamist Center Party and disrupted the first day of Parliament.

14: President and Mrs. Morsi

The *Guardian* obtained a part of the commission report that Morsi tried to suppress. "Egypt's Army Took Part in Torture and Killings During Revolution, Report Shows" by Evan Hill and Muhammad Mansour, *Guardian*, April 10, 2013. Ahmed Samir was the columnist in *El-Masry El-Youm*.

Morsi's prime minister was Hesham Qandil. His female deputy was Pakinam el-Sharkawy, who was his chief policy adviser. His Christian deputy was Samir Morcos, who was also Morsi's adviser on the democratic transition. I knew Sharkawy and she was influential. Morcos quit in December 2012. Morsi's advisers told me that rival liberal or nationalist presidential candidates had rebuffed invitations to join the government. But many sincere liberals were disappointed that Morsi did not form something closer to a coalition government, and he never explained why he did not. Still, whoever the personnel, his government did not have a chance to do much.

15: Under the Cloak

The Syrian town I visited was Tilalyan.

The fifty-five-year-old Libyan voter in Benghazi was Naema el-Gheryienne.

The anti-Islamist was Mohamed Abu Hamed.

The people who told me about Shater's reaction to Morsi's announcement included Gehad el-Haddad and Murad Ali.

It is worth noting that Morsi's team was right to fear that the court would dissolve the constitutional assembly. In a ruling on June 2, 2013, the court said that it would have done exactly that.

"What Makes Mohamed Morsi Tick: Is It a Time Bomb?" by Patrick Graham was published in the *Globe and Mail* on May 4, 2013.

The analyst who told protesters to "take to the streets and die" was Salah Eissa.

The best analysis of the 2012 Egyptian constitution in context is in Nathan J. Brown's book *Arguing Islam After the Revival of Arab Politics*. Egyptian politics produced many exaggerated claims about its merits and deficiencies, and the criticisms echoed widely in the West. But readers who want to understand that debate should read Brown's chapter titled "Arab Constitutions, the Many Voices of the Public." The comparison of constitutional plebiscites with mass loyalty oaths was Brown's as well.

The account here of the Sharia compromise around Article 219 is the product of my own reporting, including interviews with several liberal and Islamist members of the committee—among them Manar el-Shorbagy, a liberal political scientist at the American University in Cairo; Amr Moussa, a former foreign minister and presidential candidate who dropped out at the last minute to avoid signing the compromise; and Amr Darrag, of the Muslim Brotherhood. Amr Hamzawy, a liberal former parliamentarian and political scientist, also helped inform my understanding of the constitution and the compromise. Brown's account arrives at similar conclusions from a scholarly methodology.

The account of the Obama-Haddad meeting comes from aides on both sides, including Wael Haddara and Ben Rhodes.

16: A Rumble at the Palace

The protester whose death I asked about was Mohamed el-Gindy.

The Brotherhood leader I quote urging supporters to defend the palace was Essam el-Erian. A report by Human Rights Watch documented some of those appeals. Mohamed Abdel Maqsoud raised alarms about fornication in the tents. "Their dead are in hell" was said by Sheikh Fawzi el-Saeed.

Ola Shahba spoke in a television interview with the host Yosri Fouda.

Some critics of the Muslim Brotherhood note that in December 2012, Defense Minister Abdel Fattah el-Sisi offered to host a meeting for dialogue between Morsi's administration and its political opponents. Morsi's spokesmen insisted that it would be a purely social event, and Sisi ultimately scrapped it. Morsi thus effectively prevented Sisi from overseeing those talks, on the grounds that it would set a bad precedent for civilian democracy if the defense minister interceded in civilian politics or put himself above the president (like the chairman of the joint chiefs mediating a deal between Democracts and Republicans). Critics of the Brotherhood cite the aborted meeting as evidence that, on at least one occasion, Morsi was the one who walked away from an invitation to dialogue.

17: Murder, Rape, Christians, and Spies

The Interior Ministry spokesman was General Osama Ismail. The paramedic trainer was Jon Porter.

The attack on the Ikhwan Online office was January 25, 2013. The break-in at Brotherhood headquarters was on December 6, 2012.

El Sayyid el-Badawi ran the Wafd party.

The statistics on blasphemy cases against Christians come from the work of Ishak Ibrahim of the Egyptian Initiative for Personal Rights.

18: The View from the West

General James Mattis spoke about Otaiba in a speech at the Center for American Progress in Washington, on January 23, 2015, and about Adel al-Jubeir at the Aspen Institute on July 20, 2013.

Ambassador Patterson talked with Essam el-Haddad and Khaled al-Qazzaz in March about the UAE-led push for a coup. I was allowed to make an audio recording of the briefing quoted here.

Hernando de Soto Polar was among those who told me about his work for the Brotherhood; he said he was impressed with Shater.

Flynn describes his views of political Islam and his admiration for Sisi in *The Field of Fight: How We Can Win the Global War Against Radical Islam and Its Allies,* written with Michael Ledeen (New York: St. Martin's Press, 2016).

The account of Ambassador James Watt's role is based on interviews with Morsi advisers, British officials close to Watt, and members of the National Salvation Front.

General Mohamed el-Assar, who began hinting around April at the possibility of a military intervention, was also the general who, on a visit to Washington in 2011, had praised the Muslim Brotherhood for its constructive role in the transition.

European and American diplomats sometimes urged Morsi to make unilateral concessions to his opponents during this period. But his advisers say the diplomats never offered any indication that the opposition would consider any reciprocal concessions, such as recognizing Morsi's legitimacy as president or discontinuing the calls to protest and demands for his ouster. Several diplomats involved later told me that in retrospect it was doubtful that proposed concessions from Morsi, like a change of ministers, would have made any difference.

19: A New Front

The two members of the military council who stayed in contact with the National Salvation Front were General el-Assar, who was also a liaison to the Pentagon, and General Hegazy, related to Sisi through a marriage of their children.

After Sawiris boasted to me of his role promoting the music video about Tamarrod, his spokespeople asked for a correction, claiming that he had sold off his television network. But the supposed sale turned out to be a ruse. Sawiris had faked the sale for political reasons, and years later he sold the network again, for real.

Hassan Shahin of Tamarrod was also, by coincidence, the protester who had been running near the Blue Bra Girl when she was stripped by the soldiers.

In early 2014, Mohamed Heikal recounted to me his conversations with El-Baradei and showed me a picture of Sisi delivering a birthday cake. ElBaradei has declined to speak with me since he left Cairo.

General Sisi's office manager was General Abbas Kamel. The military's chief of staff was General Sedki Sobhi.

Some of the leaked audio recordings or private emails cited in this book might have been obtained by one of the Egyptian intelligence agencies or a foreign intelligence agency. I have confirmed or authenticated all of them, except those few that have been so extensively reported without credible contradiction that they have become a matter of public record in Egypt. American officials with access to intelligence reporting confirmed the accuracy of the leak indicating that the UAE sent money to the Egyptian military for Tamarrod.

20: A Dutiful Son

Wael Haddara was one of two sources from the Morsi administration who described the narcotics shipment at the airport and the secret meetings inside the palace.

The quotes from Sisi at Dahshur come from "Military Messages" by Ahmed Eleiba in *Al Ahram Weekly,* the issue of May 16–22, 2013, and from the daily *Al Ahram.* Reuters reported the comments in English as well.

The two generals who contacted the members of the National Salvation Front in May were again Assar and Hegazy.

Badawi's home was in the suburb known as October 6 City.

Two others present for the State Department meeting each independently recounted the delivery of the memorandum and Thomas Melia's response. I have the memorandum, in Arabic and English, as it was first written in Cairo and as it was translated for delivery in Washington. But Melia does not remember receiving the memorandum or making the statements that the two others attributed to him.

21: June 30

Kerry told me his side of the Addis Ababa meeting with Morsi. Multiple close aides to Morsi described his account to me.

A few days after the Salafi-dominated Syria rally in Cairo, a mob in a village on the outskirts of the city lynched four Shiites. Rights groups argued that by attending the conference Morsi had legitimated the sectarianism rising around the region. But the connection to Morsi is indirect and remote. Shiite Muslims make up a tiny minority of Egyptians, and many Egyptian Sunnis disdain Shiites as non-Muslims. It is doubtful that outrage over the killings did much to trigger a back-lash against Morsi, except perhaps in the small circle of human rights advocates.

Amr Hamzawy worried that the National Salvation Front looked obstruction-ist because it constantly refused to accept any of Morsi's invitations to dialogue or negotiations. So he broke with the group to attend the Ethiopian dam meeting, and it was a fiasco.

In addition to the quoted sources, this account of the American response to the coup during its run-up is based on conversations with more than a dozen senior officials who were closely involved.

Khaled Youssef described to me his role in filming June 30.

The account of Morsi's last days is based on extensive conversations with five people who were with him or in close contact during that period. The account of Morsi's last conversation with Obama comes from a reliable record of the call made by people in the White House.

The observation about which governors came under attack appears in *Egypt in a Time of Revolution* by Neil Ketchley (Cambridge, UK: Cambridge University Press, 2017). Ketchley also made the most systematic assessment of the crowd numbers.

The geriatric former premier Morsi proposed bringing back was Kamal Ganzouri.

The office manager who interrupted Morsi's meeting with Sisi was Ahmed Abdel Atty.

22: Coup d'État

This account of the July 4 meeting at the White House is based on interviews with more than a half dozen participants. All of the quotes were confirmed by their speaker or multiple others. The quotes and statements attributed to Obama were all recounted and confirmed by several others, but not Obama himself. The quotes from Kerry and Hagel come from their own accounts to me of their statements in the meeting (and the substance was also confirmed by others).

Michael Morrell wrote in his memoir, *The Great War of Our Time*, that he had worried the Egyptian security services under Morsi were giving a free pass to anti-Western militants. "The military, intelligence and law enforcement communi-ties in Egypt essentially stopped fighting Al Qaeda because they felt they had no political support," he wrote. Al Qaeda "was establishing new footholds in the Sinai and other parts of Egypt."

Morrell told me in an email that the Al Qaeda "foothold" he meant was Ansar Beit al-Maqdis—the group that had attacked an Egyptian military checkpoint in July 2012, before Morsi held any real power. The group's roots among the Bedouin of the North Sinai went back a decade.

Might the Egyptian soldiers, spies, and police have stopped doing their jobs to spite Morsi? I asked.

Morrell said he trusted Egypt's spies. "I do not believe that the security guys with whom I worked would ever willingly allow terrorism to run rampant for political reasons," Morrell replied by email. News reports and leaked emails later suggested that after leaving the CIA, Morrell joined a firm, Beacon Global Strategies, which was paid by the UAE.

Otaiba's meeting at the Hamilton and his messages to Blinken and Sullivan were in some of the many emails stolen from his account and leaked to the public. I have confirmed the accuracy of the content of both emails with others.

The Long Game by Derek Chollet also describes the opposition to Morsi from American allies in the region, including Israel and the Gulf monarchies. "Our other close regional partners—none of whom were sad to see Morsi go, thinking he was a stooge of Iran—were very supportive of al-Sisi," he wrote. The idea that Morsi was a stooge of Iran was absurd, even before his stance toward Damascus. But that made his views abundantly clear. In an interview, Chollet said Israeli, Saudi, and Emirati leaders ignored evidence of the differences among Islamists—even Sunni and Shiite—because they were so committed to the idea that all were the same. "It was like cognitive dissonance," he said.

23: Killing Themselves

The scholar who wrote about King Abdullah's "victory lap in Cairo" is Bruce Riedel, a veteran observer of Saudi Arabia for the CIA and the White House, in his book *Kings and Presidents* (Washington, D.C.: Brookings Institution Press, 2018).

The Salafi I quote attacking Christians from the podium at Rabaa was Assem Abdel Maged.

The name of the policeman whom Ebrahim el-Sheikh saw killed was Mohamed el-Mesairy.

I know that Morsi was still held inside the guard complex on July 8 from interviews with people who were detained with him as well as from an interview with a member of his immediate family.

The National Salvation Front's spokesman on July 8 was Khalid Talima, and the television host quoted here is Youssef el-Husseini.

Mohamad Elmasry is an Egyptian American scholar of communications who has written about the Egyptian media's portrayal of Rabaa.

24: A Lion

About Egypt's nationalist pop songs of 2013, see "5 Pop Songs That Illustrate Egypt's Cult of Personality" by Miriam Berger, on BuzzFeed, November 1, 2013, and "Egypt's Musical Nationalism, and a Little George Orwell" by Maha ElNabawi, *Mada Masr,* August 20, 2013. The joke about the Sisi underwear was made by the journalist Tom Gara.

Heikal told me that he had advised Sisi to hold a referendum or plebiscite, in the style of Abdel Nasser. The "mandate march" was Sisi's alternative.

Kerry visited Cairo in November 2013 and commended Sisi for following his "road map" to democracy. On June 22, 2014, Kerry thanked Egyptians for the work transitioning to democracy.

The two moderate Islamists were Abou Elela Mady, founder of the post-Islamist Center Party, and Saad el Katatni, former speaker of Parliament. The photo of the UAE foreign minister with the Tamarrod founders was published in the newspaper *Youm el Saba*.

25: Clearing the Square

Many journalists and rights groups confirmed that there was no safe exit from Rabaa. There was no way to move safely across the sit-in, much less in or out. Mayy and I entered and exited twice that day, and each time was terrifying. I remember passing through the medical center both times. Mayy remembers making our first entrance through a different dangerous passage and then a long search for a way to get out. Other than the path of our first entrance, our recollections differ only in a few details.

The journalist who told me he saw two guns among the demonstrators was Samer Al-Atrush of Agence France Presse. He had slept the previous night inside the sit-in and woke up there that morning.

The police general who said the demonstrators had shot first was Major General Medhat el-Menshawi, interviewed on television by Wael el-Ibrashy.

A good reference on the Rabaa massacre is the Human Rights Watch report, "All According to Plan: The Raba'a Massacre and Mass Killings of Protesters in Egypt," published on August 12, 2014.

26: Jihadis in the White House

Three Pentagon officials confirmed hearing those jokes about the White House.

27: Retribution

Human Rights Watch documents the names and circumstances around the videos of the extrajudicial killings in the North Sinai in several reports, including: "Egypt: Videos Show Army Executions in the Sinai," April 21, 2017.

The riot on the edge of Cairo was in El Matareya. Current and former Brotherhood leaders confirmed their numbers.

28: Deep State

For Mehleb's role in the Mubarak corruption case, see "The Mubarak Mansions" by Hossam Bahgat, in *Mada Masr*, May 20, 2014.

For Anwar Sadat's expulsion from Parliament, see "Egypt Parliament Removes Prominent Dissenter: Anwar Sadat" by Declan Walsh, *New York Times*, February 28, 2017. The account of corruption's toll on Egyptian archaeological treasures is based on interviews with Monica Hanna, among others. For the gluing of King Tut's beard, see "Egyptian Musuem Officials Face Tribunal for Damaging King Tutankhamen's Mask" by Declan Walsh, *New York Times*, January 25, 2016.

For the fate of Hisham Geneina, see "Graft Fighter in Egypt Finds Himself a Defendant in Court" by Declan Walsh, *New York Times*, June 7, 2016.

The former intelligence officer who ran the pro-Sisi parliamentary coalition was General Sameh Seif el-Yazel.

The senior scholar in the ministry overseeing mosques who spoke with Sheikh Ali Gomaa was Salem Abdel Galil.

The 2016 Arab Spring anniversary sermon was first reported in "Egypt's President Turns to Religion to Bolster His Authority" by Declan Walsh, *New York Times*, January 10, 2016.

On the Egyptian judiciary after the coup, see "Dissidence and Deference Among Egyptian Judges" by Mona el-Ghobashy, in *Middle East Report* (no. 279, Spring 2016).

The anchor Maha Bahnasy was on the Tahrir Channel. The anchor Moataz al-Demerdash also cut off a correspondent reporting harassment.

The account of Obama's meeting with Sisi at the United Nations about Soltan comes from multiple Obama advisers who were present, as well as from others who were briefed after the fact. The account of the meeting about ending the suspension of military aid is based on the recollections of five people involved. Derek Chollet provides a useful account of the aid debate in *The Long Game* as well. In resuming the aid, the White House discontinued an unusually favorable program that allowed Egypt to draw on future aid to acquire military equipment. This program added to the difficulty of cutting off aid because American defense manufacturers expected future aid to Egypt to pay for equipment they had already sold. Israel is the only other country to receive American military aid on those terms.

Shaimaa el-Sabbagh's poem was translated by Maged Zaher, editor and translator of *The Tahrir of Poems* (Seattle, WA: Alice Blue Books, 2014). It is used here with his permission.

The seventeen-year-old Islamist killed by the police on the same day as Sabbagh was Sondos Reda.

For the account of the autopsy of Giulio Regeni, see "Why Was an Italian Graduate Student Tortured and Murdered in Egypt?" by Declan Walsh, *New York Times Magazine*, August 15, 2017.

Index